This Was ANDERSONVILLE

This Was
ANDERSONVILLE

by

JOHN McELROY

EDITED WITH AN INTRODUCTION BY

ROY MEREDITH

*The True Story of Andersonville Military Prison as
told in the personal recollections of JOHN McELROY,
sometime Private, Co. L, 16th Illinois Cavalry.*

Illustrated by Arthur Meredith, Jr.

The Fairfax Press · New York

To Herbert Alexander, boyhood
friend and classmate, this book is
affectionately dedicated.

This edition is published by The Fairfax Press,
distributed by Crown Publishers, Inc.,
by arrangement with Ivan Obolensky, Inc.
f g h i j k l m
FAIRFAX 1979 EDITION
Manufactured in the United States of America

Library of Congress Cataloging in Publication Data

McElroy, John, 1846-1929.
This was Andersonville.

A greatly revised ed. of the author's Andersonville, a story of
rebel military prisons, first published in 1879.
Includes bibliographical references.
1. Andersonville, Ga. Military Prison.   2. United States—History
—Civil War, 1861-1865—Prisoners and prisons.   3. McElroy,
John, 1846-1929.   4. Illinois Cavalry. 16th Regiment, 1861-1865—
Biography.   5. United States—History—Civil War, 1861-1865—
Personal narratives.   6. United States—History—Civil War,
1861-1865—Regimental histories—Illinois Cavalry—16th
Regiment.   7. Prisoners of War—Georgia—Andersonville—
Biography.   I. Meredith, Roy, 1908-   II. Title.
E612.A5M4   1979   973.7'71   79-13550
ISBN 0-517-00520-4

CONTENTS

CONTENTS

ILLUSTRATIONS

[vii]

facing chapter

INTRODUCTION

W HEN JOHN MCELROY, the author of this curious narrative, first began work on a series of articles of his experiences as a prisoner of war in Andersonville for the *Toledo Blade,* he expected that what he wrote of Andersonville would be violently assailed and denied. But he was fully prepared for this.

"In my boyhood," he wrote, "I witnessed the savagery of the slavery agitation. In my youth I felt the fierceness of the hatred directed against all those who stood by the Nation. I know that Hell hath no fury like the vindictiveness of those who are hurt by the truth being told of them, but I solemnly affirm in advance the entire and absolute truth of every material fact, statement and description."

When McElroy's sketches appeared in the *Blade,* he received over three thousand letters from former Andersonville prisoners warmly endorsing his account as thoroughly accurate in every respect.

Shortly after the close of the war, when the articles appeared, D. R. Locke, the political satirist and humorist who wrote under the pen name of "Petroleum V. Nasby," persuaded his friend McElroy to put the series into book form. In 1866, fifteen months after Appomattox, McElroy agreed, saying that until that time he "had no more idea of writing this book than he had of taking up residence in China." McElroy began his book while the horrors of Andersonville were still fresh in his mind, although he felt that the task he set for himself "was more than enough for the genius of Thomas Carlyle or Victor Hugo."

No writer ever described such a deluge of hatred and villainy as that which swept over the unfortunate Federal soldiers who were confined in Andersonville, Blackshear and Florence in the last eighteen months of the Confederacy. The magnitude of McElroy's experiences overwhelmed him. So vivid were they, he was able to describe them as only a gifted writer can—one who has personally witnessed the horrifying spectacle of more than forty thousand strong, able-bodied young men starving and rotting to death within the confines of a stockade that measured one thousand feet long and eight hundred feet wide. To McElroy, Andersonville was a monstrous tragedy that stunned the mind.

McElroy's tale of unbelievable horror and human depravity would challenge the imagination of a Poe or a Bierce. Starvation, disease, pestilence and death, like the Four Horsemen of the Apocalypse, stalked hand in hand throughout the Stockade every hour of the day and night. All the base elements of fratricidal war, born of bitter sectional hatred, were confined, it seems, within the timbered walls of Andersonville. Like Pandora's box, Andersonville contained all the ills that plague the human race. Hope remained outside. Perhaps no story of the American Civil War, written before or since, strips away so completely the false aura of maudlin sentiment and romanticism that has crept into literature on this fascinating subject.

In writing his narrative, McElroy's aim was to give as accurate an account of the conditions at Andersonville as his personal experiences dictated, a factual, unadorned account. Quite naturally, and understandably so, his story is occasionally biased and partisan. But few can claim that his story, shocking as it is, does not try to tell the truth. Unquestionably, his narrative stands up uncommonly well when checked against other sources and official testimony delivered by the Surgeon General of the Confederate Army, and other Confederate officers, at the Wirz war crimes trial held in Washington shortly after the war.

McElroy, being an observant newspaperman, had a natural urge to express himself on paper precisely, as he saw things for himself, coldly and factually, with the support of the official records. In addition, he had the unqualified support of the reams of testimony submitted by Federal prisoners of Andersonville at the Wirz trial. This testimony grew to such huge proportions (almost a ton of it) that the military court decided they had heard enough and promptly convicted and sentenced Wirz to hang.

Thus Captain Henri Wirz became the first soldier sentenced to die for atrocities committed against prisoners of war. Winder escaped Wirz' fate by dying prematurely of a heart attack shortly before the end of the war.

Throughout his narrative, McElroy constantly belittles the Southerner and pictures him as an illiterate with the capabilities of a moron. He paints him as a cruel, inhuman abomination of manhood, totally devoid of feeling, ignorant and sadistic. He ridicules constantly the inability of his guards and their officers to handle elementary arithmetic without becoming hopelessly confused. Illiteracy, it is true, was more predominant in the Southern Army than in the Union forces, but there were, nevertheless, vast numbers of well educated, intelligent and sensitive men of great ability in the Southern ranks.

But, unfortunately, McElroy did not come in contact with this class of Southerner. McElroy only came in contact with those to whom he refers as "Georgia Crackers," "Goober-Grabbers" and "Clay-Eaters," illiterate farmers and share-croppers from the interior regions of South Carolina and Georgia, who comprised the rank and file of the guards of Andersonville.

But McElroy is unsparing in his criticism of both sides. While he vented his hatred on the sadistic Winder and the despicable Wirz, the "N'Yaarkers" (a large group of hoodlums, thieves and wanted murderers from the slums of New York, known to the prisoners of Andersonville as the "Raiders," who terrorized the inmates of the prison) he despised and hated even more. Comparing them with his captors, McElroy, even with his gift for graphic description, was hard put to find the proper words to describe these human hyenas.

They formed raiding parties, armed themselves with knives and clubs, and stormed the more peaceful, wounded and sick prisoners who were unable to defend themselves against their onslaughts. Like voracious wolves, they thought nothing of killing a friend or fellow soldier for a bit of bread, a uniform button or trinket with which to trade with the guards for favors, extra food and tobacco.

Perhaps in the annals of war there is nowhere to be found such a despicable collection of the dregs of society who were permitted to wear the uniform of their country. The only accountable answer for it was the bounty system which legally permitted a draftee to pay a substitute to take his place in the ranks. As a rule these bounty men made poor soldiers and deserted at the first opportunity, only to repeat the process until they were recognized and caught.

When they were caught, it went hard with them and, more often than not, they were brought back by force and in shackles. The Georgia Reservists guarding Andersonville, despite their hatred for Yankees, were almost angels when compared to these vile, ferocious, human vermin from the slums of New York who even preyed upon their own friends.

Nor did McElroy spare the incompetent Federal generals whose stupidity and military ineptitude caused such a needless loss of life as did Burnside at Fredericksburg. And to this end, Burnside, Hooker, Butler and Stoneman and, particularly, Samuel Sturgis, for his disaster at Guntown, come in for their share of his sharp criticism and contempt. Naturally, McElroy shared the opinion of the majority of his comrades in their utter contempt for his Southern captors. Beginning with the land itself, particularly Georgia, down to the last trigger-happy, sixteen-year-old Reservists who composed the guards, and who were called "Governor Joe Brown's Pets," McElroy saw it all as wasted land, unproductive, and spawning strange human products, all deserving of his contempt.

Yet, his bias is understandable. As with most Westerners of the time, McElroy hated slavery and secession and devoutly believed that the Union cause was just; that the United States flag had been assaulted at Fort Sumter; that the Southern Rebellion was sheer lawlessness and had to be crushed just as quickly and completely as the full military power of the Government could be mobilized to do it.

While McElroy held nothing against the Southern people in general, he despised Jefferson Davis and his followers as criminals who deserved to be hanged for their treachery. His only quarrel with the Southern people was for their seeming lack of intelligence in following blindly the Southern revolutionaries in the prosecution of a senseless war which could only mean utter ruin for them.

"As to the responsibility for this monstrous cataclysm of human misery and death," wrote McElroy, "that the great mass of the Southern people approved of these outrages, or even knew of them, I do not, for an instant, believe." Actually, McElroy was partly right. The Southern people did know about them. Andersonville was a matter of as much notoriety throughout the South as it was in the North. But it can never be said that the Southern people approved of it. And toward this end, McElroy mentions the kindness of the people of Charleston toward the prisoners held there, even though their city was being bombarded daily by the Federal batteries on Morris Island in the harbor.

Andersonville, like all the Confederate military prisons, was a natural outgrowth of the war. Blackshear, Millen, Florence, Libby, Castle Thunder and Belle Isle; all came into existence in the normal course of events. All were hasty makeshifts, products of an early, almost unbroken string of Confederate military victories which surprised and elated the South as much as they alarmed and dismayed the North. The mortality rate was far lower at Libby and Castle Thunder in Richmond than in the open stockades, because the former, being large tobacco and grocery warehouses, at least provided shelter for the inmates. But even though these prisons were located in the Confederate capital city, they were as poorly managed as the others farther away.

Belle Isle, the only open stockade near Richmond, was a small, pretty little island in the James River, once a favorite vacation spot of Richmonders before the war. Though it was located outside the crowded city, in no time at all the great influx of prisoners made it a place of horror. There were more men than tents to shelter them. The island itself was damp and marshy. Most of the prisoners did not have blankets and, during the harsh winter months, suffered terribly from the intense cold and rain which penetrated to the bone. Many prisoners died of exposure and, during the long winter nights, it was not an uncommon sight to find many men frozen to death.

The harsh fact is that none of the Southern military prisons was a model of military efficiency and administration. General John H. Winder, the Prison Administrator, "the most cussed man in the Confederacy," made the astounding statement that "there was not a Confederate official in the land who had any experience in taking care of prisoners of war," himself included, apparently.

Winder, fifty years old and a former physician, was appointed Provost Marshal, and a more hated man in the Confederacy cannot be found. As Provost Marshal and Commissary General of Prisoners, this apoplectic Marylander assumed a role not unlike that played in World War II by the despised Nazi, Heinrich Himmler. A *protégé* of Jefferson Davis, Winder came into this sensitive position of responsibility simply because he had been a crony of Davis' at West Point.

It seems, from the records, Winder avowed he would destroy as many Federal soldiers with his own particular brand of warfare as the Southern generals were doing with the army. "I am killing off more Yankees," he boasted, "than twenty regiments in Lee's Army," and to prove this he seems to have directed his special attention to the prisoners at Andersonville. In Wirz, Winder had a subordinate who did his bidding without question.

As for blame and causes, McElroy presents a pretty strong case against Jefferson Davis, General Winder, Captain Wirz, and others of lesser rank, who were equally responsible for the conditions existing at Andersonville, and the unnecessary brutality against Union soldiers. The Southern people themselves were undergoing great hardship and suffering for lack of food, but there was no excuse for the terrible crowding which caused such an appalling loss of life at Andersonville.

The lack of food was understandable. But McElroy asks, "Was land so scarce in the Confederacy that no more than sixteen acres could be spared for the use of thirty-five thousand prisoners?" With millions of acres of unsettled land alone, the answer seems quite obvious. McElroy also questions the fact that, since the prisons were located in the middle of heavy forests, why were the men compelled to live out in the open, in winter, without even enough wood with which to build a fire to keep warm.

McElroy also argues that with the abundance of lumber, even with the shortage of labor at hand to cut it, there was no reason why a select number of prisoners could not have undertaken the work of cutting the timber as a means of promoting their own comfort. Most of the men would have been willing to cut it for the exercise alone.

By the middle of 1863, the Southern armies in the field were in rags and often marched into battle barefoot. In one regiment alone, only fifteen men had shoes. There is no doubt that the Southern soldier suffered almost as much as the Union prisoners held in the stockades, exposed to the rigors of the elements of winter and summer. After Grant opened his campaign of 1864, and the grand movement of all the Federal armies began in unison, the South's situation became desperate as Grant's military noose tightened.

Despite the early military defeats the Union armies suffered, and the attending heavy casualties and captures, the North gave no sign of giving up the struggle. With Grant and Sherman came "total war." The South realized almost at once that in Grant the North at last had an extremely competent soldier who was more than a match for any officer it could put in the field. But, as the great battles of 1864 got under way, there was an increase in the number of prisoners sent to Andersonville and elsewhere becoming as much a problem inside the Confederacy as did the Federal armies hammering outside.

When news of the terrible conditions at Andersonville reached the North, the President and Secretary of the Chicago Board of Trade wrote President Lincoln and apprised him of the terrible death rate at Andersonville, of the calculated neglect, starvation and brutality against the prisoners there. Retaliation and revenge was their cry, and they urged the President to have the Federal Government select a like number of Confederates and subject them to the same treatment.

During the year 1864 and the first three months of 1865, twenty-five thousand Federal soldiers died in Andersonville. General Winder made good his boast that he was "killing more Yankees than twenty regiments of Lee's Army." When the horror-struck Inspector, Dr. Joseph Jones, suggested to Winder that more room be given the prisoners, he asserted that he was letting matters stand as they were, that the great mass of prisoners would soon thin out in the normal course of events, and that the fortunate survivors would soon have sufficient room in the Stockade.

History has recorded many pros and cons, accusations and counteraccusations, as to the inhuman treatment accorded prisoners on both sides. According to the records, both sides could stand indicted. As to the ever-present question of prisoner exchange, McElroy had this to say: "Our Government made overture after overture for exchange to the rebels," he wrote, "and offered to yield many of the points of difference. But it could not, with the least consideration for its own honor, yield up the negro soldiers and their officers to the unrestrained brutality of the rebel authorities, nor could it, consistent with military prudence, parole one hundred thousand well-fed, well-clothed, able-bodied rebels held by it as prisoners, and let them appear inside of a week in front of Grant or Sherman. Until it would agree to do this the rebels would not agree to exchange, and the only motive—save revenge—which could have inspired the rebel maltreatment of the prisoners was the expectation of raising such a clamor in the North as would force the Government to consent to a disadvantageous exchange, and to give back to the Confederacy, at its most critical period, one hundred thousand fresh, able-bodied soldiers. It was for this purpose, probably, that our Government and the Sanitary Commission were refused all permission to send us food and clothing."

McElroy's statement is borne out by an excerpt from a letter sent to General John H. Winder, Commissary General of Prisoners, by Robert Ould, Confederate Commissioner of Exchange, dated March 17th, 1863 "I wish you to send me on four o'clock Wednesday morning, all the military prisoners (*except officers*), and all the political prisoners you have. If any of the political prisoners have on *hand* proof enough to *convict them* of being spies, or having committed other offenses which should subject them to punishment, so state opposite their names. Also, state whether you think, under all circumstances, they should be released. *The arrangement I have made works largely in our favor. We get rid of a set of miserable wretches, and receive some of the best material I ever saw . . .*" (Italics are the editor's.)

In April, 1864, Grant issued an order that no more Confederate prisoners of war should be exchanged or paroled until certain specified conditions were met. Four months later, in August, Grant, from his headquarters in Virginia, gave his reasons for this seemingly heartless policy.

"On the subject of the exchange of prisoners," he wrote, "I differ from General Hitchcock. It is hard on our men held in Southern prisons not to exchange them, but it is humanity to those left in the ranks to fight our battles. Every man released on parole, or otherwise, becomes an active soldier against us, either directly or indirectly. If we commence a system of exchange, which liberates all prisoners taken, we will have to fight on until the whole South is exterminated. If we hold those caught, they amount to no more than dead men. At this particular time to release all rebel prisoners North, would insure Sherman's defeat, and would compromise our safety here."

Grant had a point, but it was a direct reversal from the stand he had taken earlier in the war when, after capturing Vicksburg in July, 1863, he released 29,000 prisoners on their parole word alone. When word of Grant's refusal to exchange prisoners reached the newspapers, many political and clerical pressures were brought to bear on

President Lincoln to overrule Grant's policy, which seemed inhuman and unfair. But Lincoln shrugged them off and backed his General-in-Chief, and there matters rested until November, 1864, while the press raved and threatened vengeance against the perpetrators of the atrocities inflicted on Federal soldiers in Andersonville, Millen, Blackshear and Florence.

In September of 1864, when the mortality rate at Andersonville had reached an all-time high, Dr. Joseph Jones, Surgeon, Provisional Army of the Confederate States, visited Andersonville for the purpose of "instituting a series of inquiries upon the nature and causes of the prevailing diseases." He had been furnished with the necessary letter of introduction to the Prison Surgeon, Isaiah H. White:

> *Confederate States of America*
> *Surgeon General's Office, Richmond, Va.*
> *August 6th, 1864.*
>
> Sir:
>
> The field of pathological investigations afforded by the large collection of Federal prisoners in Georgia, is of great extent and importance, and it is believed that results of value *to the profession* may be obtained by a careful investigation of the effects of disease upon the large body of men subjected to a decided change of climate and the circumstances peculiar to prison life. The surgeon in charge of the hospital for Federal prisoners, together with his assistants, will afford every facility to Surgeon Joseph Jones, in the prosecution of the labors ordered by the Surgeon General. Efficient assistance must be rendered Surgeon Jones by the medical officers, not only in his examinations into the causes and symptoms of the various diseases but especially in the arduous labors of post mortem examinations.
>
> The medical officers will assist in the performance of such post mortems as Surgeon Jones may indicate, *in order that this great field* for pathological investigation may be explored *for the benefit of the Medical Corps of the Confederate Army.*
>
> S. P. Moore, *Surgeon General*

It will be noted, in this extraordinary letter, nothing was said about relieving the prisoners or about attending to their ills, and it would seem that Andersonville was nothing more than one vast experimental laboratory, and the inmates guinea pigs.

Dr. Jones was not prepared, however, for what he saw—"a gigantic mass of human misery." When Alexander Stephens, Vice President of the Confederacy, received Dr. Jones's and other reports of prison conditions, he suggested to Jefferson Davis that he visit Andersonville, speak to the prisoners, and release them.

But Davis was compelled to yield to the more urgent and stronger pleas of General Lee for more men and supplies with which to fight what were to be the Confederacy's last battles. But, as it appeared to Davis, able-bodied prisoners need not be exchanged. To relieve the Confederacy of the responsibility of taking care of the desperately sick and wounded prisoners, Davis offered to return, without equivalents, 15,000 sick and badly wounded prisoners at an arranged meeting place at the mouth of the Savannah River. This offer would stand if the United States Government would supply the necessary transportation.

Finally, in November, 1864, the Government, having agreed to accept Davis' proposal, sent a vessel to the Savannah River to pick them up under a flag of truce. The vessel arrived in due course, and the prisoners were taken aboard. As they brought the wretched men to the deck, the ship's officers were horrified at what they saw; living skeletons, their emaciated bodies covered with sores, their clothing in rags, literally crawling with vermin, barely able to walk.

When the ship was filled to capacity, anchor was weighed and the course set for Annapolis, the receiving point and hospital for exchanged prisoners. Jefferson Davis, writing of the incident, noted:

"Accordingly, some of the worst cases, contrary to the judgment of our surgeons, but in compliance to the piteous appeals of the sick, prisoners were sent away, and after being delivered, they were taken to Annapolis, Maryland, and there photographed as specimen prisoners. The photographs were terrible indeed, but the misery they portrayed was surpassed by some of those we received at Savannah. Why was this delay between summer and November in sending vessels for the sick and wounded, for whom no equivalents were asked? Were the Federal prisoners left to suffer, and afterward photographed to aid in firing the popular heart of the North?"

For the pictorial record, the Union Army's Signal Corps sent Captain A. J. Russell, one of its best photographers, to Annapolis. The photographs were indeed "terrible," and two appear in the album section of this book.

Thus matters stood from the Southern point of view. Both sides had yelled "foul," and both were equally guilty.

The official records show that while fifteen out of every hundred Federal soldiers died in Southern prison stockades, twelve out of every hundred Southern soldiers died in Northern military prisons. Elmira, New York; Fort Delaware; and Camp Douglas at Chicago had unsavory reputations. One Union Army surgeon, after having inspected the prison at Elmira, reported that of the 8,347 prisoners there, 2,000 had scurvy, that "the entire command will be admitted to hospital in less than a year and 36 per cent die."

Elmira, an open stockade like Andersonville, with the exception of having barracks for the men, contained a small stream which had transformed itself into "a festering mass of corruption, impregnating the entire atmosphere of the camp with pestilential odors . . . the vaults give off sickly odors, and the hospitals are crowded with victims for the grave."

After the Savannah exchange had been agreed upon, 1,200 men from this camp were sent by train to Baltimore to be sent South by steamer. When the Federal Army doctors met this trainload of sick men at Baltimore, they were appalled at the "criminal neglect and inhumanity on the part of the medical officers in making the selection of the men to be transferred." The prison commandant at Elmira thought that the overcrowding there would have been relieved by the releasing of the 1,200 of his worst cases; but it was no remedy, and he wrote that "if the rate of mortality for the last two months should continue for a year you can easily calculate the number of prisoners there would be left for exchange."

Yet, it was war, and war, like its backlash, carried its thunderous undertones. The year of 1864 was a critical year for both sides. The South was being slowly strangled to death by the U.S. Naval blockade and the overwhelming might of Grant and Sherman. The North, suffering from war-weariness, appalled at the frightful toll in human life to the Army of the Potomac, was almost unwilling to go on.

Only the Army carried on the spirit of the Commander-in-Chief Lincoln and his two devoted officers, Sherman and Grant. On the Rapidan, Grant avowed that he would "fight it out on this line if it takes all summer." In Georgia, Sherman, the great invader, told his officers that he would "make Georgia howl." Both phrases were to go into history books as classic, denoting unparalleled destruction and bloodshed.

Grant's and Sherman's application of the modern concept of "total war," which is not so modern, stunned Lincoln by the ferocity of the fighting and the high casualties attendant. There could be no weakening now. Lincoln, the Commander-in-Chief, stood by his generals. Total victory was the only answer. So, in the grinding process of the war's last year, prisons and prisoners were, for the time being, put aside as relatively unimportant to the grand design.

But Andersonville was, unquestionably, a hideous blot on the military escutcheon of the Confederacy. The suffering of the men in May, 1864, was more horrifying than in the month of April; June showed a frightful increase in deaths over May, and nothing could paint the horrors of July, August and September. And Andersonville's un-surpassed record for depravity, disease, the atrocities inflicted, and the unparalleled mortality rate, cannot be denied—and there was no excuse for it, except that, despite the denials of Wirz and Winder, it seems to have been the calculated design of these men, and McElroy places the blame for Andersonville squarely where it belongs when he accuses them.

They had been placed in command by the Confederate Government. They had been given a free hand, without interference, and they, in turn, acted according to dictates of their own consciences. At the same time, Jefferson Davis, knowing of the conditions existing at Andersonville, apparently did nothing to restrain these men. Only the untimely death of Winder and the approach of Sherman's army broke their grip on the unfortunate men of Andersonville.

"I have seen little indication of any Divine interposition to mete out, at least on this earth, adequate punishment to those who were principal agents in that iniquity," wrote McElroy after the war. "Howell Cobb died as peacefully in his bed as any Chris-tian in the land, and with as few apparent twinges of remorse as if he had spent his life in good deeds and prayer. The arch-fiend, Winder, died in equal tranquility, mur-muring some cheerful hope as to his soul's future. Not one of the ghosts of his hunger-slain hovered around to embitter his dying moments, as he had theirs. Jefferson Davis 'still lives, a prosperous gentleman,' the idol of a large circle of morbid sympathies . . . only Wirz . . . small, insignificant, miserable Wirz, the underling, the tool, the servile, brainless little fetcher and carrier of these men, was punished—was hanged. . . ."

When McElroy's book appeared in 1879, some said that his exposure of the con-ditions at Andersonville was motivated by his personal hatred of the South. McElroy vehemently denied this. "Nothing can be farther from the truth," he wrote. "No one had a deeper love for every part of our common country than I, and no one today will make more efforts and sacrifices to bring the South to the same social plane and material development with the rest of the nation than I will. If I could see that the sufferings at Andersonville and elsewhere contributed in any considerable degree to that end, I should not regret that they had been. But I am naturally embittered by the fruitlessness, as well as the uselessness of the misery at Andersonville. There was never the least military or other reason for inflicting all that wretchedness upon men, and, as far as mortal eye can discern, no earthly good resulted from the martyrdom of those tens of thousands."

McElroy felt that he was speaking for all the men who survived the captivity in the Hell that was Andersonville.

A word as to method. Editing the original McElroy manuscript presented several problems. First, of course, the author's statement of facts had to be checked against known sources, which included the *Official Records Of The War Of The Rebellion*. Throughout his manuscript McElroy resorts to the use of retrospect which detailed the principal characters long after they had been introduced. In addition, McElroy quoted page after page of statistical records which tended to break the thread of the narrative.

In order to present the unbroken narrative in story form, it was necessary to reduce the long, and often tedious, reports of various officers and their official reports to footnotes. Moreover, McElroy's descriptions of the conditions of the men in Andersonville were a little too strong for even this hardened editor to accept even though they were true in every sense. Consequently, since these horrifying descriptions served no purpose other than to revolt the reader, they were deleted from the original manuscript.

Withal, few liberties were taken with the original manuscript, except to put it in story form and to catch redundancies where they existed. McElroy was extremely biased, and where he had obviously made erroneous statements in the heat of anger at his captors, these were left to stand, with the corrections added to the footnotes for the sake of accuracy. Nevertheless, taking everything into consideration, it must be admitted that McElroy's story stands up extremely well when checked against the existing records of the Andersonville Stockade.

As to the photographic illustrations, they speak for themselves. Instead of being scattered throughout the chapters, they are presented as an album, intact and chronological. Portions of McElroy's manuscript, where it applies to the pictures directly, are used as captions, not only to give a sense of immediacy to the pictures, but to place stronger emphasis on the story.

From beginning to end, this narrative belongs to John McElroy. In the final chapter, the author makes only passing reference to the trial of Captain Wirz. Actually, the trial took three months to prepare, and another three months to try the prisoner. Wirz was charged with thirteen counts in the indictment, ranging from vaccinations, the use of hounds to track escaped prisoners, murder, and conspiracy to starve Union soldiers to death. The amount of testimony taken against Wirz was almost incalcuable. Wirz' attorney, Louis Schade, felt that Wirz did not have a chance, and is reputed to have said to the prisoner, "You will be convicted." But Schade put up a strong defense.

To McElroy, the Wirz trial was a miscarriage of justice, not because he thought Wirz innocent of the charges specified in the indictment, but because, if full justice were to be done, Jefferson Davis, Alec Stephens, Howell Cobb and other members of the Confederate Government should have also faced trial. In this regard, McElroy draws some startling conclusions.

The Wirz trial caused a wave of controversy throughout the North and South. Many felt as McElroy did, that all those holding high office in the Confederacy were equally guilty of treason. Many thought the trial a farce. McElroy thought that Wirz was made the scapegoat, the victim of accumulated hates and passions brought out by the war. For these reasons, and because the editor must play an impartial role, important portions of the original transcript of this fascinating trial have been set forth in the appendix of this book.

Throughout the book, it has been the editor's purpose to present a straightforward story of this appalling incident during the Civil War, which had no precedent until the Second World War, when the prison camps of Belsen and Dachau and the unforgettable Death March in the Philippines overshadowed anything that had gone on before in warfare. All that can be said for Andersonville, after almost a century, is that it stands as an indictment against war in all its forms, and places the American Civil War in the category where it belongs, as one of the most terrible wars the world has ever known.

THE MONTHS BEFORE

To a Place Called
ANDERSONVILLE

Aᴜᴛᴜᴍɴ ᴏꜰ 1863 found High Private John McElroy, Company L, 16th Illinois Cavalry, with his regiment concentrated near Cumberland Gap in East Tennessee. Burnside's nearest base of supplies was Camp Nelson, near Lexington, Kentucky, one hundred and eighty miles away. Everything Burnside's army needed, guns, ammunition, food and clothing, supplies for both men and horses, had to be hauled that distance by mule teams over all but impassable mountain roads.

The Confederate forces in that remote region, the 64th Virginia Cavalry, a mounted regiment composed of local young bloods who had already seen two years of army service, patrolled all the roads from the Gap into Virginia, held a portion of Powell's Valley, and stripped it of all cattle, forage and food. Constant raiding on the part of this regiment against the Federal supply trains, trying to reach Burnside over this long supply route, forced Burnside into doing something to put a stop to it. The Third Battalion, 16th Illinois Cavalry, under Major C. H. Beer, about three hundred men, was chosen for the job of opening the Valley to protect the supply trains from these raids.

John McElroy, as "Boots and Saddles" sounded over the camp, buckled on his saber and revolver, saddled his horse, "Hiatoga," mounted and fell into line with his

comrades, "counted off by fours" with the listlessness of veterans and, at the sound of
the bugle, "Right! Forward! Fours Right!" walked his horse through the heavy mist
that had settled over the Valley. The weather had turned cold and penetrated to the
very marrow of every man and horse and reduced minds to a condition of limp indifference.

No one in the entire column knew where he was going and no one cared. The
patrol moved slowly over the zig-zag mountain road, their horses at a walk, past Mur-
rell's Spring, until they struck the Virginia road where they turned sharply to the left.
Before long the heavy mist turned into a downpour, the cold rain drenching men and
animals and miring the road. But the column continued on slowly for almost ten miles,
moving silently, the horses' footfalls deadened by the sound of the rain.

At nightfall, the squadron halted and went into bivouac ten miles from Cumberland Gap, where McElroy and his comrades built fires, rubbed down their horses and
fed them, and made coffee for themselves. Then they lay down on the wet ground,
wrapped themselves in their ponchos and, with their feet to the fire, caught what sleep
they could.

Before morning, they were awakened by the bitter cold. The rain had cleared
off during the night, and the campfires had burned themselves out. It had now turned
so cold that most things were frozen stiff. But campfires were lighted while designated
members of the troop made coffee, after which the cold became more endurable. Mc-
Elroy and one of the troopers then went to the horse line to tend to their mounts. At
daybreak, the bugle sounded. The troop mounted and pushed on through the in-
hospitable mountains toward the Gap.

Things were happening elsewhere. At Jonesville, forty miles away, the 64th Virginia Cavalry broke camp, mounted, and started down the Valley. Somehow news had
reached them that a Federal cavalry detachment was heading their way to drive them
out of the Valley.

It was Sunday morning and nine o'clock. For the next two hours the two oppos-
ing columns moved slowly toward each other. By noon no contact had been made. The
Federal squadron, strung out along the icy road, straggled in broken order over the
rough, frozen hillside. As if by common consent, to get warmth, horses and men drew
closely together to expose as little of themselves as they could to the bitter cold
weather. During the entire march not a word was spoken.

When the head of the Federal column reached the top of a hill, the rest of the
squadron strung out for almost a quarter of a mile to the rear, unable to see where
the head of the column was leading. Suddenly, several shots rang out. Men and horses

halted automatically, ranged themselves into fours and galloped into cavalry attack formation. Major Beer spurred his horse and dashed to the head of the column. When he reached the hilltop, he scanned the area, and, satisfied with what he had seen, turned in his saddle and ordered "Company fours! Left into line! March!"

The column swung around like a jointed toy snake, the fours coming into line on a trot. Out came sabers and revolvers, and shouts rang out as each company fell into formation and dashed forward. McElroy and the men of Company L, at the end of the column, could see nothing ahead, but a hundred yards away the 64th Virginia, in their butternut and gray uniforms, deployed their horses in line and raised their carbines.

At that instant, the Federal squadron deployed for the charge and began to advance toward the enemy at a slow trot. Seconds later, the bugle sounded the charge and the Federal squadron sprang forward like an arrow from a bow. The squadron advanced at a gallop, the horses' hooves thundering over the hard, icy ground. A blast of smoke and fire could be seen spreading from the muzzles of the guns in the Confederate line as it braced to meet the onslaught of the Federal column. In the frenzy of the charge, McElroy saw nothing more until the squadron reached the spot where stood the 64th Virginia. Before he realized it, the rebel cavalry was gone. Looking toward the bottom of the hill, he saw the woods filled with the rebel horsemen flying in disorder. In the charge, Companies I and K had reached the rebel line first, and the ground was sprinkled with men in butternut clothing wounded and dying.

One officer stopped and wheeled his horse, waved his hat to rally his companions, and attempted to make a stand. But a man at McElroy's side aimed his carbine at him, without slowing his horse's pace, and fired from the saddle. The heavy Sharpe's bullet struck the brave man and almost lifted him out of the saddle. He fell to the ground and his panic-stricken horse dashed away.

The pursuit continued, the squadron forming in two columns of fours, McElroy's taking a road, the others plunging through the forest. A gray bugler, who had become separated from his regiment, tried to leap on his horse, but McElroy and his companions brought the unfortunate man down with a hail of bullets. Minutes later the hapless and disorganized 64th Virginia, now a frightened mob of fugitives, pushing their horses to the limit of their endurance, raced down the hill leading into the main street of Jonesville, followed by their equally disorganized pursuers who were loading and firing their carbines western style and shouting at the tops of their voices.

Before long the chase was given up, but not until one hundred and fifteen prisoners, and nearly that many horses and arms, were captured. After re-forming their column, the Federal cavalrymen herded their prisoners back to Jonesville.

That night the squadron made camp outside the town, and sat around the camp-fire and talked of the battle. For the next six weeks the 16th Illinois Cavalry patrolled Powell's Valley and escorted the Army's supply wagons. The Confederate cavalry gave them no rest, and the regiment engaged in numerous little skirmishes, sharp, vicious little fights that were hard on both men and horses.

At one time the Confederates blockaded a ford of the Copper River, a deep mountain stream with a slippery bottom, making it impossible for men and horses to cross. They decoyed a detachment of McElroy's troop in pursuit, drawing them to the ford. On the opposite bank, a thin line of rebel skirmishers kept peppering away as McElroy's men tried to cross. The troop plunged into the stream at a gallop. When their horses' hooves struck the slippery rocks in the middle of the stream, horses and riders went down as if shot, horses rolling over their riders, ditching them in the icy-cold waters. But it was all in the day's work, and the war went on from there.

When it came to foraging and chicken-stealing, there was little difference between rebel and Yankee cavalrymen. McElroy and his comrades did their best to maintain the special reputation they had earned as foragers. No farm was spared. They had an uncanny way of finding delicious hams and unlimited quantities of bacon packed and hidden away in barns and smokehouses. The region abounded in apples, turnips, pumpkins, cabbages and potatoes, virtually untouched, and great quantities of these fruits and vegetables found their way into the forage wagons and saddle bags. Corn suffered the same fate, and they would take this corn to the mills in the neighborhood and have it ground to make corn bread.

Company L was never without plenty of food of all kinds, food washed down with a tincupful of coffee "strong enough to tan leather." After these meals would come the ever-ready briarwood pipe, and to young McElroy there was nothing better in life than to be with the cavalry, have a hearty meal at the end of a long patrol, and sit around a sparkling fire of cedar logs, smoke and talk of the events of the day, the merits of their individual horses, and the irregularities of the mails from home; subjects that have been topics of conversation among soldiers since time immemorial.

For the next few weeks the squadron rode up and down the narrow, granite-walled valley, patrolling deep in enemy country, surrounded on all sides by a hostile enemy. The weather had turned intensely cold, and the icicles were seen hanging from the jutting, iron-walled cliffs. It was always the same. Tattoo would sound, the men would awake from their comfortable places around the fire to look over the horse line to see that their mounts were securely tied. Then they would rub down their horses' fetlocks and legs, cleaning off the specks of mud which had escaped the first rubdown.

Many of the men would smuggle a few ears of corn or another bunch of hay for their faithful mounts; and if the men were too tired, and everything in the camp quiet and comfortable and favorable, they prepared comfortable couches of small tufts of pine or cedar to make a springy mattress-like foundation. On top of this they would place their poncho or rubber cape, covering themselves with an overcoat and two blankets, putting their feet to the fire, their boots at the foot. Belts, saber and carbine within easy reach, they would turn in, ready in the event of an alarm.

As it happened, the fatal night in question was intensely cold, colder than the region had known for years. Peach and apple trees had been killed by the frost. On the picket line, several sentinels were found frozen to death. The deep snow on which they had made their beds, the icy covering of the streams, and the limbs of the trees above them cracked with loud noises all night from the bitter cold. The experience was an unpleasant one. Incredibly, on this night, the detachment was camped just outside Jonesville, all four of the companies guarding the two main roads leading into town. McElroy's Company L lay about a mile from the Courthouse. E Company, recently arrived, was situated on a knoll at the end of the village, at a point where the roads separated. The road which led to Company L's position was covered by a three-inch Rodman rifle, belonging to the 22nd Ohio Battery. Its crew of eighteen men was commanded by Lieutenant Alger and Sergeant Davis. When the cold gray dawn came up over the mountain tops Major Beer's bugler sounded reveille. The call was taken up by the other company buglers "as fast as they could thaw out their mouthpieces."

McElroy remained on his bed of pine, hoping that some day those who planned wars would do something about confining the fighting of war to the summertime, so a soldier could go home and spend the cold weather seated beside a comfortable stove in a country store, to wait until spring, when he would return to the front wearing a straw hat and linen duster. While McElroy lay on his pine bed, ruminating this all-important question, there was a sudden excited shout from the captain. "Turn out! Company L! Turn out!"

No sooner was the order out of the captain's mouth, when a shrill, piercing rebel yell, followed by a crashing volley from a regiment of rifles, came from the woods. The men were up in an instant, the cold weather forgotten. Caps, overcoats, boots, saber and revolver belts went on in an instant. McElroy snatched up his Sharpe's carbine and looked toward the sound of the yell.

What he saw made him turn pale. Rebels, hundreds of them, were pouring out of the frozen woods and rushing toward them, firing. The officers took up position on the right front of the tents, while the troopers ran up and formed a line alongside them. As McElroy rushed toward the captain's line with his chum, the young fellow turned to him and said, "Well! This beats hell!"

But the rebel surprise was complete. Company L, firing their carbines at will, poured a rolling fire into the advancing line. Many of the charging Confederates fell, but the others still came on. Company L, firing as rapidly as the action of their carbines would permit, forced the advancing rebel line to take cover. But the Confederate colonel, mounted on a white horse, dashed to the head of the line and ordered them forward, at the same time charging up to the lieutenant of Company L and ordering him to surrender. The gray-bearded lieutenant cursed the rebel colonel with an oath, pointed his revolver into the colonel's face, and pulled the trigger. The hammer fell harmlessly. The gun was empty. The rebel colonel fired and killed him instantly.

The rest of the lieutenant's group surrendered. The main body of Company L, now pressed in front and flank, overwhelmed by numbers, fell back. It was every man for himself. The company fell back a short distance, firing sporadically, springing over fences into the fields, heading toward town.

But it was no use. Company L had almost reached the road when another rebel column swept down and headed straight for the Rodman gun. Company M, led by Sergeants Key and McWright, first in the saddle at the surprise, came forward at a swinging gallop. Seeing the new rebel column head for the gun, they spurred their horses to reach the gun first. But the rebels were closer, reached the gun and turned it. Before they could fire, Company M struck them at a headlong gallop. The rebels received the terrific impact and, for a few minutes, a fierce hand-to-hand struggle took place with sword and pistol.

The rebel officer received half a dozen wounds from that many different directions and fell dead almost under the gun. Men dropped from their saddles, the frightened, riderless horses running away. While the action was at its height, Major Beer, at the head of Company I, struck the rebel left flank. The rebels gave way slowly, and packed into a dense mass in the lane where the charge had begun. But the artillerymen swung the piece around and fired solid shot into the lane. The gun went off, recoiling with an ear-splitting crash. The heavy ball tore its way through the tightly packed, struggling mass of men and horses. The solid shot ended the action.

The Confederates broke in disorder. The Federal troopers fell back and moved out of range to allow the gunners the opportunity to open on the retreating rebels with shell and canister. But it was only a temporary respite. Every man in McElroy's troop could see that the situation was critical. The narrow throat of the Valley, through which the road back to the Gap ran, was held by a superior rebel force.

The narrow, tortuous road wound through rocks and gorges. There was not even room enough to present a platoon front against the enemy; and it would have been suicide to attempt a slow movement in columns of fours. Both ends of the town were held by strong rebel forces. To the right and left of the column rose the steep mountainsides. It was soon realized that the 16th Illinois Cavalry detachment was caught in a cul-de-sac—trapped like rats in a trap.

It was afterwards learned that the 16th Illinois had faced a rebel division commanded by Major General Sam Jones. After Longstreet's defeat at Knoxville, General Jones had been sent out to capture the 16th Illinois at Jonesville somehow to compensate for Longstreet's defeat. But Longstreet's intelligence had been faulty as to the 16th's numbers, and that had caused him to send the large force.

The battle was short and bloody, with frequent crises. At one time a shell from the Rodman crashed into a house where some of the rebel sharpshooters had taken refuge. The battle went on, broken into separate, vicious little actions, moving from knoll to knoll and fence to fence, lasting eight hours. The Rodman had fired its last shot long ago. One fourth of the men of the 16th Cavalry were lying stretched upon the snow, killed or badly wounded. Cartridges for the Sharpe's carbines were nearly all gone. Late that afternoon, while the winter sun was going down, the Southerners on the hillside, seeing how few of the Federal battalion were left, began a simultaneous charge all along the line.

Seeing that they were about to be annihilated, Major Beer raised a piece of shelter tent upon a pole in surrender. The advancing rebel line halted. A rebel officer and two privates rode out from it. Approaching Major Beer, the Confederate officer asked, "Who is in command of this force?"

"I am," replied Major Beer.

"Then, sir," said the Confederate officer, "I demand your sword."

When realization of the surrender struck the men, their first thought was to strip their new carbines and revolvers of their slides and cylinders and throw them away so as to make the guns useless. Overcome with rage and humiliation, the survivors of the 16th Illinois stood there on the bleak mountainside, while the biting wind sloughed the leafless branches of the trees, and listened to the groans and shrieks of their wounded mingling with the triumphant yells of the rebels as they plundered the tents. The shadows of the gloomy winter night closed around them.

The following night was inexpressibly dreary, its gloom intensified by the humiliation of having to give up horses and arms to the enemy. The men were sorrowful and depressed by the loss of so many of their comrades. Dejected though they were over the disaster that befell their battalion, they could not forget that they were intensely hungry. They had not eaten anything all day, and the fight, which began before they had time to get breakfast, left no interval for refreshment.

Later that evening they received a few sacks of meal from their captors, but this was of little help as they did not have anything to cook it in. For a while it looked as if they would have to eat it raw, until the happy thought struck one of the men that they could use their caps for mixing bowls. In a few minutes every cap was put to use in this manner. After getting water from a nearby spring, each man made a little wad of dough, spread it upon a flat rock, and placed it in front of the fire to bake.

It was primitive cooking, but the only way. Having eaten their rude cakes McElroy and his disgusted and dejected comrades crouched around the campfires, speculated as to what would be done with them, and tried to get as much sleep as the biting cold would permit. At dawn next morning they were rounded up by their captors, given more meal, which they cooked in the same way as the night before, and placed under heavy guard. As they prepared for the long, weary march over the mountains to a station of the Virginia and Tennessee Railroad, on the Virginia and Tennessee state line, a rebel rode up on McElroy's horse. McElroy called out to him and his horse, "Hiatoga," gave a whinny of recognition. The young sergeant riding him rode up and inquired if it was his horse. McElroy said that it was and asked the young rebel if he could take some letters, pictures and other trinkets from his saddle pockets. The rebel sergeant agreed, and McElroy and he became friends, traveling side by side as they plodded over the steep, slippery hills, whiling away the time chatting.

But to McElroy's chagrin all the rebel sergeant wanted to talk about was the horse. On the afternoon of the third day after the capture, the column of prisoners came upon a small party of "rustic belles" who were having a "quilting party." The Yankee prisoners became the immediate objects of interest and the young rebel sergeant told the girls that they were going into camp for the night a mile or so up the road, and that if they would be at a certain house he would have a live Yankee for them "for closer inspection."

Later that evening after they went into camp, the young rebel sergeant obtained leave to take McElroy out with a guard. A few moment later McElroy was ushered into a roomful of Southern belles. They entered the room, to a chorus of feminine giggles. The girls remarked about McElroy's hair and eyes, passed judgment on his nose, and called special attention to his hands and feet, all accompanied by silly laughter. McElroy's face turned scarlet and as he turned to speak to the sergeant he showed his back to the ladies. With a loud giggle they fastened their eyes on the ornamental buttons and tabs at the lower extremity of his cavalry jacket. The buttons were used to support the heavy holster and sword belt. But the unsophisticated Southern ladies thought that the two rounded tabs covered a peculiar conformation of Yankee anatomy, like the humps of a Bactrian camel or the horns which they heard all Yankees had. One of the girls was heard to inquire of the others whether it would hurt the cavalryman to cut them off. Another thought that if they did cut them off he would surely bleed to death.

Then, suddenly a new idea struck them. They all shouted together, "Make him sing! Make him sing!" The young rebel sergeant turned to McElroy and said with a very red face, "Sergeant, the girls want to hear you sing." McElroy replied that he could not sing a note, and assured him that he had no musical talent whatever, and asked him to have the ladies sing. The girls gave a fine exhibition of Southern songs and this ended the entertainment.

Four days later McElroy and his fellow prisoners arrived in Bristol, where they were packed closely in old, dilapidated box and stock cars. During the long trip to Richmond the dry journal boxes and unlubricated axles of the cars screeched and groaned, especially when rounding curves. The engine, hauling the train, running not much faster than a man could walk, ran off the track several times and gave those in the cars a severe jolting. But the engine was small and was easily pried back on the track.

Skirting along the base of the Blue Ridge Mountains, past Lynchburg and the Peaks of Otter, through the valleys of the James and Appomattox rivers, the train arrived in Richmond in the dead of night on the tenth morning of the trip. To McElroy, Richmond was a disappointment. The train crossed the long bridge over the Appomattox and came to a grinding halt in a railroad yard. The prisoners were then herded out of the cars and marched through the streets lined with stores and business houses. Many people were sauntering along the streets. Most of the men wore some sort of uniform, as nearly every able-bodied man in the city was enrolled in some sort of military organization. On their way to the prison they marched past the Capitol, a handsome marble building in the Grecian style. As they were marched through the streets they did not excite much attention. In the second year of the war, Yankee prisoners had become commonplace. Before long the march brought them to a street which ran parallel to the Kanawha Canal and the James River. It was lined on both sides by brick warehouses and tobacco factories which were now being used as prisons and military storehouses.

A few blocks further on, the column was halted in front of a warehouse larger than any of the others. Above the door a sign read:

Thomas Libby & Sons
Ship Chandlers and Grocers

This was the notorious "Libby Prison," whose name was familiar to every Union soldier. As they entered their names, rank and regiment were recorded in the prison records. All were then searched for valuables. The guard then conducted them across the street to the third story of another building where they were thrown among some four hundred men belonging to the Army of the Potomac. Thus began McElroy's first day of prison life.

During his sojourn at Libby, there were several attempts at escape on the part of the men of the Army of the Potomac, but these were always frustrated. For the next two months of the winter, McElroy and his chum, B. B. Andrews, ate food that was not fit for dogs, skimmed bugs from their soup, slept on a cold floor, and listened to the profanity exchanged between the guards and their prisoners. By the middle of February, McElroy and his friend Andrews would face the rigors of the hell of Andersonville.

Groans came forth from urns filled with the ashes of dead men. The crash of arms was heard also, and loud cries in the pathless forests, and the noise of spectral armies closing in battle. From the fields nearest the outside walls the inhabitants fled in all directions.

Lucan (Marcus Annaeus Lucanus)

44 B.C. in *The Civil Wars (Pharsalia)*

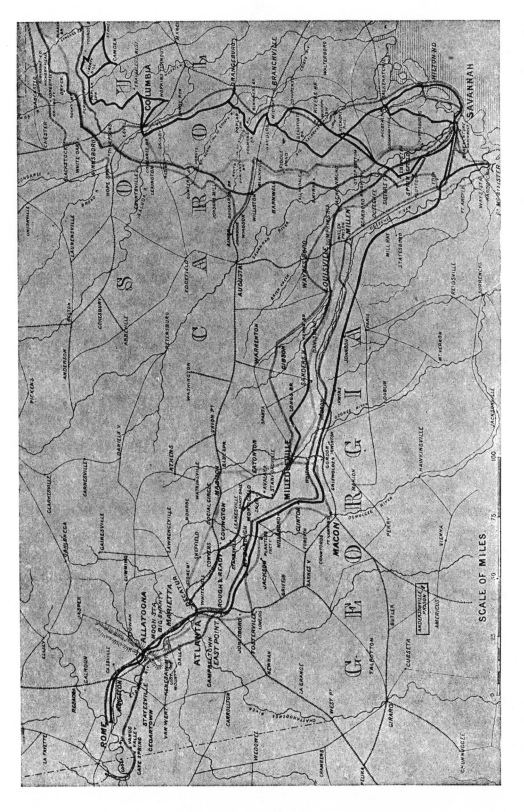

Map Showing the Location of Andersonville and the Routes Traversed by General Sherman's Army in the March to the Sea: drawn by Major General George Ward Nichols, Aide de Camp to General Sherman. Original in the collection of the author.

THE PHOTOGRAPHIC RECORD

A Note on the Photographs and Illustrations

THE ANDERSONVILLE PHOTOGRAPHS reproduced in the album of this book are extremely rare, all but two appearing in their original form for the first time. They were photographed during the months of July or August, 1864, by a Confederate photographer, A. J. Riddle, who brought his camera to the Andersonville Stockade and made his pictures from atop the catwalk used by the prison guards.

The author, John McElroy, recalled: "As a former 'star-boarder' of Andersonville, I well remember seeing a photographer with his camera in one of the sentinel boxes near the South Gate during July or August (1864), trying to take a picture of the interior of the prison. I have often wondered in later years what success this photographer had and why the public never had an opportunity of seeing a genuine photograph of Andersonville."

The photographs of Ulysses S. Grant, Clara Barton, founder of the American Red Cross, and General William Tecumseh Sherman by Mathew B. Brady, are published for the first time. The photographs of the execution of Captain Henri Wirz, Commandant of Andersonville Military Prison, in the Old Capitol Prison in Washington, which was torn down shortly after the execution of the Lincoln conspirators, were taken, presumably, by Alexander Gardner.

The illustrations that appear at the head of each chapter are adapted from the original woodcuts by a rising young modern artist, Arthur Meredith, Jr.

In order to preserve the continuity of the narrative, most of the photographs in the album are captioned with quotations by the author dealing directly with the scene, the time and the location. An original map showing Sherman's invasion of Georgia, and the location of Andersonville Stockade in relation to it, has been included as a guide for the reader.

THE PHOTOGRAPHIC RECORD
(Album Follows Page 134)

This Was ANDERSONVILLE

Captain Henri Wirz

CHAPTER I

A LEAN AND HUNGRY LAND

IN RICHMOND, a sergeant of the 7th Indiana Infantry stated his theory to me this way: "You know I'm just old lightnin' on chuck-a-luck. Now the way I bet is this: I lay down, say on the ace, an' it don't come up; I just double my bet on the ace, an' keep on doublin' every time it loses, until at last it comes up an' then I win a bushel o' money, and mebbe bust the bank. You see the thing's got to come up some time; an' every time it don't come up makes it more likely to come up next time. It's just the same way with this 'ere exchange. The thing's *got* to happen some day, an' every day that it don't happen increases the chances that it will happen the next day."

Some months later I folded the sanguine sergeant's stiffening hands across his fleshless ribs and helped carry his body out to the dead-house at Andersonville, in order to get a piece of wood to cook my ration meal with.

On the evening of the 17th of February, 1864, we were ordered to get ready to move at daybreak the next morning. We were certain this could mean nothing else than an exchange, and our exaltation was such that we did little sleeping that night. The morning was very cold, but we sang and joked as we marched over the creaking bridge on our way to the cars. We were packed so tightly in these that it was impossible even to sit down, and we rolled slowly away after a wheezing engine to Petersburg, whence we expected to march to the exchange post. We reached Petersburg before noon and the cars halted there a long time. We momentarily expected an order to get out. Then the train started up and moved out of the city toward the southeast.

This was inexplicable, but after we had proceeded this way for several hours, some one conceived the idea that the rebels, to avoid treating with Ben Butler, were taking us into the department of some other commander to exchange us. This explanation satisfied us, and our spirits rose again.

Night found us at Gaston, North Carolina, where we received a few crackers for rations, and changed cars. It was dark, and we resorted to a little strategy to secure more room. About thirty of us got into a tight box car and immediately announced that it was too full to admit any more. When an officer came along with another squad to stow away, we would yell out to him to take some of the men out, as we were crowded unbearably. In the meantime everybody in the car would pack closely around the door, so as to give the impression that the car was densely crowded. The rebel looked convinced, and demanded—"Why, how many men have you got in de cah?" Then one of us would order the imaginary host in the invisible recesses to "stand still there and be counted," while he would gravely count up to one hundred or one hundred and twenty, which was the utmost limit of the car, and the rebel would hurry off to put his prisoners somewhere else. We managed to play this successfully during the whole journey, and not only obtained room to lie down in the car, but also drew three or four times as many rations as were intended for us. While we at no time had enough, we were farther from starvation than our less strategic companions.

The second afternoon we arrived at Raleigh, the capital of North Carolina, and were camped in a piece of timber. Shortly after dark orders were issued to us to lie flat on the ground and not rise up till daylight. About the middle of the night a man belonging to a New Jersey regiment, who had apparently forgotten the order, stood up and was immediately shot dead by the guard.

For four or five days more the decrepit little locomotive strained along, dragging after it the rattling old cars. The scenery was intensely monotonous. It was a flat, almost unending stretch of pine barrens. The land was so poor, a disgusted Illinoisan, used to the fertility of the great American Bottom, said rather strongly, "By George, they'd have to manure this ground before they could even make a brick out of it." It was a surprise to all of us who had heard so much of the wealth of Virginia, North Carolina, South Carolina and Georgia, to find the soil a sterile sand bank, interspersed with swamps. We had still no idea of where we were going. We only knew that our general course was southward and that we had passed through the Carolinas and were in Georgia. We furbished up our school knowledge of geography and endeavored to recall something of the location of Raleigh, Charlotte, Columbia and Augusta, through which we passed, but the attempt was not a success.

Late on the afternoon of the 25th of February, the 7th Indiana sergeant approached with the inquiry: "Do you know where Macon is?" The place had not then become as well known as it was afterward. It seemed to me that I had read something of Macon in Revolutionary history, and that it was a fort on the seacoast. He said that the guard had told him we were to be taken to a point near that place, and we agreed that it was probably a new place of exchange. A little later we passed through the town of Macon and turned upon a road that led almost due south.

About midnight the train stopped and we were ordered off. We were in the midst of a forest of tall trees that loaded the air with the heavy balsamic odor peculiar to pine trees. A few small rude houses were scattered around near. Stretching out into the darkness was a double row of great heaps of burning pitch pine that smoked and flamed fiercely and lit up a little space around in the somber forest with a ruddy glare. Between these two rows lay a road which we were ordered to take. The scene was weird and uncanny. I recently read the *Iliad,* and the long lines of huge fires reminded me of that scene in the first book where the Greeks burn on the seashore the bodies of those smitten by Apollo's pestilential arrows:

> For nine long nights, through all the dusky air,
> The pyres, thick flaming, shot a dismal glare.

Five hundred weary men moved along slowly through the double lines of guards. Five hundred men marched silently along towards the gates that were to shut out life and hope from most of them forever. A quarter of a mile from the railroad we came to a massive palisade of great squared logs standing upright in the ground. The fires blazed up and showed us a section of these. Two massive wooden gates, with heavy iron hinges and bolts, swung open as we stood there, and we passed through into the space beyond.

We were in Andersonville.

The next nine months of the existence of those of us who survived were spent in intimate connection with the soil of Georgia, and it exercised a potential influence upon our comfort and well-being, or rather lack of these. A mention of some of its peculiar characteristics may help the reader to a fuller comprehension of the conditions surrounding us.

Georgia, which, next to Texas, is the largest state in the South and has nearly twenty-five per cent more area than the great State of New York, is divided into two distinct and widely differing sections by a geological line extending directly across the state from Augusta on the Savannah River, through Macon on the Ocmulgee, to Columbus on the Chattahoochee. That part lying to the north and west of this line is usually spoken of as "upper" Georgia; while that lying to the south and east, extending to the Atlantic Ocean and the Florida line, is called "lower" Georgia. In this part of the state, though far removed from each other, were the prisons of Andersonville, Savannah, Millen and Blackshear.

Upper Georgia, the capital of which is Atlanta, is a fruitful, productive, metalliferous region that will in time become quite wealthy. Lower Georgia, which has an extent about equal to that of Indiana, is poorer now than a worn-out province of Asia Minor, and in all probability will ever remain so. It is a starved, sterile land, impressing one as a desert in the first stages of reclamation into productive soil, or as productive soil in the last steps of deterioration into a desert. It is a vast expanse of arid yellow sand, broken at intervals by foul swamps, with a jungle-like growth of unwholesome vegetation, teeming with venomous snakes and all manner of hideous crawling things. The original forest which still stands almost unbroken on this wide stretch of thirty thousand square miles does not entirely *cover* it. The tall solemn pines, upright and symmetrical as huge masts, wholly destitute of limbs except for the little, umbrella-like crests at the very top, stand far apart from each other in an unfriendly isolation. There is no fraternal interlacing of branches to form a kindly umbrageous shadow. Between them there is no genial undergrowth of vines, shrubs and demi-trees, generous in fruits, berries and nuts, such as make one of the charms of northern forests. On the ground is no rich springing sod of emerald green, fragrant with the elusive sweetness of white clover and dainty flowers, but a sparse, wiry, famished grass, scattered thinly over the surface in tufts and patches like the hair on a mangy cur. The giant pines seem to have sucked up into their immense boles all the nutriment in the earth and to have starved out every minor growth. So wide and clean is the space between them, that one can look through the forest in any direction for miles, with almost as little interference with the view as on a prairie. In the swampier parts, the trees are lower and their limbs are hung with heavy festoons of the gloomy Spanish moss or "death moss." Where it grows rankest, the malaria is the deadliest. Everywhere Nature seems sad, subdued and somber.

I have long entertained a peculiar theory to account for the decadence and ruin of countries. My reading of the world's history seems to teach me that when a strong people takes possession of a fertile land, they reduce it to cultivation, thrive upon its bountifulness, multiply into millions the mouths to be fed from it, tax it to the last limit of production of the necessaries of life, take from it continually and give nothing back, starve and overwork it as cruel grasping men do a servant or a beast. And when at last it breaks down under the strain, it revenges itself by starving thousands with great famines, while others go off in search of new countries to put through the same process of exhaustion. We have seen one country after another undergo this process as the seat of empire took its westward way, from the cradle of the race on the banks of the Oxus to the fertile plains in the valley of the Euphrates. Impoverishing these, men next sought the valley of the Nile, then the Grecian peninsula, next Syracuse and the Italian peninsula, and the African shores of the Mediterranean. Exhausting all these, they then deserted these for the French, German and English portions of Europe. The turn of the latter is now come; famines are becoming terribly frequent, and mankind is pouring into the virgin fields of America.

Lower Georgia, the Carolinas and eastern Virginia have all the characteristics of these starved and worn-out lands. It would seem as if, away back in the distance of ages, some numerous and civilized race had drained from the soil the last atom of food-producing constituents and that it is now slowly gathering back, as the centuries pass, the elements that have been wrung from the land. Lower Georgia is very thinly settled. Much of the land is still in the hands of the Government. The three or four railroads which pass through it have little reference to local traffic. There are no towns along them as a rule; stations are made every ten miles and are not named but numbered, as Station No. 4, No. 10, etc. The roads were built as through lines, to bring to the seaboard the rich products of the interior.

Andersonville is one of the few stations dignified with a name, probably because it contained some half a dozen shabby houses. At the others, there was usually nothing more than a mere open shed to shelter goods and travellers. Andersonville is on a rudely constructed, rickety railroad that runs from Macon to Albany, the head of navigation on the Flint River, which is one hundred and six miles from Macon and two hundred and fifty from the Gulf of Mexico. Andersonville is about sixty miles from Macon, and about three hundred miles from the Gulf. The camp was merely a hole cut in this wilderness. It was as remote a point from our armies, as they then lay, as the Southern Confederacy could give. The nearest was Sherman's at Chattanooga four hundred miles away, on the other side of a range of mountains hundreds of miles wide.

To us it seemed beyond the last forlorn limits of civilization, and we felt that we were more completely at the mercy of our foes than ever. While in Richmond, we were in the heart of the Confederacy. We were in the midst of the rebel military and civil forces, surrounded on every hand by visible evidences of the great magnitude of that power. But this, while it enforced our ready submission, did not overawe us depressingly. We knew that, though the rebels were all about us in great force, our own men were also near and in still greater force; that while they were very strong, our army was still stronger, and there was no telling what day this superiority of strength might be demonstrated in such a way as to decisively benefit us.

We roused up promptly with the dawn to take a survey of our new abiding place. We found ourselves in an immense pen about one thousand feet long by eight hundred wide. A young surveyor, a member of the 34th Ohio, informed us after he had paced it off that it contained about sixteen acres. The walls were formed by pine logs twenty-five feet long, from two to three feet in diameter, hewn square, set into the ground to a depth of five feet and placed so close together as to leave no crack through which the country outside could be seen. There being five feet of the logs in the ground the wall was, of course, twenty feet high. This manner of enclosure was in some respects superior to a wall of masonry. It was equally unscalable, and much more difficult to undermine or batter down. The pen was longest due north and south. It was divided in the center by a creek about a yard wide and ten inches deep, running from west to east. On each side of this was a quaking bog of slimy ooze one hundred and fifty feet wide and so yielding that one attempting to walk upon it would sink to the waist. From this swamp, the sandhills sloped north and south to the Stockade. All the trees inside the Stockade, save two, had been cut down and used in its construction. All the rank vegetation of the swamp had also been cut off.

There were two entrances to the Stockade, one on each side of the creek, midway between it and the ends, called respectively the North Gate and the South Gate. These had been constructed double by building smaller stockades around them on the out-side with another set of gates. When prisoners or wagons with rations were brought in, they were first brought inside the outer gates which were then carefully secured before the inner gates were opened. This was done to prevent the gates being carried by a rush by those confined inside. At regular intervals along the palisades were little perches, upon which stood guards who overlooked the whole inside of the prison. The only view we had of the outside was that obtained by looking from the highest points of the north and south sides across the depression where the stockade crossed the swamp. In this way we could see about forty acres at a time of the adjoining wood-land, or say one hundred and sixty acres altogether, and this meager landscape had to content us.

Before our inspection was finished, a wagon drove in with rations. A quart of meal, a sweet potato and a few ounces of salt beef were issued to each one of us and in a few minutes we were all hard at work preparing our first meal in Andersonville. The debris of the forest left a temporary abundance of fuel, and we already had a cheerful fire blazing for every little squad. There were a number of tobacco presses in the rooms we occupied in Richmond and for each of these was a quantity of sheets of tin evidently used to put between the layers of tobacco. The deft hands of the mechanics among us now bent these up into square pans which were real handy cooking utensils, holding about a quart. Water was carried in them from the creek; the meal was mixed in them to a dough or else boiled as mush in the same vessels; in them our potatoes were boiled; and their final service was to hold first a little meal to be carefully browned and then the water boiled upon it, so as to form a feeble imitation of coffee.

I found my education at Jonesville in the art of baking hoe-cake now came in good play, both for myself and my companions. Taking one of the pieces of tin which had not yet been made into a pan, we spread upon it a layer of dough about a half-inch thick. We propped this up nearly upright before the fire, and it was soon nicely browned over. This process made it sweat itself loose from the tin, when it was turned over and the bottom browned also. Save that it was destitute of salt, it was quite a toothsome bit of nutriment for a hungry man, and I recommend that my readers try making a "pone" of this kind once, just to see what it was like.

The supreme indifference with which the rebels always treated the matter of cooking utensils for us excited my wonder. It never seemed to occur to them that we could have any more need of vessels for our food than cattle or swine. Never during my whole prison life did I see so much as a tin cup or a bucket issued to a prisoner. Starving men were driven to all sorts of shifts for want of these. Pantaloons or coats were pulled off and their sleeves or legs used to draw a mess's meal in. Boots were common vessels for carrying water, and when the feet of these gave way, the legs were ingeniously closed up with pine pegs so as to form rude leathern buckets. Men whose pocket-knives had escaped search at the gates made very ingenious little tubs and buckets, and these devices enabled us to get along after a fashion.

After our meal was disposed of, we held a council on the situation. Though we had been sadly disappointed in not being exchanged, it seemed that on the whole our condition had been bettered. This first ration was a decided improvement on those of the Pemberton Building; we had left the snow and ice behind at Richmond—or rather at some place between Raleigh, North Carolina, and Columbia, South Carolina—and the air here, though chill, was not nipping, but bracing. It looked as if we would have plenty of wood for shelter and fuel; it was certainly better to have sixteen acres to roam over than the stifling confines of a building; and, still better, it seemed as if there would be plenty of opportunities to get beyond the Stockade and attempt a journey through the woods to that blissful land—our lines.

We settled down to make the best of things. A rebel sergeant came in presently and arranged us in hundreds. We subdivided these into messes of twenty-five, and began devising means for shelter. Nothing showed the inborn capacity of the Northern soldier to take care of himself better than the way in which we accomplished this with the rude materials at our command. No ax, spade or mattock was allowed us by the rebels, who treated us in regard to these the same as in respect to culinary vessels. The only tools were a few pocket-knives and perhaps half a dozen hatchets which some infantrymen, principally members of the 3rd Michigan, were allowed to retain.

Yet, despite all these drawbacks, we had quite a village of huts erected in a few days—nearly enough, in fact, to afford tolerable shelter for the whole five hundred of us first-comers. The withes and poles that grew in the swamps were bent into the shape of the semicircular bows that support the canvas covers of army wagons, and both ends were thrust in the ground. These formed the timbers of our dwellings. They were held in place by weaving in, basket-wise, a network of briers and vines. Tufts of the long leaves which are the distinguishing characteristic of the Georgia pine, popularly known as the "long-leafed pine," were brought into this network until a thatch was formed that was a fair protection against the rain—it was like the Irishman's unglazed window-sash which "kep' out the coarsest uv the cold."

The results accomplished were as astonishing to us as to the rebels, who would have lain unsheltered upon the sand until bleached out like field-rotted flax before thinking to protect themselves in this way. As our village was approaching completion, the rebel sergeant who called the roll entered. He was very odd-looking. The cervical muscles were distorted in such a way as to suggest the name of "Wry-necked Smith," and so we always designated him. Pete Bates of the 3rd Michigan, who was the wag of our squad, accounted for Smith's condition by saying that once, while on dress parade, the colonel of Smith's regiment had commanded "eyes right," and then forgot to give the order "front." Smith, being a good soldier, had kept his eyes in the position of gazing at the buttons of the third man to the right, waiting for the order to restore them to their natural direction, until they had become permanently fixed in their obliquity and he was compelled to go through life taking a biased view of all things. Smith made a diagonal survey of the encampment which, if he had ever seen *Mitchell's Geography,* probably reminded him of the picture of a Kaffir village in that instructive but awfully dull book, and then expressed the opinion that usually welled up to every rebel's lips: "Well, I'll be durned, if you Yanks don't just beat the devil." Of course we replied with the well-worn prison joke, that we supposed we did, since we beat the rebels, who were worse than the devil.

There rode in among us, a few days after our arrival, an old man whose collar bore the wreathed stars of a Major General. Heavy white locks fell from beneath his slouched hat nearly to his shoulders. Sunken gray eyes, too dull and cold to light up, marked a hard stony face, the salient feature of which was a thin-lipped compressed mouth, with corners drawn down deeply—the mouth which seems the world over to be the index of selfish, cruel, sulky malignance. It is such a mouth as has the school-boy, the coward of the playground, who delights in pulling off the wings of flies. It is such a mouth as we can imagine some remorseless inquisitor to have had—that is, not an inquisitor filled with holy zeal for what he mistakenly thought the cause Christ demanded, but a spleeny, envious, rancorous shaveling, who tortured men from hatred of their superiority to him and sheer love of inflicting pain.

The rider was General John H. Winder, Commissary General of Prisoners, a Baltimorean renegade and the malign genius to whose account should be charged the deaths of more gallant men than all the inquisitors of the world ever slew by the less dreadful rack and wheel. It was he who, in August, could point to the three thousand and eighty-one new-made graves for that month and exultingly tell his hearer that he was "doing more for the Confederacy than twenty regiments." His lineage was in accordance with his character. His father was that General William H. Winder whose poltroonery at Bladensburg in 1814 nullified the resistance of the gallant Commodore Barney and gave Washington to the British. The father was a coward and an incompetent. The son, John, always cautiously distant from the scene of hostilities, was the tormentor of those whom the fortunes of war and the arms of brave men threw into his hands.

Winder was an obscure, dull old man, the commonplace descendant of a pseudo-aristocrat whose cowardly incompetence had once cost us the loss of the national capital. More prudent than his runaway father, he held himself aloof from the field. His father had lost reputation—and almost his commission—by coming into contact with the enemy. He would take no such foolish risks, and he did not. When false expectations of the ultimate triumph of secession led him to cast his lot with the Southern Confederacy, he did not solicit a command in the field but took up his quarters in Richmond, to become a sort of Informer-General, High Inquisitor and Chief Eaves-dropper for his intimate friend, Jefferson Davis.

He pried and spied around every man's bedroom and family circle to discover traces of Union sentiment. The wildest tales malice and vindictiveness could concoct found welcome reception in his ears. He was only too willing to believe, that he might find an excuse for harrying and persecuting. He arrested, insulted, imprisoned, banished and shot people, until the patience even of the citizens of Richmond gave way, and pressure was brought upon Jefferson Davis to secure the suppression of his satellite. For a long while Davis resisted, but at last yielded, and transferred Winder to the office of Commissary General of Prisoners. The delight of the Richmond people was great. One of the papers expressed it in an article, the keynote of which was, "Thank God that Richmond is at last rid of old Winder. God have mercy upon those to whom he has been sent." Remorseless and cruel as his conduct of the office of Provost Marshal was, it gave little hint of the extent to which he would go in that of Commissary General of Prisoners. Before, he was restrained somewhat by public opinion and the laws of the land. These no longer deterred him.

Winder gazed at us stonily for a few minutes without speaking and, turning, rode out again. Our troubles from that hour rapidly increased.

Prize Fight for the Skillet

CHAPTER II

ANDERSONVILLE

THE STOCKADE was not quite finished at the time of our arrival, a gap of several hundred feet appearing at the southwest corner. A gang of about two hundred Negroes were at work felling trees, hewing logs and placing them upright in the trenches. We had an opportunity, soon to disappear forever, of studying the workings of the "peculiar institution" in its very home.

These Negroes were of the lowest field-hand class, strong, dull, ox-like but each having, in our eyes, an admixture of cunning and secretiveness that their masters pretended was not in them. Their demeanor toward us illustrated this. We were the objects of the most supreme interest to them but, when near us and in the presence of a white rebel, this interest took the shape of stupid, open-eyed, open-mouthed wonder, something akin to the look on the face of a rustic lout gazing for the first time upon a locomotive or a steam threshing-machine. But if chance threw one of them near us and he thought himself unobserved by the rebels, the blank vacant face lighted up with an entirely different expression. He was no longer the credulous yokel who believed the Yankees were only slightly modified devils, ready at any instant to return to their original horn-and-tail condition and snatch him away to the bluest kind of perdition. He knew, apparently quite as well as his master, that they were in some way his friends and allies, and he lost no opportunity in communicating his appreciation of that fact, offering his services in any possible way. And these offers were sincere. It is the testimony of every Union prisoner in the South that he was never betrayed by, or disappointed in, a field Negro, but could always approach any one of them with perfect confidence in his extending all the aid in his power, whether as a guide to escape, as a sentinel to signal danger, or a purveyor of food. These services were frequently attended with the greatest personal risk, but they were none the less readily undertaken. This applies only to the field hands; the house servants were treacherous and wholly unreliable. Very many of our men who managed to get away from the prisons were recaptured through the betrayal of house servants, but none were retaken where a field hand could prevent it.

We were much interested in watching the Negro work. They wove in a great deal of their peculiar, wild, mournful music whenever the character of the labor permitted. They seemed to sing the music for the music's sake alone, and were as heedless of the fitness of the accompanying words as the composer of a modern opera is of his libretto.

One middle-aged man, with a powerful mellow baritone like the round full notes of a French horn played by a virtuoso, was the musical leader of the party. He never seemed to bother himself about air, notes or words, but improvised all as he went along, singing as the spirit moved him. He would suddenly break out with, "Oh, he's gone up dah, nevah to come back again." At this every darky within hearing would roll out, in admirable consonance with the pitch, air, and time started by the leader, "O-o-o-o-o-o-o-o-o-o-o!" Then would ring out from the leader as from the throbbing lips of a silver trumpet, "Lord bress him soul; I done think he is happy now!" And the antiphonal two hundred would chant back. And so on for hours. They never seemed to weary of singing, and we certainly did not tire of listening to them. The absolute independence of conventionalities of tune and sentiment gave them freedom to wander through a kaleidoscopic variety of harmonic effects, as spontaneous and changeful as the song of a bird.

I sat up one evening, long after the shadows of night had fallen upon the hillside, with one of my chums, Frank Berkstresser of the 9th Maryland Infantry, who, before enlisting, was a mathematical tutor in a college at Hancock, Maryland. As we listened to the unwearying flow of melody from the camp of laborers, I thought of, and repeated to him, Longfellow's lines:

> And the voice of his devotion
> Filled my soul with strong emotion:
> For its tones by turns were glad,
> Sweetly solemn, wildly sad.

"Now, isn't that fine, Berkstresser?" I said. He was a Democrat of fearfully pro-slavery ideas, and he replied, sententiously, "Oh, the poetry's tolerable, but the sentiment's damnable."

The official designation of our prison was "Camp Sumter," but this was scarcely known outside of the rebel documents, reports and orders. It was the same way with the prison five miles from Millen to which we were afterward transferred. The rebels styled it officially "Camp Lawton" but we always called it "Millen." Having our huts finished, the next solicitude was about escape. This was the burden of our thoughts day and night. We held conferences at which every man was required to contribute all the geographical knowledge of that section of Georgia that he might have left over from his school days and also that gained by persistent questioning of such guards and other rebels as he had come in contact with. When first landed in the prison, we were as ignorant of our whereabouts as if we had been dropped in the center of Africa. But one of the prisoners was found to have a fragment of a school atlas in which was an outline map of Georgia that had Macon, Atlanta, Milledgeville and Savannah laid down upon it.

As we knew we had come southward from Macon, we felt pretty certain we were in the southwestern corner of the state. Conversations with guards and others gave us the information that the Chattahoochee flowed some two score miles to the westward and that the Flint River lay a little nearer on the east. Our map showed that these two united and flowed together into Appalachicola Bay where, some of us remembered, a newspaper item had said we had gunboats stationed. The creek that ran through the Stockade flowed to the east, and we reasoned that if we followed its course we would be led to the Flint River, down which we could float on a log or raft to the Bay. This was the favorite scheme of the party with which I sided. Another party believed the most feasible plan was to go northward and endeavor to gain the mountains, and thence get into East Tennessee. But the main thing was to get away from the Stockade. This, as the French say of all first steps, was what would cost.

Our first attempt was made about a week after our arrival. We found two logs on the east side that were a couple feet shorter than the rest and it seemed as if they could be successfully scaled. About fifty of us resolved to make the attempt. We made a rope twenty-five or thirty feet long, strong enough to bear a man, out of strips of cloth. A stout stick was fastened to the end, so that it would catch on the logs on either side of the gap. On a night dark enough to favor our scheme, we gathered together, drew cuts to determine each boy's place in line, fell in single rank, according to this arrangement, and marched to the place. The line was thrown skillfully, the stick caught fairly in the notch, and the boy who had drawn number one climbed up amid suspense so keen that I could hear my heart beating. It seemed ages before he reached the top and that the noise he made must certainly attract the attention of the guard. It did not.

We saw our comrade's figure outlined against the sky as he slid over the top, and then heard the dull thump as he sprang to the ground on the other side. "Number two," was whispered by the leader, and he too performed the feat as successfully as his predecessor. Thus it went on until, just as we heard number fifteen drop, we also heard a rebel voice say in a vicious undertone, "Halt! Halt, there, damn you!" This was enough. The game was up. We were discovered, and the remaining thirty-five of us left that locality with all the speed in our heels, getting away just in time to escape a volley which a squad of guards, posted in the lookouts, poured upon the spot where we had been standing.

The next morning, the fifteen who had got over the Stockade were brought in, each chained to a sixty-four-pound ball. Their story was that one of the N'Yaarkers,[1] who had become cognizant of our scheme, had sought to obtain favor in the rebel eyes by betraying us. The rebels stationed a squad at the crossing place and as each man dropped down from the Stockade, he was caught by the shoulder, the muzzle of a revolver thrust into his face, and an order to surrender whispered into his ear. It was expected that the guards in the sentry-boxes would do such execution among those of us still inside as would prove a warning to other would-be escapees. They were defeated in this benevolent intention by the readiness with which we divined the meaning of that incautiously loud halt and our alacrity in leaving the unhealthy locality. The traitorous "N'Yaarker" was rewarded with a detail in the Commissary Department where he fed and fattened like a rat that had secured undisturbed homestead rights in the center of a cheese. When the miserable remnant of us were leaving Andersonville months afterward, I saw him, sleek, rotund and well-clothed, lounging leisurely in the door of a tent. He regarded us a moment contemptuously and then went on conversing with a fellow N'Yaarker in the foul slang that none but such as he were low enough to use. I have always imagined that the fellow returned home at the close of the war to become a prominent member of Tweed's gang.

We protested against the barbarity of compelling men to wear irons for exercising their natural right of attempting to escape, but no attention was paid to our protest. Another result of this abortive affair was the establishment of the notorious Dead Line. A few days later a gang of Negroes came in and drove a line of stakes down at a distance of twenty feet from the Stockade. They nailed upon this a strip of stuff four inches wide, and then an order was issued that if this was crossed or even touched, the guards would fire upon the offender without warning. Our surveyor figured this new contraction of space, and came to the conclusion that the Dead Line and the swamp took up about three acres. This was not of much consequence then, however, as we still had plenty of room.

The first man to be killed after the Dead Line was established was a German wearing the white crescent of the 2nd Division of the 11th Corps, whom we had nick-named "Sigel." Hardship and exposure had crazed him and brought on a severe attack of St. Vitus's dance. As he went hobbling around with a vacuous grin upon his face, he spied an old piece of cloth lying on the ground inside the Dead Line. He stooped down and reached under for it. At that instant the guard fired. The charge of ball-and-buck entered the poor fellow's shoulder and tore through his body. He fell dead, still clutching the dirty rag that had cost him his life.

The emptying of the prisons at Danville and Richmond into Andersonville went on slowly during the month of March. They came in, by trainloads of from five to eight hundred, at intervals of two or three days. By the end of the month there were about five thousand in the Stockade. There was a fair amount of space for this number, and as yet we suffered no inconvenience from our crowding, though most persons would fancy that thirteen acres of ground was a rather limited area for five thousand men to live, move and have their being upon. Yet a few weeks later we were to see seven times that many packed into that space.

One morning a new rebel officer came in to superintend calling the roll. He was an undersized, fidgety man with an insignificant face and a mouth that protruded like a rabbit's. His bright little eyes, like those of a squirrel or a rat, assisted in giving his countenance a look of kinship to the family of rodent animals, a genus which lives on stealth and cunning, subsisting on that which it can steal away from stronger and braver creatures. He was dressed in a pair of gray trousers with the other part of his body covered with a calico garment like that which small boys used to wear called waists. This was fastened to the pantaloons by buttons precisely as was the custom with the garments of boys still struggling with the orthography of words in two syllables. Upon his head was perched a little gray cap. Sticking in his belt and fastened to his wrist by a strap two or three feet long was one of those formidable-looking but harm-less English revolvers that have ten barrels around the edge of the cylinder and fire a musket bullet from the center. The wearer of this composite costume and bearer of this amateur arsenal stepped nervously about and sputtered volubly in broken Eng-lish. He said to Wry-Necked Smith, "Py Gott, you don't vatch dem damn Yankees glose enough! Dey are schlippin' rount, and peatin' you efery dimes."

This was Captain Henri Wirz, the new Commandant of the interior of the prison.

There has been a great deal of misapprehension of the character of Wirz. He is usually regarded as a villain of large mental caliber, with a genius for cruelty. He was nothing of the kind. He was simply contemptible from whatever point of view he was studied. Gnat-brained, cowardly and feeble-natured, he had not a quality that commanded respect from anyone who knew him. His cruelty did not seem so much designed, but rather the ebullitions of a peevish, snarling little temper, united to a mind incapable of conceiving the results of his acts or of understanding the pain he was inflicting. I never heard anything of his profession or vocation before entering the army. I always believed, however, that he had been a cheap clerk in a small dry-goods store, a third- or fourth-rate bookkeeper or something similar.

Imagine, if you please, one such, who never had brains or self-command sufficient to control himself, placed in command of thirty-five thousand men. Being a fool, he could not help being an infliction to them, even with the best of intentions. And Wirz was not troubled with good intentions. I mention the probability of his having been a dry-goods clerk or bookkeeper, not with any disrespect to two honorable vocations, but because Wirz had had some training as an accountant, and this was what gave him the place over us. Rebels, as a rule, are astonishingly ignorant of arithmetic and accounting. Generally they are good shots, fine horsemen, ready speakers and ardent politicians. But like all non-commercial people, they flounder hopelessly in what people of this section would consider simple mathematical processes.

One of our constant amusements was in befogging and "beating" those charged with calling the rolls and issuing rations. It was not at all difficult at times to make a hundred men count as a hundred and ten and so on. Wirz could count beyond one hundred, and this had determined his selection for the place. His first move was a stupid change. We had been grouped in the natural way into hundreds and thousands. He rearranged the men in squads of ninety, and three of these—two hundred and seventy men—into a detachment. The detachments were numbered in order from the North Gate, and the squads were numbered one, two, three. On the rolls this was stated after the man's name. For instance, a chum of mine in the same squad with me, was Charles L. Soule of the 3rd Michigan Infantry. His name appeared on the rolls: "Chas. L. Soule, priv. Co. E, 3d Mich. Inf., 1-2." That is, he belonged to the 2nd Squad of the 1st Detachment. Where Wirz got his preposterous idea of organization from has always been a mystery to me. It was awkward in every way—in drawing rations, counting and dividing into messes.

Wirz was not long in giving us a taste of his quality. The next morning after his first appearance, he came in when roll call was sounded and ordered all the squads and detachments to form and remain standing in ranks until all were counted. Any soldier will say that there is no duty more annoying and difficult than standing still in ranks for any considerable length of time, especially when there is nothing to do or engage the attention. It took Wirz between two and three hours to count the whole camp, and by that time we of the first detachments were almost all out of ranks. Thereupon Wirz announced that no rations would be issued to the camp that day. The orders to stand in ranks were repeated the next morning, with a warning that a failure to obey would be punished as that of the previous day had been.

We were so hungry that, to use the words of a 35th Pennsylvanian standing next to me, his "big intestines were eating his little ones up." It was impossible to keep the rank formation during the long hours. One man after another straggled away, and again we lost our rations. That afternoon we became desperate. Plots were considered for a daring assault to force the gates or scale the Stockade. The men were crazy enough to attempt anything rather than sit down and patiently starve. Many offered themselves as leaders in any attempt that it might be thought best to make. The hopelessness of any such venture was apparent, even to famished men, and the proposition went no farther than inflammatory talk.

The third morning the orders were again repeated. This time we succeeded in remaining in ranks in such a manner as to satisfy Wirz and we were given our rations for that day, but those for the other days were permanently withheld. That afternoon Wirz ventured into camp alone. He was assailed with a storm of curses, execrations and a shower of clubs. He pulled out his revolver as if to fire upon his assailants. A yell was raised to take his pistol away from him and a crowd rushed forward to do this. Without waiting to fire a shot, he turned and ran to the gate for dear life. He did not come in again for a long while, and never afterward without a retinue of guards.

One of the trainloads from Richmond was almost wholly made up of our old acquaintances, the N'Yaarkers. The number of these had swelled to four or five hundred, all leagued together in the fellowship of crime. We did not manifest any keen desire for intimate social relations with them, and they did not seem to hunger for our society, so they moved across the creek to the unoccupied south side, and established their camp there at a considerable distance from us.

One afternoon a number of us went across to their camp, to witness a fight, according to the rules of the prize ring, which was to come off between two professional pugilists. These were a couple of bounty-jumpers [2] who had some little reputation in New York sporting circles under the names of the "Staleybridge Chicken" and the "Haarlem Infant." On the way from Richmond a cast-iron skillet—or spider—had been stolen by the crowd from the rebels. It was a small affair, holding a half gallon and worth today about fifty cents. In Andersonville its worth was literally above rubies.

Two men belonging to different messes each claimed the ownership of the utensil, on the ground of being most active in securing it. Their claims were strenuously supported by their respective messes, at the heads of which were the aforesaid "Infant" and "Chicken." A great deal of strong talk and several indecisive knock-downs resulted in an agreement to settle the matter by wager of battle between the "Infant" and "Chicken."

When we arrived, a twenty-four-foot ring had been prepared by drawing a deep mark in the sand. In diagonally opposite corners of these, the seconds were kneeling on one knee and supporting their principals on the other. By their sides they had little vessels of water and bundles of rags to answer for sponges. Another corner was occupied by the umpire, a foul-mouthed, long-tongued Tombs shyster named Pete Bradley. A long-bodied, short-legged hoodlum nicknamed "Heenan," armed with a club, acted as ring keeper and belted back remorselessly any of the spectators who crowded over the line. Did he see a foot obtruding itself so much as an inch over the mark in the sand, and the pressure from the crowd behind was so great that it was difficult for the front fellows to keep off the line, his heavy club and a blasting curse would fall upon the offender simultaneously.

Every effort was made to have all things conform as nearly as possible to the recognized practices of the London Prize Ring. At Bradley's call of time, the principals would rise from their seconds' knees, advance briskly to the scratch across the center of the ring and spar away sharply for a little time, until one got in a blow that sent the other to the ground where he would lie until his second picked him up, carried him back, washed his face off and gave him a drink. He then rested until the next call of time. This sort of performance went on for an hour or more, with the knock-downs and other casualties pretty evenly divided between the two. Then it became apparent that the "Infant" was getting more than he had storage room for. His interest in the skillet was evidently abating, the leering grin he wore upon his face during the early part of the engagement had disappeared long ago, as the successive "hot ones" which the "Chicken" had succeeded in planting upon his mouth, put it out of his power to "smile and smile, e'en though he might still be a villain." He began coming up to the scratch as sluggishly as a hired man starting out for his day's work, and finally he did not come up at all. A bunch of blood-soaked rags was tossed into the air from his corner, and Bradley declared the "Chicken" to be the victor amid enthusiastic cheers from the crowd. We voted the thing rather tame. In the whole hour and a half there was not so much savage fighting, not so much damage done as a couple of earnest but unscientific men who have no time to waste will frequently crowd into an impromptu affair not exceeding five minutes in duration.

Our next visit to the N'Yaarkers was on a different errand. The moment they arrived in camp we began to be annoyed by their depredations. Blankets, the sole protection of men, would be snatched off as they slept at night. Articles of clothing and cooking utensils would go the same way, and occasionally a man would be robbed in open daylight. All these, it was believed with good reason, were the work of the N'Yaarkers, and the stolen things were conveyed to their camp. Occasionally depredators would be caught and beaten, but they would give a signal which would bring to their assistance the whole body of N'Yaarkers, and turn the tables on their assailants.

We had in our squad a little watchmaker named Dan Martin, of the 8th New York Infantry. Other boys let him take their watches to tinker up, so as to make a show of running and be available for trading to the guards. One day, when Martin was at the creek, a N'Yaarker asked him to let him look at a watch. Martin incautiously did so. The N'Yaarker snatched it and sped away to the camp of his crowd. Martin ran back to us and told his story. This was the feather which broke the camel's back of our patience. Peter Bates of the 3rd Michigan, the sergeant of our squad, had considerable confidence in his muscular ability. He flamed up into mighty wrath and swore a sulphurous oath that we would get that watch back, whereupon about two hundred of us avowed our willingness to help reclaim it.

Each of us providing ourselves with a club, we started on our errand. The rest of the camp, about four thousand at that time, gathered on the hillside to watch us. We thought they might have sent us some assistance, as it was about as much their fight as ours, but they did not, and we were too proud to ask it. The crossing of the swamp was quite difficult. Only one could go over at a time, and he very slowly. The N'Yaarkers understood that trouble was pending, and they began mustering to receive us. From the way they turned out, it was evident that we should have come over with three hundred instead of two hundred, but it was too late then to alter the program.

As we came up, a stalwart Irishman stepped out and asked us what we wanted. Bates replied, "We have come over to get a watch that one of your fellows took from one of ours, and by God we're going to have it." The Irishman's reply was equally explicit, though not strictly logical in construction. "We haven't got your blasted watch, and begorra ye can't have it!" This joined the issue just as fairly as if it had been done by all the documentary formulae that passed between Turkey and Russia prior to the late war.[3] Bates and the Irishman then exchanged very derogatory opinions of each other and began striking with their clubs. The rest of us took this as our cue and, each selecting as small a N'Yaarker as he could find, sailed in. There is a very expressive bit of slang coming into general use in the West, which speaks of a man "biting off more than he can chew." That is what we had done. We had taken a contract that we should have divided and sublet the bigger half. Two minutes after the engagement became general, there was no doubt that we would have been much better off if we had stayed on our own side of the creek. The watch was a very poor one anyhow. We thought we would just say good day to our New York friends and return home hastily. But they declined to be left so precipitately. They wanted to stay with us awhile. It was lots of fun for them and for the four thousand yelling spectators on the opposite hill who were greatly enjoying our discomfiture. There was hardly enough of the amusement to go clear around, however, and it all fell short just before it reached us. We earnestly wished that some of the boys would come over and help us let go of the N'Yaarkers, but they were enjoying the thing too much to interfere. We were driven down the hill, pell-mell, with the N'Yaarkers pursuing hotly with yell and blow.

At the swamp we tried to make a stand to secure our passage across, but it was only partially successful. Very few got back without some severe hurts, and many received blows that greatly hastened their death. After this, the N'Yaarkers became bolder in their robberies and more arrogant in their demeanor than ever, and we had the poor revenge upon those who would not assist us of seeing a reign of terror inaugurated over the whole camp.

Shot at the Creek by a Guard

CHAPTER III

THE DEAD LINE

THE RATIONS diminished perceptibly day by day. When we first entered we each received something over a quart of tolerably good meal, a sweet potato, a piece of meat about the size of one's two fingers, and occasionally a spoonful of salt. First the salt disappeared. Then the sweet potato took unto itself wings and flew away never to return.

An attempt was ostensibly made to issue us cow-peas [4] instead, and the first issue was only a quart to a detachment of two hundred and seventy men! This was two-thirds of a pint to each squad of ninety, and made but a few spoonfuls for each of the four messes in the squad. When it came to dividing among the men, the beans had to be counted. Nobody received enough to pay for cooking, and we were at a loss what to do until somebody suggested that we play poker for them. This met general acceptance, and after that, as long as beans were drawn, a large portion of the day was spent in absorbing games of "bluff and draw," at a bean ante and no limit. After a number of hours' diligent playing, some lucky or skillful player would be in possession of all the beans in the mess, and a squad and sometimes even a detachment would then have enough for a good meal. Next, the meal began to diminish in quantity and deteriorate in quality. It became so exceedingly coarse that the common remark was that the next step was to bring us the corn in the shock and feed it to us like cattle. Then meat followed suit with the rest. The rations decreased in size, and the number of days that we did not get any kept constantly increasing in proportion to the days that we did, until eventually the meat bade us a final adieu and joined the sweet potatoes in that undiscovered country from whose bourne no ration ever returned.

The fuel and building material in the Stockade were speedily exhausted. The later comers had nothing whatever to build shelters with. But, after the spring rains had fairly set in, it seemed that we had not tasted misery until then. About the middle of March, the windows of heaven opened and it began to rain like that of the time of Noah. It was tropical in quantity and persistency and arctic in temperature. For dreary hours that lengthened into weary days and nights and these again into never-ending weeks, the driving, drenching flood poured down upon the sodden earth, searching the very marrow of the five thousand hapless men against whose chilled frame it beat with pitiless monotony, and soaking the sandbank upon which we lay until it was like a sponge filled with ice-water.

It seems to me now that it must have been two or three weeks that the sun was wholly hidden behind the dripping clouds, not shining out once in all that time. The intervals when it did not rain were rare and short. An hour's respite would be followed by a day of steady, regular pelting of the great raindrops. I find that the report of the Smithsonian Institute gives the average annual rainfall in the section around Andersonville at fifty-six inches, nearly five feet, while that of foggy England is only thirty-two. Our experience would lead me to think that we got the five feet all at once.

We first-comers who had huts were measurably better off than the later arrivals. It was much dryer in our leaf-thatched tents, and we were spared much of the annoyance that comes from the steady dash of rain against the body for hours. The condition of those who had no tents was truly pitiable. They sat or lay on the hillside the live-long day and night, and took the washing flow with such gloomy composure as they could muster. All soldiers will agree with me that there is no campaign hardship comparable to a cold rain. One can brace up against the extremes of heat and cold and mitigate their inclemency in various ways. But there is no escaping a long-continued, chilling rain. It seems to penetrate to the heart, and leach away the very vital force.

The only relief attainable was found in huddling over little fires kept alive by small groups with their slender stocks of wood. As this wood was all pitch-pine that burned with a very sooty flame, the effect upon the appearance of the hoverers was startling. Face, neck and hands became covered with a mixture of lampblack and turpentine, forming a coating as thick as heavy brown paper, and absolutely irremovable by water alone. The hair also became of midnight blackness, and gummed up into elf-locks of fantastic shape and effect. Any one of us could have gone on the Negro minstrel stage, without changing a hair, and put to blush the most elaborate make-up of the grotesque burnt-cork artists. No wood was issued to us. The only way of getting it was to stand around the gate for hours until a guard off duty could be coaxed or hired to accompany a small party to the woods, to bring back a load of such knots and limbs as could be picked up. Our chief persuaders to the guards to do us this favor were rings, pencils, knives, combs and such trifles as we might have in our pockets and, more especially, the brass buttons on our uniforms. Rebel soldiers, like Indians, Negroes and other imperfectly civilized people, were passionately fond of bright and gaudy things. A handful of brass buttons would catch every one of them as swiftly and as surely as a piece of red flannel will a gudgeon. Our regular fee for an escort for three of us to the woods was six overcoat or dress coat buttons, or ten or twelve jacket buttons. All in the mess contributed to this fund, and the fuel obtained was carefully guarded and husbanded.

This manner of conducting the wood business is a fair sample of the management, or rather the lack of it, of every other detail of prison administration. All the hardships we suffered from lack of fuel and shelter could have been prevented without the slightest expense or trouble to the Confederacy. Two hundred men allowed to go out on parole and supplied with axes, could, in a week's time, have brought in from the adjacent woods enough material to make everybody comfortable tents and to supply all the fuel needed. The mortality caused by the storm was, of course, very great. The official report says the total number in the prison in March was four thousand six hundred and three, of whom two hundred and eighty-three died.

Among the first to die was the one whom we expected to live longest. He was by much the largest man in prison, and because of this was called Big Joe. He was a sergeant in the 5th Pennsylvania Cavalry, and seemed the picture of health. One morning the news ran through the prison that Big Joe was dead, and a visit to his squad showed his stiff, lifeless form occupying as much ground as Goliath's after his encounter with David. His early demise was an example of a general law, the workings of which few in the army failed to notice.

It was always the large and strong who first succumbed to hardship. The stalwart, huge-limbed, toil-inured men sank down earliest on the march, yielded soonest to malarial influences, and fell first under the combined effects of homesickness, exposure and the privations of army life. The slender, wiry boys, as supple and weak as cats, had apparently the nine lives of those animals. There were few exceptions to this rule in the army; there were none in Andersonville. I can recall few or no instances where a large, strong, "hearty" man lived through more than a few months of imprisonment. The survivors were invariably youths at the verge of manhood, slender, quick, active, medium-statured fellows, of a cheerful temperament, in whom one would have expected comparatively little powers of endurance. The theory which I constructed for my own private use in accounting for this phenomenon I offer with proper diffidence to others who may be in search of a hypothesis to explain facts that they have observed. It is this: no strong man is a healthy man, from the athlete in the circus who lifts pieces of artillery and catches cannon balls, to the exhibitions "swell" in a country gymnasium. If my theory is not a sufficient explanation of this, there is nothing to prevent the reader from building up one to suit him better.

There were two regiments guarding us—the 26th Alabama and the 55th Georgia. Never were two regiments of the same army more different. The Alabamians were the superiors of the Georgians in every way that one set of men could be superior to another. They were manly, soldierly and honorable, where the Georgians were treacherous and brutal. We had nothing to complain of at the hands of the Alabamians; we suffered from the Georgians everything that mean-spirited cruelty could devise. The Georgians were always on the look-out for something that they could torture into such apparent violations of orders as would justify them in shooting men down; the Alabamians never fired until they were satisfied that a deliberate offense was intended. I can recall of my own seeing at least a dozen instances where men of the 55th Georgia killed prisoners under the pretense that they were across the Dead Line, when the victims were a yard or more from the Dead Line and had not the remotest idea of going any nearer.

The only man I ever knew to be killed by one of the 26th Alabama was named Hubbard from Chicago, a member of the 38th Illinois. He had lost one leg, and went hobbling about the camp on crutches, chattering continually in a loud, discordant voice, saying all manner of hateful and annoying things, whenever he saw an opportunity. This and his beak-like nose gained for him the name of "Poll Parrot." His misfortune caused him to be tolerated where another man would have been suppressed. By and by he gave still greater cause for offense by his obsequious attempts to curry favor with Captain Wirz, who took him outside several times for purposes that were not well explained. Finally, some hours after one of Poll Parrot's visits outside, a rebel officer came in with a guard, and proceeding with suspicious directness to a tent which was the mouth of a large tunnel that a hundred men or more had been quietly been pushing forward, broke the tunnel in and took the occupants of the tent outside for punishment.

The question that demanded immediate solution was who was the traitor who informed the rebels. Suspicion pointed very strongly to Poll Parrot. By the next morning the evidence collected seemed to amount to a certainty, and a crowd caught the Parrot with the intention of lynching him. He succeeded in breaking away from them and ran under the Dead Line near where I was sitting in my tent. At first it looked as if he had done this to secure the protection of the guard. The latter, a 26th Alabamian, ordered him out. Poll Parrot rose up on his one leg, put his back against the Dead Line, faced the guard and said in his harsh cackling voice, "No! I won't go out. If I lost the confidence of my comrades, I want to die!" Part of the crowd were taken aback by this move, and felt disposed to accept it as a demonstration of the Parrot's innocence. The rest thought it was a piece of bravado, because of his belief that the rebels would not injure him after he had served them. They renewed their yells, the guard again ordered the Parrot out, but the latter, tearing open his blouse, cackled out, "No! I won't go; fire at me, guard. There's my heart; shoot me right there!" There was no help for it. The rebel leveled his gun and fired. The charge struck the Parrot's lower jaw and carried it completely away, leaving his tongue and the roof of his mouth exposed. As he was carried back to die, he wagged his tongue vigorously in attempting to speak, but it was of no use. The guard set his gun down and buried his face in his hands. It was the only time that I saw a sentinel show anything but exultation at killing a Yankee.

A ludicrous contrast to this took place a few nights later. The rains had ceased, the weather had become warmer and, our spirits rising with this increase in the comfort of our surroundings, a number of us were sitting around Nosey, a boy with a superb tenor voice, who was singing patriotic songs. We were coming in strong on the chorus, in a way that spoke vastly more for our enthusiasm for the Union than for our musical knowledge. Nosey sang the "Star-Spangled Banner," the "Battle Cry of Freedom," "Brave Boys Are They," and other airs capitally, and we threw our whole lungs into the chorus.

It was quite dark, and while our noise was going on the guards changed, new men coming on duty. Suddenly, bang! went the gun of the guard in the box about fifty feet away from us. We knew it was a 55th Georgian and supposed that, irritated at our singing, he was trying to kill some of us for spite. At the sound of the gun we jumped up and scattered. As no one gave the usual agonized yell of a prisoner when shot, we supposed the ball had not taken effect. We could hear the sentinel ramming down another cartridge, hear him "return rammer" and cock his rifle. Again the gun cracked, and again there was no sound of anybody being hit. Again we could hear the sentry churning down another cartridge. The drums began beating the long roll in the camps, the officers could be heard turning the men out.

The thing was becoming exciting, and one of us sang out to the guard: "SAY! What the hell are you shooting at, anyhow?"

"I'm a shootin' at that goddam Yank thar, by the Dead Line, and by God if you'uns don't take him in, I'll blow the whole damn head off'n him."

"What Yank? Where's any Yank?"

"Why thar, right thar, a-standin' agin the Dead Line."

"Why, you blasted rebel fool, that's a chunk of wood. You can't get any furlough for shooting that!"

At this there was a general roar from the rest of the camp which the other guards took up and, as the reserves came double-quicking up and learned the occasion of the alarm, they gave the rascal who had been so anxious to kill somebody a torrent of abuse for having disturbed them. A part of our crowd had been out after wood during the day and secured a piece of a log as large as two of them could carry and, bringing it in, stood it up near the Dead Line. When the guard mounted to his post, he was sure he saw a Yankee in front of him and hastened to slay him. It was an unusual good fortune that nobody was struck. It was very rare that the guards fired into the prison without hitting at least one person.

The Georgia Reserves, who formed our guards later in the season, were armed with an old gun called a Queen Anne musket, altered to percussion. It carried a bullet as big as a large marble, and three or four buckshot. When fired into a group of men it was sure to bring several down. I was standing one day in the line at the gate, waiting for a chance to go out after wood. A 55th Georgian was the gate guard, and he drew a line in the sand with his bayonet which we should not cross. The crowd behind pushed one man till he put his foot a few inches over the line to save himself from falling. The guard sank a bayonet through the foot as quick as a flash.

So far, only old prisoners, those taken at Gettysburg, Chickamauga and Mine Run, had been brought in. The armies had been very quiet during the winter, preparing for the death grapple in the spring. There had been nothing done save a few cavalry raids, such as our own, and Averill's attempt to gain and break up the rebel salt works at Wytheville and Saltville. Consequently, none but a few cavalry prisoners were added to the number already in the hands of the rebels. The first lot of new ones came in about the middle of March. There were about seven hundred of them, who had been captured at the Battle of Olustee, Florida, on the 20th of February. About five hundred of them were white and belonged to the 7th Connecticut, the 7th New Hampshire, the 47th, 48th and 115th New York, and Sherman's Regular Battery. The rest were colored and belonged to the 8th United States, and 54th Massachusetts.

The story they told of the battle was one which had many shameful reiterations during the war. It was the story told whenever Banks, Sturgis, Butler or one of a host of similar smaller failures were intrusted with commands. It was a senseless waste of the lives of private soldiers and the property of the United States by pretentious blunderers who, in some inscrutable manner, had attained to responsible command. In this instance, a bungling brigadier named Seymour had marched his forces across the State of Florida, to do he hardly knew what, in the neighborhood of an enemy of whose numbers, disposition, location, and intentions he was profoundly ignorant. The rebels, under General Finigan, waited till Seymour had strung his command along through swamps and canebrakes, scores of miles from his supports, and then fell unexpectedly upon his advance. The regiment was overpowered, and another regiment that hurried to its support suffered the same fate. The balance of the regiments were sent in in the same manner, each arriving on the field just after its predecessor had been thoroughly whipped by the concentrated force of the rebels. The men fought gallantly, but the stupidity of a commanding general is a thing that the gods themselves strive against in vain. We suffered a humiliating defeat, with a loss of two thousand men and a fine rifled battery, which was brought to Andersonville and placed in position to command the prison.

The majority of the 7th New Hampshire were an unwelcome addition to our numbers. They were N'Yaarkers, old time colleagues of those already in with us, veteran bounty-jumpers, that had been drawn to New Hampshire by the size of the bounty there, and had been assigned to fill up the wasted ranks of the veteran 7th Regiment. They had tried to desert as soon as they received their bounty, but the Government clung to them literally with hooks of steel, sending many of them to the regiment in irons. Thus foiled, they deserted to the rebels during the retreat from the battlefield. They were quite an accession to the force of our N'Yaarkers, and helped much to establish the hoodlum reign which was shortly inaugurated over the entire prison.

The 48th New Yorkers who came in were a set of chaps so odd in every way as to be a source of never-failing interest. The name of their regiment was *Les Enfants Perdus,* "The Lost Children," which we anglicized into "The Lost Ducks." It was believed that every nation in Europe was represented in their ranks, and it used to be said jocularly that no two of them spoke the same language. As correctly as I could discover, they were all or nearly all south Europeans, Italians, Spaniards, Portuguese, Levantines, with a predominance of the French element. They wore a little cap with an upturned brim and a strap resting on the chin, a coat with funny little tails about two inches long, and a brass chain across the breast; and for pantaloons they had a sort of petticoat reaching to the knees and sewed together down the middle. They were just as singular otherwise as in their looks, speech and uniform. On one occasion the whole mob of us went over in a mass to their squad to see them cook and eat a large water snake which two of them had succeeded in capturing in the swamps and carried off to their mess, jabbering in high glee over their treasure trove. Any of *us* were ready to eat a piece of dog, cat, horse or mule if we could get it, but it was generally agreed, as Dawson of my company expressed it, that "nobody but one of them darned queer Lost Ducks would eat a varmint like a water snake."

Major Albert Bogle, of the 8th United States Colored, had fallen into the hands of the rebels by reason of a severe wound in the leg, which left him helpless upon the field at Olustee. The rebels treated him with studied indignity. They utterly refused to recognize him as an officer, or even as a man. Instead of being sent to Macon or Columbia where the officers were, he was sent to Andersonville as an enlisted man. No care was given his wound. No surgeon would examine or dress it. He was thrown into a stock car, without bed or blanket, and hauled over the rough, jolting road to Andersonville. Once a rebel officer rode up and fired several shots at him as he lay helpless on the car floor. Fortunately the rebel's marksmanship was as bad as his intentions, and none of the shots took effect. Bogle was placed in a squad near me, and was compelled to get up and hobble into line when the rest were mustered for roll-call. No opportunity to insult the Negro officer was neglected, and the N'Yaarkers vied with the rebels in heaping abuse upon him. He was a fine, intelligent young man and bore it all with dignified self-possession, until after a lapse of some weeks the rebels changed their policy and took him from the prison to send him to where the other officers were.

The Negro soldiers were also treated as badly as possible. The wounded were turned into the stockade without having their hurts attended to. One stalwart, soldierly sergeant had received a bullet which had forced its way under the scalp for some distance and partially imbedded itself in the skull, where it still remained.[5] He suffered intense agony, and would pass the whole night walking up and down the street in front of our tent, moaning distressingly. The bullet could be felt plainly with the fingers, and we were sure that it would not be a minute's work with a sharp knife to remove it and give the man relief. But we could not prevail upon the rebel surgeons even to see the man. Finally, inflammation set in and he died.

The Negroes were put into a squad by themselves and taken out every day to work around the prison. A white sergeant was placed over them who was the object of the contumely of the guards and other rebels. One day as he was standing near the gate, waiting his orders to come out, the gate guard, without any provocation whatever, dropped his gun until the muzzle rested against the sergeant's stomach, and fired, killing him instantly. The sergeantship was then offered to me, but as I had no accident policy, I was constrained to decline the honor.

A Plymouth Pilgrim

CHAPTER IV

A LITTLE BLOOD SPILT

APRIL BROUGHT SUNNY SKIES and balmy weather. Existence became much more tolerable. With freedom it would have been enjoyable, even had we been no better fed, clothed and sheltered. But imprisonment had never seemed so hard to bear, even in the first few weeks, as now. It was easier to submit to confinement to a limited area, when cold and rain were aiding hunger to benumb the faculties and chill the energies than it was now, when Nature was rousing her slumbering forces to activity, and earth and air and sky were filled with stimulus to man to imitate her example. The yearning to be up and doing something, to turn these golden hours to good account for self and country, pressed into heart and brain as the vivifying sap pressed into tree-duct and plant cell, awakening all vegetation to energetic life.

To be compelled, at such a time, to lie around in vacuous idleness, to spend days that should be crowded full of action in a monotonous objectless routine of hunting lice, gathering at roll call, and drawing and cooking our scanty rations, was torturing. But to many others of our number the aspirations for freedom were not—as with us— the desire for a wider, manlier field of action so much as an intense longing to get where care and comforts would arrest their swift progress to the shadowy hereafter. The cruel rains had sapped away their stamina, and they could not recover it with the meager and unnutritious diet of coarse meal and an occasional scrap of salt meat. Quick consumption, bronchitis, pneumonia, low fever and diarrhea seized upon these ready victims for their ravages and bore them off at the rate of nearly a score a day.

It now became a part of the day's regular routine to take a walk past the gates in the morning, inspect and count the dead, and see if any friends were among them. Clothes having by this time become a very important consideration with the prisoners, it was the custom of the mess in which a man died to remove from his person all garments that were of any account, and so many bodies were carried out nearly naked. The hands were crossed upon the breast, the big toes tied together with a bit of string, and a slip of paper containing the man's name, rank, company and regiment was pinned on the breast of his shirt. The appearance of the dead was indescribably ghastly. The unclosed eyes shone with a stony glitter. The lips and nostrils were distorted with pain and hunger, the sallow dirt-grimed skin drawn tensely over the facial bones, and the whole framed by long, lank, matted hair and beard. Millions of lice swarmed over the wasted limbs and ridged ribs.

These verminous pests had become so numerous, owing to our lack of changes of clothing and of facilities for boiling what we had, that the most a healthy man could do was to keep the number feeding upon his person down to a reasonable limit, say a few tablespoonfuls. When a man became so sick as to be unable to help himself, the parasites speedily increased into millions or, to speak more comprehensively, into pints and quarts. It did not even seem exaggeration when someone declared that he had seen a dead man with more than a gallon of lice on him. There is no doubt that the irritation from the biting of these myriads of insects abridged very materially the days of those who died. Where a sick man had friends or comrades, part of their duty in taking care of him was to "louse" his clothing. One of the most effectual ways of doing this was to turn the garments wrong side out and hold the seams as close to the fire as possible, without burning the cloth. In a short time the lice would swell up and burst open like popcorn. This method was a favorite one for another reason than its efficacy—it gave one a keener sense of revenge upon his rascally little tormentors than he could get in any other way. As the weather grew warmer and the number in the prison increased, the lice became more unendurable. They even filled the hot sand under our feet, and voracious troops would climb up on one like streams of ants, swarming up a tree.

We began to have a full comprehension of the third plague with which the Lord visited the Egyptians. The total number of deaths in April, according to the official report, was five hundred and seventy-six, or an average of over nineteen a day. There was an average of five thousand prisoners in the pen during all but the last few days of the month, when the number was increased by the arrival of the captured garrison of Plymouth. This would make the loss over eleven per cent, and so worse than decimation. At that rate we should all have died in about eight months. We could have gone through a sharp campaign lasting those thirty days and not lost so great a proportion of our forces. The British had about as many men as were in the Stockade at the Battle of New Orleans, yet their loss in killed fell much short of the deaths in the pen in April.[6]

A makeshift of a hospital was established in the northeastern corner of the Stockade. A portion of the ground was divided from the rest of the prison by a railing, a few tent flies were stretched, and in these the long leaves of the pine were made into apologies for beds of about the goodness of the straw on which a northern farmer beds his stock. The sick taken there were no better off than if they had stayed with their comrades. What they needed to bring about their recovery was clean clothing, nutritious food, shelter and freedom from the tortures of the lice. They obtained none of these. Save a few decoctions of roots, there were no medicines; the sick were fed the same coarse corn meal that brought about the malignant dysentery from which they all suffered; they wore and slept in the same vermin-infested clothes. There could be but one result. The official records show that seventy-six per cent of those taken to the hospitals died there.[7]

The establishment of the hospital was specially unfortunate for my little squad. The ground required for it compelled a general reduction of the space we all occupied. We had to tear down our huts and move. By this time the materials had become so dry that we could not rebuild with them, as the pine tufts fell to pieces. This reduced the tent and bedding material of our party, now numbering five, to a cavalry overcoat and a blanket. We scooped a hole a foot deep in the sand and stuck our tent-poles around it. By day we spread our blanket over the poles for a tent. At night we lay down upon the overcoat and covered ourselves with the blanket. It required considerable stretching to make it go over five. The two outside fellows used to get very chilly and so squeezed the three inside ones until they felt no thicker than a wafer. But it had to do, and we took turns sleeping on the outside. In the course of a few weeks, three of my chums died and left myself and B. B. Andrews [8] sole heirs to and occupants of the overcoat and blanket.

We awoke one morning, in the last part of April, to find about two thousand freshly arrived prisoners lying asleep in the main streets near the gates. They were attired in stylish new uniforms, with fancy hats and shoes; the sergeants and corporals wore patent leather or silk chevrons, and each man had a large well-filled knapsack of the kind new recruits usually carried on coming first to the front, which the older soldiers spoke of humorously as "bureaus." They were the snuggist, nattiest lot of soldiers we had ever seen, outside of the "paper collar" fellows forming the headquarter guard of some general in a large city. As one of my companions surveyed them, he said, "Hulloa! I'm blanked if the Johnnies haven't caught a regiment of brigadier generals, somewhere." By and by the "fresh fish," as all new arrivals were termed, began to wake up, and then we learned that they belonged to a brigade consisting of the 85th New York, 101st and 103rd Pennsylvania, 16th Connecticut, 24th New York Battery, two companies of Massachusetts heavy artillery and a company of the 12th New York Cavalry.

They had been garrisoning Plymouth, North Carolina, an important seaport on the Roanoke River. Three small gunboats assisted them in their duties. The rebels constructed a powerful ironclad called the *Albermarle,* at a point further up the Roanoke, and on the afternoon of the 17th, with her and three brigades of infantry, made an attack upon the post. The *Albermarle* ran past the forts unharmed, sank one of the gunboats, and drove the others away. She then turned her attention to the garrison, which she took in the rear while the infantry attacked in front. Our men held out until the 20th, when they capitulated. They were allowed to retain their personal effects of all kinds and, as is the case with all men in garrison, these were considerable.

The 101st and 103rd Pennsylvania and 85th New York had just "veteranized" and received their first installment of veteran bounty. Had they not been attacked, they would have sailed for home in a day or two on their veteran furlough, and this accounted for their fine raiment. They were made up of boys from good New York and Pennsylvania families and were, as a rule, intelligent and fairly educated. Their horror at the appearance of their place of incarceration was beyond expression. At one moment they could not comprehend that these dirty and haggard tatterdemalions had once been clean, self-respecting, well-fed soldiers like themselves; at the next they would affirm that they could not stand it a month, where we had then endured it from four to nine months. They took it, in every way, the hardest of any prisoners that came in, except some of the "Hundred Days" [9] men who were brought in in August from the valley of Virginia. They had served nearly all their time in various garrisons along the seacoast, from Fortress Monroe to Beaufort, where they had had comparatively little of the actual hardships of soldiering in the field.

They had nearly always had comfortable quarters, an abundance of food, few hard marches or other severe service. Consequently, they were not so well hardened for Andersonville as the majority who came in. In other respects they were better prepared, as they had an abundance of clothing, blankets and cooking utensils, and each man had some of his veteran bounty still in possession. It was painful to see how rapidly many of them sank under the miseries of the situation. They gave up the moment the gates were closed upon them and began pining away. We older prisoners buoyed ourselves up continually with hopes of escape or exchange. We dug tunnels with the persistence of beavers, and we watched every possible opportunity to get outside the accursed walls of the pen. But we could not enlist the interest of these discouraged ones in any of our schemes or talk. They resigned themselves to Death, and waited despondently till he came.

A middle-aged 101st Pennsylvanian who had taken up his quarters near me was an object of peculiar interest. Reasonably intelligent and fairly read, I presumed that he was a respectable mechanic before entering the army. He was evidently a very domestic man whose whole happiness centered in his family. When he first came in, he was thoroughly dazed by the greatness of his misfortune. He would sit for hours with his face in his hands and his elbows on his knees, gazing out upon the mass of men and huts with vacant, lack-luster eyes. We could not interest him in anything. We tried to show him how to fix his blanket up to give him some shelter, but he went at the work in a disheartened way and finally smiled feebly and stopped. He had some letters from his family and a melaneotype [10] of a plain-faced woman, his wife, and her children, and spent much time in looking at them. At first he ate his rations when he drew them, but finally began to reject them. In a few days he was delirious with hunger and homesickness. He would sit on the sand for hours imagining that he was at his family table, dispensing his frugal hospitalities to his wife and children. Making a motion, as if presenting a dish, he would say, "Janie, have another biscuit, do!"; or, "Eddie, son, won't you have another piece of this nice steak?"; or, "Maggie, have some more potatoes," and so on, through a whole family of six or more. It was a relief to us when he died in about a month after he came in.

The Plymouth men brought in a large amount of money, variously estimated at from ten thousand to one hundred thousand dollars. The presence of this quantity of money immediately started a lively commerce. All sorts of devices were resorted to by the other prisoners to get a little of this wealth. Rude chuck-a-luck boards were constructed out of such material as was obtainable and put in operation. Dice and cards were brought out by those skilled in such matters. As those of us already in the stockade occupied all the ground, there was no disposition on the part of many to surrender a portion of this space without exacting heavy compensation. Messes having ground in a good location would frequently demand and get ten dollars for permission for two or three to quarter with them. Then there was a great demand for poles to stretch blankets over to make tents. The rebels, with their usual stupid cruelty, would not supply these nor allow the prisoners to go out and get them themselves. Many of the older prisoners had poles to spare which they were saving for fuel. They sold these to the Plymouth folks at the rate of ten dollars for three, enough to put up a blanket.

The most considerable trading was done through the gates. The rebel guards were found quite as keen to barter as they had been in Richmond. Though the laws against their dealing in the money of the enemy were still as stringent as ever, their thirst for greenbacks was not abated one whit and they were ready to sell anything they had for the coveted currency. The rate of exchange was seven or eight dollars in Confederate money for one dollar in greenbacks. Wood, tobacco, meat, flour, beans, molasses, onions and a villainous kind of whiskey, made from sorghum, were the staple articles of trade. A whole race of little traffickers in these articles sprang up, and finally Selden, the rebel Quartermaster, established a sutler shop in the center of the north side, which he put in charge of Ira Beverly of the 100th Ohio, and Charley Huckleby of the 8th Tennessee. It was a fine illustration of the development of the commercial instinct in some men. No more unlikely place for making money could be imagined, yet starting in without a cent they contrived to turn and twist and trade until they had transferred to their pockets a portion of the funds which were in some-one else's.

The rebels, of course, got nine out of every ten dollars there were in the prison, but these middlemen contrived to have a little of it stick to their fingers. It was only the very few who were able to do this. Nine hundred and ninety-nine out of every thousand were like myself, either wholly destitute of money and unable to get it from anybody else, or they paid out what money they had to the middleman in exorbitant prices for articles of food. The N'Yaarkers had still another method for getting food, money, blankets and clothing. They formed little bands called raiders, under the leadership of a chief villain. One of these bands would select as their victim a man who had good blankets, clothes, a watch or greenbacks. Frequently he would be one of the little traders, with a sack of beans, a piece of meat, or something of that kind. Pouncing upon him at night, they would snatch away his possessions, knock down his friends who came to his assistance, and scurry away into the darkness.

To our minds the world now contained but two grand divisions, as widely differ-ent from each other as happiness and misery. The first, that portion over which our flag floated, was usually spoken of as "God's country": the other, that under the bane-ful shadow of rebellion, was designated by the most opprobrious epithets at the speak-er's command. To get from the latter to the former was to attain, at one bound, the highest good. Better to be a doorkeeper in the House of the Lord under the Stars and Stripes, than to dwell in the tents of wickedness under the hateful Southern Cross. To take even the humblest and hardest of service in the field now would be a delightsome change. We did not ask to go home; we would be content with anything, so long as it was in that blest place, "within our lines."

Only let us get back once and there would be no more grumbling at rations or guard duty; we would willingly endure all the hardships and privations that soldier flesh is heir to. There were two ways of getting back, exchange and escape. Exchange was like the ever-receding mirage of the desert that lures the thirsty traveller on over the parched sands with illusions of refreshing springs, only to leave his bones at last to whiten by the side of those of his unremembered predecessors. Every day there came something to build up the hopes that exchange was near at hand and every day brought something to extinguish the hopes of the preceding one. We took these varying phases according to our several temperaments. The sanguine built themselves up on the encouraging reports; the desponding sank down and died under the discouraging ones.

Escape was a perpetual allurement. To the actively inclined among us it seemed always possible, and daring busy brains were indefatigable in concocting schemes for it. The only bit of rebel brainwork that I ever saw for which I did not feel contempt was the perfect precaution taken to prevent our escape. This is shown by the fact that, although from first to last there were nearly fifty thousand prisoners in Andersonville, and three out of every five of these were ever on the alert to take French leave of their captors, only three hundred and twenty-eight succeeded in getting so far away from Andersonville as to leave it to be presumed that they had reached our lines.[11]

The first and almost superhuman difficulty was to get outside the Stockade. It was simply impossible to scale it. The guards were too close together to allow an instant's hope to the most sanguine that he could even pass the Dead Line without being shot by some one of them. This same closeness prevented any hope of bribing them. To be successful half those on post would have to be bribed, as every part of the Stockade was clearly visible from every other part, and there was no night so dark as not to allow a plain view to a number of guards of the dark figure, outlined against the light-colored logs, of any Yankee who should essay to clamber towards the top of the palisades. The gates were so carefully guarded every time they were opened as to preclude hope of slipping out through them. They were only opened twice or thrice a day——to admit the men to call the roll, to let them out again, to let the wagons come in with rations, and once more perhaps to admit new prisoners. At all these times every precaution was taken to prevent anyone getting out surreptitiously.

This narrowed down the possibilities of passing the limits of the pen alive to tunneling. This was also surrounded by almost insuperable difficulties. First, it required not less than fifty feet of subterranean excavation to get out, which meant enormous work with our limited means. Then the logs forming the Stockade were set in the ground to a depth of five feet, and the tunnel had to go down beneath them. These logs had an unpleasant habit of dropping down into the burrow under them. It added much to the discouragements of tunneling to think of one these massive timbers dropping upon a fellow as he worked his mole-like way under it, either crushing him to death outright or pinning him there to die of suffocation and hunger.

In one instance, in a tunnel near me but one in which I was not interested, the logs slipped down after the digger had got out beyond it. He immediately began digging for the surface for dear life and was fortunately able to break through before he suffocated. He got his head above the ground and then fainted. The guard outside saw him, pulled him out of the hole and, when he recovered sensibility, hurried him back into the Stockade. In another tunnel, also near us, a broad-shouldered German of the 2nd Minnesota, went in to take his turn at digging. He was so much larger than any of his friends that he stuck fast in a narrow part. Despite all the efforts of himself and comrades, it was found impossible to move him one way or the other. His comrades were at last reduced to the humiliation of informing the officer of the guard of their tunnel and the condition of their friend and of asking assistance to release him, which was given.

The great tunneling tool was the indispensable half-canteen. The inventive genius of our people, stimulated by the war, produced nothing for the comfort and effectiveness of the soldier equal in usefulness to this humble and unrecognized utensil. It will be remembered that a canteen was composed of two pieces of tin stuck up into the shape of saucers, soldered together at the edges. After a soldier had been in the field a little while and had thrown away or lost the curious and complicated kitchen furniture he started out with, he found that by melting the halves of his canteen apart he had a vessel much handier in every way than any he had parted with. It could be used for anything, to make soup or coffee in, bake bread, brown coffee and stew vegetables. A sufficient handle was made with a split stick. When the cooking was done, the handle was thrown away and the half-canteen slipped into the haversack. There seemed to be no end of the uses to which this ever-ready disc of blackened sheet-iron [12] could be turned.

Several instances are on record where infantry regiments, with no other tools than this, covered themselves on the field with quite respectable rifle pits. The starting point of a tunnel was always some tent close to the Dead Line, and sufficiently well closed to screen the operations from the sight of the guards nearby. The party engaged in the work organized by giving each man a number to secure the proper apportionment of the labor. Number one began digging with his half-canteen. After he had worked until tired, he came out and number two took his place, and so on. The tunnel was simply a round rat-like burrow, a little larger than a man's body. The digger lay on his stomach, dug ahead of him, threw the dirt under him, and worked it back with his feet till the man behind him, also lying on his stomach, could catch it and work it back to the next. As the tunnel lengthened, the number of men behind each other had to be increased, so that in a tunnel seventy-five feet long there would be from eight to ten men lying one behind the other. When the dirt was pushed to the mouth of the tunnel, it was taken up in improvised bags made by tying up the bottoms of pantaloon legs, carried to the swamp, and emptied. The work in the tunnel was very exhausting, and the digger had to be relieved every half hour. The greatest trouble was to carry the tunnel forward in a straight line. As nearly everybody dug most of the time with the right hand, there was an almost irresistible tendency to make the course veer to the left.

The first tunnel I was connected with was a ludicrous illustration of this. About twenty of us had devoted our nights for over a week to the prolongation of a burrow. We had not yet reached the Stockade, which astonished us, as measurement with a string showed that we had gone nearly twice the distance necessary for the purpose. The thing was inexplicable, and we ceased operations to consider the matter. The next day a man walking by a tent some little distance from the one in which the hole began, was badly startled by the ground giving way under his feet and his sinking nearly to his waist in a hole. This was very singular, but after wondering over the matter for some hours, there came a glimmer of suspicion that it might be in some way connected with the missing end of our tunnel. One of us started through on an exploring expedition and confirmed the suspicions by coming out where the man had broken through. Our tunnel was shaped like a horseshoe, and the beginning and end were not fifteen feet apart. After that, we practiced digging with our left hands and made certain compensations for the tendency to the sinister side. Another trouble connected with tunneling was the number of traitors and spies among us. There were many, principally among the N'Yaarker crowd, who were always zealous to betray a tunnel in order to curry favor with the rebel officers. Then again, the rebels had numbers of their own men in the pen at night as spies. It was hardly even necessary to dress these in our uniform, because a great many of our own men came into the prison in rebel clothes, having been compelled to trade garments with their captors.

One day in May, quite an excitement was raised by the detection of one of these "tunnel traitors" in such a way as left no doubt of his guilt. At first everybody was in favor of killing him, and they actually started to beat him to death. This was arrested by a proposition to have Captain Jack "tattoo" him, and the suggestion was immediately acted upon. Captain Jack was a sailor who had been with us in the Pemberton Building at Richmond. He was a very skillful tattoo artist but, I am sure, could make the process nastier than any other that I ever saw attempted. He chewed tobacco enor-

mously. After pricking away for a few minutes at the design on the arm or some portion of the body, he would deluge it with a flood of tobacco spit which, he claimed,
acted as a kind of mordant. Wiping this off with a filthy rag, he would study the effect
for an instant, and then go ahead with another series of prickings and tobacco juice
drenchings. The tunnel-traitor was taken to Captain Jack. That worthy decided to
brand him with a great T, the top part to extend across his forehead and the stem to
run down his nose. Captain Jack got his tattooing kit ready, and the fellow was thrown
upon the ground and held there. The Captain took the rascal's head between his legs
and began operations. After an instant's work with the needles, the Captain opened
his mouth and filled the wretch's face and eyes full of the disgusting saliva. The crowd
round-about yelled with delight at this new process.

For an hour, that was doubtless an eternity to the rascal undergoing branding,
Captain Jack continued his alternate prickings and drenchings. At the end of that
time the traitor's face was disfigured with a hideous mark that he would bear to his
grave. We learned afterwards that he was not one of our men, but a rebel spy. This
added much to our satisfaction with the manner of his treatment. He disappeared
shortly after the operation was finished, being, I suppose, taken outside. I hardly think
Captain Jack would be pleased to meet him again.

Hounds Tearing a Prisoner

CHAPTER V

IN THE WAY OF ESCAPE

ESCAPE WAS ALWAYS foremost in our minds. Those who succeeded one way or another in passing the stockade limits found still more difficulties lying between them and freedom than would discourage ordinarily resolute men. The first was to get away from the immediate vicinity of the prison. All around were rebel patrols, pickets and guards watching every avenue of escape. Several packs of hounds formed efficient coadjutors of these and were more dreaded by possible escapees than any other means at the command of our jailors. Guards and patrols could be evaded or circumvented, but the hounds could not. Nearly every man brought back from a futile attempt at escape told the same story——he had been able to escape the human rebels, but not their canine colleagues.

Three of our detachment, members of the 20th Indiana, had an experience of this kind that will serve to illustrate hundreds of others. They had been taken outside to do some work upon the cook-house that was being built. A guard was sent with the three a little distance into the woods to get a piece of timber. The boys sauntered along carelessly with the guard and managed to get pretty near him. As soon as they were fairly out of sight of the rest, the strongest of them, a Tom Williams, snatched the rebel's gun away from him, and the other two springing upon him, swift as wild cats, throttled him so that he could not give the alarm. Still keeping a hand on his throat, they led him off some distance and tied him to a sapling with strings made by tearing up one of their blouses. He was also securely gagged and the boys, bidding him a hasty but not specially tender farewell, struck out, as they fondly hoped, for freedom.

It was not long until they were missed, and the parties sent in search found and released the guard, who gave all the information he possessed as to what had become of his charges. All the packs of hounds, the squads of cavalry and the foot patrols were sent out to scour the adjacent country. The Yankees kept in the swamps and creeks and no trace of them was found that afternoon or evening. By this time they were ten or fifteen miles away and thought that they could safely leave the creeks for better walking on solid ground. They had gone but a few miles when the pack of hounds Captain Wirz was with took their trail and came after them in full cry. The boys tried to run but, as exhausted as they were, they could make no headway. Two of them were soon caught, but Tom Williams, who was so desperate that he preferred death to re-capture, jumped into a mill pond nearby.

When he came up, it was in a lot of driftwood and saw-logs that hid him from being seen from the bank. The dogs stopped at the bank and bayed after the disap-pearing prey. The rebels with them who had seen Tom spring in came up and made a pretty thorough search for him. As they did not think to probe around the drift-wood, this was unsuccessful and they came to the conclusion that Tom had been drowned. Wirz marched the other two back and, for a wonder, did not punish them, probably because he rejoiced so at his success in capturing them. He was beaming with delight when he returned them to our squad and said with a chuckle, "Brisoners, I pring you pack two of dem tam Yankees wat got away yesterday, unt I run de oder rascal into a millt-pont and trowntet him." What was our astonishment, about three weeks later, to see Tom, fat and healthy, and dressed in a new suit of butternut, come stalking into the pen. He had nearly reached the mountains when a pack of hounds, patrolling for deserters or Negroes, took his trail where he had crossed the road from one field to another and speedily ran him down. He had been put in a little country jail and well fed till an opportunity occurred to send him back.

This patrolling for Negroes and deserters was another of the great obstacles to a successful passage through the country. The rebels had put every able-bodied man in the ranks and were bending every energy to keep them there. The whole countryside was carefully policed by Provost Marshals to bring out those who were shirking military duty or had deserted the colors, and to check any movement by the Negroes. One could not go anywhere without a pass, as every road was continually watched by hounds and men. It was the policy of our men, when escaping, to avoid roads as much as possible by travelling through the woods and fields. From what I saw of the hounds and what I could learn from others, I believe that each pack was made up of two bloodhounds and from twenty-five to fifty other dogs.

The bloodhounds were debased descendants of the strong fierce hounds imported from Cuba, many of them by the United States Government, for hunting Indians during the Seminole War. The other dogs were the mongrels that are found in such plentifulness about every Southern house, increasing, as a rule, in numbers as the inhabitants of the houses get lower down and poorer. They are like wolves, sneaking and cowardly when alone, fierce and bold when in packs. Each pack was managed by a well-armed man who rode a mule and carried, slung over his shoulders by a cord, a cowhorn, scraped very thin, with which he controlled the band by signals. What always puzzled me much was why the hounds took only Yankee trails, in the vicinity of the prison. There were about the Stockade from 6,000 to 10,000 rebels and Negroes, including guards, officers, servants and workmen. These were, of course, continually in motion and must have daily made trails leading in every direction. It was the custom of the rebels to send a pack of hounds around the prison every morning, to examine if any Yankees had escaped during the night.

It was believed that they rarely failed to find a prisoner's tracks and still more rarely ran off upon a rebel's. If those outside the Stockade had been confined to certain paths and roads, we could have understood this but, as I understand it, they were not. It was part of the interest of the day for us to watch the packs go yelping around the pen searching for tracks. We got information in this way as to whether any tunnels had been successfully opened during the night. The use of hounds furnished us a crushing reply to the ever-recurring rebel question, "Why are you'uns puttin' niggers in the field to fight we'uns?" The questioner was always silenced by the return interrogatory, "Is that as bad as running white men down with bloodhounds?"

In May, the long-gathering storm of war burst with angry violence all along the line held by the contending armies. The campaign began which was to terminate eleven months later in the obliteration of the Southern Confederacy: May 1, Sigel moved up the Shenandoah Valley with thirty thousand men; May 3, Butler began his blundering movement against Petersburg; May 3, the Army of the Potomac left Culpeper, and on the 5th began its deadly grapple with Lee in the Wilderness; May 6th, Sherman moved from Chattanooga and engaged Joe Johnston at Rocky Face Ridge and Tunnel Hill. Each of these columns lost heavily in prisoners. It could not be otherwise; it was a consequence of the aggressive moments. An army acting offensively usually suffers more from capture than one on the defensive. Our armies were penetrating the enemy's country in close proximity to a determined and vigilant foe. Every scout, every skirmish line, every picket, every foraging party ran the risk of falling into a rebel trap. This was in addition to the risk of capture in action.

The bulk of the prisoners was taken from the Army of the Potomac. For this there were two reasons: first, there were many more men in that army than in any other; and second, the entanglement in the dense thickets and shrubbery of the Wilderness enabled both sides to capture great numbers of the other's men. Grant lost in prisoners from May 5 to May 31, 7450. He probably captured two thirds of that number from the Johnnies.[13]

Wirz' headquarters were established in a large log house which had been built in the fort a little distance from the southeast corner of the prison. Every day, and sometimes two or three times a day, we would see great squads of prisoners marched to these headquarters where they would be searched, their names entered upon the prison records by clerks (few rebels had the requisite clerical skill), and then be marched into the prison. As they entered, the rebel guards would stand to arms. The infantry would be in line of battle, the cavalry mounted, and the artillerymen standing by their guns ready to open at the instant with grape and canister. The disparity between the number coming in from the Army of the Potomac and Western armies was so great that we Westerners began to take some advantage of it. If we saw a squad of one hundred and fifty or thereabouts at the headquarters, we felt pretty certain they were from Sherman and gathered to meet them and learn the news from our friends. If there were from five hundred to two thousand, we knew they were from the Army of the Potomac and there were none of our comrades among them.

There were three exceptions to this rule while we were in Andersonville. The first was in June, when the drunken and incompetent Sturgis shamefully sacrificed a superb division at Guntown, Mississippi. The next was after Hood made his desperate attack on Sherman on the 22nd of July, and the third was when Stoneman was captured at Macon. At each of these times about two thousand prisoners were brought in. By the end of May there were eighteen thousand, four hundred and fifty-four prisoners in the Stockade. Before the reader dismisses this statement from his mind, let him reflect how great a number this is. It is more active able-bodied men than there are in any of our leading cities save New York and Philadelphia. It is more than the average population of an Ohio county. It is four times as many troops as Taylor won the victory of Buena Vista with, and about twice as many as Scott went into battle with at any time in his march to the City of Mexico.

These eighteen thousand, four hundred and fifty-four men were couped up on less than thirteen acres of ground, making about fifteen hundred to the acre. No room could be given up for streets or for the usual arrangements of a camp, and most kinds of exercise were wholly precluded. The men crowded together like pigs nesting in the woods on cold nights. The ground, despite all our efforts, became indescribably filthy, and this condition grew rapidly worse as the season advanced and the sun's rays gained fervency.

As it is impossible to describe this adequately, I must again ask the reader to assist with a few comparisons. He has an idea of how much filth is produced on an ordinary city lot in a week by its occupation by a family, say, of six persons. Now let him imagine what would be the result if that lot, instead of having upon it six persons with every appliance for keeping themselves clean and for removing and concealing filth, was the home of one hundred and eight men with none of these appliances. That he may figure these proportions for himself, I will repeat some of the elements of the problem.

We will say that an average city lot is thirty feet front by one hundred deep. This is more front than most of them have, but we will be liberal. This gives us a surface of three thousand square feet. An acre contains forty-three thousand, five hundred and sixty square feet. Upon thirteen of these acres, we had eighteen thousand four hundred and fifty-four men. After the reader has found the number of square feet that each man had for sleeping apartment, dining room, kitchen, exercise grounds and outhouses, and has decided that nobody could live for any length of time in such contracted space, I will tell him that a few weeks later, double that many men were crowded upon that space—that over thirty-five thousand were packed upon those twelve and a half or thirteen acres. But I will not anticipate. With the warm weather the condition of the swamp in the center of the prison became simply horrible. We hear so much nowadays of blood-poisoning from the effluvia of sinks and sewers that, reading this, I wonder how a man inside the Stockade, into whose nostrils came a breath of that noisomeness, escaped being carried off by a malignant typhus.

In the slimy ooze were billions of white maggots. They would crawl out by thousands on the warm sands and, lying there a few minutes, would sprout a wing or pair of them. With these they would essay a clumsy flight, ending by dropping down upon some exposed portion of a man's body and stinging him like a gadfly. Still worse, they would drop into what he was cooking. The utmost care could not prevent a mess of food from being contaminated with them. All the water we had to use was that in the creek which flowed through this seething mass of corruption and received its sewerage. How pure the water was when it came into the Stockade was a question. We always believed that it received the drainage from the camps of the guards a half mile away. A road was made across the swamp, along the Dead Line at the west side where the creek entered the pen. Those getting water would go to this spot and reach as far up the stream as possible to get water that was least filthy.

As they could reach nearly to the Dead Line, this furnished an excuse to such of the guards as were murderously inclined to fire upon them. I think I hazard nothing in saying that for weeks at least one man a day was killed at this place. The murders became monotonous; there was a dreadful sameness to them. A gun would crack and looking up we would see, still smoking, the muzzle of the musket of one of the guards on either side of the creek. At the same instant would rise a piercing shriek from the man struck, now floundering in the creek in his death agony. Then thousands of throats would yell out curses and denunciations, shouting, "Oh! Give the rebel son of a bitch a furlough!" It was our belief that every guard who killed a Yankee was rewarded with a thirty-day furlough.

Mr. Frederick Holliger, now of Toledo, formerly a member of the 72nd Ohio and captured at Guntown, tells me that as his introduction to Andersonville life, a few hours after his entry, he went to the brook to get a drink, reached out too far, and was fired upon by the guard who missed him but killed another man and wounded a second. The other prisoners standing near then attacked him and beat him nearly to death for having drawn the fire of the guard.

Nothing could be more inexcusable than these murders. Whatever defense there might be for firing on men who touched the Dead Line in other parts of the prison, there could be none here. The men had no intention of escaping; they had no designs upon the stockade; and they were not leading any party to assail it. They were in every instance killed in the act of reaching out with their cups to dip up a little water. Let the reader understand that in any strictures I make, I do not complain of the necessary hardships of war. I understood fully and accepted the conditions of a soldier's career. My going into the field uniformed and armed implied an intention, at least, of killing, wounding or capturing some of the enemy. There was consequently no ground of complaint if I was myself killed, wounded or captured. If I did not want to take these chances I ought to have stayed at home. In the same way, I recognized the right of our captors or guards to take proper precautions to prevent our escape. I never questioned for an instant the right of a guard to fire upon those attempting to escape, and to kill them. Had I been posted over prisoners, I should have had no compunction about shooting at those trying to get away and consequently I could not blame the rebels for doing the same thing. It was a matter of soldierly duty.

But not one of the men assassinated by the guards at Andersonville was trying to escape, nor could he have got away if not arrested by a bullet. In a majority of instances there was not even a transgression of a prison rule, and when there was such a transgression it was a mere harmless inadvertence. The slaying of every man there was a foul crime. Most of this was done by very young boys, some of it by old men. The 26th Alabama and 55th Georgia had guarded us since the opening of the prison. But now they were ordered to the field and their places filled by the Georgia Reserves, an organization of boys under, and men over, military age. As General Grant aptly phrased it, they had "robbed the cradle and the grave" in forming these regiments. The boys, who had grown up from children since the war began, could not comprehend that a Yankee was a human being, or that it was any more wrongful to shoot one than to kill a mad dog. Their young imaginations had been inflamed with stories of the total depravity of the Unionists until they believed it was a meritorious thing to seize every opportunity to exterminate them.

Early one morning I overheard a conversation between two of these youthful guards:

"Say, Bill, I hear that you shot a Yank last night?"

"Now, you just bet I did. God! You jest ought to've heered him holler."

Evidently the juvenile murderer had no more conception that he had committed a crime than if he had killed a rattlesnake.

Among those who came in about the last of the month were two thousand men from Butler's command lost in the disastrous action of May 15 in which Butler was "bottled up" at Bermuda Hundred.[14] At that time the rebels' hatred for Butler verged on insanity, and they vented this upon these men who were so luckless, in every sense, as to be in his command. Every pains was taken to mistreat them. Stripped of every article of clothing, equipment and cooking utensils, everything except a shirt and a pair of pantaloons, they were turned bareheaded and barefooted into the prison, and the worst possible place in the pen was hunted out to locate them upon. This was under the bank, at the edge of the swamp and at the eastern side of the prison where the sinks were. All filth from the upper part of the camp flowed to them. The sand upon which they lay was dry and burning as that of a tropical desert; they were without the slightest shelter of any kind; the maggot flies swarmed over them; and the stench was frightful. If one of them survived, the germ theory of disease is a hallucination.

The increasing number of prisoners made it necessary for the rebels to improve their means of guarding and holding us in check. They threw up a line of rifle pits around the stockade for the infantry guards. At intervals along this were piles of hand grenades [15] which could be used with fearful effect in case of an outbreak. A strong star fort was thrown up at a little distance from the southwest corner. Eleven field pieces were mounted in this in such a way as to rake the Stockade diagonally. A smaller fort, mounting five guns, was built at the northwest corner, and at the northeast and southeast corners were small lunettes, with a couple of howitzers each. Packed as we were, we had reason to dread a single round from any of those works, which could not fail to produce fearful havoc. Still, a plot was concocted for a break, and it seemed to the sanguine portions of us that it must prove successful.

First, a secret society was organized, bound by the most stringent oaths that could be devised. The members of this were divided into companies of fifty men each, under officers regularly elected. The secrecy was assumed in order to shut out rebel spies and the traitors from a knowledge of the contemplated outbreak. A man named Baker, belonging, I think, to some New York regiment, was the grand organizer of the scheme. We were careful in each of our companies to admit none to membership except such as long acquaintance gave us entire confidence in. The plan was to dig large tunnels to the Stockade at various places, and then hollow out the ground at the foot of the timbers, so that a half dozen or so could be pushed over with a little effort and so make a gap ten or twelve feet wide. All these were to be thrown down at a preconcerted signal and the companies were to rush out and seize the eleven guns of the headquarters fort.

The Plymouth Brigade was then to man these and turn them on the camp of the Reserves who, it was imagined, would drop their arms and take to their heels after receiving a round or so of shell. We would gather what arms we could and place them in the hands of the most active and determined. This would give us from eight to ten thousand fairly armed, resolute men with which we thought we could march to Appalachicola Bay or to Sherman. We worked energetically at our tunnels which soon began to assume such shape as to give assurance that they would answer our expectations in opening the prison walls. Then came the usual blight to all such enterprises. A spy or a traitor revealed everything to Wirz.

One day a guard came in, seized Baker and took him out. What was done with him I do not know; we never heard of him after he passed the inner gate. Immediately afterward all the sergeants of detachments were summoned outside. There they met Wirz, who made a speech informing them that he knew all the details of the plot and had made sufficient preparations to defeat it. The guard had been strongly reinforced and disposed in such a manner as to protect the guns from capture. The stockade had been secured to prevent its falling even if undermined. He said, in addition, that Sherman had been badly defeated by Johnston and driven back across the river, so that any hopes of co-operation by him would be ill-founded. When the sergeants returned, he caused the following notice to be posted on the gates:

NOTICE

Not wishing to shed the blood of hundreds not connected with those who concocted a mad plan to force the stockade and make in this way their escape, I hereby warn the leaders and those who formed themselves into a band to carry out this, that I am in possession of all the facts and have made my dispositions accordingly so as to frustrate it. No choice would be left me but to open with grape and canister on the Stockade, and what effect this would have, in this densely crowded place, need not be told.

May 25, 1864.
Signed H. WIRZ.

The next day a line of tall poles, bearing white flags, were put up at some little distance from the Dead Line, and a notice was read to us at roll call, that if, except at roll call, any gathering exceeding one hundred was observed closer to the Stockade than these poles, the guns would open with grape and canister without warning.

The number of deaths in the Stockade in May was seven hundred and eight, about as many as had been killed in Sherman's army during the same time. After Wirz' threat of grape and canister upon the slightest provocation, we lived in daily apprehension of some pretext being found for opening the guns upon us for a general massacre. Bitter experience had long since taught us that the rebels rarely threatened in vain. Wirz especially was much more likely to kill without warning, than to warn without killing. This was because of the essential weakness of his nature. He knew no art of government, no method of discipline save "kill them!" His petty little mind's scope reached no further. He could conceive of no other way of managing men than the punishment of every offense, or seeming offense, with death. Men who have any talent for governing find little occasion for the death penalty. The stronger they are in themselves, the more fitted for controlling others, the less their need of enforcing their authority by harsh measures.

There was a general expression of determination among the prisoners to answer any cannonade with a desperate attempt to force the Stockade. It was agreed that anything was better than dying like rats in a pit or wild animals in a bateau. It was believed that if anything would occur which would rouse half those in the pen to make a headlong effort in concert, the palisade could be scaled and the gates carried and though it would be at a fearful loss of life, the majority of those making the attempt would get out. If the rebels would discharge grape and canister or throw a shell into the prison, it would lash everybody to such a pitch that they would see that the sole forlorn hope of safety lay in wresting the arms away from our tormentors. The great element in our favor was the shortness of the distance between us and the cannon. We could hope to traverse this before the guns could be reloaded more than once.

Whether it would have been possible to succeed, I am unable to say. It would have depended wholly upon the spirit and unanimity with which the effort was made. Had ten thousand rushed at once, each with a determination to do or die, I think it would have been successful without a loss of a tenth of the number. But the insuperable trouble, in our disorganized state, was want of concerted action. I am quite sure, however, that the attempt would have been made had the guns opened.

One day, while the agitation of this matter was feverish, I was cooking my dinner—that is, boiling my pitiful little ration of unsalted meal in my fruit can, with the aid of a handful of splinters I had been able to pick up by a half day's diligent search. Suddenly the long rifle in the headquarters fort rang out angrily. A fused shell shrieked across the prison, close to the tops of the logs, and burst in the woods beyond. It was answered with a yell of defiance from ten thousand throats. I sprang up, my heart in my throat. The long-dreaded time had arrived; the rebels had opened the massacre in which they must exterminate us or we them. I looked across to the opposite bank on which were standing twelve thousand men, erect, excited, defiant. I was sure that at the next shot they would surge straight against the stockade like a mighy human billow, and then a carnage would begin the like of which modern times had never seen.

The excitement and suspense were terrible. We waited for what seemed ages for the next gun. It was not fired. Old Winder was merely showing the prisoners how he could rally the guards to oppose an outbreak. Though the gun had a shell in it, it was merely a signal, and the guards came double-quicking up by regiments, going into position in the rifle-pits and by the hand-grenade piles. As we realized what the whole affair meant, we relieved our surcharged feelings with a few general yells of execration upon rebels generally and upon those around us in particular, and resumed our occupation of cooking rations, killing lice and discussing the prospects of exchange and escape.

The rations, like everything about us, had steadily grown worse. A bakery was built outside of the Stockade in May, and our meal was baked there into loaves about the size of a brick. Each of us got a half of one of these for a day's ration. This and, occasionally, a small slice of salt pork, was all that we received. I wish the reader would prepare himself an object lesson as to on how little life can be supported for a length of time, by procuring a piece of corn bread the size of an ordinary brickbat, and a thin slice of pork, and then imagine how he would fare with that as his sole daily ration for long hungry weeks and months.

Dio Lewis satisfied himself that he could sustain life on sixty cents a week. I am sure that the food furnished us by the rebels would not, at present prices, cost one third that. They pretended to give us one third of a pound of bacon and one and one-fourth pounds of corn meal. A week's rations then would be two and one-third pounds of bacon, worth ten cents, and eight and three-fourths pounds of meal worth, say, ten cents more. As a matter of fact, I do not presume that at any time we got this full ration. It would surprise me to learn that we averaged two thirds of it. The meal was ground very coarse and produced great irritation in the bowels. We used to have the most frightful cramps that men ever suffered from. Those who were predisposed to intestinal infections were speedily carried off by incurable diarrhea and dysentery. Of the twelve thousand and twelve men who died, four thousand died of chronic diarrhea, eight hundred and seventeen died of acute diarrhea, and one thousand three hundred and eighty-four died of dysentery, making a total of six thousand two hundred and one victims to enteric disorders.

Let the reader reflect a moment upon this number, till he comprehends fully how many six thousand two hundred and one men are, and how much force, energy, training and rich possibilities for the good of the community and country died with those six thousand and more young active men. It may help his perception of the magnitude of this number to remember that the total loss of the British during the Crimean War, by death in all shapes, was four thousand five hundred and ninety-five, or one thousand seven hundred and six less than the deaths in Andersonville from dysentery and diseases alone.

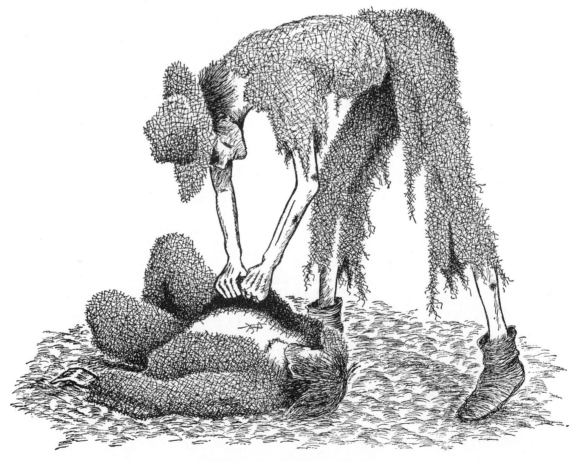

Stripping the Dead for Clothes

CHAPTER VI

A FETID, BURNING DESERT

DURING THE MONTH of May, more and more prisoners answered to roll call and it
was not long until the bakery became inadequate to supply bread for all the
prisoners. Worse still, the loathsome maggot flies swarmed about the bakery and
dropped into the trough where the dough was being mixed, so that it was rare to get
a ration of bread not contaminated with them. When the bread ration fell short, great
iron kettles were set up, and mush was issued to a number of detachments instead of
bread. There was not so much cleanliness and care in preparing this as a farmer shows
in cooking food for livestock. A deep wagon bed would be shoveled full of smoking
paste which was then hauled inside and issued out to the detachments, the latter receiving it on blankets, pieces of shelter tents or, lacking even these, upon the bare
sand.

As still more prisoners came in, neither bread nor mush could be furnished them,
and a part of the detachments received their rations in meal. Earnest solicitation at
length resulted in having occasional scanty issues of wood to cook with. My detachment was allowed to choose which it would take, bread, mush or meal. It took the
latter. Cooking the meal was the daily topic of interest. There were three ways of
doing it—bread, mush and "dumplings." In the last, the meal was dampened until it
would hold together and was rolled into little balls the size of marbles, which were
then boiled. The bread was the most satisfactory and nourishing; the mush the bulki-
est—it made a bigger show but did not stay with one so long. The dumplings held an

intermediate position, the water in which they were boiled becoming a sort of a broth that helped to stay the stomach. We received no salt as a rule. No one knows the intense longing for this when one goes without it for a while. When, after a privation of weeks, we would get a teaspoonful of salt apiece, it seemed as if every muscle in our bodies was invigorated.

We traded buttons to the guards for red peppers, and made our mush or bread or dumplings hot with the fiery pods, in hopes that this would make up for the lack of salt, but it was a failure. One pinch of salt was worth all the pepper pods in the Southern Confederacy. My little squad, now diminished by death from five to three, cooked our rations together to economize wood and waste of meal, and quarreled among ourselves daily as to whether the joint stock should be converted into bread, mush or dumplings. The decision depended upon the state of the stomach. If very hungry, we made mush; if less famished, dumplings; if disposed to weigh matters, bread. This may seem a trifling matter, but it was far from it. We all remember the man who was very fond of white beans but, after having fifty or sixty meals of them in succession, he began to find a suspicion of monotony in the provender. We had now had six months of unvarying diet of corn meal and water, and even so slight a change as a variation in the way of combining the two was an agreeable novelty.

At the end of June there were twenty-six thousand three hundred and sixty-seven prisoners in the Stockade, and one thousand two hundred—just forty a day—had died during the month. May and June made sad havoc in the already thin ranks of our battalion. Nearly a score died in my company, L, and the other companies suffered proportionately. Among the first to die of my company comrades was a genial little corporal, Billy Phillips, who was a favorite with us all. Everything was done for him that kindness could suggest, but it was of little avail. Then Bruno Weeks, the son of a preacher, a young boy who had run away from his home in Fulton County, Ohio, to join us, succumbed to hardship and privation.

The next to go was good-natured, harmless Victor Seitz, a Detroit cigar maker, a German, and one of the slowest of created mortals. How he ever came to go in the cavalry was beyond the wildest surmises of his comrades. Why his supernatural slowness and clumsiness did not result in his being killed at least once a day while in the service was even still farther beyond the power of conjecture. No accident ever happened in the company that Seitz did not have some share in. Did a horse fall on a slippery road, it was almost sure to be Seitz', and that imported son of the Fatherland was equally sure to be caught under him. Did somebody tumble over a bank of a dark night, it was Seitz that we soon heard making his way back, swearing in deep guttural oaths with frequent allusion to *tausend teufeln*. Did a shanty blow down, we ran over and pulled Seitz out of the debris, when he would exclaim, "Zo! Dot vos pretty vunny now, ain't it?" And as he surveyed the scene of his trouble with true German phlegm, he would fish a brier-wood pipe from the recesses of his pockets, fill it with tobacco, and go plodding off in a cloud of smoke in search of some fresh way narrowly to escape destruction.

Seitz did not know enough about horses to put a snaffle-bit in one's mouth, and yet he would draw the friskiest, most mettlesome animal in the corral, upon whose back he was scarcely more at home than he would be on a slack rope. It was no uncommon thing to see a horse break out of ranks and go past the battalion like the wind, with poor Seitz clinging to his mane like the traditional grim Death to a deceased African. We then knew that Seitz had thoughtlessly sunk the keen spurs he would persist in wearing deep into the flanks of his high-mettled horse. These accidents became so much a matter of course that when anything unusual occurred in the company, our first impulse was to go out and help Seitz. When the bugle sounded "Boots and Saddles," the rest of us would pack up, mount, "count off by fours from the right," and be ready to move out before the last notes of the call had fairly died away.

Just then we would notice an unsaddled horse still tied to the hitching post. It was Seitz', and that worthy would be seen approaching, pipe in mouth and bridle in hand, with calm equable steps, as if any time before the expiration of his enlistment would be soon enough to accomplish the saddling of his steed. A chorus of derisive remarks would go up from his impatient comrades: "For heaven's sake, Seitz, hurry up!" "Seitz! You're like a cow's tail—always behind!" "Seitz, you are slower than the second coming of the Saviour!" "Christmas is a railroad train alongside of you, Seitz!" "If you ain't on that horse in half a second, Seitz, we'll go off and leave you, and the Johnnies will skin you alive!" Not a ripple of emotion would roll over Seitz' placid features under the sharpest of these proddings. At last, losing all patience, two or three of the boys would dismount, run to Seitz' horse, pack, saddle and bridle him as if he were struck with a whirlwind. Then Seitz would mount and we would move off. For all this, we liked him. His good nature was boundless and his disposition to oblige equal to the severest test. He did not lack a grain of his full share of the calm, steadfast courage of his race, and would stay where he was put, though Erebus yawned and bade him fly. He was very useful, despite his unfitness for many of the duties of a cavalryman. He was a good guard, always ready to take charge of prisoners or be sentry around wagons or a forage pile, duties that most of the boys cordially hated.

But he came into the last trouble at Andersonville. He stood up pretty well under the hardships of Belle Isle, but lost his cheerfulness, his unrepining calmness, after a few weeks in the Stockade. One day we remembered that none of us had seen him for several days and we started in search of him. We found him in a distant part of the camp, lying near the Dead Line. His long fair hair was matted together, his blue eyes had the flush of fever. Every part of his clothing was gray with lice that were hastening death with their torments. He uttered the first complaint I ever heard him make, as I came up to him. "My Gott," he said, "dis is vorse dan a dog's det!" In a few days we gave him a funeral, the best in our power. We tied his toes together, folded his hands across his breast, pinned to his shirt a slip of paper, upon which was written—

> Victor E. Seitz
> Company L, 16th Illinois Cavalry.

We then laid his body at the South Gate beside some scores of others that were awaiting the arrival of the six-mule wagon that hauled them to Potter's Field, which was to be their last resting place.

John Emerson and John Stiggall, of my company, were two Norwegian boys and fine specimens of their race—intelligent, faithful and always ready to do their duty. They had an affection for each other that reminded one of stories told of the sworn attachment and unfailing devotion that were common between two Gothic warrior youths. Coming into Andersonville some little time after the rest of us, they found all the desirable ground taken up, and they established their quarters at the base of the hill near the swamp. There they dug a hole to lie in and put a layer of pine leaves in the bottom. Between them they had an overcoat and a blanket. At night they lay upon the coat and covered themselves with the blanket. By day the blanket served as a tent.

The hardships and annoyances that we endured made everybody else cross and irritable. At times it seemed impossible to say or listen to pleasant words, and nobody was ever allowed to go any time spoiling for a fight. He could usually be accommodated on the spot to any extent he desired by simply making his wishes known. Even the best of chums would have sharp quarrels and brisk fights, and this disposition increased as disease made greater inroads upon them. I saw, in one instance, two brothers, both of whom died the next day of scurvy and who were so helpless as to be unable to rise, pull themselves up on their knees by clenching the poles of their tents in order to strike each other with clubs, and they kept striking each other until the bystanders interfered and took their weapons away from them.

But Stiggall and Emerson never quarreled with each other. Their tenderness and affection were remarkable to witness. They began to go the way that so many were going. Diarrhea and scurvy set in and they wasted away till their muscles and tissues almost disappeared, leaving the skin lying flat upon the bones. But their principal solicitude was for each other, and each seemed actually jealous of any person else doing for the other. I met Emerson one day, with one leg drawn clear out of shape and rendered almost useless by the scurvy. He was very weak but was hobbling down towards the creek with a bucket made from a bootleg.

"Johnny," I said, "I'll fill it for you and bring it up to your tent."

"No. Much obliged, Mac," he wheezed out. "My pardner wants a cool drink, and I guess _I_ better get it for him." Stiggall died in June. He was one of the first victims of scurvy which, in the succeeding few weeks, carried off so many. When Stiggall died we thought Emerson would certainly follow him in a day or two but, to our surprise, he lingered along until August before dying.

All of us who had read much of this disease and its horrors in sea stories had little conception of the dreadful reality. It usually manifested itself first in the mouth. The breath became unbearably fetid; the gums swelled until they protruded, livid and disgusting, beyond the lips. The teeth became so loose that they frequently fell out, and the sufferer would pick them up and put them back in the sockets. In attempting to bite the hard corn bread furnished by the bakery, the teeth often stuck fast and had to be pulled out. The gums had a way of breaking off in large chunks which would be swallowed or spit out. All the time one was eating, his mouth would be filled with blood, fragments of gums and loosened teeth. Frightful malignant ulcers appeared in other parts of the body, the ever-present maggot flies laid eggs in these, and soon worms swarmed therein. The sufferer looked and felt as if, though he yet lived and moved, his body was anticipating the rotting it would undergo a little later in the grave.

The last change was ushered in by the lower parts of the legs swelling. When this appeared, we considered the man doomed. We all had scurvy, more or less, but as long as it kept out of our legs, we were hopeful. First, the ankle joints swelled, then the foot became useless. The swelling increased until the knees became stiff and the skin from these down was distended until it looked pale, colorless and transparent as a tightly blown bladder. The leg was so much larger at the bottom than at the thigh that the sufferers used to make grim jokes about being modeled like a churn, "with the biggest end down." The man then became utterly helpless and usually died in a short time. The official report puts down the number of deaths from scurvy at three thousand five hundred and seventy-four, but Dr. Jones, the rebel surgeon, reported to the Confederate Government his belief that nine tenths of the great mortality of the prison was due, either directly or indirectly, to this cause. The only effort made by the rebel doctors to check its ravages was occasionally to give a handful of sumach berries to some particularly bad case.

The gradually lengthening summer days were insufferably long and wearisome. Each was hotter, longer and more tedious than its predecessors. In my company was a not-too-bright fellow named Dawson. During the chilly rains or the nipping winds of our first days in prison, Dawson would, as he rose in the morning, survey the forbidding skies with lack-luster eyes and remark, "Well, Ole Boo gits us agin today." He was so unvarying in this salutation to the morn that his designation of disagreeable weather as Ole Boo became generally adopted by us. When the hot weather came on, Dawson's remark, upon rising and seeing excellent prospects for a scorcher, changed to "Well, Ole Sol the Haymaker is going to git in his work on us agin today." As long as he lived and was able to talk, this was Dawson's invariable observation at the break of day.

He was quite right. The "Ole Haymaker" would do some famous work before he descended in the west, sending his level rays through the wide interstices between the somber pines. By nine o'clock in the morning his beams would begin to fairly singe everything in the crowded pen. The hot sand would blow as one sees it in the center of the unshaded highway some noon in August. The high walls of the prison prevented the circulation inside of any breeze that might be in motion, while the foul stench rising from the putrid swamp and the rotting ground seemed to reach the skies. One can readily comprehend the horrors of death on the burning sands of a desert. But the desert sand is at least clean; there is nothing worse about it than heat and intense dryness. It is not, as that was at Andersonville, poisoned with the excretions of thousands of sick and dying men, filled with disgusting vermin, and loading the air with the germs of death. The difference is as that between a brick-kiln and a sewer. Should the fates ever decide that I shall be flung out upon sands to perish, I beg that the hottest place in the Sahara may be selected, rather than such a spot as the interior of the Andersonville Stockade.

It may be said that we had an abundance of water, which made a decided improvement on a desert. Doubtless, had the water been pure, things might have been better, but every mouthful of it was a blood poison and helped promote disease and death. Even before reaching the Stockade it was so polluted by the drainage of the rebel camps as to be utterly unfit for human use. In our part of the prison we sank several wells, some as deep as forty feet, to procure water. We had no other tools for this than our faithful half-canteens, and nothing wherewith to wall the wells. But a firm clay was reached a few feet below the surface which afforded tolerable strong sides for the lower part and furnished material to make adobe bricks for curbs to keep out the sand of the upper part. The sides were continually giving away, however, and the fellows were perpetually falling down the holes, to the great damage of their legs and arms. The water which was drawn up in little cans or boot-leg buckets, by strings made of strips of cloth, was much better than that of the creek. But it was still far from pure, as it contained the seepage from the filthy ground.

The intense heat led men to drink great quantities of water, and this super-induced malignant, dropsical complaints which, next to diarrhea, scurvy and gangrene, were the ailments most active in carrying men off. Those affected in this way swelled up frightfully from day to day. Their clothes speedily became too small for them and were ripped off, leaving them entirely naked, and they suffered intensely until death at last came to their relief. Among those of my squad who died in this way was a young man named Baxter of the 5th Indiana Cavalry, taken at Chickamauga. He was very fine looking, tall and slender, with regular features and intensely black hair and eyes. He sang nicely, and was generally liked. A more pitiable object than he, when last I saw him just before his death, cannot be imagined. His body was swollen until it seemed marvelous that the human skin could bear so much distention without disruption. All the old look of bright intelligence had been driven from his face by the distortion of his features. His swarthy hair and beard, grown long and ragged, had that peculiar repulsive look which the black hair of the sick is prone to assume.

I attributed much of my freedom from the diseases to which others succumbed to abstention from water drinking. Long before I entered the army, I had constructed a theory, on premises that were doubtless as insufficient as those that boyish theories are usually based upon, that drinking water was a habit and a pernicious one which sapped away the energy. I took some trouble to curb my appetite for water and soon found that I got along very comfortably without drinking anything beyond that which was contained in my food. I followed this up after entering the army, drinking nothing at any time but a little coffee and finding no need, even on the dustiest marches, for anything more. I presume that in a year I did not drink a quart of cold water. Experience seemed to confirm my views, for I noticed that the first to sink under fatigue or to yield to sickness were those who were always on the lookout for drinking water, springing from their horses and struggling around every well or spring on the line of march to fill their canteens.

I made liberal use of the creek for bathing purposes, however, visiting it four or five times a day during the hot days to wash myself all over. This did not cool one off much, for the shallow stream was nearly as hot as the sand, but it seemed to do some good and it helped pass away the tedious hours. The stream was crowded nearly all the time, filled as full of bathers as could stand. The water could do little towards cleansing so many. The occasional rain storms that swept across the prison were welcomed, not only because they cooled the air temporarily but because they gave us a shower-bath. As they came up, nearly every one stripped naked and got out where he could enjoy the full benefit of the falling water. Fancy, if possible, the spectacle of twenty-five thousand or thirty thousand men without a stitch of clothing upon them. The like has not been seen, I imagine, since the naked followers of Boadicea gathered in force to do battle to the Roman invaders. But it was impossible to get really clean. Our bodies seemed covered with a varnish-like gummy matter that defied removal by water alone. I imagine that it came from the rosin or turpentine arising from the little pitch pine fires over which we hovered when cooking our rations. It would yield to nothing except strong soap, and soap, as I have before stated, was nearly as scarce in the Southern Confederacy as salt. We in prison saw even less of it, or rather, none at all. The scarcity of it and our desire for it recall a bit of personal experience.

I had steadfastly refused all offers of positions outside the prison on parole as, like the great majority of the prisoners, my hatred of the rebels grew more bitter day by day. I felt as if I would rather die than accept the smallest favor at their hands, and I shared the common contempt for those who did. But the movement for a grand attack on the Stockade, mentioned previously, was apparently rapidly coming to a head. I was offered a temporary detail outside to assist in making up some rolls. I resolved to accept. First, because I thought I might get some information that would be of use in our enterprise; and next, because I foresaw that the rush through the gaps in the stockade would be bloody business and that by going out in advance I would avoid that much of the danger and still be able to give effective assistance.

I was taken up to Wirz' office. He was writing at a desk at one end of a large room when the sergeant brought me in. He turned around, told the sergeant to leave me and ordered me to sit down upon a box at the other end of the room. Turning his back and resuming his writing, in a few minutes he had forgotten me. I sat quietly, taking in the details for a half hour and then, having exhausted everything else in the room, I began wondering what was in the box I was sitting upon. The lid was loose. I hitched it forward a little without attracting Wirz' attention, and slipped my left hand down on a voyage of discovery. It seemed very likely that there was something there that a loyal Yankee deserved better than a rebel. I found that it was a fine article of soft soap. A handful was scooped up and speedily shoved into my left pantaloons pocket.

Expecting every instant that Wirz would turn around and order me to come to the desk to show my handwriting, I hastily and furtively wiped my hands on the back of my shirt and watched Wirz with as an innocent an expression as a schoolboy assumes when he has just flipped a chewed paper wad across the room. Wirz was still engrossed in his writing, and did not look around. I was emboldened to reach down for another handful. This was also successfully transferred, the hand wiped off on the back of the shirt, and the face wore its expression of infantile ingenuousness. Still Wirz did not look up. I kept dipping up handful after handful, until I had gotten about a quart in the left-hand pocket. After each handful I rubbed my hand off on the back of my shirt and waited an instant for a summons to the desk. Then the process was repeated with the other hand, and a quart of the sapindaceous mush was packed in the right-hand pocket. Shortly after, Wirz rose and ordered a guard to take me away and keep me until he decided what to do with me.

The day was intensely hot, and soon the soap in my pockets and on the back of my shirt began burning like double-strength Spanish fly blisters. There was nothing to do but grin and bear it. I set my teeth, squatted down under the shade of the parapet of the fort and stood it silently and sullenly. For the first time in my life I thoroughly appreciated the story of the Spartan boy who stole the fox and suffered the animal to tear his bowels out rather than give a sign which would lead to the exposure of his theft.

Between four and five o'clock, after I had endured the thing for five or six hours, a guard came with orders from Wirz that I should be returned to the Stockade. Upon hastily removing my clothes after coming inside, I found I had a blister on each thigh and one down my back that would have delighted an old practitioner of the heroic school. But I also had a half gallon of excellent soft soap. My chums and I took a magnificent wash and gave our clothes the same. We still had soap enough left to barter for some onions that we had long coveted and which tasted as sweet to us as manna to the Israelites.

The time moved with leaden feet. Do the best we could, there were very many tiresome hours for which no occupation whatever could be found. All that was *necessary* to be done during the day—attending roll call, drawing and cooking rations, killing lice and washing—could be disposed of in an hour's time, and we were left with fifteen or sixteen waking hours for which there was absolutely no employment. Very many tried to escape both the heat and ennui by sleeping as much as possible through the day, but I noticed that those who did this soon died, and consequently I did not do it.

Card playing had sufficed to pass away the hours at first, but our cards soon wore out and deprived us of this resource. My chum Andrews and I constructed a set of chessmen with an infinite deal of trouble. We found a soft white root in the swamp which answered our purpose. A boy near us had a tolerably sharp pocket-knife for the use of which a couple of hours each day we gave a few spoonfuls of meal. The knife was the only one among a large number of prisoners. The rebel guards had an affection for that style of cutlery which led them to search incoming prisoners very closely and the fortunate owner of this one derived quite a little income of meal by shrewdly loaning it to his knifeless comrades. The shapes that we made for pieces and pawns were necessarily very crude, but they were sufficiently distinct for identification. We blackened one set with pitch-pine soot, found a piece of plank that would answer for a board and purchased it from its possessor for part of a ration of meal, and so were fitted out with what served until our release to distract our attention from much of the surrounding misery.

Everyone else procured such amusement as they could. Newcomers who still had money and cards gambled as long as their means lasted. Those who had books read them until the leaves fell apart. Those who had paper and pen and ink tried to write descriptions and keep journals, but this was usually given up after being in prison a few weeks. I was fortunate enough to know a boy who had brought a copy of *Gray's Anatomy* into prison with him. I was not specially interested in the subject, but it was Hobson's choice—I could read anatomy or nothing. And so I tackled it with such good will that before my friend became sick and was taken outside, and his book with him, I had obtained a very fair knowledge of the rudiments of physiology.

There was a little band of devoted Christian workers, among whom was Orderly Sergeant Thomas J. Sheppard, 97th Ohio Volunteer Infantry, now a leading Baptist Minister in eastern Ohio; Boston Corbett,[16] who afterwards slew John Wilkes Booth; and Frank Smith, now at the head of the railroad Bethel work at Toledo. They were indefatigable in trying to evangelize the prison. A few of them would take their station in some part of the Stockade—a different one every time—and begin singing some old familiar hymn like "Come, Thou Fount of Every Blessing," and in a few minutes they would have an attentive audience of as many thousand as could get within hearing. The singing would be followed by regular services, during which Sheppard, Smith, Corbett and some others would make short, spirited, practical addresses which no doubt did much good to all who heard them, though the grains of leaven were entirely too small to leaven such an immense measure of meal. They conducted several funerals as nearly like the way it was done at home as possible. Their ministrations were not confined to mere lip service, but they labored assiduously in caring for the sick and made many a poor fellow's way to the grave much smoother for him.

This was about all the religious service that we were favored with. The rebel preachers did not make that effort to save our misguided souls which one would have imagined they would. Having us where we could not choose but hear, they might have taken advantage of our situation to rake us fore and aft with their theological artillery They only attempted it in one instance. While in Richmond, a preacher came into our room and announced in an authoritative voice that he would address us on religious subjects. We uncovered respectfully and gathered around him. He was a loud-tongued, brawling Boanerges,[17] who addressed the Lord as if drilling a brigade. He spoke but a few minutes before making apparent his belief that the worst of crimes was that of being a Yankee, and that a man must not only be saved through Christ's blood, but also serve in the rebel army before he could attain to Heaven. Of course we raised such a yell of derision that the sermon was brought to an abrupt conclusion.

The only minister who came into the Stockade was middle-aged, tall, slender and unmistakably devout. He was unwearied in his attention to the sick, and the whole day he could be seen moving around through the prison attending those who needed spiritual consolation. Though full of commiseration for the unhappy lot of the prisoners, nothing could betray him into the slightest expression of opinion regarding the war or those who were the authors of all this misery. In our impatience at our treatment and hungry for news, we forgot his churchly character and importuned him for tidings of the exchange. His invariable reply was that he lived apart from these things and kept himself ignorant of them. "When I leave the prison in the evening," he said, "full of sorrow at what I have seen here, I find that the best use I can make of my time is in studying the Word of God, and especially the Psalms of David."

"The N'Yaarker"

CHAPTER VII

MAGGOTS, LICE AND RAIDERS

WITH EACH LONG hot summer hour, the lice, the maggot flies and the N'Yaarkers increased in numbers and venomous activity. They were ever-present annoyances and troubles; no time was free from them. The lice worried us by day and tormented us by night; the maggot flies fouled our food and laid in sores and wounds larvae that speedily became masses of wriggling worms; the N'Yaarkers were human vermin that preyed upon and harried us unceasingly. They formed themselves into bands numbering from five to twenty-five, each led by a bold, unscrupulous, energetic scoundrel. We now called them Raiders, and the most prominent and best known of the bands were called by the names of their ruffian leaders, Mosby, also known as Collins, Curtis, Delaney, Sarsfield, Sullivan and so on.

As long as we old prisoners formed the bulk of those inside the Stockade, the Raiders had slender picking. They would occasionally snatch a blanket from the tent poles or knock a boy down at the Creek and take his silver watch from him; but this was all. Abundant opportunities for securing richer swag came to them with the advent of the Plymouth Pilgrims. These boys had brought in with them a large installment of veteran bounty,[18] aggregating in amount to between twenty-five thousand and one hundred thousand dollars. The Pilgrims were likewise well clothed, had an abundance of blankets and camp equipage, and a plentiful supply of personal trinkets that could be readily traded off to the rebels. An average one of them, even if his money was all gone, was a bonanza to any band which could succeed in plundering him. His watch and chain, shoes, knife, ring, handkerchief, combs and similar trifles would net several hundred dollars in Confederate money. The Blockade, which cut off the rebel communication with the outer world, made these in great demand. Many of the prisoners that came in from the Army of the Potomac repaid robbing equally well. As a rule, those from that army were not searched so closely as those from the west, and not unfrequently they came in with all their belongings untouched, where as Sherman's men, arriving the same day, would be stripped nearly to the buff.

The methods of the Raiders were various, ranging all the way from sneak thievery to highway robbery. All the arts learned in the prisons and purlieus of New York were put into exercise. Decoys, "bunko steerers" at home, would be on the lookout for promising subjects as each crowd of fresh prisoners entered the gate and, by kindly offers to find them a sleeping place, would lure them to where they could be easily despoiled during the night. If the victim resisted, there was always sufficient force at hand to conquer him, and not seldom his life paid the penalty for his rashness. I have known as many as three of these to be killed in a night, and their bodies, their throats cut or skulls crushed in, would be found in the morning among the dead at the gates. All men having money or valuables were under continual observation and, when found in places convenient for attack, a rush was made for them. They were knocked down and their persons rifled with such swift dexterity that it was done before they realized what had happened.

At first these depredations were only perpetrated at night. The quarry was selected during the day and arrangements made for a descent. After the victim was asleep, the band dashed down upon him and sheared him of his goods with incredible swiftness. Those near would raise the cry, "Raiders!" and attack the robbers. If the latter had secured their booty, they retreated with all possible speed and were soon lost in the crowd. If not, they would offer battle, and signal for assistance from the other bands. Severe engagements of this kind were of continual occurrence, in which men were so badly beaten as to die from the effects. The weapons used were fists, clubs, axes, tent-poles and stones. The Raiders were plentifully provided with the usual weapons of their class—slingshots and brass knuckles. Several of them had succeeded in smuggling bowie knives into prison.

They had the great advantage in these rows of being well acquainted with each other while, except for the Plymouth Pilgrims, the rest of the prisoners were made up of small squads of men from each regiment in the service and total strangers to all outside of their own little band. The Raiders could concentrate, if necessary, four hundred or five hundred men upon any point of attack, and a member of the gang had become so familiarized with all the rest, by long association in New York and elsewhere, that he never dealt a blow amiss, while their opponents were nearly as likely to attack friends as enemies. By the middle of June, the continual success of the Raiders emboldened them so that they no longer confined their depredations to the night but made their forays in broad daylight, and there was hardly an hour in the twenty-four that the cry of "Raiders! Raiders!" did not go up from some part of the pen. And looking in the direction of the cry, one would see a surging commotion, men struggling and clubs being plied vigorously. This was even more common than the guards shooting men at the creek crossing.

One day I saw Dick Allen's Raiders, eleven in number, attack a man wearing the uniform of Ellett's Marine Brigade. He was a recent comer and alone, but he was brave. He had come into possession of a spade by some means or another and he used this with delightful vigor and effect. Two or three times he struck one of his assailants so fairly on the head, and with such good will, that I congratulated myself that he had killed him. Finally, Dick Allen managed to slip around behind unnoticed and, striking him on the head with a slingshot, knocked him down, when the whole crowd pounced upon him to kill him but were driven off by others rallying to his assistance.

The proceeds of these forays enabled the Raiders to wax fat and lusty while others were dying from starvation. They all had good tents constructed of stolen blankets, and their headquarters was a large, roomy tent with a circular top, situated on the street leading to the South Gate, and capable of accommodating from seventy-five to one hundred men. All the material for this had been wrested from others. While hundreds were dying from scurvy and diarrhea, these fellows had flour, fresh meat, onions, potatoes, green beans and other things, the very looks of which were a torture to the hungry, scorbutic, dysenteric men. They were on the best possible terms with the rebels, whom they fawned upon and groveled before and were in return allowed many favors in the way of trading, going out upon detail and making purchases.

Among their special objects of attack were the small traders in the prison. We had quite a number of these whose genius for barter was so strong that it took root and flourished even in that unpropitious soil, and during the time when new prisoners were constantly coming with money they managed to accumulate small sums of from ten dollars upward by trading between the guards and the prisoners. In the period immediately following a prisoner's entrance, he was likely to spend all his money and trade off all his possessions for food, trusting to fortune to get him out of there when these were gone. Then was when he was profitable to these go-betweens, who managed to make him pay handsomely for what he got. The Raiders kept watch of these traders, and plundered them whenever occasion served. It reminded one of the habits of the fishing eagle, which hovers around until some other bird catches a fish and then takes it away.

To appreciate fully the condition of affairs, let it be remembered that we were a community of twenty-five thousand boys and young men, none too regardful of control at best, and now wholly destitute of government. The rebels never made the slightest attempt to maintain order in the prison. Their whole energies were concentrated in preventing our escape. So long as we stayed inside the Stockade, they cared as little what we did there as for the performances of savages in the interior of Africa. I doubt if they would have interfered had one half of us killed and eaten the other half. They rather took a delight in such atrocities as came to their notice. It was an ocular demonstration of the total depravity of the Yankees. Among ourselves there was no one in position to lay down law and enforce it. Being all enlisted men, we were on a dead level as far as rank was concerned, the highest being only sergeants whose stripes carried no weight of authority.

The time of our stay was, it was hoped, too transient to make it worth while bothering about organizing any form of government. The great bulk of the boys were recent comers who hoped that in another week or so they would be out again. There were no fat salaries to tempt anyone to take upon himself the duty of ruling the masses, and all were left to their own devices to do good or evil, according to their several bents and as fear of consequences swayed them. Each little squad of men was a law unto itself, and made and enforced its own regulations on its own territory. The administration of justice was reduced to its simplest terms. If a fellow did wrong, he was pounded, if there was anybody capable of doing it. If not, he went free. The almost unvarying success of the Raiders in their forays gave the general impression that they were invincible—that is, that not enough men could be concentrated against them to whip them.

Our ill success in the attack we made on them in April helped us to the same belief. If we could not beat them then, we could not now, after we had been enfeebled by months of starvation and disease. It seemed to us that the Plymouth Pilgrims, whose organization was yet very strong, should undertake the task. But as is usually the case in this world when we think somebody else ought to undertake the performance of a disagreeable public duty, they did not see it in the light that we wished them to. They established guards around their squads and helped beat off the Raiders when their own territory was invaded, but this was all they would do. The rest of us formed similar guards.

In the southwest corner of the Stockade where I was, we formed ourselves into a company of fifty active boys, mostly belonging to my own battalion and to other

Illinois regiments, of which I was elected captain. My first lieutenant was a tall, taciturn, long-armed member of the 100th Illinois whom we called "Egypt," as he came from that section of the State. He was wonderfully handy with his fists. I think he could knock a fellow down so that he would fall harder and lie longer than any person I ever saw. We made a tacit division of duties—I did the talking and Egypt went through the manual labor of knocking our opponents down. In the numerous little encounters in which our company was engaged, Egypt would stand by my side, silent, grim and patient, while I pursued the dialogue with the leader of the other crowd. As soon as he thought the conversation had reached the proper point, his long left arm stretched out like a flash, and the other fellow dropped as if he had suddenly come in range of a mule that was feeling well.[19] That unexpected left-hander never failed. It would have made Charles Reed's heart leap for joy to see it.

In spite of our company and our watchfulness, the Raiders beat us badly on one occasion. Marion Friend of Company I of our battalion was one of the small traders. He had accumulated forty dollars by his bartering. One evening at dusk, Delaney's Raiders, about twenty-five strong, took advantage of the absence of most of us, drawing rations, to make a rush for Marion. They knocked him down, cut him across the wrist and neck with a razor and robbed him of his forty dollars. By the time we could rally, Delaney and his attendant scoundrels were safe from pursuit in the midst of their friends. This state of things had become unendurable. Sergeant Leroy L. Key of Company M, our battalion, resolved to make an effort to crush the Raiders. He was a printer from Bloomington, Illinois, tall, dark, intelligent and strong-willed, and one of the bravest men I ever knew. He was ably seconded by "Limber Jim" of the 67th Illinois, whose lithe, sinewy form and striking features reminded one of a young Sioux brave. He had all of Key's desperate courage but not his brains or his talent for leadership.

Though fearfully reduced in numbers, our battalion had still about one hundred well men in it, and these formed the nucleus for Key's band of "Regulators," as they were styled. Among them were several who had no equals in physical strength and courage in any of the Raider's chiefs. Our best man was Ned Carrigan, corporal of Company I, from Chicago, who was so manifestly the best man in the whole prison that he was never called upon to demonstrate it. He was a big-hearted, genial Irish boy who was never known to get into trouble on his own account but only used his fists when some of his comrades were imposed upon. He had fought in the ring, and on one occasion had killed a man with a single blow of his fist in a prize fight near St. Louis. We were all very proud of him, and it was as good as an entertainment to us to see the noisiest roughs subside into deferential silence as Ned would come among them, like some grand mastiff in the midst of a pack of yelping curs. Ned entered into the regulating scheme heartily. Other stalwart specimens of physical manhood in our battalion were Sergeant Goody, Ned Johnson, Tom Larkin and others who, while not approaching Carrigan's perfect manhood, were still more than a match for the best of the Raiders.

Key proceeded with the greatest secrecy in the organization of his forces. He accepted none but western men, and preferred Illinoisans, Iowans, Kansans, Indianians and Ohioans. The boys from those states seemed to naturally go together and be moved by the same motives. He informed Wirz what he proposed doing, so that any unusual commotion within the prison might not be mistaken for any attempt upon the stockade and made the excuse for opening with the artillery. Wirz, who happened to be in a complaisant humor, approved of the design and allowed him the use of the enclosure of the North Gate to confine his prisoners in.

In spite of Key's efforts at secrecy, information as to his scheme reached the Raiders. It was debated at their headquarters and decided there that Key must be killed. Three men were selected to do this work. They called on Key at dusk on the evening of the second of July. In response to their inquiries, he came out of the blanket-covered hole on the hillside that he called his tent. They told him what they had heard and asked if it was true. He said it was. One of them then drew a knife and the other two "billies," to attack him. But, anticipating trouble, Key had procured a revolver which one of the Pilgrims had brought in his knapsack and, drawing this, he drove them off, but without firing a shot.

The occurrence caused the greatest excitement. To us of the Regulators, it showed that the Raiders had penetrated our designs and were prepared for them. To the great majority of the prisoners, it was the first intimation that such a thing was contemplated; the news spread from squad to squad with the greatest rapidity, and soon everybody was discussing the chances of the movement. For a while men ceased their interminable discussion of escape and exchange, let those overworked words and themes have a rare spell of repose, and debated whether the Raiders would whip the Regulators or the Regulators conquer the Raiders. The reasons which I have previously enumerated induced a general disbelief in the probability of our success. The Raiders were in good health, well fed, used to operating together and had the confidence begotten by a long series of successes. The Regulators lacked in all these respects.

Whether Key had originally fixed on the next day for making the attack or whether this affair precipitated the crisis, I know not, but later in the evening he sent us all orders to be on our guard all night, and ready for action the next morning.

There was very little sleep anywhere that night. The rebels learned through their spies that something unusual was going on inside, and as their only interpretation of anything unusual there was a design upon the Stockade, they strengthened the guards, took additional precautions in every way and spent the hours in anxious anticipation. We, fearing that the Raiders might attempt to frustrate the scheme by an attack in overpowering force on Key's squad which would be accompanied by the assassination of him and Limber Jim, held ourselves in readiness to offer any assistance that might be needed. The Raiders, though confident of success, were no less exercised. They threw out pickets to all the approaches to their headquarters and provided otherwise against surprise. They had smuggled in some canteens of a cheap, vile whiskey, made from sorghum, and they grew quite hilarious in their big tent over their potations.

Two songs had long ago been accepted by us as peculiarly the Raiders' own, as someone in their crowd sang them nearly every evening, and we never heard them anywhere else. The first began:

> In Athol lived a man named Jerry Lanigan;
> He battered away till he hadn't a pound——

The other song related the exploits of an Irish highway man named Brennan whose chief virtue was that "What he robbed from the rich he gave unto the poor." And this was the villainous chorus in which they all joined and sang in such a way as suggested highway robbery, murder, mayhem and arson:

> Brennan on the moor!
> Proud and Undaunted stood
> John Brennan on the moor.

They howled these two songs nearly the livelong night. They became eventually quite monotonous to us who were waiting and watching. It would have been quite a relief if they had thrown in a new one every hour or so by way of variety.

Morning at last came. Our companies mustered on their grounds, and then marched to the space on the south side where the rations were issued. Each man was armed with a small club, secured to his wrist by a string. The rebels, with their chronic fear of an outbreak animating them, had all the infantry in line of battle with loaded guns. The cannon in the works were shotted, the fuses thrust into the touch-holes, and the men stood with lanyards in hand ready to mow down everybody at any instant. The sun rose rapidly through the clear sky which soon glowed down on us like a brazen oven. The whole camp gathered where it could best view the encounter. This was on the north side. As I have before explained, the two sides sloped toward each other like those of a great trough. The Raiders' headquarters stood upon the center of the southern slope and consequently those standing on the northern slope saw everything as if upon the stage of a theater.

While standing in ranks waiting the orders to move, one of my comrades touched me on the arm and said, "My God! Just look over there!" I turned from watching the rebel artillerists, whose intentions gave me more uneasiness than anything else, and looked in the direction indicated by the speaker. The sight was the strangest one my eyes ever encountered. There were at least fifteen thousand—perhaps twenty thousand—men packed together on the bank, and every eye was turned on us. The slope was such that each man's face showed over the shoulders of the one in front of him, making acres on acres of faces. It was as if the whole broad hillside was paved or thatched with human countenances.

When all was ready we moved down upon the Raider headquarters in as good order as we could preserve while passing through the narrow, tortuous paths between the tents. Key, Limber Jim, Ned Carrigan, Goody, Tom Larkin and Ned Johnson led the advance with their companies. The prison was a silent graveyard. As we approached, the Raiders massed themselves in a strong, heavy line, with the center, against which our advance was moving, held by the most redoubtable of their leaders. How many there were of them could not be told, as it was impossible to say where their line ended and the mass of spectators began. They could not themselves tell, as the attitude of a large portion of the spectators would be determined by which way the battle went. Not a blow was struck until the lines came close together. Then the Raiders' center launched itself forward against ours, and grappled savagely with the leading Regulators. For an instant—it seemed an hour—the struggle was desperate. Strong, fierce men clenched and strove to throttle each other; great muscles strained almost to bursting; and blows with fists and clubs, dealt with the energy of mortal hate, fell like hail. For one seemingly endless minute the lines surged and throbbed backward and forward, a step or two. And then, as if by a concentration of mighty effort, our men flung the Raider line from it, broken, shattered.

The next instant our leaders were striding through the mass like raging lions. Carrigan, Limber Jim, Larkin, Johnson and Goody each smote down a swath of men before them, as they moved resistlessly forward. We lightweights had been sent around on the flanks to separate the spectators from the combatants, strike the Raiders in reverse, and, as far as possible, keep the crowd from reinforcing them. In five minutes after the first blow was struck, the overthrow of the Raiders was complete. Resistance ceased, and they sought safety in flight. As the result became apparent to the watchers on the opposite hillside, they vented their pent-up excitement in a yell that made the very ground tremble, and we answered them with a shout that expressed not only our exultation over our victory but our great relief from the intense strain we had long borne. We picked up a few prisoners on the battlefield and retired without making any special effort to get any more then, as we knew that they could not escape us. We were very tired and very hungry. The time for drawing rations had arrived. Wagons containing bread and mush had driven to the gates, but Wirz would not allow these to be opened lest in the excited condition of the men an attempt might be made to carry them. Key ordered operations to cease, that Wirz might be reassured and let the rations enter. It was in vain. Wirz was thoroughly scared. The wagons stood out in the hot sun until the mush fermented and soured and had to be thrown away, while we went rationless to bed, and rose the next day with more than usually empty stomachs to goad us on to our work.

I may not have made it wholly clear to the reader why we did not have the active assistance of the whole prison in the struggle with the Raiders. There were many reasons for this. First, the great bulk of the prisoners were newcomers, having been at the farthest but three or four weeks in the Stockade. They did not comprehend the situation of affairs as we older prisoners did. They did not understand that all the outrages, or very nearly all, were the work of a relatively small crowd of graduates of the metropolitan school of vice. The activity and audacity of the Raiders gave them the impression that at least half the able-bodied men in the Stockade were engaged in these depredations.

This is always the case. A half dozen burglars or other active criminals in a town will produce the impression that a large portion of the population are law-breakers. We never estimated that the raiding N'Yaarkers, with their spies and other accomplices, exceeded five hundred, but it would have been difficult to convince a new prisoner that there were not thousands of them.

Secondly, the prisoners were made up of small squads from every regiment at the front along the whole line from the Mississippi to the Atlantic. These were strangers to and distrustful of all outside their own little circles. The eastern men were especially so. The Pennsylvanians and New Yorkers each formed groups and did not fraternize readily with those outside their state lines. The New Jerseyans held aloof from all the rest, while the Massachusetts soldiers had very little in common with anybody, even their fellow New Englanders. The Michigan men were modified New Englanders. They had the same tricks of speech. They said "I be" for "I am," and "haag" for "hog," "let me look at your knife half a second" or "give me just a sup of that water," where we said simply "lend me your knife" or "hand me a drink." They were less reserved than the true Yankees, more disposed to be social and, with all their eccentricities, were as manly and honorable a set of fellows as it was my good fortune to meet with in the army. I could ask no better comrades than the boys of the 3rd Michigan Infantry, who belonged to the same Ninety with me. The boys from Minnesota and Wisconsin were very much like those from Michigan.

Those from Ohio, Indiana, Illinois, Iowa, and Kansas all seemed cut off the same piece. To all intents and purposes they might have come from the same county. They spoke the same dialect, read the same newspapers, had studied *McGuffey's Readers, Mitchell's Geography* and *Ray's Arithmetics* at school, admired the same great men and generally held the same opinions on any given subject. It was never difficult to get them to act in unison. They did it spontaneously, while it required an effort to bring about harmony of action with those of other sections. Had the western boys in prison been thoroughly apprised of our enterprise, we could doubtless have commanded their cordial assistance, but they were not, and there was no way in which it could be done readily until after the decisive blow was struck.

The work of arresting the leading Raiders went on all day on the Fourth of July. They made occasional shows of fierce resistance, but the events of the day before had destroyed their prestige, broken their confidence and driven away from their support many who followed their lead when they were considered all-powerful. They scattered from their former haunts and mingled with the crowds in other parts of the prison, but were recognized and reported to Key who sent parties to arrest them. Several times they managed to collect enough adherents to drive off the squads sent after them, but this only gave them a short respite, for the squad would return reinforced and make short work of them.

Besides, the prisoners generally were beginning to understand and approve of the Regulators' movement, and were disposed to give all the assistance needed. Myself and Egypt, my taciturn lieutenant of the sinewy left arm, were sent with our company to arrest Pete Donnelly, a notorious character and leader of a bad crowd. He was more "knocker" than Raider, however. He was an old Pemberton Building acquaintance and, as we marched up to where he was standing at the head of his gathering clan, he recognized me and said, "Hello, Illinoy—" the name I was generally known by in prison—"what do you want here?"

I replied, "Pete, Key has sent me for you. I want you to go to headquarters."

"What the hell does Key want with me?"

"I don't know, I'm sure; he only said to bring you."

"But I haven't had anything to do with them or those other snoozers you have been having trouble with."

"I don't know anything about that; you can talk to Key as to that. I only know that we are sent for you."

"Well, you don't think you can take me unless I choose to go? You hain't got anybody in that crowd big enough to make it worth while for him to waste his time trying it."

I replied diffidently that one never knew what he could do until he tried, that while none of us were very big, we were as willing a lot of little fellows as he ever saw and if it were all the same to him, we would undertake to waste a little time getting him to headquarters. The conversation seemed unnecessarily long to Egypt who stood by, about half a step in advance. Pete was becoming angrier and more defiant every minute. His followers were crowding up to us, clubs in hand. Finally Pete thrust his fist in my face and roared out, "By God, I ain't a-going with ye, and ye can't take me, you son of a bitch!"

This was Egypt's cue. His long left arm uncoupled like the loosening weight of a pile-driver. It caught Mr. Donnelly under the chin, fairly lifted him from his feet and dropped him on his back among his followers. It seemed to me that the predominating expression on his face as he went over was that of profound wonder as to where that blow could have come from and why he did not see it in time to dodge or ward it off. As Pete dropped, the rest of us stepped forward with our clubs to engage his followers, while Egypt and one or two others tied his hands and otherwise secured him. But his henchmen made no effort to rescue him, and we carried him over to headquarters without molestation.

The work of arresting increased in interest and excitement until it developed into the furor of a hunt, with thousands eagerly engaged in it. The Raiders' tents were torn down and pillaged. Blankets, tent-poles and cooking utensils were carried off as spoils and the ground was dug over for secretive property. A large quantity of watches, chains, knives, rings, gold pens, the booty of many a raid, was found, and helped to give impetus to the hunt. Even the rebel quartermaster, with the characteristic keen scent of the rebels for spoils, smelled from the outside the opportunity for gaining plunder and came in with a squad of rebels equipped with spades, to dig for buried treasures. How successful he was I know not, as I took no part in any of the operations of that nature. It was claimed that several skeletons of victims of the Raiders were found buried beneath the tents. I cannot speak with any certainty as to this, though my impression was that at least one was found. By evening Key had perhaps one hundred and twenty-five of the most noted Raiders in his hands. Wirz had allowed him the use of the small stockade forming the entrance to the North Gate to confine them in. The next thing was the judgment and punishment of the arrested ones.

For this purpose Key organized a court-martial composed of thirteen sergeants, chosen from the latest arrivals of prisoners, that they might have no prejudice against the Raiders. I believe that a man named Dick McCullough belonging to the 3rd Missouri Cavalry was the President of the Court. The trial was carefully conducted, with all the formality of a legal procedure that the Court and those managing the matter could remember as applicable to the crimes with which the accused were charged. Each of these was confronted by the witnesses who testified against him, and he was allowed to cross-examine them to any extent he desired. The defense was managed by one of their crowd, the foul-tongued Tombs shyster, Peter Bradley of whom I have before spoken. Such was the fear of the vengeance of the Raiders and their friends that many who had been badly abused dared not testify against them, dreading midnight assassination if they did. Others would not go before the Court except at night. But for all this there was no lack of evidence. There were thousands who had been robbed and maltreated or who had seen these outrages committed on others, and the boldness of the leaders in their height of power rendered their identification a matter of no difficulty whatever.

The trial lasted several days, and concluded with sentencing quite a large number to run the gauntlet, a smaller number to wear balls and chains, and the following six to be hanged: John Sarsfield, William Collins, alias "Mosby," Charles Curtis, Patrick Delaney, A. Muir, Terrence Sullivan. These names are of little consequence, however, as I believe all the rascals were professional bounty-jumpers and did not belong to any regiment longer than they could find an opportunity to desert and join another. Those sentenced to ball and chain were brought in immediately and had the irons fitted to them that had been worn by some of our men as a punishment for trying to escape. It was not yet determined how punishment should be meted out to the remainder, but circumstances themselves decided the matter. Wirz became tired of guarding so large a number as Key had arrested, and he informed Key that he should turn them back into the Stockade immediately. Key begged for a little more time to consider the disposition of the cases, but Wirz refused it and ordered the officer of the guard to return all arrested, save those sentenced to death, to the Stockade.

In the meantime the news had spread through the prison that the Raiders were to be sent in again unpunished, and an angry mob, numbering some thousands, mostly composed of men who had suffered injuries at the hands of the marauders, gathered at the South Gate, clubs in hand, to get such satisfaction as they could out of the rascals. They formed in two long, parallel lines, facing inward, and grimly awaited the incoming of the objects of their vengeance. The officer of the guard opened the wicket in the gate and began forcing the Raiders through it, one at a time, at the point of the bayonet, and each as he entered was told what he already realized well, that he must run for his life. They did this with all the energy that they possessed, and as they ran blows rained on their heads, arms and backs. If they could succeed in breaking through the line at any place, they were generally let go without any further punishment. Three of the number were beaten to death. I saw one of these killed. I had no liking for the gauntlet performance and refused to have anything to do with it, as did most if not all of my crowd.

While the gauntlet was in operation, I was standing by my tent at the head of a little street about two hundred feet from the line, watching what was being done. A sailor was let in. He had a large bowie knife concealed about his person somewhere, which he drew and struck savagely with at his tormentors on either side. They fell back from before him, but closed in behind and pounded him terribly. He broke through the line, and ran up the street towards me. About midway of the distance stood a boy who had helped carry a dead man out during the day, and while out had secured a large pine rail which he had brought in with him. He was holding this straight up in the air as if at a "present arms." He seemed to have known from the first that the Raider would run that way. Just as he came squarely under it, the boy dropped the rail like the bar of a toll gate. It struck the Raider across the head, felled him as if by a shot, and his pursuers then beat him to death.

Execution of the Raiders

CHAPTER VIII

SIX ARE HANGED

IT BEGAN TO BE pretty generally understood through the prison that six men had been sentenced to be hanged, though no authoritative announcement of the fact had been made. There was much canvassing as to where they should be executed, and whether an attempt to hang them inside the stockade would not rouse their friends to make a desperate effort to rescue them which would precipitate a general engagement of even larger proportions than that of the 3rd. Despite the result of the affairs of that and the succeeding days, the camp was not yet convinced that the Raiders were really conquered. The Regulators were themselves not thoroughly at ease on that score. Some five or six thousand new prisoners had come in since the first of the month, and it was claimed that the Raiders had received large reinforcements from those, a claim rendered probable by most of the newcomers being from the Army of the Potomac.

Key and those immediately about him kept their own counsel in the matter and suffered no secret of their intentions to leak out. But on the morning of the 11th, it became generally known that the sentences were to be carried out that day, and inside the prison. My first direct information as to this was by messenger from Key with an order to assemble my company and stand guard over the carpenters who were to erect the scaffold. He informed me that all the Regulators would be held in readiness to come to our relief if we were attacked in force. I had hoped that if the men were to be hanged I would be spared the unpleasant duty of assisting, for though I believed they richly deserved the punishment, I had much rather someone else administer it upon them. There was no way out of it, however, that I could see, and so Egypt and I got the boys together and marched down to the designated place, an open space near the end of the street running from the South Gate and kept vacant for the purpose of issuing rations. It was quite near the spot where the Raiders' big tent had stood and afforded as good a view to the rest of the camp as could be found.

Key had secured the loan of a few beams and rough planks, sufficient to build a scaffold with. Our first duty was to care for these as they came in, for such was the need for wood and plank for tent purposes that they would have scarcely have fallen to the ground before they were spirited away had we not stood over them all the time with clubs. The carpenters sent by Key came over and set to work. The N'Yaarkers gathered around in considerable numbers, sullen and abusive. They cursed us with all their rich vocabulary of foul epithets, vowed that we should never carry out the execution, and swore that they had marked each one of us for vengeance. We returned the compliments in kind, and occasionally it seemed as if a general collision was imminent. But we succeeded in avoiding this, and by noon the scaffold was finished.

It was a very simple affair. A stout beam was fastened on the top of two posts about fifteen feet high. At about the height of a man's head, a couple of boards stretched across the space between the posts and met in the center. The ends at the posts were laid on cleats, those in the center rested upon a couple of boards standing upright, each having a piece of rope fastened through a hole in it in such a manner that a man could snatch it from under the planks serving as the floor of the scaffold, and let the whole thing drop. A rude ladder to ascend by completed the preparations. As the arrangements neared completion, the excitement in and around the prison grew intense. Key came over with the balance of the Regulators, and we formed a hollow square around the scaffold, our company making the line on the east side.

There were now thirty thousand in the prison. Of these about one third packed themselves as tightly about our square as they could stand. The remaining twenty thousand were wedged together in a solid mass on the north side. Again I contemplated the wonderful startling spectacle of a mosaic pavement of human faces covering the whole broad hillside. Outside the rebel artillery were in place about their loaded and trained pieces, the No. 4 of each gun holding the lanyard cord in his hand ready to fire the piece at the instant of command. The rebel infantry was standing in the rifle pits. The small squad of cavalry was drawn up on the hill near the Star Fort, and near it were the masters of hounds with their yelping packs. All the hangers-on of the rebel camp—clerks, teamsters, employees, Negroes, hundreds of white and colored women, in all forming a motley crowd of between one and two thousand—were gathered in a group between the end of the rifle pits and the Star Fort. They had a good view from there, but a still better one could be had a little farther to the right, in front of the guns. They kept edging up in that direction as crowds will, though they knew the danger they would incur if the artillery opened. The day was broiling hot. The sun shot his perpendicular rays down with blistering fierceness, and the densely packed motionless crowds made the heat almost insupportable.

Key took up his position inside the square to direct matters. With him were Limber Jim, Dick McCullough and one or two others. Also Ned Johnson, Tom Larkin, Sergeant Goody and three others who were to act as hangmen. Each of these six was provided with a white sack, such as the rebels brought meal in with. Two corporals of my company, "Stag" Harris and Wat Payne, were appointed to pull the stays from under the platform at the signal. A little after noon the South Gate opened and Wirz rode in, dressed in a suit of white duck, and mounted on his white horse, a conjunction which had gained for him the appellation of "Death on a Pale Horse." [20] Behind him walked the faithful old minister reading the service for the condemned. The six doomed men followed, walking between the double ranks of rebel guards. All came inside the hollow square and halted. Wirz then spoke: "Brizners, I return to you dese men so goot as I got dem. You have tried dem yourselves and found dem guilty. I haf had notting to do with it. I vash my hands of eferyting connected wit dem. Do wit dem as you like, and may Gott haf mercy on you and on dem. Garts, about face! Vorwarts, march!" With this he marched out and left us.

For a moment the condemned looked stunned. They seemed to comprehend for the first time that it was really the determination of the Regulators to hang them. Before that they had evidently thought that the talk of hanging was merely bluff. One of them gasped, "My God, men, you don't really mean to hang us up there?" Key answered grimly and laconically: "That seems to be about the size of it." At this they burst out in a passionate storm of intercessions and imprecations which lasted for a minute or so, when it was stopped by one of them saying, "All of you stop now, and let the preacher talk for us." At this the preacher closed the book upon which he had kept his eyes bent since his entrance and, facing the multitude on the North Side, began a plea for mercy. The condemned faced in the same direction, to read their fate in the countenances of those whom he was addressing.

This movement brought Curtis, a low-statured, massively built man, on the right of their line and about ten or fifteen steps from my company. The whole camp had been as still as death since Wirz' exit. The silence seemed to become even more profound as the preacher began his appeal. For a minute every ear was strained to catch what he said. Then, as the nearest of the thousands comprehended what he was saying, they raised a shout of "No! No! NO!! Hang them! Hang them! Don't let them go! Never! Hang the rascals! Hang the villains! Hang 'em! Hang 'em! Hang 'em!" This was taken up all over the prison, and tens of thousands of throats yelled in a fearful chorus.

Curtis turned from the crowd with desperation convulsing his features. Tearing off the broad-brimmed hat which he wore, he flung it on the ground with the exclamation, "By God, I'll die this way first!" and, drawing his head down and folding his arms about it, he dashed forward for the center of my company like a great stone hurled from a catapult. Egypt and I saw where he was going to strike and ran down the line to help stop him. As he came up we rained blows on his head with our clubs, but so many of us struck at him at once that we broke each others' clubs to pieces, and only knocked him on his knees. He rose with an almost superhuman effort and plunged into the mass beyond. The excitement almost became delirium. For an instant I feared that everything was gone to ruin. Egypt and I strained every energy to restore our lines before the break could be taken advantage of by the others.

Our boys behaved splendidly, standing firm, and in a few seconds the line was restored. As Curtis broke through, Delaney, a brawny Irishman standing next to him, started to follow. He took one step. At the same instant Limber Jim's long legs took three great strides and placed him directly in front of Delaney. Jim's right hand held an enormous bowie knife, and as he raised it above Delaney he hissed out, "If you dare move another step, you bastard, I'll open you from one end to the other." Delaney stopped. This checked the others till our lines reformed. When Wirz saw the commotion, he was panic-stricken with fear that the long-dreaded assault on the Stockade had begun. He ran down from the headquarters steps to the captain of the battery, shrieking, "Fire! Fire! Fire!" The captain, not being a fool, could see that the rush was not towards the Stockade but away from it, and he refrained from giving the order.

But the spectators who had gotten before the guns heard Wirz' excited yell, and remembering the consequences to themselves should the artillery be discharged, became frenzied with fear and screamed and fell down over and trampled upon each other in endeavoring to get away. The guards on that side of the Stockade ran down in a panic, and the ten thousand prisoners immediately around us, expecting no less than that the next instant we would be swept with grape and canister, stampeded tumultuously. There were quite a number of wells right around us, and all of these were filled full of men that fell into them as the crowd rushed away. Many had legs and arms broken and I have no doubt that several were killed. It was the stormiest five minutes that I ever saw.

While this was going on two of my company, belonging to the 5th Iowa Cavalry, were in hot pursuit of Curtis. I had seen them start and shouted to them to come back, as I feared they would be set upon by the Raiders and murdered. But the din was so overpowering that they could not hear me, and doubtless would not have come back if they had heard. Curtis ran diagonally down the hill, jumping over the tents and knocking down the men who happened in his way. Arriving at the swamp he plunged in, sinking nearly to his hips in the fetid filthy ooze. He forged his way through with terrible effort. His pursuers followed his example, and caught up to him just as he emerged on the other side. They struck him on the back of the head with their clubs, and knocked him down.

By this time order had been restored about us. The guns remained silent and the crowd massed around us again. From where we were, we could see the successful end of the chase after Curtis, and could see his captors start back with him. Their success was announced with a roar of applause from the north side. Both captors and captured were greatly exhausted and they were coming back very slowly. Key ordered the balance up onto the scaffold. They obeyed promptly. The preacher resumed his reading of the service for the condemned. The excitement seemed to make the doomed ones exceedingly thirsty. I never saw men drink such inordinate quantities of water. They called for it continually, gulped down a quart or more at a time, and kept two men going nearly all the time carrying it to them.

When Curtis finally arrived, he sat on the ground for a minute or so to rest and then, reeking with filth, slowly and painfully climbed the steps. Delaney seemed to think he was suffering as much from fright as anything else and said to him, "Come on up, now, show yourself a man, and die game." Again the preacher resumed his reading, but it had no interest to Delaney, who kept calling out directions to Pete Donnelly, who was standing in the crowd, as to dispositions to be made of certain bits of stolen property—to give a watch to this one, a ring to another, and so on. Once the preacher stopped and said, "My son, let the things of this earth go, and turn your attention toward those of Heaven." Delaney paid no attention to this admonition. The whole six then began delivering farewell messages to those in the crowd. Key pulled a watch from his pocket and said, "Two minutes more to talk." Delaney said cheerfully, "Well, goodby, b'ys; if I've hurted any of yez, I hope ye'll forgive me. Shpake up, now, any of yez that I've hurted, and say ye'll forgive me." We called upon Marion Friend, whose throat Delaney had tried to cut three weeks before while robbing him of forty dollars, to come forward, but Friend was not in a forgiving mood and refused with an oath.

Key then said, "Time's up," put the watch back in his pocket, and raised his hand like an officer commanding a gun. Harris and Payne laid hold of the ropes to the supports of the planks. Each of the six hangmen tied a condemned man's hands, pulled a meal sack down over his head, placed the noose around his neck, drew it up tolerably close and sprang to the ground. The preacher began praying aloud. Key dropped his hand. Payne and Harris snatched the supports out with a single jerk. The planks fell with a clatter. Five of the bodies swung around dizzily in the air. The sixth, that of Mosby, a large, powerful, raw-boned man, one of the worst in the lot, who, among other crimes, had killed Limber Jim's brother, broke the rope and fell with a thud to the ground. Some of the men ran forward, examined the body and decided that he still lived. The rope was cut off his neck, the meal sack removed, and water thrown in his face until consciousness returned.

At the first instant he thought he was in eternity. He gasped out, "Where am I? Am I in the other world?" Limber Jim muttered that they would soon show him where he was and went on grimly fixing up the scaffold anew.

Mosby soon realized what had happened, and the unrelenting purpose of the Regulator chiefs. Then he began to beg piteously for his life, saying, "Oh, for God's sake, don't put me up there again! God has spared my life once. He meant that you should be merciful to me." Limber Jim deigned him no reply. When the scaffold was rearranged, and a stout rope had replaced the broken one, he pulled the meal sack once more over the head of Mosby, who never ceased his pleadings. Then, picking up the large man as if he were a baby, he carried him to the scaffold and handed him up to Tom Larkin, who fitted the noose around his neck and sprang down. The supports had not been set with the same delicacy as at first and Limber Jim had to set his heel and wrench desperately at them before he could force them out. Then Mosby passed away without a struggle. After hanging till life was extinct, the bodies were cut down, the meal sacks pulled off their faces, and the Regulators formed two parallel lines, through which all the prisoners passed and took a look at the bodies. Pete Donnelly and Dick Allen knelt down and wiped the froth off Delaney's lips, and swore vengeance against those who had done him to death.

After the executions Key, knowing that he and all those prominently connected with the hanging would be in hourly danger of assassination if they remained inside, secured details as nurses and wardmasters in the hospital and went outside. In this crowd were Key, Ned Carrigan, Limber Jim, Dick McCullough, the six hangmen, the two corporals who pulled the props from under the scaffold and perhaps some others whom I do not now remember. In the meanwhile, provision had been made for the future maintenance of order in the prison by the organization of a regular police force which in time came to number twelve hundred men. These were divided into companies, under appropriate officers. Guards were detailed for certain locations, patrols passed through the camp in all directions continually, and signals with whistles could summon sufficient assistance to suppress any disturbance or carry out any orders from the chief. The chieftainship was first held by Key but when he went outside, he appointed Sergeant A. R. Hill of the 100th Ohio Volunteers as his successor.

Hill was one of the notables of that immense throng. A great broad-shouldered giant in the prime of his manhood, the beginning of his thirtieth year, he was as good-natured as big and as mild-mannered as brave. He spoke slowly, softly, and with a slightly rustic twang that was very tempting to a certain class of sharps to take him up for a "lubberly greenie." The man who did so usually repented his error in sackcloth and ashes. Hill first came into prominence as the victor in the most stubbornly contested fist fight in the prison history of Belle Isle. When the squad of the 100th Ohio, captured at Limestone Station, East Tennessee, in September, 1863, arrived on Belle Isle, a certain Jack Oliver of the 19th Indiana was the undisputed monarch of the island. He did not bear his blushing honors modestly—few kings of muscle can or do. The possession of a right arm capable of knocking an ordinary man into that indefinite locality known as the "middle of next week" is something that the possessor can as little resist showing as a girl showing her first solitaire ring. To know that one can certainly strike a disagreeable fellow out of time is pretty sure to breed a desire to do that thing whenever occasion serves. Jack Oliver was one who did not let his biceps rust in inaction, but thrashed everybody on the island whom he thought needed it, and his ideas as to those who should be included in this class widened daily, until it began to appear that he would soon feel it his duty to let no unwhipped man escape, but pound everybody on the island.

One day his evil genius led him to abuse a rather elderly man belonging to Hill's mess. As he fired off his tirade of scornful insolence, Hill said with more than his usual "soft" rusticity, "Mister, I don't think it just right for a young man to call an old one such bad names." Jack Oliver turned on him savagely. "Well! Maybe you want to take it up?" The grin on Hill's face looked still more verdant as he answered with gentle deliberation, "Well, mister, I don't go around a-hunting things, but I ginerally take care of all that's sent me!" Jack foamed, but his fiercest bluster could not drive that infantile smile from Hill's face, nor provoke a change in the calm slowness of his speech.

It was evident that nothing would do but a battle-royal, and Jack had sense enough to see that the imperturbable rustic was likely to give a job of some difficulty. He went off and came back with his clan, while Hill's comrades of the 100th gathered around to insure him fair play. Jack pulled off his coat and vest, rolled up his sleeves and made other elaborate preparations for the fray. Hill, without removing his garment, said as he surveyed him with a mocking smile, "Mister, you seem to be one of them particular fellers." Jack roared out, "By God, I'll make you partickler before I get through with you. Now, how shall we settle this? Regular, stand-up-and-knock-down, or rough-and-tumble?" If anything Hill's face was more vacantly serene, and his tones blander than ever as he answered, "Strike any gait that suits you, mister, I guess I will be able to keep up with you." They closed. Hill feinted with his left, and as Jack uncovered to guard he caught him fairly on the lower left ribs by a blow from his mighty right fist that sounded, as one of the bystanders expressed it "like striking a hollow log with a maul."

The color in Jack's face paled. He did not seem to understand how he had laid himself open to such a pass and made the same mistake, receiving a resounding blow in the short ribs. This taught him nothing, either, for again he opened his guard in response to a feint and again caught a blow on his luckless left ribs that drove the blood from his face and the breath from his body. He reeled back among his supporters for an instant to breathe. Recovering his wind, he dashed at Hill, feinted strongly with his right, but delivered a terrible kick against the lower part of the latter's abdomen. Both closed and fought savagely at half-arms' length for an instant, during which Hill struck Jack so fairly in the mouth as to break out three front teeth which the latter swallowed. Then they clinched and struggled to throw each other.

Hill's superior strength and skill crushed his opponent to the ground and he fell upon him. As they grappled there, one of Jack's followers sought to aid his leader by catching Hill by the hair, intending to kick him in the face. In an instant he was knocked down by a stalwart member of Hill's regiment and then literally lifted out of the ring by kicks. Jack was soon so badly beaten as to be unable to cry "enough!" One of his friends did that service for him. The fight ceased, and thenceforth Mr. Oliver resigned his pugilistic crown and retired to the shade of private life. He died of scurvy and diarrhea some months afterward in Andersonville.

The almost hourly scenes of violence and crime that marked the days and nights before the Regulators began operations were now succeeded by the greatest order. The prison was freer from crime than the best-governed city. There were frequent squabbles and fights, of course, and many petty larcenies. Rations of bread and of wood, articles of clothing and the wretched little cans and half-canteens that formed our cooking utensils were still stolen, but all these in a sneak-thief way. There was an entire absence of the audacious open-day robbery and murder, the raiding of the previous few weeks. The summary punishment inflicted on the condemned was sufficient to cow even bolder men than the Raiders and they were frightened into at least quiescence.

Sergeant Hill's administration was vigorous and secured the best results. He became a judge of all infractions of morals and law, and sat at the door of his tent to dispense justice to all comers like the cadi of a Mohammedan village. His judicial methods and punishment also reminded one strongly of the primitive judicature of Oriental lands. The wronged one came before him and told his tale; he had had his blouse or his quart cup or his shoes or his watch or his money stolen during the night. The suspected one was also summoned, confronted with his accuser, and sharply interrogated. Hill would resolve the stories in his mind, decide the innocence or guilt of the accused and, if he thought the accusation sustained, order the culprit to punishment. He did not imitate his Mussulman prototypes to the extent of bow-stringing or decapitating the condemned, nor did he cut any thief's hands off, nor yet nail his ears to a door post, but he introduced a modification of the bastinado that made those who were punished by it even wish they were dead.

The instrument used was what is called in the South a "shake," a split shingle a yard or more long, with one end whittled down to form a handle. The culprit was made to bend down until he could catch around his ankles with his hands. The part of the body thus brought into most prominence was denuded of clothing and spanked from one to twenty times, as Hill ordered, by the "shake" in some strong and willing hand. It was very amusing to the bystanders. The "spankee" never seemed to enter very heartily into the mirth of the occasion. As a rule he slept on his face for a week or so after and took his meals standing.

The fear of the spanking and Hill's skill in detecting the guilty ones had a very salutary effect upon the smaller criminals. The Raiders who had been put into irons were very restive under the infliction and begged Hill daily to release them. They professed the greatest penitence and promised the most exemplary behavior for the future. Hill refused to release them, declaring that they should wear the irons until delivered up to our Government. One of the Raiders named Heffron had, shortly after his arrest, turned State's evidence and given testimony that assisted materially in the conviction of his companions. One morning, a week or so after the hanging, his body was found lying among the other dead at the South Gate. The impression made by the fingers of the hand that had strangled him were still plainly visible about the throat. There was no doubt as to why he had been killed or that the Raiders were his murderers, but the actual perpetrators were never discovered.

Denouncing the Southern Confederacy

CHAPTER IX

"SO THIS IS ANDERSONVILLE, IS IT?"

ALL DURING JULY the prisoners came streaming in by hundreds and thousands from every portion of the long line of battle, stretching from the eastern bank of the Mississippi to the shores of the Atlantic.[21] Over one thousand squandered by Sturgis at Guntown came in; two thousand of those captured in the desperate blow dealt by Hood against the Army of the Tennessee on the 22nd of the month before Atlanta; Hunter's luckless column in the Shenandoah Valley; thousands from Grant's lines in front of Petersburg.

In all, seven thousand one hundred and twenty-eight were, during the month, turned into the seething mass of corrupting humanity, to be polluted and tainted by it, and to assist in turn to make it fouler and deadlier. Over seventy hecatombs of chosen victims—of fair youths in the first flush of hopeful manhood, at the threshold of lives of honor to themselves and of usefulness to the community; beardless boys rich in the priceless affections of homes, fathers, mothers, sisters and sweethearts, with minds thrilling with high aspirations for the bright future—were sent in as the monthly sacrifice to this Minotaur of the Rebellion who, couched in his foul lair, slew them not with the merciful delivery of speedy death as his Cretan prototype did the annual tribute of Athenian youths and maidens, but, gloating over his prey, doomed them to lingering destruction. He rotted their flesh with the scurvy, racked their minds with intolerable suspense, burned their bodies with the slow fire of famine, and delighted in each separate pang until they sank beneath the fearful accumulation.

Theseus, the deliverer, was coming. His terrible sword could be seen gleaming as it rose and fell on the banks of the James and in the mountains beyond Atlanta where he was hewing his way towards them and the heart of the Confederacy. But he came too late to save them. Strike as swiftly and as heavily as he would, he could not strike so hard nor so sure at his foes with saber blow and musket shot as this Minotaur could at the hapless youths with his dreadful armament of starvation and disease.

Though the deaths were one thousand eight hundred and seventeen, more than killed at the battle of Shiloh,[22] this left the number in the prison at the end of the month thirty-one thousand six hundred and seventy-eight. It was more soldiers than could be raised today under strong pressure in twenty-five states of the Union. These thirty-one thousand six hundred and seventy-eight active young men, who were likely to find the confines of a state too narrow for them, were cooped up on thirteen acres of ground, less than a farmer gives for a playground to half a dozen colts or a small flock of sheep. There was hardly room for all to lie down at night, and to walk a few hundred feet in any direction would require an hour's patient threading of the mass of men and tents. The weather became hotter and hotter. At midday the sand would burn the hand. The thin skins of fair and auburn-haired men blistered under the sun's rays and swelled up in great watery puffs which soon became the breeding grounds of the hideous maggots or the still more deadly gangrene. The loathsome swamp grew in rank offensiveness with every burning hour. The pestilence literally stalked at noonday and struck his victims down on every hand. One could not look a rod in any direction without seeing at least a dozen men in the last frightful stages of rotting death.

Let me describe the scene immediately around my own tent during the last two weeks of July as a sample of the condition of the whole prison. I will take a space not larger than a good-sized parlor or sitting room. On this were at least fifty of us. Directly in front of me lay two brothers named Sherwood belonging to Company I of my battalion, who came originally from Missouri. They were in the last stages of scurvy and diarrhea. Every particle of muscle and fat about their limbs and bodies had apparently wasted away, leaving the skin clinging close to the bones of the face, arms, hands, ribs and thighs, everywhere except the feet and legs where it was swollen tense and transparent, distended with gallons of purulent matter. Their livid gums from which most of the teeth had already fallen protruded far beyond their lips. To their left lay a sergeant and two others of their company, all three slowly dying from diarrhea. Beyond was a fair-haired German, young and intelligent-looking, whose life was ebbing tediously away. To my right was a handsome young sergeant of an Illinois infantry regiment captured at Kenesaw. His left arm had been amputated between the shoulder and elbow, and he was turned into the Stockade with the stump all undressed save the litigating of the arteries. Of course, he had not been inside an hour before the maggot flies had laid eggs in the open wound, and before the day was gone the worms were hatched out and rioting amid the inflamed and super-sensitive nerves, where their every motion was agony. Accustomed as we were to misery, we found a still lower depth in his misfortune, and I would be happier could I forget his pale drawn face as he wandered uncomplainingly to and fro, holding his maimed limb with his right hand, occasionally stopping to squeeze it as one does a boil and press from it a stream of maggots and pus. I do not think he ate or slept for a week before he died. Next to him was an Irish sergeant of a New York regiment, a fine soldierly man who, with pardonable pride, wore conspicuously on his left breast a medal gained by gallantry while a British soldier in the Crimea. He was wasting away with diarrhea and died before the month was out.

This was what one could see in every square rod of the prison. Where I was was not only no worse than the rest of the prison, but was probably much better and healthier, as it was the highest ground inside, farthest from the swamp and, having the Dead Line on two sides, had a ventilation that those nearer the center could not possibly have. Yet, with all these conditions in our favor, the mortality was as I have described.

Near us an exasperating idiot who played the flute had established himself. Like all mournful players, he affected low mournful notes as plaintive as the distant cooing of the dove in lowering weather. He played or rather tooted away in his "blues"—inducing strain hour after hour, despite our energetic protests and an occasional fling of a club at him. There was no more stop to him than to a man with a hand-organ, and to this day the low sad notes of a flute are the swiftest reminder of those sorrowful, death-laden days.

I had an illustration one morning of how far decomposition would progress in a man's body before he died. My chum and I found a treasure trove in the streets in the shape of a body of a man who died during the night. The value of this "find" was that if we took it to the gate we would be allowed to carry it outside to the deadhouse, and on our way back have an opportunity to pick up a chunk of wood to use in cooking. While discussing our good luck, another party came up and claimed the body. A verbal dispute led to one of blows in which we came off victorious and I hastily caught hold of the arm near the elbow to help bear the body away. The skin gave way under my hand and slipped with it down to the wrist like a torn sleeve. It was sickening, but I clung to my prize and secured a very good chunk of wood while outside with it. The wood was very much needed by my mess as our squad had had none for more than a week.

Naturally we had a consuming hunger for news of what was being accomplished by our armies toward crushing the Rebellion. Now more than ever, had we reason to ardently wish for the destruction of the rebel power. Before capture, we had love of country and a natural desire for the triumph of her flag to animate us. Now we had a hatred of the rebels that passed expression, and a fierce longing to see those who daily tortured and insulted us trampled down in the dust of humiliation.

The daily arrival of prisoners kept us tolerably well informed as to the general progress of the campaign,[23] and we added to the information thus obtained by getting, almost daily, in some manner or another, a copy of the rebel papers. Most frequently these were Atlanta papers or an issue of the "Memphis-Corinth-Jackson-Grenada-Chattanooga-Resaca-Marietta-Atlanta" *Appeal,* as they used to facetiously term a Memphis paper that left that city when it was taken in 1862 and for two years fell back from each new location as Sherman's army advanced, until at last it gave up the struggle in September 1864, in a little town south of Atlanta after about two thousand miles of weary retreat from an indefatigable pursuer. The papers were brought in by "fresh fish," [24] purchased from the guards at from fifty cents to one dollar apiece, or occasionally thrown into us when we had some specially disagreeable intelligence like the defeat of Banks or Sturgis or Hunter to brood over. I was particularly fortunate in getting hold of these. Becoming installed as general reader for a neighborhood of several thousand men, everything of this kind was immediately brought to me, to be read aloud for the benefit of everybody. All the older prisoners knew me by the nickname of "Illinoy," a designation arising from my wearing on my cap, when I entered prison, a neat little white metal badge marked ILLS. When any reading matter was brought into our neighborhood, there would be a general cry of "take it up to 'Illinoy,'" and then hundreds would mass around my quarters to hear the news read. The rebel papers usually had very meager reports of the operations of the armies and these were greatly distorted, but they were still very interesting, and as we always started in to read with the expectation that the whole statement was a mass of perversions and lies and truth an infrequent accident, we were not likely to be much impressed with it.

There was a marked difference in the tone of the reports brought in from different armies. Sherman's men were always sanguine. They had no doubt that they were pushing the enemy straight to the wall and that every day brought the Southern Confederacy much nearer its downfall. Those from the Army of the Potomac were never so hopeful. They would admit that Grant was pounding Lee terribly, but the shadow of the frequent defeats of the Army of the Potomac seemed to hang depressingly over them.[25] There came a day, however, when our sanguine hopes as to Sherman were checked by a possibility that he had failed, this his long campaign toward Atlanta had culminated in such a reverse under the very walls of the city as would compel an abandonment of the enterprise and possibly a humiliating retreat.

We knew that Jeff Davis and his Government were strongly dissatisfied with the Fabian policy of Joe Johnston. The papers had told us of the rebel President's visit to Atlanta, of his bitter comments on Johnston's tactics, of his going so far as to sneer about the necessity of providing pontoons at Key West so that Johnston might continue his retreat, even to Cuba. Then came the news of Johnston's replacement by Hood, and the papers were full of the exulting predictions of what would now be accomplished "when that gallant young soldier is once fairly in the saddle."

All this meant one supreme effort to arrest the onward course of Sherman. It indicated a resolve to stake the fate of Atlanta and the fortunes of the Confederacy in the West upon the hazard of one desperate fight. We watched the summoning up of every rebel energy for the blow with apprehension. We dreaded another Chickamauga. The blow fell on the 22nd of July. It was well planned.

The Army of the Tennessee, the left of Sherman's forces, was the part struck. On the night of the 21st, Hood marched a heavy force around its left flank and gained its rear. On the 22nd, this force fell on the rear with the impetuous violence of a cyclone, while the rebels in the works immediately around Atlanta attacked furiously in front. It was an ordeal that no other army ever passed through successfully. The steadiest troops in Europe would think it foolhardiness to attempt to withstand an assault in force in front and rear at the same time. The finest legions that follow any flag today must almost inevitably succumb to such a mode of attack. But the seasoned veterans of the Army of the Tennessee encountered the shock with an obstinacy which showed that the finest material for soldiery this planet held was that in which undaunted hearts beat beneath blue blouses. Springing over the front of their breastworks, they drove back with a withering fire the force assailing them in the rear. This beaten off, they jumped back to their proper places and repulsed the assault in front. This was the way the battle was waged until night compelled a cessation of operations. Our boys were alternately behind the breastworks firing at rebels advancing upon the front and in front of the works firing upon those coming up in the rear. Sometimes part of our line would be on one side of the works and part on the other.

In the prison we were greatly excited over the result of the engagement, of which we were uncertain for many days. A host of new prisoners, perhaps two thousand, was brought in from there, but as they were captured during the progress of the fight, they could not speak definitely as to its issue. The rebel papers exulted without stint over what they termed a "glorious victory." They were particularly jubilant over the death of McPherson who, they claimed, was the brain and guiding hand of Sherman's army.

One paper likened him to the pilot fish which guides the shark to his prey. Now that he was gone, said the paper, Sherman's army became a great lumbering hulk with no one in it capable of directing it and must soon fall to utter ruin under the skillfully delivered strokes of the gallant Hood.

We also knew that great numbers of wounded had been brought to the prison hospital, and this seemed to confirm the rebel claim of a victory, as it showed they retained possession of the battlefield. About the 1st of August a large squad of Sherman's men captured in one of the engagements subsequent to the 22nd came in. We gathered around them eagerly. Among them I noticed a bright, curly-haired, blue-eyed infantryman—or boy, rather, as he was yet beardless. His cap was marked 68th Ohio Volunteer Infantry, his sleeves were garnished with re-enlistment stripes, and on the breast of his blouse was a silver arrow. To the eye of the soldier, this said that he was a veteran member of the 68th Regiment of Ohio Infantry. That is, having already served three years, he had re-enlisted for the war, and he belonged to the 3rd Division of the 17th Army Corps. He was so young and fresh-looking that one could hardly believe him to be a veteran. But even if his stripes had not said this, the soldierly arrangement of clothing and accoutrements and the graceful self-possessed pose of limbs and body would have told the observer that he was one of those "Old Reliables" with whom Sherman and Grant had already subdued a third of the Confederacy. His blanket which, for a wonder, the rebels had neglected to take from him, was tightly rolled, its ends tied together and thrown over his shoulder scarf-fashion. His pantaloons were tucked inside his stocking tops that were pulled up as far as possible and tied tightly around his ankle with a string. A none-too-clean haversack, containing the inevitable sooty quart cup and even blacker half-canteen, was slung easily from the shoulder opposite to that on which the blanket rested.

Hand him his faithful Springfield rifle, put three days' rations in his haversack and forty rounds in his cartridge box, and he would be ready without an instant's demur or question to march to the ends of the earth and fight anything that crossed his path. He was a type of the honest, honorable, self-respecting American boy who as a soldier the world has not equalled in the sixty centuries that war has been a profession. I suggested that he was rather a youngster to be wearing veteran's chevrons.

"Yes," said he, "I am not so old as some of the rest of the boys, but I have seen about as much service and been in the business about as long as any of them. They call me 'Old Dad.' I suppose I was the youngest boy in the Regiment when we first entered the service, though our whole company, officers and all, were only a lot of boys, and the regiment today—what's left of 'em—are about as young a lot of officers and men as there are in the service. Why, our old colonel ain't only twenty-four years old now, and he has been in command ever since we went into Vicksburg. I have heard it said by our boys that since we veteranized, the whole regiment—officers and men—average less than twenty-four years old. But they are greyhounds to march and stayers in a fight, you bet. Why, the rest of the troops over in West Tennessee used to call our Brigade 'Leggett's Cavalry,' for they always had us chasing 'Old Forrest,' and we kept him skedaddling too, pretty lively. But I tell you we did get into a red hot scrimmage on the 22nd. It just laid over Champion Hills, or any of the big fights around Vicksburg, and they were lively enough to amuse anyone."

"So you were in the affair on the 22nd, were you?" I asked. "We are awful anxious to hear all about it. Come over here to my quarters and tell us all you know. All we know is that there has been a big fight, with McPherson killed and a heavy loss of life besides, and the rebels claim a great victory."

"Oh, they be." The boy grinned. "It was the sickest victory they ever got. About one more victory of that kind would make their infernal old Confederacy ready for a coroner's inquest. Well, I can tell you pretty much all about that fight, for I reckon if the truth was known, our regiment fired about the first and last shot that opened and closed the fighting on that day. . . .

"Well, you see the whole army got across the river, and were closing in around the city of Atlanta. Our Corps, the 17th, was the extreme left of the army and was moving up toward the city from the east. The Fifteenth, Logan's Corps, joined us on the right, then the Army of the Cumberland further to the right. We ran onto the rebs about sundown the 21st. They had some breastworks on a ridge in front of us, and we had a pretty sharp fight before we drove them off. We went right to work, and kept at it all night in changing and strengthening the old rebel barricades, fronting them towards Atlanta, and by morning had some good solid works along our whole line. During the night we fancied we could hear wagons or artillery moving away in front of us, apparently going south or towards our left. About three or four o'clock in the morning, while I was shoveling dirt like a beaver out on the works, the Lieutenant came to me and said the Colonel wanted to see me, pointing to a large tree in the rear, where I could find him.

"I reported and found him with General Leggett, who commanded our Division, talking mighty serious, and Bob Wheeler of F Company, standing there with his Springfield at parade rest. As soon as I came up, the Colonel says, 'Boys, the General wants two level-headed chaps to go out beyond the pickets to the front and toward the left. I have selected you for the duty. Go as quietly as possible and as fast as you can; keep your eyes and ears open; don't fire a shot if you can help it, and come back and tell us exactly what you have seen and heard, and not what you imagine or suspect.' He gave us the countersign, and off we started over the breastworks and through the thick woods. We soon came to our skirmish or pickets only a few rods in front of our works, and cautioned them not to fire on us in going or returning. We went out as much as half a mile or more, until we could plainly hear the sound of wagons and artillery. We then crept forward until we could see the main road leading south from the city filled with marching men, artillery and teams. We could hear the commands of the officers and see the flags and banners of regiment after regiment as they passed us. We got back quietly and quickly, past through our picket line all right, and found the General and our Colonel sitting on a log where we had left them, waiting for us.

"We reported what we had seen and heard, and gave it as our opinion that the Johnnies were evacuating Atlanta. The General shook his head and the Colonel says, 'You may return to your company.' Bob says to me, 'The old General shakes his head as though he thought them damn rebs ain't evacuating Atlanta so mighty sudden, but are up to some devilment again. I ain't sure but he's right. They ain't going to keep falling back and falling back to all eternity, but are just agoin' to give us a rip-roaring great big fight one o' these days, when they get a good ready. You hear me?' It was about daylight then, and I must have snoozed away until near noon, when I heard the order 'Fall in!' and found the regiment getting into line, and the boys all talking about going right into Atlanta, that the rebels had evacuated the city during the night, and that we were going to have a race with the 15th Corps as to which would get into the city first.

"We could look away out across a large field in front of our works and see the skirmish line advancing steadily towards the main works around the city. Not a shot was being fired on either side. To our surprise, instead of marching to the front and toward the city, we filed off into a small road cut through the woods and marched rapidly to the rear. We could not understand what it meant. We marched at quick time feeling pretty mad that we had to go to the rear, when the rest of our Division were going into Atlanta. We passed the 16th Corps lying on their arms back in some open fields and the wagon trains of our Corps all comfortably corralled, and finally found ourselves out by the 17th Corps Headquarters. Two or three companies were sent out to picket several roads that seemed to cross at that point, as it was reported that rebel cavalry had been seen on these roads but a short time before, and this accounted for our being rushed out in such a great hurry. We had just stacked arms and were going to take a little rest after our rapid march, when several rebel prisoners were brought in by some of our boys who had straggled a little. They found the rebels on the road we had just marched out on.

"Up to this time not a shot had been fired. All was quiet back at the main works we had just left, when suddenly we saw several staff officers come tearing up to the Colonel, who ordered us to fall in, take arms, about face! The Lieutenant-Colonel dashed down one of the roads where one of the companies had gone on out picket. The Major and Adjutant galloped down the others. We did not wait for them to come back though, but moved right back on the road we had just come out, in line of battle, our colors in the road, and our flanks in open timber. We soon reached a fence enclosing a large field and there could see a line of rebels moving by the flank and forming, facing toward Atlanta but to the left and in the rear of the position occupied by our Corps. As soon as we reached the fence, we fired a round or two into the backs of these gray coats, who broke into confusion. Just then the other companies joined us, and we moved off on double-quick by the right flank, for you see we were completely cut off from the troops up at the front, and we had to get well over to the right to get around the flank of the rebels. Just about the time we fired on the rebels, the 16th Corps opened up a hot fire of musketry and artillery on them, some of their shot coming over mighty close to where we were. We marched pretty fast, and finally turned in through some open fields to the left and came out just in the rear of the 16th which was fighting like devils along its whole line.

"As we came out into the open field, we saw General Scott, who commanded our Brigade, come tearing toward us with one or two aides or orderlies. He was on his big claybank horse—'Old Hatchie' as we called him—as we had captured him on the battlefield at the battle of Matamora, 'Hell on the Hatchie,' our boys always called it. He rode up to the Colonel, said something hastily, when all at once we heard the allfiredest crash of musketry and artillery way up at the front where we had built the works the night before and had left the rest of our brigade and division getting ready to prance into Atlanta when we were sent off to the rear. Scott put spurs to his old horse, who was one of the fastest runners in our division, and away he went towards the position where his brigade and the troops to their left were now hotly engaged. He rode right along in the rear of the 16th, paying no mind to the shot and shell and bullets that were tearing the earth and exploding and striking all around him. His aides and orderlies vainly tried to keep up with him.

"We could plainly see the rebel lines as they came out of the woods into the open grounds to attack the 16th which was fighting hand-to-hand in the open field, without any signs of works. We were just far enough in the rear so that every blasted shot or shell that was fired too high to hit their ranks came rattling over amongst us. All this time we were marching fast following in the direction General Scott had taken—guess he'd ordered the Colonel to join his brigade up at the front. Anyway we were down under the crest of a little hill, following along the bank of a little creek, keeping under cover of the bank as much as possible to protect us from the shots of the enemy.

"Suddenly we saw General Logan and one or two of his staff up on the right bank of the ravine racing toward us. As he neared the head of the regiment, he shouted, 'Halt! What regiment is that and where are you going?' The Colonel, in a loud voice that all could hear, told him. 'The 68th Ohio, going to join our brigade of the 3rd Division—your old Division, General—of the 17th Corps.' Logan says, 'You had better go right in here on the left of Dodge. The 3rd has hardly ground enough left now to bury their dead. God knows they need you. But try it on, if you think you can get to them.'

"Just at this moment a staff officer came riding up on the opposite side of the ravine from where Logan was and interrupted Logan who was about telling the Colonel not to try to get to the position held by the division by the road cut through the woods, but to keep off to the right towards the 15th Corps, as the woods were full of rebels. The officer saluted Logan and shouted across, 'General Sherman directs me to inform you of the death of General McPherson and orders you to take command of the Army of the Tennessee. Have Dodge get close to the 17th Corps and Sherman will reinforce you to the extent of the whole army.' Logan, standing in his stirrups on his beautiful black horse, formed a picture against the blue sky as we looked up the ravine at him, his black eyes fairly blazing and his long black hair waving in the wind. He replied in a ringing, clear tone that we all could hear, 'Say to General Sherman I have heard of McPherson's death, and have assumed the command of the Army of the Tennessee, that I have already anticipated his orders in regard to closing the gap between Dodge and the 17th Corps.' Logan put spurs to his horse and rode in one direction, General Sherman's staff officer in another, and we started in a rapid step toward the front. This was the first we had heard of McPherson's death and it made us feel very bad. Some of the officers and men cried as though they had lost a brother; others swore to avenge his death. He was a great favorite with all his army, particularly with our Corps, which he commanded for a long time.[26] Our company, especially, knew him well and loved him dearly, for we had been his headquarters guard for over a year.

"As we marched along to the front, we could see brigades, regiments and batteries of artillery coming over on the right of the army and taking position in new lines in rear of the 16th and 17th Corps. Major generals and their staffs, brigadier generals and their staffs, were mighty thick along the ravine we were following. From the stragglers and wounded men pouring into the safe shelter formed by the broken ground along which we marched, we heard of divisions, brigades and regiments that these men belonged to having been all cut to pieces, officers all killed, and the man we were talk-ing to the only one of his command not killed, wounded or captured.

"The battle raged furiously all this time. Part of the time the 16th Corps seemed to be in the worst; then it would let up on them and the 17th would be right in it along their whole front. We had probably marched half an hour since leaving Logan and were getting pretty near back to our main line of works, when the Colonel or-dered a halt and knapsacks unslung and piled up. I tell you it was a relief to get them off, for it was a fearful hot day and we had been marching almost double quick. We knew that this meant business though, and that we were stripping for the fight which we would soon be in. Just at this moment we saw an ambulance, with the horses on a dead run, followed by two or three mounted officers and men, coming right towards us out of the woods Logan had cautioned the Colonel to avoid. When the ambulance got to where we were, it halted. We recognized Major Strong of McPherson's staff, whom we all knew, as he was the Chief Inspector of our Corps. In the ambulance he had the body of General McPherson.

"During a slight let-up in the fighting at that part of the line, the Major had taken an ambulance and driven into the line of fire to get the General. He found the body right by the side of the little road that we had gone out on when we went to the rear. The General was dead when he found him, having been shot off his horse, the bullet striking him in the back just below his heart, probably killing him instantly. There was a young fellow with him who was wounded also when Strong found them. He be-longed to our 1st Division, and he had recognized General McPherson and stood by him until Major Strong came up. He was in the ambulance with the body of McPher-son when they stopped by us. It seems that when the fight opened away back in the rear where we had been, at the left of the 16th which was almost directly in the rear of the 17th, McPherson sent his staff and orderlies with various orders to different parts of the line and he started to ride over from the 17th to the 16th, taking the same course our regiment had about an hour before. But the rebels had discovered the gap and, meeting no opposition to their advances in this strip of woods where they were hidden from view, they had marched right along down in the rear, and with their line at right angles with the line of works occupied by the left of the 17th Corps. They were parallel and close to the little road McPherson had taken, and probably he rode right into them and was killed before he realized the true situation.

"Having piled our knapsacks and left a couple of our older men who were played out with the heat and most ready to drop with sunstroke to guard them, we started on again. The ambulance with the corpse of General McPherson moved off towards the right of the army, which was the last we ever saw of the brave and handsome soldier.

We bore off a little to the right of a large open field on top of a high hill where one of our batteries was pounding away at a tremendous rate. We came up to the main line of works just about at the left of the 15th Corps. They seemed to be having an easy time of it just then, no fighting going on in their front except occasional shots from some heavy guns on the main line of rebel works around the city. We crossed right over the 15th's works and filed to the left, keeping along on the outside of our works. We had not gone far before the rebel gunners in the main works around the city discovered us, and the way they did tear loose at us was a caution! Their aim was pretty bad, however, and most of their shots went over us. We saw one of them—I think it was a shell—strike an artillery caisson belonging to one of our batteries. It exploded as it struck, and then the caisson, which was full of ammunition, exploded with an awful noise, throwing pieces of wood and iron and its own load of shot and shell high into the air, scattering death and destruction to the men and horses attached to it. We thought we saw arms and legs and parts of bodies of men flying in every direction, but we were glad to learn afterwards that it was the contents of the knapsacks the battery boys had strapped on the caissons for transportation.

Just after we passed the hill where our battery was making things so lively, they stopped firing to let us pass. We saw General Leggett, our Division Commander, come riding toward us. He was outside of our line of works, too. You know how we build breastworks—sort of zigzag-like, you know, so they cannot be enfiladed. Well, that's just the way the works were along there, and you never saw such a curious shape as we formed our division in. Why, part of them were on one side of the works, and go along a little further and here was a regiment or part of a regiment on the other side, both sets firing in opposite directions. No sir-ee, they were not demoralized or in confusion—they were cool and as steady as on parade. But the old division had, you know, never been driven from any position they had once taken in all their long service, and they did not propose to leave that ridge until they got orders from someone beside the rebs. There were times when a fellow did not know which side of the works was the safest, for the Johnnies were in front of us and in rear of us. You see, our 4th Division, which had been to the left of us, had been forced to quit their works when the rebs got into the works in their rear, so that our division was now at the point where our line turned sharply to the left and rear in the direction of the 16th Corps.

"We got into business before we had been there over three minutes. A line of the rebs tried to charge across the open fields in front of us, but by the help of the old twenty-four pounders which proved to be Cooper's Illinois Battery that we had been alongside of in many a hard fight before, we drove them back a-flying, only to have to jump over on the outside of our works the next minute to tackle a heavy force that came for our rear through that blasted strip of woods. We soon drove them off, and the firing on both sides seemed to have pretty much stopped. Our brigade, which we discovered, was now commanded by Old Whiskers"—[Colonel Wiles]—"of the 78th Ohio. I'll bet he's got the longest whiskers of any man in the Army. You see, General Scott had not been seen or heard since he had started to the rear after our regiment when the fighting first commenced. We all believed that he was either killed or captured, or he would have been with his command. He was a splendid soldier, and a bulldog of a fighter. His absence was a great loss.

"But we had not much time to think of such things, for our brigade was ordered to leave the works and to move to the right about twenty or thirty rods across a large ravine where we were placed in position in an open cornfield, forming a new line at an angle from the line of works we had just left, extending to the left and getting us back nearer onto a line with the 16th Corps. The battery of howitzers, now reinforced by a part of the 3rd Ohio's heavy guns, still occupied the old works on the highest part of the hill just to the right of our new line. We took our position just on the brow of a hill and were ordered to lie down and the rear rank to go for rails, which we discovered a few rods behind us in the shape of a good ten-rail fence.

"Every rear-rank chap came back with all the rails he could lug, and we barely had time to lay them down in front of us, forming a little barricade of six to eight or ten inches high, when we heard the most unearthly rebel yell directly in front of us. It got louder and came nearer and nearer, until we could see a solid line of the gray coats coming out of the woods and down the opposite slope, their battle flags flying, officers in front with drawn swords, arms at right shoulder, and every one of them yelling like so many Sioux Indians.

"The line seemed to be massed six or eight ranks deep, followed closely by the second line, and that by the third, each, if possible, yelling louder and appearing more desperately reckless than the one ahead. At their first appearance we opened on them, and so did the bully old twenty-pounders—with canister. On they came. The first line staggered and wavered back onto the second which was coming on the double quick. Such a raking as we did give them. O, Lordy, how we did wish that we had the breech-loading Spencers or Winchesters.[26] But we had the old reliable Springfields,[27] and we poured it in hot and heavy. By the time the charging column got down the opposite slope, and was struggling through the thicket of undergrowth in the ravine, it was one confused mass of officers and men, the three lines now forming one solid column, which made several desperate efforts to rush up to the top of the hill where we were punishing them so.

"One of their first surges came mighty near going right over the left of our regi-

ment lying behind their little rail piles. But the boys clubbed their guns and the officers used their revolvers and swords and drove them back down the hill. The 78th and
20th Ohio, our right and left bowers who had been brigaded with us ever since Shiloh,
were into it as hot and heavy as we had been. They had lost numbers of their officers
and men, but they were still hanging on to their little rail piles when the fight was
over. At one time the rebs were right in on top of the 78th. One big Reb grabbed their
colors and tried to pull them out of the hands of the color-bearer. But old Captain Orr,
a little, short, dried-up fellow about sixty years old, struck him with his sword across
the back of the neck and killed him deader than a mackerel right in his tracks.

"It was now getting dark, and the Johnnies concluded they had taken a bigger
contract in trying to drive us off that hill in one day than they had counted on, so they
quit charging on us and drew back under cover of the woods and along the old line
of works that we had left and kept up a-pecking away and sharpshooting at us all night
long. They opened fire on us from a number of pieces of artillery from the front,
from the left, and from some heavy guns away over to the right of us in the main works
around Atlanta. We did not fool away much time that night either. We got our shovels
and picks and while part of us were sharpshooting and trying to keep the rebels from
working up too close to us, the rest of the boys were putting up some good solid earthworks right where our rail piles had been. By morning we were in splendid shape to
receive our friends no matter which way they came at us, for they kept up such an
all-fired shelling of us from so many different directions that the boys had built
traverses and bomb-proofs at all sorts of angles and in all directions.

"There was one point off to our right, a few rods up along our old line of works,
where there was a crowd of rebel sharpshooters that annoyed us more than all the rest
by their constant firing at us through the night. They killed one of Company H's boys
and wounded several others. Finally, Captain Williams of D Company came along and
said he wanted a couple good shots out of our company to go with him. So I went—for
one. He took about ten of us, and we crawled down into the ravine in front of where
we were building the works and got behind a large fallen tree, and we laid there and
could just fire right up into the rear of those fellows as they lay in behind a traverse
coming out from our old line of works. It was so dark we could only see where to fire
by the flash of guns, but every time they would shoot, some of us would let them have
one. They stayed there until almost daylight when they concluded that as things
looked, since we were going to stay, they had better be going.

"It was an awful night. Down in the ravine below us lay hundreds of killed and
wounded rebels, groaning and crying aloud for water and for help. We did do what we
could for those right around us, but it was so dark and so many shells bursting and

bullets flying around that a fellow could not get about much. I tell you it was pretty tough next morning to go along to the different companies of our regiment and hear who were among the killed and wounded, and to see the long row of graves that were being dug to bury our comrades and our officers. There was the Captain of Company E, Nelson Skeeles, of Fulton County, Ohio, one of the bravest and the best officers in the regiment. By his side lay First Sergeant Lesnit. The next were the two great powerful Sheppards, cousins, but more like brothers. One, it seems, was killed while supporting the head of the other who had just received a death wound, thus dying in each other's arms. But I can't begin to think or tell you the names of all the poor boys that we laid away to rest in their last, long sleep on that gloomy day. Our Major was severely wounded, and several other officers had been hit more or less badly. It was a frightful sight to go over the field in front of our works on that morning.

"The rebel dead and badly wounded laid where they had fallen. The bottom and opposite side of the ravine showed how destructive our fire and that of the canister from the howitzers had been. The underbrush was cut, slashed and torn into shreds, and the larger trees were scarred, bruised and broken by the thousands of bullets and other missiles that had been poured into them from almost every conceivable direction during the day before.

"A lot of us boys went way over to the left into Fuller's Division of the 16th Corps, to see how some of our boys over there had got through the scrimmage, for they had about as nasty a fight as any part of the Army, and if it had not been for their being just where they were, I am not sure but what the old 17th would have had a different story to tell now. We found our friends had been way out by Decatur where their brigade had got into a pretty lively fight on their own hook. We got back to camp, and the first I knew I was detailed for picket duty.

"We were posted over a few rods across the ravine in our front. We had not been out but a short time, when we saw a flag of truce, borne by an officer, coming towards us. We halted him and made him wait until a report was sent back to Corps Headquarters. The rebel officer was quite chatty and talkative with our picket officer while waiting. He said he was on General Cleburne's staff, and that the troops that charged us so fiercely the evening before were Cleburne's whole division, and that after their last repulse, knowing the hill where we were posted was the most important position along our line, he felt that if they would keep close to us during the night and keep up a show of fight, that we would pull out and abandon the hill before morning. He said that he, with about fifty of their best men, had volunteered to keep up the demonstration, and it was his party that had occupied the traverse in our old works the night before, and had annoyed us and the batterymen by their constant sharpshooting which we fellows, behind the old tree, had finally tired out. They had stayed until almost daylight and he lost more than half his men before he left. He also told us that General Scott was captured by their division at about the time and almost the same spot as where General McPherson was killed and that he was not hurt or wounded and was now a prisoner in their hands. Quite a lot of our staff officers soon came out. As near as we could learn, the rebels wanted a truce to bury their dead. Our folks tried to get up an exchange of prisoners that had been taken by both sides the day before, but for some reason they could not bring it about. But the truce for burying the dead was agreed to.

Along about dusk some of the boys on my post got to telling about a lot of silver and brass instruments that belonged to one of the bands of the 4th Division which had been hung up in some small trees a little way over in front of where we were when the fight was going on the day before, and that when a bullet would strike one of the horns, they could hear it go 'ping,' and in a few minutes, 'pang' would go another bullet through one of them. A new picket was just coming on, and I had picked up my blanket and haversack and was about ready to start back to camp when, thinks I, 'I'll just go out there and see about them horns.' I told the boys what I was going to do. They all seemed to think it was safe enough, so out I started.

I had not gone more than a hundred yards, I should think, when I found the horns all hanging around on the trees just as the boys had described. Some of them had lots of bullet holes in them. But I saw a beautiful nice-looking silver bugle hanging off to one side a little. Says I, 'I'll just take that little toot-horn in out of the wet and take it back to camp.'

"I was just reaching up after it when I heard someone say 'Halt!' and I'll be dog-goned if there wasn't two of the meanest-looking rebels standing not ten feet from me with their guns cocked and pointed at me, an' of course I knew I was a goner. They walked me back about one hundred and fifty yards, where their picket line was. From there I was kept going for an hour or two until we got over to a place on the railroad called East Point. There I got in with a big crowd of our prisoners who were taken the day before, and we have been fooling along in a lot of old cattle cars getting down here ever since—

"So *this* is Andersonville, is it? Well, by God! . . ."

Little Red Cap

CHAPTER X

"ONLY AN AVERAGE MAN STANDS THE MISERY"

CLOTHING HAD NOW become an object of real solicitude to us older prisoners. The veterans of our crowd, the surviving remnant of those captured at Gettysburg, had been prisoners over a year. The next in seniority, the Chickamauga boys, had been ten months. The Mine Run fellows were eight months old, and my battalion had had seven months' incarceration. None of us were models of well-dressed gentlemen when captured. Our garments told the whole story of the hard campaigning we had undergone. Now, with months of the wear and tear of prison life, sleeping on the sand, working in tunnels and digging wells, we were tattered and torn to an extent that a second-class tramp would have considered disgraceful.

This is no reflection upon the quality of the clothes furnished by the Government. We simply reached the limit of the wear of textile fabrics. I am particular to say this because I want to contribute my little mite towards doing justice to a badly abused part of our Army organization, the Quartermaster's Department. It is fashionable to speak of "shoddy" clothing and utter some stereotyped sneers about "brown paper shoes" and "muskeeto-netting overcoats" when any discussion of the Quartermaster service is the subject of conversation, but I have no hesitation in asking the endorsement of my comrades to the statement that we have never found anywhere else as durable garments as those furnished by the Government during our service in the Army. The clothes were not as fine in texture nor so stylish in cut as those we wore before or since, but when it came to wear they could be relied on to the last shred. It was always marvelous to me that they lasted so well, with the rough usage a soldier in the field must give them. But to return to my subject.

I can best illustrate the way our clothes dropped off us, piece by piece, like the petals from the last rose of summer, by taking my own case as an example. When I entered prison, I was clad in the ordinary garb of an enlisted man of the cavalry: stout comfortable boots, woolen socks, drawers, pantaloons with a reinforcement or "ready-made patches" as the infantry called them, vest, warm snug-fitting jacket, under and over shirts, heavy overcoat and a forage cap.

First my boots fell into cureless ruin. This was no hardship as the weather had become quite warm and it was more pleasant than otherwise to go barefoot. Then, part of the underclothing retired from service. The jacket and vest followed, their end being hastened by having their best portions taken to patch up the pantaloons which kept giving out at the most embarrassing places. Then, the cape of the overcoat was called upon to assist in repairing these continually recurring breaches in the nether garments. The same insatiate demand finally consumed the whole coat in a vain attemp to prevent an exposure of person greater than consistent with the usages of society. The pantaloons or what, by courtesy, I call such were a monument of careful and ingenious, but hopeless, patching that should have called forth the admiration of a Florentine artist in mosaic. I have been shown for years many table tops ornamented in marquetry, inlaid with thousands of little bits of wood, cunningly arranged and patiently joined together. I always look at them with interest, for I know the work spent upon them. I remember my Andersonville pantaloons.

The clothing upon the upper part of my body had been reduced to the remains of a knit undershirt. It had fallen into so many holes that it looked like the coarse "riddles" through which ashes and gravel are sifted. Wherever these holes were, the sun had burned my back, breast and shoulders deeply black. The parts covered by the threads and fragments forming the boundaries of the holes were still white. When I pulled my alleged shirt off to wash or to free it from some of its teeming population, my skin showed a fine lace pattern in black and white that was very interesting to my comrades and the subject of countless jokes by them. They used to descant loudly on the chaste elegance of the design, the richness of the tracing and beg me to furnish them with a copy of it when I got home for their sisters to work window curtains or tidies by. They were sure that so striking a novelty in patterns would be very acceptable. I would reply to their witticisms in the language of Portia's Prince of Morocco:

> Mislike me not for my complexion—
> The shadowed livery of the burning sun—

One of the stories told me in my childhood by an old Negro nurse was of a poverty-stricken little girl "who slept on the floor and was covered with a door," and she once asked, "Mamma, how do poor folks get along who haven't any door?" In the same spirit I used to wonder how poor fellows got along who hadn't any shirt.

One common way of keeping up one's clothing was by stealing mealsacks. The meal furnished as rations was brought in in white cotton sacks. Sergeants of detachments were required to return these when the rations were issued the next day. I have before alluded to the general incapacity of the rebels to deal accurately with even simple numbers. It was never very difficult for a shrewd sergeant to make nine sacks count as ten. After a while, the rebels began to see through this sleight-of-hand manipulation and to check it. Then the sergeants resorted to the device of tearing the sacks in two and turning each half in as a whole one. The cotton cloth gained in this way was used for patching. If a boy could succeed in beating the rebels out of enough of it, he would fabricate himself a shirt or a pair of pantaloons. We obtained all our thread in the same way. A half sack, carefully ravelled out, would furnish a couple of handfuls of thread. Had it not been for this resource, all our sewing and mending would have had to come to a standstill.

Most of our needles were manufactured by ourselves from bones. A piece of bone, split as near as possible to the required size, was carefully rubbed down upon a brick, and then had an eye laboriously worked through it with a bit of wire or something else available for the purpose. The needles were about the size of ordinary darning needles and answered the purpose very well. These devices gave one some conception of the way savages provide for the wants of their lives. Time was with them, as with us, of little importance. It was no loss of time to them, nor to us, to spend a large portion of the waking hours of a week in fabricating a needle out of bone, where a civilized man could purchase a much better one with the product of three minutes' labor. I do not think any Indian of the Plains exceeded us in the patience with which we worked away at these minutiae of life's needs.

Of course, the most common source of clothing was the dead. No body was carried out with any clothing on it that could be of service to the survivors. The Plymouth Pilgrims, who were so well clothed on coming in and who were now dying off very rapidly, furnished many good suits to cover the nakedness of the older prisoners. Most of the prisoners from the Army of the Potomac were well dressed and since many died within a month or six weeks after their entrance, they left their clothes in pretty good condition for those who constituted themselves their heirs, administrators and assigns. For my own part, I had the greatest aversion to wearing a dead man's clothes and could only bring myself to it after I had been a year in prison and it became a question between doing that or freezing to death.

Every new batch of prisoners was besieged with anxious inquiries on the subject which lay closest to all our hearts—"What *are* they doing about exchange?" Nothing in human experience, save the anxious expectancy of a sail by castaways on a desert island, could equal the intense eagerness with which this question was asked and the answer awaited. To thousands now hanging on the verge of eternity, it meant life or death. Between the first day of July and the first of November, over twelve thousand men died who would doubtless have lived had they been able to reach our lines or "get to God's country," as we expressed it. Newcomers brought little reliable news of contemplated exchange. There was none to bring in the first place and in the next, soldiers in active service in the field had other things to busy themselves with than reading up on the details of the negotiations between the Commissioners of Exchange. They had all heard rumors, however, and by the time they reached Andersonville they had crystallized these into actual statements of fact. A half hour after they entered the Stockade, a report like this would spread like wildfire: "An Army of the Potomac man has just come in who was captured in front of Petersburg. He says that he read in the New York *Herald* the day before he was taken that an exchange had been agreed upon, and that our ships had already started for Savannah to take us home."

Our hopes would soar up like balloons at hearing this. We fed ourselves on such stuff from day to day and, doubtless, many lives were prolonged by the continual encouragement. There was hardly a day when I did not say to myself that I would much rather die than endure imprisonment another month, and had I believed that another month would see me still there, I am pretty certain that I should have ended the matter by crossing the Dead Line. I was firmly resolved not to die the disgusting, agonizing death that so many around me were dying.

One of our best purveyors of information was a bright, blue-eyed, fair-haired little drummer boy, as handsome as a girl, well bred as a lady, and evidently the darling of some refined loving mother. He belonged, I think, to some loyal Virginia regiment, was captured in one of the actions in the Shenandoah Valley, and had been with us in Richmond. We called him "Red Cap," from his wearing a jaunty gold-laced crimson cap. Ordinarily, the smaller a drummer boy is the harder he is, but no amount of attrition with rough men could coarsen the ingrained refinement of Red Cap's manners. He was between thirteen and fourteen and it seemed utterly shameful that men, calling themselves soldiers, should make war on such a tender boy and drag him off to prison. But no six-footer had a more soldierly heart than little Red Cap, and none was more loyal to the cause. It was a pleasure to hear him tell the story of the fights and movements his regiment had been engaged in. He was a good observer and told his tale with boyish fervor.

Shortly after Wirz assumed command, he took Red Cap into his office as orderly. His bright face and winning manners fascinated the women visitors at Headquarters and numbers of them tried to adopt him, but with poor success. Like the rest of us, he could see few charms in an existence under the rebel flag and turned a deaf ear to their blandishments. He kept his ears open to the conversation of the rebel officers around him and frequently secured permission to visit the interior of the Stockade, when he would communicate to us all that he had heard. He received a flattering reception every time he came in, and no orator ever secured a more attentive audience than would gather around him to listen to what he had to say.

He was, beyond a doubt, the best known and most popular person in the prison, and I know all the survivors among his old admirers share my great interest in him and my curiosity as to whether he yet lives, and whether his subsequent career has justified the sanguine hopes we all had as to his future. I hope that if he, or anyone who knows anything about him, sees this, he will communicate with me. There are thousands who will be glad to hear from him.[28]

Speaking of the manner in which the Plymouth Pilgrims were now dying, I am reminded of my theory that the ordinary man's endurance of this prison life did not average over three months. The Plymouth boys arrived in May; the bulk of those who died passed away in July and August. The great increase in prisoners from all sources was in May, June and July. The greatest mortality among these was in August, September and October.

Many came in who had been in good health during their service in the field but who seem utterly overwhelmed by the appalling misery they saw on every hand, and, giving away to despondency, died in a few days or weeks. I do not mean to include them in the above class, as their sickness was more mental than physical. My idea is that, taking one hundred ordinarily healthy young soldiers from a regiment in active service and putting them in Andersonville, by the end of the third month at least thirty-three of those weakest and most vulnerable to disease would have succumbed to exposure, pollution of ground and air, and the insufficiency of the ration of coarse corn meal. After this the mortality would be somewhat less—say at the end of six months, fifty of them would be dead. The remainder would hang on still more tenaciously, and at the end of a year there would be fifteen or twenty still alive. There were sixty-three of my company taken; thirteen lived through. I believe this was the usual proportion for those who were in as long as we. In all, there were forty-five thousand six hundred and thirteen prisoners brought into Andersonville. Of these, twelve thousand nine hundred and twelve died there, to say nothing of thousands that died in other prisons in Georgia and the Carolinas immediately after their removal from Andersonville.

One of every three and a half men upon whom the gates of the Stockade closed never repassed them alive. Twenty-nine per cent of the boys who so much as set foot in Andersonville died there. Let it be kept in mind all the time that the average stay of a prisoner there was not four months. The great majority came in after the first of May and left before the middle of September. May 1st, 1864, there were ten thousand four hundred and twenty-seven in the Stockade; August 8th, there were thirty-three thousand one hundred and fourteen; September 30th, all these were dead or gone except eight thousand two hundred and eighteen, of whom four thousand five hundred and ninety died inside the next thirty days. The records of the world can show no parallel to this astounding mortality.[29]

Certainly in no other great community that ever existed upon the face of the globe was there so little daily ebb and flow as in this. Dull as an ordinary town or city may be, however monotonous, eventless, even stupid, the lives of its citizens, there is yet a flow every day of its life-blood, its population, towards its heart, and an ebb of the same every evening towards its extremities. These recurring tides mingle all classes together and promote the general healthfulness just as the constant motion hither and yon of the ocean's waters purifies and sweeten them. The lack of these helped vastly to make the living mass inside the Stockade a human Dead Sea, or rather a "Dying Sea," a putrefying stinking lake, resolving itself into phosphorescent corruption, like those rotting southern seas whose seething filth burns in hideous reds and ghastly greens and yellows.

There being little call for motion of any kind, and no room to exercise whatever wish there might be in that direction, very many succumbed unresistingly to the apathy which was so strongly favored by despondency and the weakness induced by continual hunger and, lying supinely on the hot sand day in and day out, speedily brought themselves into such a condition as invited attacks of disease. It required both determination and effort to take a little walking exercise. The ground was so densely crowded with holes and other devices for shelter that it took one at least ten minutes to pick his way through the narrow and tortuous labyrinth which served as paths for communication between different parts of the camp.

Still further, there was nothing to see anywhere or to form sufficient inducement for anyone to make so laborious a journey. One simply encountered at every new step the same unwelcome sights that he had just left; there was a monotony in the misery as in everything else, and consequently the temptation to sit or lie still in one's own quarters became very great. I used to make it a point to go to some of the remoter parts of the Stockade once every day simply for exercise. One can gain some idea of the crowd and the difficulty of making one's way through it when I say that no point in the prison could be more than fifteen hundred feet from where I stayed. Had the way been clear, I could have walked thither and back in at most a half hour. Yet, it usually took me from two to three hours to make one of these journeys. This daily trip, a few visits to the creek to wash all over, a few games of chess, attendance upon roll call, drawing rations, cooking and eating the same, "lousing" my fragments of clothes, and doing some little duties for my sick and helpless comrades, constituted the daily routine for myself, as for most of the active youths in the prison.

The creek was the great meeting point for all inside the stockade. All able to walk were certain to be there at least once during the day, and we made it a rendezvous, a place to exchange gossip, discuss the latest news, canvass the prospects of exchange and, most of all, to curse the rebels. Indeed no conversation ever progressed very far without both speaker and listener taking frequent rests to say bitter things as to the rebels generally and Wirz, Winder and Davis in particular. A conversation between two boys, strangers to each other, who came to the creek to wash themselves, or for some other purpose, would go like this: "I belong to the Second Corps, Hancock's," said one. "They got me at Spotsylvania when they were butting their heads against our breastworks, trying to get even with us for gobbling up Johnston in the morning." Stopping suddenly and changing his tone, he continued, "I hope to God that when our folks get Richmond, they will put old Ben Butler in command of it with orders to limb, skin and jayhawk it worse than he did New Orleans." [30]

"I wish to God he would," replied the second boy fervently, "and that he'd catch old Jeff and the gray-haired devil, Winder, and the Old Dutch Captain, strip 'em just as we were, put 'em in this pen, with just the rations they are givin' us, and set a guard of plantation niggers over 'em with orders to blow their whole infernal heads off if they dared so much as look at the Dead Line."

"Old Hancock caught the Johnnies that morning the neatest you ever saw in your life," said the first boy, seeming to want to talk about his capture. "After the two armies had murdered each other for four or five days in the Wilderness by fighting so close together that much of the time you could almost shake hands with the Gray-backs, both hauled off a little and lay and glowered at each other. Each side had lost about twenty thousand men in learning that if it attacked the other it would get mashed fine. So each built a line of works and lay behind them, and tried to nag the other into coming out and attacking. At Spotsylvania our lines and those of the Johnnies weren't twelve hundred yards apart. The ground was clear and clean between them, and any force that attempted to cross it to attack would be cut to pieces as sure as anything. We laid there three or four days watching each other, just like boys at school who shake fists and 'dare' each other.

"At one place the rebel line ran out towards us like the top of a great letter 'A'. The night of the 11th of May, it rained very hard and then came a fog so thick that you couldn't see the length of a company. Hancock thought he'd take advantage of this. We were all turned out very quietly about four o'clock in the morning. Not a bit of noise was allowed. We even had to take off our canteens and tin cups that they might not rattle against our bayonets. The ground was so wet that our footsteps couldn't be heard. It was one of those deathly still movements when you think your heart is making as much noise as a bass drum. The Johnnies didn't seem to have the faintest suspicion of what was coming, though they ought, because we would have expected such an attack from them if we hadn't made it ourselves. Their pickets were out just a little ways from their works and we were almost on them before they discovered us. They fired and ran back. At this we raised a yell and dashed forward at a charge.

"As we poured over the works, the rebels came double-quicking up to defend them. We flanked Johnston's Division quicker'n you could say 'Jack Robinson,' and had four thousand of 'em in our grip just as nice as you please. We sent them to the rear under guard and started for the next line of rebel works about a half mile away. But we had now waked up the whole of Lee's army and they all came straight for us, like packs of mad wolves. Ewell struck us in the center, Longstreet let drive at our left flank, and Hill tackled our right. We fell back to the works we had taken, Warren and Wright came up to help us, and we had it hot and heavy for the rest of the day and part of the night. The Johnnies seemed so mad over what we'd done that they were half crazy. They charged us five times, coming up every time just as if they were going to lift us right out of the works with the bayonet.

"About midnight, after they'd lost over ten thousand men, they seemed to understand that we had pre-empted that piece of real estate, and didn't propose to allow anybody to jump our claim, so they fell back sullen-like to their main works. When they came on that last charge, our Brigadier walked behind each of our regiments and said, " 'Boys, we'll send 'em back for keeps this time. Give it to 'em by the acre, and when they begin to waver, we'll all jump over the works and go for them with the bayonet.' We did it just that way. We poured such a fire on them that the bullets knocked up the ground in front just like you have seen the deep dust in a road in the middle of summer fly up when the first great big drops of a rain storm strike it. But they came on, yelling and swearing, officers in front waving swords and shouting, all that business, you know. When they got to about one hundred yards from us, they did not seem to be coming so fast and there was a good deal of confusion among them.

"The brigade bugle sounded, 'Cease firing!' We all ceased instantly. The rebels looked up in astonishment. Our General sang out, 'Fix Bayonets!' But we knew what was coming and were already executing the order. You can imagine the crash that ran down the line as every fellow snatched his bayonet out and slapped it on the muzzle of his gun. Then the General's voice rang out like a bugle: 'Ready— Forward— Charge!' We cheered till everything seemed to split and jumped over the works, almost every man at the same minute. The Johnnies seemed to have been puzzled at the stoppage of our fire. When we all came sailing over the works with guns brought right down where they meant business, they were so astonished for a minute that they stood stock still, not knowing whether to come for us or run.

"We did not allow them long to debate, but went right towards them on the double-quick with the bayonets looking awful savage and hungry. It was too much for Mr. Johnny Reb's nerves. They all seemed to 'about face' at once, and they lit out of there as if they had been sent for in a hurry. We chased them as fast as we could and picked up just lots of 'em. Finally it began to be real funny. A Johnny's wind would begin to give out; he'd fall behind his comrades; he'd hear us yell and think that we were right behind him, ready to sink a bayonet through him; he'd turn around, throw up his hands, and sing out, 'I surrender! Mister, I surrender!' and find that we were a hundred feet off, and would have to have a bayonet as long as one of McClernand's general orders to touch him.[31]

"Well, my company was the left of our regiment, and our regiment was the left of the brigade, and we swung out ahead of all the rest of the boys. In our excitement of chasing the Johnnies, we didn't see that we had passed an angle of their works. About thirty of us had become separated from the company and were chasing a squad of about seventy-five or one hundred. We had got so close to them that we hollered, 'Halt there, now, or we'll blow your heads off!' They turned round. 'Halt yourselves, you damn Yankee sons of bitches!'

"We looked around at this and saw that we were not one hundred feet away from the angle of the works which were filled with rebels waiting for our fellows to get where they could have a good flank fire upon them. There was nothing to do but to throw down our guns and surrender, and we had hardly gone inside of the works before the Johnnies opened on our brigade and drove it back. This ended the battle at Spotsylvania Court House."

"Some day the underpinning will fly out from under the damn South and let it sink right into the middle kittle o' Hell," answered the second boy irrelevantly.

"I only wish the whole Southern Confederacy was hanging over Hell by a single string," said the first boy, "and I had a knife."

"Flagstaff"

CHAPTER XI

LIKE NEEDLES IN PUMPKIN SEEDS

Illinoy," said tall gaunt Jack North of the 114th Illinois to me one day as we sat contemplating our naked and sadly attenuated underpinnings, "what do our legs and feet most look like?"

"Give it up, Jack," I replied.

"Why, darning needles stuck in pumpkin seeds, of course." I never heard a better comparison for our wasted limbs. The effects of the great bodily emaciation were sometimes very startling. Boys of fleshy habit would change so in a few weeks as to lose all resemblance to their former selves. Comrades who came into the prison later would utterly fail to recognize them. Most fat men, as most large men, died in a little while after entering, though there were exceptions.

One of these was a boy of my own company named George Hicks. George had shot up within a few years to over six feet in height and then, as such boys do occasionally, had, after enlisting, taken on such a development of flesh that we nicknamed him "The Giant" and he became a pretty good load for even the strongest horse. George held his flesh through Belle Isle and the earlier weeks in Andersonville. But June, July and August "fetched him," as the boys said. He seemed to melt away like an icicle on a spring day, and he grew so thin that his height seemed preternatural. We called him "Flagstaff" and cracked all sorts of jokes about putting an insulator on his head and setting him up for a telegraph pole, braiding his legs and using him for a whip lash, letting his hair grow a little longer and trading him off to the rebels for a sponge and staff for the artillery. We all expected him to die and looked continually for the development of the fatal scurvy symptoms which were to seal his doom. But he worried through and came out at last in good shape, a happy result due as much as to anything else to his having in Chester Hayward of Prairie City, Illinois, one of the most devoted chums I ever knew. Chester nursed and looked out for George with wife-like fidelity and had his reward in bringing him safe through our lines. There were thousands of instances of this generous devotion to each other by chums in Andersonville, and I know nothing that reflects any more credit upon our boy soldiers.

There was little chance for anyone to accumulate flesh on the rations we were receiving. I say it in all soberness that I do not believe that a healthy hen could have grown fat upon them. I am sure that any good-sized "Shanghai" eats more every day than the meager half-loaf that we had to maintain life upon. Scanty as this was and hungry as all were, very many could not eat it. Their stomachs revolted against the trash; it became so nauseous to them that they could not force it down even when famishing, and they died of starvation with the chunks of the so-called bread under their head.

I found myself rapidly approaching this condition. I had been blessed with a good digestion and a talent for sleeping under the most discouraging circumstances. These, I have no doubt, were of the greatest assistance in my struggle for existence. But now the rations became fearfully obnoxious to me and it was only with the greatest effort pulling the bread into little pieces and swallowing each of these as one would a pill, that I succeeded in worrying the stuff down. I had not as yet fallen away very much but as I never, up to that time, weighed so much as one hundred and twenty-five pounds, there was no great amount of adipose tissue to lose. It was evident that unless some change occurred, my time was near at hand.

There was not only hunger for more food but a longing with an intensity beyond expression for alteration of some kind in the rations. The changeless monotony of the miserable saltless bread—or worse, mush—for days, weeks and months, became unbearable. If those wretched mule teams had only once a month hauled in something different, if they had come in loaded with sweet potatoes, green corn or wheat flour, there would be thousands of men still living who now slumber beneath those melancholy pines. It would have given something to look forward to and remember when past. But to know each day that the gates would open to admit the same distasteful apologies for food took away the appetite and raised one's gorge even while famishing for something to eat. We could forget for a while the stench, the lice, the heat, the maggots, the dead and dying around us, the insulting malignance of our jailors; but it was very hard work to banish thoughts and longings for food from our minds.

Hundreds actually became insane from brooding over it. Crazy men could be found in all parts of the camp. Numbers of them wandered around entirely naked. Their babblings and maunderings about something to eat were painful to hear. I have before mentioned the case of the Plymouth Pilgrim near me, whose insanity took the form of imagining that he was sitting at the table with his family and who would go through the motions of helping them to imaginary viands and delicacies. The cravings for green food of those afflicted with scurvy were agonizing. Large numbers of watermelons were brought to the prison and sold to those who had the money to pay for them at from one to five dollars, greenbacks, apiece. A boy who had the means to buy a piece of these would be followed about while eating it by a crowd of perhaps twenty-five or thirty livid-gummed scorbutics, each imploring for the rind when he was through with it.

We thought of food all day and were visited with torturing dreams of it at night. One of the pleasant recollections of my pre-military life was a banquet at the Planter's House, St. Louis, at which I was a boyish guest. It was, doubtless, an ordinary affair as banquets go, but to me then, with all the keen appreciation of youth and first experiences, it was a feast worthy of Lucullus. But now this delightful reminiscence became a torment. Hundreds of times I dreamed I was again at the Planter's. I saw wide corridors with their mosaic pavement. I entered the grand dining room, keeping timidly near the friend to whose kindness I owed this wonderful favor. I saw again the mirror-lined walls, the evergreen-decked ceilings, the festoons and mottoes, the tables gleaming with cut glass and silver, the buffets with wines and fruits, the brigade of sleek black, white-aproned waiters, headed by one who had the presence of a major general. Again I reveled in all the dainties and dishes on the bill of fare, calling for everything that I dared to, just to see what each was like and to be able to say afterwards that I had partaken of it. All these bewildering delights of the first realization of what a boy has read of and wondered over and longed for would dance their rout and reel through my somnolent brain. Then I would awake to find myself, a half-starved, half-naked, vermin-eaten wretch, crouching in a hole in the ground, waiting for my keepers to fling me a chunk of corn bread.

Naturally, the boys, especially the country boys and new prisoners, talked much of victuals, what they had had, and what they would have again when they got out. Take this as a sample conversation which might be heard in any group of boys sitting together on the sand, killing lice and talking of exchange: "Well, Bill," Tom would say, "when we get back to God's country, you and Jim and John must all come to my house and take dinner with me. I want to give you a square meal. I want to show you just what good livin' is. You know my mother is just the best cook in all that section.

When she lays herself out to get up a meal, all the other women in the neighborhood just stand back and admire."

"Oh, that's all right," replies Bill, "but I'll bet she can't hold a candle to my mother when it comes to good cooking."

"No, nor to mine," answered Jim.

"Oh shucks!" chimed in John with patronizing contempt, "none of you fellers were ever at our house, even when we had one of our common weekday dinners."

Tom, unheedful of the counterclaims, spoke up, "I have been studyin' up the dinner I'd like and the bill of fare I'd set out for you fellers when you come over to see me. First, of course, we'll lay the foundation-like with a nice juicy loin roast and some mashed potatoes."

"Now, do you like mashed potatoes with beef?" interrupted Bill. "The way *my* mother does it is to pare the potatoes and lay them in the pan along with the beef. Then, you know, they come out just as nice and crisp and brown. They have soaked up all the beef gravy and they crinkle between your teeth."

"Now, I tell you," said Jim, "mashed Neshannocks with butter on 'em is plenty good enough for me."

"If you'd et some of the new kind of peachblows that we raised in the old pasture lot the year before I enlisted, you'd never say another word about your Neshan-nocks," said John with finality.

Taking in a breath and starting afresh, Tom said, "Then we'll hev some fried spring chickens of our Dominic breed. Them Dominics of ours have the nicest, tenderest meat, better'n quail a derned sight, and the way my mother can fry spring chickens—!"

Bill, turning aside to Jim in exasperation, said, "Every derned woman in the country thinks she can 'spry ching frickens,' but *my* mother— You fellers all know that there's nobody knows half as much about chicken doin's as these 'tinerant Meth-odis' preachers. They give 'em chicken wherever they go, and folks do say that out in the new settlements they can't get no preachin', no gospel nor nothin' until the chicks become so plenty that a preacher is reasonably sure of having one for his dinner wherever he may go. Now, there's old Peter Cartright who has travelled our Illinoy and Indiany since the Year One and preached more good sermons than any other man who ever set on saddle-bags and has et more chickens than there are birds in a big pi-geon roost. Well, he took dinner at our house when he came up to dedicate the big white church at Simpkin's Corners, and when he passed up his plate the third time for more chicken, he sez—sez he, 'I've et at a great many hundred tables in the fifty years I have labored in the vineyard of the Redeemer, but I mus' say, Mrs. Kiggins, that your way of frying chickens is a leetle the nicest that I ever knew. I only wish that the sisters generally would get your reseet.' Yes, that's what he said, 'a leetle the nicest'."

"An' we'll have bisquits an' butter," said Tom. "I'll just bet five hundred dollars to a cent—and give back the cent if I win—that we have the best butter at our house that there is in Central Illinoy. You can't ever have good butter onless you have a spring house. There's no use of talkin' all the patent churns thet lazy men ever invented; all the fancy milk pans an' coolers can't make up for a spring house. Locations for a spring house are scarcer than hen's teeth in Illinoy, but we hev one and there ain't a better one in Orange County, New York. *Then* you'll see some of the bisquits my mother makes."

"Well, now," replied Bill, "my mother's a boss bisquit-maker, too."

"You kin just gamble that mine is," answered Jim.

"Oh, that's the way you fellers ought to think an' talk," said John. "But my mother—"

Joining in the conversation with fresh vigor, Tom spoke up. "They're just as light and fluffy as a dandelion puff and they melt in your mouth like a ripe Bartlett pear. You just pull 'em open—now you know that I think there's nothin' that shows a person's raisin' so well as to see him eat bisquits an' butter. If he's been raised mostly on corn bread an' common doin's, an' don't know much about good things to eat, he'll most likely cut his bisquit open with a case knife an' make it fall as flat as one o' yesterday's pancakes. But if he is used to bisquits, has had 'em often at his house, he'll just pull 'em open, slow and easy-like, then he'll lay a little slice of butter inside, an' drop a few drops of clear honey on this an' stick the two halves back together again, an'——"

"Oh, for God Almighty's sake, stop talking that infernal nonsense," roar out a half-dozen of the surrounding crowd, whose mouths have been watering over this unctuous recital of the good things of the table. "You blamed fools, do you want to drive yourselves and everybody else crazy with such stuff as that. Dry up and try to think of something else."

I have before mentioned that among the things that grew upon one with increasing acquaintance with the rebels on their heath, was astonishment at their lack of mechanical skill and at their inability to grapple with numbers and the simpler processes of arithmetic. Another characteristic of the same nature was their amazing lack of musical ability or of any kind of tuneful creativeness. Elsewhere, all over the world, people living under similar conditions to the Southerners are exceedingly musical, and we owe the great majority of the sweetest compositions which delight the ear and subdue the senses to unlettered song-makers of the Swiss mountains, the Tyrolese valleys, the Bavarian highlands and the minstrels of Scotland, Ireland and Wales.

The music of English-speaking people is very largely made up of these contributions from the folk-songs of dwellers in the wilder and more mountainous parts of the British Isles. One rarely goes far out of the way in attributing to this source any air that he may hear that captivates him with its seductive opulence of harmony. Exquisite melodies, limpid and unstrained as the carol of a bird in springtime and as plaintive as the cooing of a turtle-dove, seem as natural products of the Scottish Highlands as the gorse which blazons on their hillsides in August. Debarred from expressing their aspirations, as people of broader culture do, in painting, in sculpture, in poetry and prose, these mountaineers make song the flexible and ready instrument for the communication of every emotion that sweeps across their souls. Love, hatred, grief, revenge, anger and especially war, seem to tune their minds to harmony and awaken the voice of song in their hearts.

The battles which the Scotch and Irish fought to replace the luckless Stuarts upon the British throne, the bloody rebellions of 1715 and 1745, left a rich legacy of sweet song, the outpouring of loving passionate loyalty to a wretched cause—songs which are today esteemed and sung, wherever the English language is spoken, by people who have long since forgotten what burning feelings gave birth to their favorite melodies. For a century the bones of both the Pretenders have mouldered in alien soil. The names of James Edward and Charles Edward, which were once trumpet blasts to rouse armed men, mean as little to the multitudes of today as those of the Saxon Ethelbert and Danish Hardicanute. Yet the world goes on singing, and will probably as long as the English language is spoken, "Wh'all be king but Charlie," "When Jamie Comes Hame," "Over the Water to Charlie," "Charlie is My Darling," "The Bonnie Blue Bonnets Are over the Border," "Saddle Your Steeds and Awa," and a myriad others whose infinite tenderness and melody no modern composer can equal.

Yet these same Scotch and Irish, the same Jacobite English, transplanted on account of their chronic rebelliousness to the mountains of Virginia, the Carolinas and Georgia, seemed to have lost their tunefulness, as some fine singing birds do when carried from their native shores. The descendants of those who drew swords for James and Charles at Prestonpans and Culloden dwell today in the dales and valleys of the Alleghenies, as their fathers did in the dales and valleys of the Grampians, but their voices are mute. As a rule, the Southerners are fond of music. They are fond of singing and listening to old-fashioned ballads, most of which have never been printed, but handed down from one generation to the other, like the *volklieder* of Germany. They sing these with a wild fervid impressiveness characteristic of the ballad singing of unlettered people.

Very many play tolerably on the violin and banjo, and occasionally one is found whose instrumentation may be called good. But above this height they never soar The only musician produced by the South of whom the rest of the country has ever heard is Blind Tom, the Negro idiot. No composer, no song writer of any kind has appeared within the borders of Dixie. It was a disappointment to me that even the stress of the war, the passion and fierceness with which the rebels felt and fought, could not stimulate any adherent of the Stars and Bars into the production of a single lyric worthy in the remotest degree of the magnitude of the struggle, and the depth of the popular feeling.

Where two million Scotch, fighting to restore the fallen fortunes of the worse than worthless Stuarts, filled the world with immortal music, eleven million Southerners, fighting for what they claimed to be individual freedom and national life, did not produce any original verse, or a bar of music that the world could recognize as such. This is the fact; and an undeniable one.

Searching for peculiar causes we find but two that make the South differ from the ancestral home of these people. These two are climate and slavery. Climatic effects will not account for the phenomenon, because the peasantry of the mountains of Spain and the South of France, as ignorant as these people, and dwelling in a still more enervating atmosphere, are very fertile in musical composition, and their songs are to the Romanic languages what the Scotch and Irish ballads are to the English.

Then it must be ascribed to the incubus of slavery upon the intellect, which has repressed this as it has all other healthy growths in the South. Slavery seems to benumb all the faculties except the passions. The fact that the mountaineers had but few or no slaves does not seem to be of importance in the case. They lived under the deadly shadow of the Upas Tree, and suffered the consequences of its stunting their development in all directions, as the ague-smitten inhabitant of the Roman Campagna finds every sense and every muscle clogged by the filtering in of the insidious miasma. They did not compose songs and music, because they did not have the intellectual energy for that work.

As a matter of fact it was the Negroes who supplied most of the musical creativeness of that section. Their wonderful prolificness in wild, rude songs, with strangely melodious airs that burned themselves into the memory, was one of the salient characteristics of that down-trodden race. Like the Russian serfs, and the bondmen of all ages and lands, the songs they made and sang all had an undertone of touching plaintiveness, born of ages of dumb suffering. The themes were exceedingly simple, and the range of subjects limited. The joys and sorrows, hopes and despairs of love's gratification or disappointment, of struggles for freedom, contests with maligned persons and influences, of rage, hatred, jealousy, revenge, such as formed the *motifs* for the majority of the poetry of free and strong races, were wholly absent from their lyrics. Religion, hunger and toil were their main inspirations. They sang of the pleasures of idling in the genial sunshine; the delights of abundance of food; the eternal happiness that awaited them in the heavenly future, where the slave-driver ceased from troubling and the weary were at rest; where Time rolled around in endless cycles of days spent in basking, harp in hand, and silken-clad, in golden streets, under the soft effulgence of cloudless skies, glowing with warmth and kindness emanating from the Creator himself.

Had their masters condescended to borrow the music of their slaves, they would have found none whose sentiments were suitable for the odes of a people undergoing the pangs of what was hoped to be the birth of a new nation. The three songs most popular in the South and generally regarded as distinctively Southern were "The Bonnie Blue Flag," "Maryland, My Maryland," and "Stonewall Jackson Crossing into Maryland." The first of these was the greatest favorite by long odds. Women sang, men whistled and the so-called musicians played it wherever we went. While in the field before capture, it was the commonest of experiences to have rebel women sing it at us tauntingly from the houses that we passed or near which we stopped. If ever near enough to a rebel camp, we were sure to hear its wailing crescendos rising upon the air from the lips or instruments of some of those quartered there.

At Richmond we heard it constantly from some source or another, and the same was true wherever we went in the Confederacy. I give the words:

> We are a band of brothers, and native to the soil,
> Fighting for our liberty, with treasure, blood, and toil,
> And when our rights were threatened, the cry rose near and far,
> Hurrah for the Bonnie Blue Flag, that bears a single star;
> Hurrah, hurrah for Southern rights, hurrah, hurrah for the
> Bonnie Blue Flag that bears a single star!

All familiar with Scotch songs will readily recognize the name and air as an old friend and one of the fierce Jacobite melodies that for a long time disturbed the tranquility of the Brunswick family on the English throne. The new words supplied by the rebels are the merest doggerel and fit the music as poorly as the unchanged name of the song fitted its new use. The flag of the Rebellion was not a bonnie blue one. It had quite as much red and white as azure. It did not have a *single* star—there were thirteen.

A Lean and Hungry Land: "It is a starved, sterile land, broken at intervals by foul swamps, with a jungle-like growth of unwholesome vegetation, and teeming with venomous snakes and all manner of crawling things."

The Andersonville Stockade: "We found ourselves in an immense pen, about one thousand feet long by eight hundred feet wide. The walls were formed by pine logs twenty-five feet long, from two to three feet in diameter. It was divided in the center by a creek about a yard wide and ten inches deep, running east to west."

General John Henry Winder, C.S.A.: "Winder was an obscure, dull old man, a sort of Informer-General, High Inquisitor and Chief Eavesdropper for his intimate friend Jefferson Davis. Remorseless and cruel, he gave little hint of the extent to which he would go as Commissary General of Prisoners."

Andersonville: Interior of the Stockade Looking North, Showing the Dead Line. The Blurred Area is the Guards' Catwalk: "I can recall of my own seeing men of the 55th Georgia kill prisoners under the pretense that they were across the Dead Line."

Andersonville: Interior of the Stockade—The Creek at the East Side: "The vast majority appeared to lose all repulsion to filth, and both sick and well disregarded all the laws of hygiene and personal cleanliness."

Andersonville: Interior of the Stockade Looking North: "The living mass inside the Stockade was a human Dead Sea—or rather a Dying Sea—a putrefying, stinking lake, whose seething filth burns in hideous reds and ghastly greens and yellows."

Andersonville Stockade: Interior, a Closer View: "By the end of May there were eighteen thousand four hundred and fifty-four prisoners in the Stockade. These men were cooped up on less than thirteen acres of ground, making about fifteen hundred to the acre. The ground became indescribably filthy."

Andersonville: Waiting for Rations: "All during July the prisoners came streaming in by hundreds and thousands. In all, seven thousand one hundred and twenty-eight were turned into the seething mass of corrupting humanity to be polluted and tainted by it."

Lieutenant-General Ulysses S. Grant, Commander-in-Chief of the Union Armies: "It is hard on our men held in Southern prisons not to exchange them, but it is humanity to those left in the ranks to fight our battles."

Jefferson Davis, President of the Confederacy: "On two occasions we were asked to send the very sick and desperately wounded prisoners, and a particular request was made for men who were so seriously sick that it was doubtful whether they would survive a removal a few miles down the James River."

Andersonville Cemetery. Burying the Dead: "The dead were buried without coffins, side by side, in trenches four feet deep."

The Graveyard at Andersonville as the Rebels Left it: "The manner of disposing of the dead was also calculated to depress the already desponding spirits of the men. When a patient dies, he is simply laid in the narrow street in front of his tent until he is removed by Federal Negroes."

Members of the Annapolis Medical Commission, as photographed on the steps of one of the hospital buildings on the Academy grounds. The man in uniform on the right is a police guard.

A Federal Soldier Before Entering Andersonville. This soldier, in full regimentals, is believed to be Private Calvin Bates. The photograph was made in July or August of 1862, by C. H. Greer.

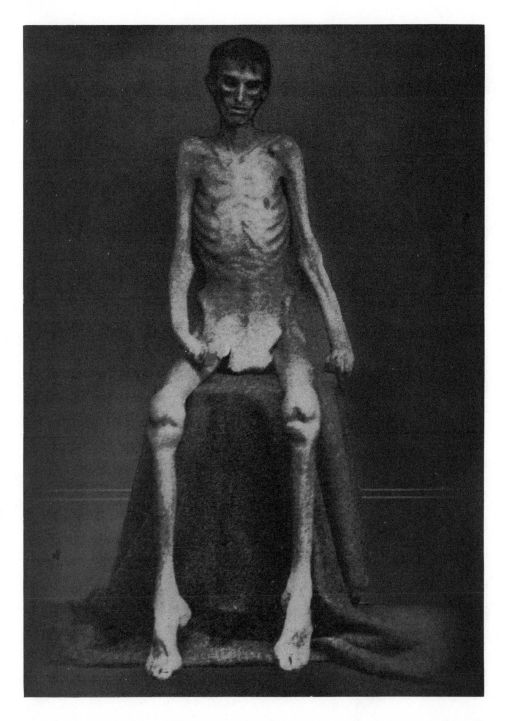

A Prisoner of Andersonville as Seen by the Camera of Captain A. J. Russell:
A victim of scurvy and gangrene, this living skeleton displays his cadaverous body
for the camera as a "specimen" prisoner. "The photographs were terrible, indeed," wrote Jefferson Davis, "but the misery portrayed was surpassed by some of
those we received at Savannah."

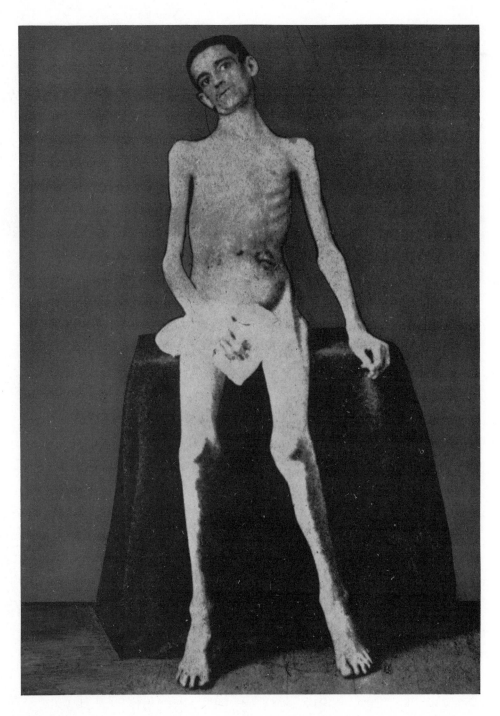

A Union Soldier, a Prisoner of Andersonville. Photographed at Annapolis by Captain A. J. Russell, this soldier is a victim of scurvy, malnutrition and cancer.

Cavalry Chieftains of the Federal Army. L. to R. Seated: General Wesley Merritt, Major General James Harrison Wilson. Standing: Major General Alfred Torbert: "When the Confederacy went to pieces in April, 1865, Wirz was still at Andersonville. General Wilson sent Captain H. E. Noyes, with a squad to the Stockade to arrest him. Captain Noyes took Wirz and the Andersonville records to Washington."

The Execution of Captain Wirz: "The Court declared the prisoner guilty on all charges and sentenced him to be hanged, Friday, November 10th, 1865 . . ."

The Execution of Captain Wirz: The noose is being adjusted and the execution order read. An officer in the foreground shields his eyes from the sun. Soldiers on the ground stand at attention.

The Execution of Captain Wirz: The sentence is carried out. A husky soldier, minutes later, lowers the body. Soldiers, not invited to attend Wirz' hanging, climbed trees to witness it.

Major General William Tecumseh Sherman. The prisoners waited hopefully for Sherman to reach Andersonville, but Sherman's line of march bypassed the Stockade by fifty miles.

Miss Clara Barton. Clara Barton, founder of the American Red Cross, made every effort to relieve the terrible suffering of the prisoners at Andersonville and other prisons, but her efforts proved fruitless. She was able only to improve the conditions of the cemetery at Andersonville.

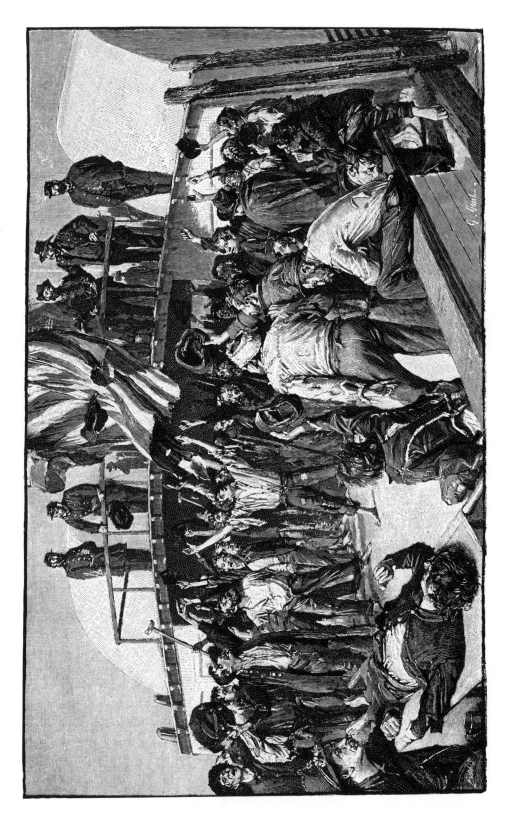

Exchanged Prisoners from Andersonville Cheering the Colors. Aboard ship, released prisoners bound for Annapolis. From an original drawing by Gilbert Gaul made in 1870.

The Andersonville Stockade Looking Southwest. The Confederate Military Prison as it looked at the peak of its occupancy. To the right is the railroad. At the upper left can be seen the creek. A guard has just shot a prisoner for crossing the Dead Line. From an original color lithograph of a painting made in 1884.

Next in popularity was "Maryland, My Maryland." The versification of this was of a much higher order, being fairly respectable. The air is old and a familiar one to all college students and belongs to one of the most common of German household songs:

> O, Tannenbaum! O, Tannenbaum, wie treu sind deine Blätter!
> Du grünst nicht nur zur Sommerzeit, nein auch im Winter,
> Wenn es Schneit——

Longfellow translated this to:

> O, Hemlock tree! O, Hemlock tree, How faithful are thy branches;
> Green not alone in Summertime, But in the Winter's frost and rime.
> O, Hemlock tree! O, Hemlock tree! How faithful are thy branches——

The rebel version ran:

> The despot's heel is on thy shore, Maryland, My Maryland!
> His touch is at thy temple door, Maryland, My Maryland!
> Avenge the patriotic gore, that flecked the streets of Baltimore,
> And be the battle queen of yore, Maryland, My Maryland!

"Stonewall Jackson Crossing into Maryland" was another travesty of about the same literary merit—or rather demerit—as "The Bonnie Blue Flag." Its air was that of the well-known and popular Negro minstrel song "Billy Patterson." For all that, it sounded very martial and stirring when played by a brass band.

We heard these songs with tiresome iteration, daily and nightly, during our stay in the Southern Confederacy. Some one of the guards seemed to be perpetually beguiling the weariness of his watch by singing in all keys, in every sort of voice and with the wildest latitude as to air and time. They became so terribly irritating to us that to this day the remembrance of those soul-lacerating lyrics abides with me as one of the chief minor torments of our situation. They were, in fact, nearly as bad as the lice. We revenged ourselves as best we could by constructing fearfully wicked, obscene and insulting parodies on these and by singing them with irritating effusiveness in the hearing of the guards who were inflicting these nuisances upon us.

Of the same nature was the garrison music. One fife, played by an asthmatic old fellow whose breathings were nearly as audible as his notes, and one rheumatic drummer constituted the entire band for the post. The fifer knew but one tune, "The Bonnie Blue Flag," and did not know that well. But it was all that he had and he played it with wearisome monotony for every camp call, five or six times a day and seven days a week. He called us up in the morning with it for Reveille; he sounded the Roll Call, and Drill Call, breakfast, dinner and supper with it, and finally sent us to bed with the same dreary wail that had rung in our ears all day. I never hated any piece of music as I came to hate that threnody of treason. It would have been such a relief if the old asthmatic who played could have been induced to learn another tune to play on Sundays and so give us one day of rest. He did not but desecrated the Lord's Day by playing as vilely as on the rest of the week.

The rebels were fully conscious of their musical deficiencies and made repeated but unsuccessful attempts to induce the musicians among the prisoners to come outside and form a band.

Morning Assemblage of the Sick
at the South Gate

CHAPTER XII

THE LAME, THE HALT AND THE DISEASED

EARLY IN AUGUST Merriott, our Company Bugler, died. Previous to coming to America, he had been for many years an English soldier, and I accepted him as a type of that stolid, doggedly brave class which forms the bulk of the English armies and has for centuries carried the British flag with dauntless courage into every land under the sun. Rough, surly and unsocial, he did his duty with the unemotional steadiness of a machine. He knew nothing but to obey orders and obeyed them under all circumstances promptly but with stony impassiveness. Was the command to move forward into action, he moved forward without a word and with face as blank as a side of sole leather. He went as far as ordered, halted at the word, and retired at command as phlegmatically as he advanced. If he cared a straw whether he advanced or retreated, if it mattered to the extent of a pinch of salt whether we whipped the rebels or they defeated us, he kept that feeling so deeply hidden in the recesses of his sturdy bosom that no one ever suspected it.

In the excitement of action the rest of the boys shouted and swore and expressed their tense feelings in various ways, but Marriott might as well have been a graven image for all the expression that he suffered to escape. Doubtless, if the captain had ordered him to shoot one of the company through the heart, he would have executed the command according to the manual of arms, brought his carbine to a "recover" and, at the word, marched back to his quarters without an inquiry as to the cause of the proceedings. He made no friends and, though his surliness repelled us, he made few enemies. Indeed he was rather a favorite, since he was a genuine character. His gruffness had no taint of selfish greed in it, he minded his own business strictly, and wanted others to do the same. When he first came into the company, it is true, he gained the enmity of everyone in it, but an incident occurred which turned the tide in his favor.

Some annoying little depredations had been practised on the boys, and it needed but a word of suspicion to inflame all their minds against the surly Englishman as the unknown perpetrator. The feeling intensified until about half the company were in a mood to kill the bugler outright. As we were returning from stable duty one evening, some little occurrence fanned the smoldering into a fierce blaze; a couple of the smaller boys began an attack upon him; others hastened to their assistance, and soon half the company were engaged in the assault. He succeeded in disengaging himself from his assailants, and squaring himself off, said, defiantly, "Dom your cowardly hides; jest come hat me one hat a time, hand hi'll wallop the 'ole gang uv ye's." One of our sergeants styled himself proudly a "Chicago rough" and was as vain of his pugilistic abilities as a small boy is of a father who plays in the band. We all hated him cordially, even more than we did Marriott.

He thought this was a good time to show off, and forcing his way through the crowd, he said, vauntingly: "Just fall back and form a ring, boys, and see me polish off the fool!" The ring was formed, with the bugler and the sergeant in the center. Though the latter was the younger and stronger, the first round showed him that it would have profited him much more to have let Marriott's challenge pass unheeded. As a rule, it is as well to ignore all invitations of this kind from Englishmen, and specially from those who, like Marriott, had served a term in the army, for they are likely to be so handy with their fists as to make the consequences of an acceptance more lively than desirable. So the sergeant found. Marriott, as one of the spectators expressed it, went around him like a cooper around a barrel. He planted his blows just where he wished, to the intense delight of the boys, who yelled enthusiastically whenever he got in a hot one, and their delight in seeing the sergeant drubbed so thoroughly and artistically worked an entire revolution in his favor.

Thenceforward, we viewed Marriott's eccentricities with lenient eyes and became rather proud of his bulldog stolidity and surliness. The whole battalion soon came to share this feeling, and everybody enjoyed hearing his deep-toned growl which mischievous boys would incite by some petty annoyances deliberately designed for that purpose. I will mention, incidentally, that after his encounter with the sergeant no one ever again volunteered to "polish" him off. Andersonville did not improve either his temper or his communicativeness. He seemed to want to get as far away from the rest of us as possible and took up his quarters in a remote corner of the stockade among utter strangers. Those of us who wandered up in his neighborhood occasionally to see how he was getting along were received with such scant courtesy that we did not hasten to repeat the visit.

At length, after none of us had seen him for weeks, we thought that comradeship demanded another visit. We found him in the last stages of scurvy and diarrhea. Chunks of uneaten corn bread lay by his head. They were at least a week old. The rations since then had evidently been stolen from the helpless man by those around him. The place where he lay was indescribably filthy and his body was swarming with vermin. Some good Samaritan had filled his little black oyster can with water, and placed it within his reach. For a week, at least, he had not been able to rise from the ground; he could hardly reach for the water near him. He gave us such a glare of recognition as I remember to have seen light up the fast-darkening savage old mastiff that I and my boyish companions once found dying in the woods of disease and hurts. Had he been able, he would have driven us away, or at least assailed us with biting English epithets. Thus he had doubtless driven all those who had attempted to help him. We did what little we could, and stayed with him until the next afternoon when he died. We prepared his body in the customary way, folded the hands across his breast, tied the toes together and carried it outside, not forgetting—each of us—to bring back a load of wood.

The scarcity of mechanics of all kinds in the Confederacy and the urgent needs of the people for many things which the war and the blockade prevented their obtaining led to continual inducements being offered to the artisans among us to go outside and work at their trade. Shoemakers seemed most in demand; next to these black- smiths, machinists, molders and metal-workers generally. Not a week passed during my imprisonment that I did not see a rebel emissary of some kind about the prison seeking to engage skilled workmen for some purpose or another. While in Richmond the managers of the Tredegar Iron Works were brazen and persistent in their efforts to seduce what are termed "malleable iron workers" to enter their employ. A boy who was master of any one of the commoner trades had but to make his wishes known and he would be allowed to go out on parole to work. I was a printer, and I think that at least a dozen times I was approached by rebel publishers with offers of a parole and work at good prices. One from Columbia, South Carolina, offered me two dollars and a half a "thousand" for composition. As the highest price for such work that I had received before enlisting was thirty cents a thousand, this seemed a chance to accumu- late untold wealth. Since a man working in daytime can set from thirty-five to fifty thousand a week, this would make my weekly wages run from eighty-seven dollars and fifty cents to one hundred and forty-five dollars. But it was in Confederate money, then worth from ten to twenty cents on the dollar.

Still better offers were made to iron workers of all kinds, to shoemakers, tanners, weavers, tailors, hatters, engineers, machinists, millers, railroad men and similar tradesmen. Any of these could have made a handsome thing by accepting the offers made them almost weekly. As nearly all in the prison had useful trades, it would have been of immense benefit to the Confederacy if they could have been induced to work at them. There is no measuring the benefit it would have been to the Southern Cause if just the hundreds of tanners and shoemakers in the stockade could have been persuaded to go outside and labor in providing leather and shoes for the almost shoeless people and soldiery. The machinists could have done more good to the Southern Confederacy than one of our brigades was doing harm by consenting to go to the railroad shops at Griswoldville and ply their handicraft.

The lack of material resources in the South was one of the strongest allies our arms had. This lack of resources was primarily caused by a lack of skilled labor to develop those resources, and nowhere could there be found a finer collection of skilled laborers than in the thirty-three thousand prisoners incarcerated in Andersonville. Yet all solicitations to accept paroles and go outside to work at one's trade were treated with the scorn they deserved. If any mechanic yielded to them, the fact did not come under my notice. The usual reply to invitations of this kind was "No, sir! by God, I'll stay in here till I rot, and the maggots carry me out through the cracks in the Stockade, before I'll so much as raise my little finger to help the infernal Confederacy or rebels in any shape or form." In August a Macon shoemaker came in to get some of his trade to go back with him to work in the Confederate shoe factory. He persisted in his search for these until he reached the center of the camp on the north side, when some of the shoemakers who had gathered around him, apparently considering his propositions, seized him and threw him into a well. He was kept there a whole day and only released when Wirz cut off the rations of the prison for that day and announced that no more would be issued until the man was returned safe and sound to the gates.

The terrible crowding was somewhat ameliorated by the opening in July of an addition, six hundred feet long, to the north side of the Stockade. This increased the room inside to twenty acres, giving about an acre to every one thousand seven hundred men, a preposterously contracted area still. The new ground was not a hot-bed of virulent poison like the old, however, and those who moved on to it had that much in their favor. The palisades between the new and the old portions of the pen were left standing when the new portion was opened. We were still suffering a great deal of inconvenience from lack of wood. That night the standing timbers were attacked by thousands of prisoners armed with every species of tool to cut wood, from a case-knife to an ax. They worked the livelong night with such energy that by morning not only every inch of the logs above ground had disappeared, but that below had been dug up and there was not enough left of the eight-hundred-foot wall of twenty-five-foot logs to make a box of matches.

One afternoon early in August, one of the violent rainstorms common to that section sprung up and in a little while the water was falling in torrents. The little creek running through the camp swelled up immensely and swept out large gaps in the Stockade, both in the west and east sides. The rebels noticed the breaches as soon as the prisoners. Two guns were fired from the Star Fort and all the guards rushed out and formed so as to prevent any egress if one was attempted. Taken by surprise, we were not in a condition to profit by the opportunity until it was too late. The storm did one good thing. It swept away a great deal of filth and left the camp much more wholesome. The foul stench rising from the camp made an excellent conductor, and the lightning struck several times within one hundred feet of the prison.

Toward the end of August there happened what the religiously inclined termed a "providential dispensation." The water in the creek was indescribably bad. No amount of familiarity with it, no increase of intimacy with our offensive surroundings, could lessen the disgust at the polluted water. As I have said previously, before the stream entered the Stockade it was rendered too filthy for any use by the contaminations from the camps of the guards situated about a half mile above. Immediately upon entering the Stockade, the contamination became terrible. The oozy seep at the bottom of the hillsides drained directly into it all the mass of filth from a population of thirty-three thousand. Imagine the condition of an open sewer, passing through the heart of a city of that many people and receiving all the offensive product of so dense a gathering into a shallow sluggish stream, a yard wide and five inches deep, and heated by the burning rays of the sun in the thirty-second degree of latitude. Imagine, if one can without becoming sick at the stomach, all of these people having to wash in and drink of this foul flow.

There is not a scintilla of exaggeration in this statement. That it is within the exact truth is demonstrable by the testimony of any man, rebel or Union, who ever saw the inside of the Stockade at Andersonville. I am quite content to have its truth, as well as that of any other statement made in this book, be determined by the evidence of anyone, no matter how bitter his hatred of the Union, who had any personal knowledge of the condition of affairs at Andersonville. No one can successfully deny that there were at least thirty-three thousand prisoners in the Stockade, nor that the one shallow narrow creek which passed through the prison was at once their main sewer and their source of supply of water for bathing, drinking and washing. With these main facts admitted, the reader's common sense of natural consequences will furnish the rest of the details.

It is true that some of the more fortunate of us had wells, thanks to our own energy in overcoming extraordinary obstacles, no thanks to our jailers for making the slightest effort to provide these necessities. We dug the wells with case and pocket knives and half-canteens to a depth of twenty to thirty feet, pulling up the dirt in pantaloon legs and running continual risk of being smothered to death by the caving in of the unwalled sides. Not only did the rebels refuse to give us boards with which to wall the wells and buckets for drawing the water, but they did all in their power to prevent us from digging the wells, and made continual forays to capture the digging tools because the wells were frequently used as the starting places for tunnels.

The great majority of the prisoners who went to the creek for water went as near as possible to the Dead Line on the west side where the creek entered the Stockade, that they might get water with as little filth in it as possible. In the crowds struggling there for their turn to take a dip, someone nearly every day got so close to the Dead Line as to arouse a suspicion in the guard's mind that he was touching it. This suspicion was the unfortunate one's death warrant and also its execution. As the sluggish brain of the guard conceived it, he leveled his gun; the distance to his victim was not over one hundred feet; he never failed his aim. The first warning the wretched prisoner got that he was suspected of transgressing a prison rule was the charge of ball-and-buck that tore through his body. It was lucky if he was the only one of the group killed. More wicked and unjustifiable murders never were committed than these almost daily assassinations at the creek.

One morning the camp was astonished beyond measure to discover that during the night a large bold spring had burst out on the north side, about midway between the swamp and the summit of the hill. It poured out its grateful flood of pure sweet water in an apparently exhaustless quantity. To the many who looked in wonder upon it, it seemed as truly a heaven-wrought miracle as when Moses' enchanted rod smote the parched earth in Sinai's desert waste, and the living waters gushed forth. The police took charge of the spring, and everyone was compelled to take his regular turn in filling his vessel. This was kept up during our whole stay in Andersonville, and every morning shortly after daybreak, a thousand men could be seen standing in line, waiting their turns to fill their cans and cups with the precious liquid.

I am told by comrades who have revisited the Stockade of recent years that the spring is yet running as when we left, and is held in most pious veneration by the Negroes of that vicinity, who still preserve the tradition of its miraculous origin and ascribe to its water wonderful grace-giving and healing properties. When I hear of people bringing water for baptismal purposes from the Jordan, I say in my heart, "How much more would I value for myself and friends the administration of the chrismal sacrament with the divine flow from that low sandhill in western Georgia."

Every morning after roll call, thousands of sick gathered at the South Gate, where the doctors made some pretense of affording medical relief. The scene there reminded me of the illustrations in my Sunday School lessons of that time when "great multitudes came unto Him" by the shores of the Sea of Galilee, "having with them those that were lame, blind, dumb, maimed and many others." Had the crowds worn the flowing robes of the East, the picture would have lacked nothing but the presence of the Son of Man to make it complete. Here were the burning sands and parching sun; hither came scores of groups of three or four comrades, laboriously staggering under the weight of a blanket in which they had carried a disabled and dying friend from some distant part of the Stockade. Beside them hobbled the scorbutics with swollen and distorted limbs, each more loathsome and near death than the lepers whom Christ's divine touch made whole. Dozens, unable to walk and having no comrades to carry them, crawled painfully along, with frequent stops on their hands and knees. Every form of intense physical suffering that it is possible for disease to induce in the human frame was visible at these daily parades of the sick of the prison.

As over three thousand and seventy-six died in August, there were probably twelve thousand dangerously sick at any given time during the month, and a large part of these collected at the South Gate every morning. Measurably calloused as we had become by the daily sights of horror around us, we encountered spectacles in these gatherings which no amount of visible misery could accustom us to. I remember one especially that burned itself deeply into my memory. It was of a young man, not over twenty-five, who a few weeks ago had been the picture of manly beauty and youthful vigor. He had had a well-knit lithe form, dark curling hair fell over a forehead which had once been fair and his eyes still showed that they had gleamed with a bold adventurous spirit. The red clover leaf on his cap showed that he belonged to the 1st Division of the 2nd Corps, the three chevrons on his arm that he was a sergeant and the stripe at his cuff that he was a veteran.

Some kind-hearted boys had found him in a miserable condition on the north side and carried him over in a blanket to where the doctors could see him. He had but little clothing on save his blouse and cap. Ulcers of some kind had formed in his abdomen and these were now masses of squirming worms. It was so much worse than the usual forms of suffering that quite a little crowd of compassionate spectators gathered around and expressed their pity. The sufferer turned to one who lay beside him with

"Comrade, if we were only under the old Stars and Stripes, we wouldn't care a God-damn for a few worms, would we?" This was not profane. It was an utterance from the depths of a brave man's heart, couched in the strongest language at his command. It seemed terrible that so gallant a soul should depart from earth in this miserable fashion. Some of us, much moved by the sight, went to the doctors and put the case as strongly as possible, begging them to do something to alleviate his suffering. They declined to see the case, but got rid of us by giving us a bottle of turpentine with directions to pour it upon the ulcers to kill the maggots. We did so. It must have been cruel torture and as absurd remedially as cruel, but our hero set his teeth and endured it without a groan. He was then carried out to the hospital to die.

I said the doctors made a "pretense" of affording medical relief. It was hardly that since about all the prescription for those inside the Stockade consisted of giving a handful of sumach berries to each of those complaining of scurvy. The berries might have done some good, had there been enough of them and had their action been assisted by proper food. As it was, they were probably nearly, if not wholly, useless. Nothing was given to arrest the ravages of dysentery. A limited number of the worst cases were admitted to the hospital each day. As this only had capacity for about one quarter of the sick in the Stockade, new patients could only be admitted as the others died. It seemed, anyway, like signing a man's death warrant to send him to the hospital, as three out of every four who went out there died.

Early in August, I made a successful effort to get out to the hospital. I had several reasons for this. First, one of my chums, W. W. Watts of my own company, had been sent out a little while before very sick with scurvy and pneumonia and I wanted to see if I could do anything for him if he still lived. I have mentioned before that for a while after our entrance into Andersonville five of us slept on one overcoat and covered ourselves with one blanket. Two of these had already died, leaving as possessors of the blanket and overcoat W. W. Watts, B. B. Andrews and myself. Next, I wanted to go out to see if there was any prospect of escape. I had long since given up hopes of escaping from the Stockade. All our attempts at tunneling had resulted in dead failures, and now to make us wholly despair of success in that direction, another stockade was built clear around the prison at a distance of one hundred and twenty feet from the first palisades.

It was manifest that though we might succeed in tunneling past one stockade, we could not go beyond the second one. I had the scurvy rather badly, and being naturally slight in frame, I presented a very sick appearance to the physicians and was passed out to the hospital. While this was a wretched affair, it was still a vast improvement on the Stockade. About five acres of ground, a little southeast of the Stockade and bordering on a creek, were enclosed by a board fence around which the guard walked. Trees shaded the ground tolerably well. There were tents and flies to shelter part of the sick, and in these were beds made of pine leaves. There were regular streets and alleys running through the grounds and as the management was in the hands of our own men, the place was kept reasonably clean and orderly—for Andersonville. There was also some improvement in the food. Rice in some degree replaced the nauseous and unnutritious corn bread and, if served in sufficient quantities, would doubtless have promoted the recovery of many men dying from dysenteric diseases. We also received small quantities of okra, a plant peculiar to the South, whose pods contained a mucilaginous matter that made a soup very grateful to those suffering from scurvy.

But all these ameliorations of condition were too slight to even arrest the progress of the disease of the thousands of dying men brought out from the Stockade. These still wore the same lice-infested garments as in prison; no baths or even ordinary applications of soap and water cleaned their dirt-grimed skins, to give their pores an opportunity to assist in restoring them to health; even their long, lank and matted hair, swarming with vermin, was not trimmed. The most ordinary and obvious measures for their comfort were neglected. If a man recovered, he did it almost in spite of fate. The medicines given were scanty and crude. The principal remedial agent, as far as my observation extended, was a rank, fetid species of unrectified spirits which, I was told, was made from sorghum seed. It had a light green tinge and was about as inviting to the taste as spirits of turpentine. It was given to the sick in small quantities mixed with water. I had had some experience with Kentucky "Apple-Jack" which, it was popularly believed among the boys, would dissolve a piece of the fattest pork thrown into it. But that seemed balmy and oily alongside of this. After tasting some, I ceased to wonder at the atrocities of Wirz and his associates. Nothing would seem too bad to a man who made that his habitual tipple.

Certainly this continent has never seen and, I fervently trust, will never again see such a gigantic concentration of misery as that hospital displayed daily. The official statistics tell the story of this with terrible brevity: there were three thousand seven hundred and nine in the hospital in August; one thousand one hundred and eighty-nine—nearly every other man—died. The rate afterwards became much higher than this.

The most conspicuous suffering was in the gangrene wards. Horrible sores, spreading almost visibly from hour to hour, devoured men's limbs and bodies. I remember one ward in which the ulcerations appeared to be altogether in the back, where they ate out the tissue between the skin and the ribs. The attendants seemed trying to arrest the progress of the sloughing by drenching the sores with a solution of blue vitriol. This was exquisitely painful, and in the morning when the drenching was going on, the whole hospital rang with the most agonizing screams. But gangrene mostly attacked the arms and legs, and the legs more than the arms. Sometimes it killed men inside of a week; sometimes they lingered indefinitely. I remember one man in the Stockade who cut his hand with the sharp corner of a *card* of corn bread he was lifting from the ration wagon; gangrene set in immediately and he died four days after. One form that was quite prevalent was a cancer of the lower lip. It seemed to start at one corner of the mouth and it finally ate the whole side of the face out. Of course the sufferer had the greatest trouble in eating and drinking. For the latter, it was customary to whittle out a little wooden tube, and fasten it in a tin cup so he could suck up the water. As this mouth cancer seemed contagious, none of us would allow anyone afflicted with it to use any of our cooking utensils. The rebel doctors at the hospital resorted to wholesale amputations to check the progress of the gangrene. They had a two-hour session of limb-lopping every morning, each of which resulted in quite a pile of severed members.

I presume more bungling operations are rarely seen outside of Russian or Turkish hospitals. Their unskillfulness was apparent even to non-scientific observers like myself. The standard of medical education in the South, as indeed of every other form of education, was quite low. The Chief Surgeon of the prison, Dr. Isaiah White, and perhaps two or three others seemed to be gentlemen of fair abilities and attainments. The remainder were of that class of illiterate and unlearning quacks who physic and blister the poor whites and Negroes in the country districts of the South; who believe they can stop bleeding of the nose by repeating a verse from the Bible; who think that if, in gathering their favorite remedy of boneset,[32] they cut the stem "upwards" it will purge their patients, and if "downwards" it will vomit them; and who hold that there is nothing so good for "fits" as a black cat killed in the dark of the moon, cut open and bound, while yet warm, upon the naked chest of the victim of the convulsions. They had one case of instruments captured from some of our field hospitals, which were dull and fearfully out of order. With poor instruments and unskilled hands the operations became mangling.

In the hospital I saw an admirable illustration of the affection which a sailor will lavish on a ship's boy whom he takes a fancy to and makes his "chicken," as the phrase is. The United States sloop *Water Witch* had recently been captured in Ossabaw Sound, and her crew brought into prison. One of her boys, a bright, handsome little fellow of about fifteen, had lost one of his arms in the fight. He was brought into the hospital and the old fellow whose "chicken" he was was allowed to accompany and nurse him. This "old barnacle-back" was as surly a growler as ever went aloft but to his "chicken" he was as tender and thoughtful as a woman. They found a shady nook in one corner, and any moment one looked in that direction he could see the old tar hard at work at something for the comfort and pleasure of his pet. Now he was dressing the wound as deftly and gently as a mother caring for a new-born babe; now he was trying to concoct some relish out of the slender materials he could beg or steal from the Quartermaster; now trying to arrange the shade of the bed of pine leaves in a more comfortable manner; now repairing or washing his clothes, and so on.

All sailors were particularly favored by being allowed to bring their bags in untouched by the guards. This "chicken" had a wonderful supply of clothes, the handiwork of his protector who, like most good sailors, was very skillful with the needle. He had suits of fine white duck embroidered with blue in a way that would ravish the heart of a fine lady, and blue suits similarly embroidered with white. No belle ever kept her clothes in better order than these were and when the ducks came up from the old sailor's patient washing they were as spotless as new-fallen snow.

I found my chum in a very bad condition. His appetite was entirely gone, but he had an inordinate craving for tobacco, for strong black plug which he smoked in a pipe. He had already traded off all his brass buttons to the guards for this. I had accumulated a few buttons to bribe the guard to take me out for wood, and I gave these also for tobacco for him. When I awoke one morning the man who lay next to me on the right was dead, having died sometime during the night. I searched his pockets and took what was in them. These were a silk pocket-handkerchief, a gutta-percha finger ring, a comb, a pencil, and a leather pocketbook, making in all quite a nice little find. I hied over to the guard and succeeded in trading the personal estate which I had inherited from the intestate deceased for a handful of peaches, a handful of hardly ripe figs and a long plug of tobacco. I hastened back to Watts, expecting that the figs and peaches would do him a world of good. At first I did not show him the tobacco, as I was strongly opposed to his using it, thinking that it was making him much worse. But he looked at the tempting peaches and figs with lack-luster eyes; he was too far gone to care for them.

He pushed them back to me, saying faintly, "No, you take 'em, Mac. I don't want 'em, I can't eat 'em!" I then produced the tobacco and his face lighted up. Concluding that this was all the comfort that he could have and that I might as well gratify him, I cut up some of the weed, filled his pipe and lighted it. He smoked calmly and almost happily all the afternoon, hardly speaking a word to me. As it grew dark he asked me to bring him a drink. I did so and as I raised him up, he said, "Mac, this thing's ended. Tell my father that I stood it as long as I could, an'——" The death rattle sounded in his throat and when I laid him back it was all over. Straightening out his limbs, folding his hands across his breast and composing his features as best I could, I lay down beside the body and slept till morning, when I did what little else I could toward preparing for the grave all that was left of my long-suffering little friend.

Spanking a Thief

CHAPTER XIII

THE FUTILITY OF SUCCESSFUL EXPLANATION

FTER WATTS' DEATH, I set about earnestly seeing what could be done in the way of escape. Frank Harney of the 1st West Virginia Cavalry, a boy of about my own age and disposition, joined with me in the scheme. I was still possessed with my original plan of making my way down the creeks to the Flint River, down the Flint River to where it emptied into the Appalachicola, and down that stream to its *debouchure* into the bay that connected with the Gulf of Mexico. I was sure of finding my way by this route because, if nothing else offered, I could get astride of a log and float down the current. The way to Sherman, in the other direction, was long, tortuous and difficult, with a fearful gauntlet of blood-hounds, patrols and scouts of Hood's Army to be run. I had but little difficulty in persuading Harney into an acceptance of my views, and we began arranging for a solution of the first great problem—how to get outside of the hospital guards.

As I have explained before, the hospital was surrounded by a board fence, with guards walking their beats on the ground outside. A small creek flowed through the southern end of the grounds. Its lower end was used as a sink. The boards of the fence came down to the surface of the water where the creek passed out, but we found by careful prodding with a stick that the hole between the boards and the bottom of the creek was sufficiently large to allow the passage of our bodies, and that there had been no stakes driven or other precautions used to prevent egress by this channel. The guard posted there had probably been ordered to stand at the edge of the stream, but it smelled so vilely in those scorching days that he had consulted his feelings and had decided to protect his health by retiring to the top of the bank a rod or more distant. We watched night after night, and at last were gratified to find that none went nearer the creek than the top of the bank.

Then we waited for the moon to come right so that the first part of the night should be dark. This took several days, but at last we knew that the next night she would not rise until between 9 and 10 o'clock, which would give us nearly two hours of the dense darkness of a moonless summer night in the South. We had first thought of saving up some rations for the trip, but then reflected that these would be ruined by the filthy water into which we must sink to go under the fence. It was not difficult to abandon the food idea, since it was very hard to force ourselves to lay by even the smallest portion of our scanty rations.

As the next day wore on, our minds were wrought up into exalted tension by the rapid approach of the supreme moment with all its chances and consequences. The experience of the past few months was not such as to fit us mentally for such a hazard. It had prepared us for sullen, uncomplaining endurance, for calmly contemplating the worst that would come. But it did not strengthen the fiber of mind that leads to venturesome activity and daring exploits. Doubtless the weakness of our bodies reacted upon our spirits. We contemplated all the perils that confronted us—perils that, now looming with impending nearness, took a clearer and more threatening shape than they had ever done before. We considered the desperate chances of passing the guard unseen; or, if noticed, of escaping his fire without death or severe wounds. But supposing him fortunately evaded, then came the gauntlet of the hounds and the patrols hunting deserters. After this, a long, weary journey, with bare feet and almost naked bodies, through an unknown country abounding with enemies; the dangers of assassination by the embittered populace; the risks of dying with hunger and fatigue in the gloomy depths of a swamp; the scanty hopes that, if we reached the seashore, we could get to our vessels.

Not one of all these contingencies failed to expand itself to all its alarming proportions and unite with its fellows to form a dreadful vista, like the valleys filled with demons and genii, dragons and malign enchantments which confronted the heroes of the Arabian Nights when they set out to perform their exploits. But behind us lay more miseries and horrors than a riotous imagination could conceive. Before us could certainly be nothing worse. We would put life and freedom to the hazard of a touch, and win or lose it all.

The day had been intolerably hot. The sun's rays seemed to sear the earth like heated irons, and the air that lay on the burning sand was broken by wavy lines, such as one sees indicate the radiation from a hot stove. Except the wretched chain gang plodding tortuously back and forward on the hillside, not a soul nor animal could be seen in motion outside the Stockade. The hounds were panting in their kennel; the rebel officers, half or wholly drunken with villainous sorghum whiskey, were stretched at full length in the shade at Headquarters; the half-naked gunners crouched under the shadow of the embankments of the forts; the guards hung limply over the Stockade in front of their little perches; and the thirty thousand boys inside the Stockade, prone or supine upon the glowing sand, gasped for breath—for one draft of sweet, cool, wholesome air that did not bear on its wings the subtle seeds of rank corruption and death. Everywhere was the prostration of discomfort, the inertia of sluggishness. Only the sick moved; only the pain-racked cried out; only the dying struggled; only the agonies of dissolution could make life assert itself against the exhaustion of the heat.

Harney and I, lying in the scanty shade of the trunk of a tall pine, our hearts filled with solicitude as to the outcome of what the evening would bring us, looked out over the scene as we had done daily for long months, and remained silent for hours, until the sun, as if weary with torturing and slaying, began going down in the blazing west. The groans of the thousands of sick around us, the shrieks of the rotting ones in the gangrene wards rang incessantly in our ears.

As the sun disappeared and the heat abated, the suspended activity was restored. The master of hounds came out with his yelping pack and started on his rounds; the rebel officers roused themselves from their siestas and went lazily about their duties; the fifer produced his cracked fife and piped forth his unvarying "Bonnie Blue Flag" as a signal for dress parade, and the drums, beaten by unskilled hands in the camps of the different regiments, repeated the signal. In the Stockade, the mass of humanity became full of motion as an ant hill and resembled it very much from our point of view, with the boys threading their way among the burrows, tents and holes.

It was becoming dark quite rapidly. The moments seemed galloping onward toward the time when we must make the decisive step. We drew from the dirty rag in which it was wrapped the little piece of corn bread that we had saved for our supper, carefully divided it into equal parts, and each took one and ate it in silence. This done, we held a final consultation as to our plans and went over each detail carefully, that we might fully understand each other under all possible circumstances and act in concert. One point we laboriously impressed upon each other, and that was that under no circumstances were we to allow ourselves to be tempted to leave the creek until we reached its junction with the Flint River. I then picked up two pine leaves, broke them off to unequal lengths, rolled them in my hands behind my back for a second and, presenting them to Harney with their ends sticking out of my closed hand, said:

"The one that gets the longest one goes first." Harney reached forth and drew the longer one.

We made a tour of reconnaissance. Everything seemed as usual and wonderfully calm compared with the tumult in our minds. The hospital guards were pacing their beats lazily, and those on the Stockade were drawling listlessly the first "call around" of the evening: "Post numbah foah! Half-past seven o'clock! and all's well!" Inside the Stockade was a babel of sounds, above all of which rose the melody of religious and patriotic songs sung in the various parts of the camp. From the headquarters came the shouts and laughter of the rebel officers having a little frolic in the cool of the evening. The groans of the sick around us were gradually hushing, as the abatement of the terrible heat let all but the worst cases sink into a brief slumber from which they awoke before midnight to renew their outcries. But those in the gangrene wards seemed to be denied even this scanty blessing. Apparently they never slept, for their shrieks never ceased. A multitude of whippoorwills in the woods around us began their usual dismal cry, which had never seemed so unearthly and full of dreadful presages as now.

It was now quite dark, and we stole noiselessly down to the creek and reconnoitered. We listened. The guard was not pacing his beat, as we could not hear his footsteps. A large ill-shapen lump against the trunk of one of the trees on the bank showed that he was leaning there resting himself. We watched him for several minutes, but he did not move, and the thought shot into our minds that he might be asleep. But it seemed impossible—it was too early in the evening.

Now, if ever, was the opportunity. Harney squeezed my hand, stepped noiselessly into the creek, let himself gently down into the filthy water and, while my heart was beating so that I was certain it could be heard some distance from me, began making toward the fence. He passed under easily. Anxiously I raised my eyes toward the guard, while on my strained ears fell the soft plashing made by Harney as he pulled himself cautiously forward. It seemed as if the sentinel must hear this, as if he could not help it, and every second I expected to see the black lump address itself to motion, and the musket flash out fiendishly. But the lump remained motionless; the musket silent. When I thought that Harney had gained sufficient distance, I followed. It seemed as if the disgusting water would smother me as I laid myself down in it. Such was my agitation that it appeared almost impossible that I should escape making such a noise as would attract the guard's notice.

Catching hold of the roots and limbs at the side of the stream, I pulled myself slowly along as noiselessly as possible. I passed under the fence without difficulty and was outside and within fifteen feet of the guard. I had lain down in the creek on my right side, that my face might be toward the guard and I could watch him all the time.

As I came under the fence, he was still leaning motionless against the tree, but to my heated imagination he appeared to have turned and be watching me. I hardly breathed; the filthy water rippling past me seemed to roar to attract the guard's attention. I reached my hand out cautiously to grasp a root to pull myself along by and caught instead a dry branch which broke with a loud crack. My heart stood absolutely still. The guard evidently heard the noise. The black lump separated itself from the tree, and a straight line which I knew to be his musket separated itself from the lump.

In a brief instant I lived a year of mortal apprehension. So certain was I that he had discovered me and was leveling his piece to fire, that I could scarcely restrain myself from springing up and dashing away to avoid the shot. Then I heard him take a step and, to my unutterable surprise and relief, he walked farther from the creek, evidently to speak to the man whose beat joined his. I pulled away more swiftly but still with the greatest caution, until after half an hour's painful effort I had gotten fully one hundred and fifty yards away from the hospital fence. I found Harney crouched on a cypress tree, close to the water's edge, watching me.

We struggled on determinedly for nearly an hour, and were perhaps a mile from the hospital. The moon came up and its light showed that the creek continued its course through a dense jungle like that we had been traversing; while on high ground to our left were the open pine woods I have previously described. We stopped and debated for a few minutes. We recalled our decision to keep in the creek, remembering the experiences of other boys who had tried to escape and been caught by the hounds. If we stayed in the creek we were sure the hounds would not find our trail, but it was equally certain that at this rate we would be exhausted and starved before we got out of sight of the prison. It seemed that we had gone far enough to be out of reach of the packs patrolling immediately around the Stockade, and there could be little risk in trying a short walk on dry ground. We decided to take the chance and, ascending the bank, we walked and ran as fast as we could for about two miles further.

All at once it struck me that with all our progress the hounds sounded as near as when we started. I shivered at the thought and, though nearly ready to drop with fatigue, urged myself and Harney on. An instant later their baying rang out on the still night air right behind us with fearful distinctness. There was no mistake now. They had found our trail and were running us down. The change from fearful apprehension to the crushing reality stopped us stock-still in our tracks. At the next breath the hounds came bursting through the woods in plain sight and in full cry. We obeyed our first impulse and, rushing back into the swamp, forced our way for a few yards through the flesh-tearing impediments until we gained a large cypress upon whose great knees we climbed, thoroughly exhausted, just as the yelping pack reached the edge of the water and stopped there and bayed at us. It was a physical impossibility for us to go another step.

In a moment a low-browed villain who had charge of the hounds came galloping up on his mule, tooting signals to his dogs as he came on a cow-horn slung from his shoulders. He immediately discovered us, covered us with his revolver, and yelled out, "Come ashore there, quick, you goddamed Yankees!" There was no help for it. We climbed down off the knees [33] and started towards the land. As we neared it, the hounds became almost frantic and it seemed as if we would be torn to pieces the moment they could reach us. But their master dismounted and drove them back. He was surly, even savage, to us but seemed in too much of a hurry to get back to waste any time annoying us with the dogs. He ordered us to get around in front of the mule and start back to camp.

We moved as rapidly as our fatigue and our lacerated feet would allow us, and before midnight we were again in the hospital, fatigued, filthy, torn, bruised and wretched beyond description or conception. The next morning we were turned back into the Stockade as punishment. Harney and I were specially fortunate in being turned back without being brought before Captain Wirz. We subsequently learned that we owed this good luck to Wirz's absence on sick leave, his place being supplied by Lieutenant Davis.

Davis was a moderate-brained Baltimorean and one of that horde of Marylanders in the rebel army whose principal service to the Confederacy consisted of working themselves into "bomb-proof" places and forcing those whom they displaced into the field. Winder was the illustrious head of this crowd whose enthusiasm for the Southern Cause, and consistency in serving it only in such places as were out of range of the Yankee artillery, was the subject of many bitter jibes by the rebels. Lieutenant Davis went into the war with great brashness. He was one of the mob which attacked the 6th Massachusetts [34] in its passage through Baltimore but, like all that class of roughs, he got his stomach full of war as soon as the real business of fighting began, and he retired to where the chances of attaining ripe old age were better than in front of the Army of the Potomac's muskets. We shall hear of Davis again.

Encountering Captain Wirz was one of the terrors of an abortive attempt to escape. When recaptured prisoners were brought before him, he would frequently give way to paroxysms of screaming rage, so violent as to verge closely on insanity. Brandishing the fearful and wonderful revolver of which I have spoken, in such a manner as to threaten the luckless captives with instant death, he would shriek out imprecations, curses and foul epithets in French, German and English until he fairly frothed at the mouth. There were plenty of stories current in camp of his having several times given way to his rage so far as to actually shoot men down in these interviews, and still more of his knocking down boys and jumping upon them until he inflicted injuries that soon resulted in death. How true these rumors were I am unable to say of my own personal knowledge, since I never saw him kill anyone nor have I talked with anyone who did.

There were a number of cases of this kind testified to upon his trial, but they all happened among "paroles" outside the Stockade, or among the prisoners inside after we left, so I knew nothing about them. One of the "Old Switzer's" [35] favorite ways of ending these *séances* was to inform the boys that he would have them shot in an hour or so and bid them prepare for death. After keeping them in fearful suspense for hours, he would order them to be punished with the stocks, the ball-and-chain, the chain gang or, if his fierce mood had burned itself out, as was quite likely with a man of his shallow brain and vacillating temper, simply to be returned to the Stockade.

Nothing, I am sure, since the days of the Inquisition or—still later—since the terrible punishments visited upon the insurgents of 1848 by the Austrian aristocrats, has been so diabolical as the stocks and the chain gangs used by Wirz. At one time seven men, sitting in the stocks near the Star Fort in plain view of the camp, became objects of interest to everybody inside. They were never relieved from their painful position but were kept there until all of them died. I think it was nearly two weeks before the last one succumbed. What they endured in that time even imagination cannot conceive. I do not think that an Indian tribe ever devised keener torture for its captives. The chain gang consisted of a number of men, varying from twelve to twenty-five, all chained to one sixty-four pound ball. They were also stationed near the Star Fort, out in the hot sun without a particle of shade over them. When one moved, they all had to move. They were scourged with the dysentery, and the necessities of some of their number kept them constantly in motion. I see them distinctly yet, tramping laboriously and painfully back and forward over that burning hillside every moment of the long, weary summer days.

A comrade writes to remind me of the beneficent work of the Masonic Order. I mention it most gladly, as it was the sole recognition on the part of any of our foes of our claims to human kinship. The churches of all denominations ignored us as wholly as if we were dumb beasts. Lay humanitarians were equally indifferent, and the only interest manifested by any rebel in the welfare of any prisoner was by the Masonic brotherhood. The rebel Masons interested themselves in securing details outside the Stockade in the cook-house, the commissary and elsewhere for the brethren among the prisoners who would accept such favors. Such as did not feel inclined to go outside on parole received frequent presents in the way of food, especially of vegetables, which were literally beyond price. Materials were sent inside to build tents for the Masons, and I think such as made themselves known before death received burial according to the rites of the Order. Doctor White and some of the other surgeons belonged to the fraternity, and the wearing of a Masonic emblem by a new prisoner was pretty sure to catch their eyes and be the means of securing for the wearer the tender of good offices, such as a detail in the hospital as a nurse or wardmaster.

I was not fortunate enough to be one of the mystic brethren, and so missed all share in any of these benefits as well as in any others. I take special pride in one thing: that during my whole imprisonment, I was not beholden to a rebel for a single favor of any kind. The rebel does not live who can say that he ever gave me so much as a handful of meal, a spoonful of salt, an inch of thread or a stick of wood. From first to last I received nothing but my rations, except occasional trifles that I succeeded in stealing from the stupid officers charged with issuing rations. I owe no man in the Southern Confederacy gratitude for anything, not even for a kind word.

Speaking of secret society pins recalls a noteworthy story which has been told me since the war, of boys whom I knew. At the breaking out of hostilities there existed in Toledo a festive little secret society such as larking boys frequently organize, with no other object than fun and the usual adolescent love of mystery. There were a dozen or so members in it who called themselves "The Royal Reubens." They were headed by a bookbinder named Ned Hopkins. Someone started a branch of the order in Napoleon, Ohio, and among the members was Charles E. Reynolds of that town. The badge of that society was a peculiarly shaped gold pin. Reynolds and Hopkins never met and had no acquaintance with each other. When the war broke out, Hopkins enlisted in Battery H, 1st Ohio Artillery, and was sent to the Army of the Potomac, where he was captured in the fall of 1863 while scouting in the neighborhood of Richmond. Reynolds entered the 68th Ohio Volunteer Infantry and was taken in the neighborhood of Jackson, Mississippi, two thousand miles from the place of Hopkins' capture. At Andersonville, Hopkins became one of the officers in charge of the hospital. One day a rebel sergeant who called the roll in the Stockade, after studying Hopkins' pin a minute, said, "I seed a Yank in the Stockade today a-wearin' a pin egzackly like that'ere." This aroused Hopkins' interest, and he went in search of this other "Yank." Knowing his squad and detachment, he had little difficulty in finding him. He recognized the pin, spoke to its wearer, gave him the grand hailing sign of the Royal Reubens, and it was duly responded to. The upshot of the matter was that he took Reynolds out with him as clerk and so saved his life, as the latter was going downhill very rapidly. Reynolds, in turn, secured the "detail" of a comrade of the 68th who was failing fast and succeeded in saving his life, all of which happy results were attributable to that insignificant boyish society and its equally unimportant badge of membership.

Along in the last of August, the rebels learned that there were between two and three hundred captains and lieutenants in the Stockade passing themselves off as enlisted men. The motive of these officers was two-fold: first, a chivalrous wish to share the fortunes and fate of their boys; and second, a disinclination to gratify the rebels by the knowledge of the rank of their captives. The secret was so well kept that none of us suspected it until the fact was announced by the rebels themselves. They were taken out immediately and sent to Macon where the commissioned officers' prison was. It would not do to trust such possible leaders with us another day.

"Half Past Eight O'Clock and Atlanta's Gone to Hell!"

CHAPTER XIV

A GENERAL EXCHANGE

I HAVE IN OTHER PLACES dwelt upon the insufficiency and the nauseousness of the food. No words that I can use, no insistence upon this theme, can give the reader any idea of its mortal importance to us. Let the reader consider for a moment the quantity, quality and variety of food that he now holds to be necessary for the maintenance of health and life. I trust that everyone that peruses this book, that everyone in fact over whom the Stars and Stripes wave, has his cup of coffee, his biscuits and his beefsteak for breakfast; a substantial dinner of roast and "boiled," and a lighter but still sufficient meal in the evening. In all, certainly not less than fifty different articles are set before him during the day for his choice of nourishment.

Let him scan this extended bill of fare which long custom has made so commonplace as to be uninteresting, perhaps even wearisome, to think about and see what he could omit from it if necessity compelled him. After a reluctant farewell to fish, butter, eggs, milk, sugar, green and preserved fruits and vegetables, he thinks that perhaps under extraordinary circumstances he might be able to merely sustain life for a limited period on a diet three times a day of bread and meat washed down with creamless, unsweetened coffee, and varied occasionally with additions of potatoes, onions and beans. It would astonish the innocent to have one of our veterans inform him that this was not even the first stage of destitution; that a soldier who had these was expected to be on the summit level of contentment.

Any of the boys who followed Grant to Appomattox Court House, Sherman to the Sea, or "Pap" Thomas [36] till his glorious career culminated with the annihilation of Hood, will tell him of many weeks when a slice of fat pork on a piece of "hard tack" had to do duty for the breakfast of beefsteak and biscuits; when another slice of fat pork and another cracker served for the dinner of roast beef and vegetables, and a third cracker and a slice of pork was a substitute for the supper of toast and chops. I say to these veterans in turn that they did not arrive at even the first stages of destitution, compared with the depths to which we were dragged. The restriction for a few weeks to a diet of crackers and fat pork was certainly a hardship; but the crackers alone, chemists tell us, contain all the elements necessary to support life, and in our army they were always well made and very palatable. I believe I risk nothing in saying that one of the ordinary square crackers of our Commissary Department contained much more real nutriment than the whole of our average ration.

I have before compared the size, shape and appearance of the daily half-loaf of corn bread issued to us to a half-brick, and I do not yet know of a more fitting comparison. At first we got a small piece of rusty bacon along with this; but the size of this diminished steadily until at last it faded away entirely, and during the last six months of our imprisonment I do not believe that we received rations of meat above half a dozen times. To this smallness was added ineffable badness. The meal was ground very coarsely, by dull, weakly propelled stones that imperfectly crushed the grains and left the tough, hard coating of the kernels in large, sharp, mica-like scales which cut and inflamed the stomach and intestines like handfuls of pounded glass. The alimentary canals of all compelled to eat it were kept in a continual state of irritation that usually terminated in incurable dysentery.

The old adage says that "hunger is the best sauce for poor food," but hunger failed to render this detestable stuff palatable, and it became so loathsome that very many actually starved to death, being unable to force their organs of deglutition to receive the nauseous dose and pass it to the stomach. I was always much healthier than the average of the boys and my appetite consequently much better; yet, for the last month that I was in Andersonville, it required all my determination to crowd the bread down my throat, and I could only do this by breaking off small bits at a time and forcing each down as I would a pill.

A large part of this repulsiveness was due to the coarseness and foulness of the meal, the wretched cooking and the lack of salt, but there was a still more potent reason than all these. Nature does not intend that man shall live by bread alone nor by any one kind of food. She indicates this by the varying tastes and longings that she gives him. If his body needs one kind of constituents, his tastes lead him to desire the food that is richest in these constituents. When he has taken as much as his system requires, a sense of satiety supervenes and he becomes tired of that particular food. If tastes are not perverted but allowed a free but temperate exercise, they are the surest indicators of the way to preserve health and strength by a judicious selection of elimination. In this case, Nature was protesting by a rebellion of the tastes against any further use of that species of food. She was saying, as plainly as she ever spoke, that death could only be averted by a change of diet which would supply our bodies with the constituents they so sadly needed and which could not be supplied by corn meal. How needless was this confinement of our rations to corn meal, and especially to such wretchedly prepared meal, is conclusively shown by the rebels' testimony.

It would have been very little extra trouble to the rebels to have had our meal sifted. We would have gladly done it ourselves if allowed the utensils and opportunity. It would been as little trouble to have varied our rations with green corn and sweet potatoes, of which the country was then full. A few wagonloads of roasting ears and sweet potatoes would have banished every trace of scurvy from the camp, healed up wasting dysentery and saved thousands of lives. Any day that the rebels had chosen they could have gotten a thousand volunteers who would have given their solemn parole not to escape, who would have gone any distance into the country to gather the potatoes and corn and such other vegetables as were readily obtainable, and bring them into camp.

Whatever else may be said in defense of the Southern management of the military prisons, the permitting of seven thousand men to die of the scurvy in the summertime, in the midst of an agricultural region filled with all manner of green vegetables, must forever remain impossible of explanation.

We again began to be exceedingly solicitous over the fate of Atlanta and Sherman's army. We had heard but little directly from that front for several weeks. Few prisoners had come in since those captured in the bloody engagements of the 20th, 22nd and 28th of July. In spite of their confident tones, and our own sanguine hopes, the outlook admitted of very grave doubts. The battles of the last week of July had been, to look at them in the best light possible, indecisive. Our men had held their own, it is true, but an invading army cannot afford simply to hold its own. Anything short of an absolute success is disguised defeat.

Then we knew that the cavalry column sent out by Stoneman had been so badly handled by that inefficient commander that it had failed ridiculously in its object, being beaten in detail and suffering the loss of its commander and a considerable portion of its numbers. This had been followed by a defeat of our infantry at Etowah Creek, and then came a long interval in which we received no news save what the rebel papers contained, and they pretended no doubt that Sherman's failure was already demonstrated. Next came the well-authenticated news that Sherman had raised the siege and fallen back to the Chattahoochee and we felt something of the bitterness of despair.

For days thereafter we heard nothing, though the hot, close summer air seemed supercharged with the premonitions of a war storm about to burst, even as Nature heralds in the same way a concentration of the mighty force of the elements for the grand crash of the thunderstorm. We waited in tense expectancy for the decision of the fates whether final victory or defeat should end the long, arduous campaign. At night the guards in the perches around the Stockade called out every half hour, so as to show the officers that they were awake and attending to their duty: "Post Numbah One; half past eight o'clock, and a-l-l-s w-e-l-l!" Post Number Two repeated this cry, and so it went around.

One evening when our anxiety as to Atlanta was wrought to the highest pitch, one of the guards sang out: "Post Numbah Foah, half past eight o'clock and Atlanta's gone to Hell!" The heart of every man within hearing leaped to his mouth. We looked toward each other, almost speechless with glad surprise, and then gasped out, "Did you *hear* that?" The next instant such a ringing cheer burst out as wells spontaneously from the throats and hearts of men in the first ecstatic moments of victory, a cheer to which our saddened hearts and enfeebled lungs had long been strangers. It was the genuine, honest, manly Northern cheer, as different from the shrill rebel yell as the honest mastiff's deep-voiced welcome is from the howl of a prowling wolf. The shout was taken up all over the prison. Even those who had not heard the guard understood that it meant that "Atlanta was ours and fairly won." They took up the acclamation with as much enthusiasm as we had begun it. All thoughts of sleep were put to flight; we would have a season of rejoicing.

Little groups gathered together, debated the news and indulged in the most sanguine hopes as to the effect upon the rebels. In some parts of the Stockade, stump speeches were made. I believe that Boston Corbett [37] and his party organized a "prayer and praise" meeting. In our corner we stirred up our tuneful friend Nosey, who sang again the grand old patriotic hymns that set our thin blood to bounding and made us remember that we were still Union soldiers with higher hopes than that of starving and dying in Andersonville. He sang the everlasting, glorious, "Star-Spangled Banner" as he used to sing it around the campfire in happier days when we were in the field, and the rousing "Rally Round the Flag" with all its wealth of patriotic fire and martial vigor. And we, with throats hoarse from shouting, joined in the chorus until the welkin rang again.

The rebels became excited lest our exultation of spirits would lead to an assault upon the Stockade. They got under arms and remained so until the enthusiasm became less demonstrative. A few days later, on the evening of September 6th, the rebel sergeants who called the roll entered the Stockade, and each assembling his squads, addressed them as follows: "Prisoners, I am instructed by General Winder to inform you that a general exchange has been agreed upon. Twenty thousand men will be exchanged at Savannah where your vessels are waiting for you. Detachments from One to Ten will prepare to leave tomorrow morning."

The excitement that this news produced was simply indescribable. I had seen men in every possible exigency that could confront men, and a large proportion had viewed that which impended with at least outward composure. These boys around me had endured all that we had suffered with stoical firmness. Groans from pain-wracked bodies could not be repressed, and bitter curses and maledictions against the rebels leaped unbidden to the lips at the slightest occasion, but there was no murmuring or whining. There was not a day, hardly an hour, in which one did not see such exhibitions of manly fortitude as made him proud of belonging to a race of which every individual was a hero. But the emotion which pain and suffering and danger could not develop, joy could, and boys sang and shouted and cried and danced as if in a delirium. "God's Country," fairer than that sweet Promised Land of Canaan appeared to the rapt vision of the Hebrew poet-prophet, spread out in glad vista before the mind's eye of everyone. It had come—at last it had come—that which we had so longed for, wished for, prayed for, dreamed of; which we had schemed, planned, toiled for; which had been the last wish of those thousands of our comrades who would now know no exchange save into that eternal "God's Country" where

> sickness and sorrow, pain and death
> are felt and feared no more.

Our preparations for leaving were few and simple. When the morning came and shortly after the order to move, Andrews and I picked up our well-worn blanket, our tattered overcoat, our rude chessmen and no less rude board, our little black can and the spoon made of hoop-iron, and bade farewell to the hole in the ground that had been our home for eight long months. My feet were still in miserable condition from the lacerations received in the attempt to escape, but I took one of our tent poles and hobbled away.

We re-passed the gates which we had entered on that February night, ages since, it seemed, and crawled slowly over to the depot. I had come to regard the rebels around us as such measureless liars that my first impulse was to believe the reverse of anything they said to us. Even now, while I hoped for the best, my old habit of mind was so strongly upon me that I had some doubts of our going to be exchanged, simply because it was a rebel who said so. But in the crowd of rebels who stood close to the road along which we were walking was a young second lieutenant who said to a colonel as I passed, "Well, those fellows *can* sing 'Homeward Bound,' can't they?" This set my misgiving at rest. Now I was certain that we were going to be exchanged, and my spirits soared to the skies.

Entering the cars, we thumped and pounded toilsomely along after the manner of Southern railroads at the rate of six or eight miles an hour. Savannah was two hundred and forty miles away, and to our impatient minds it seemed as if we would never get there. The route lay the whole distance through the cheerless pine barrens which cover the greater part of Georgia. The only considerable town on the way was Macon, which then had a population of five thousand or thereabouts. For scores of miles there would not be a sign of a human habitation. In the one hundred and eighty miles between Macon and Savannah there were but three insignificant villages. There was a station every ten miles where the only building was an open shed to shelter from the sun and rain a casual passenger or a bit of goods.

The occasional specimens of the poor white "cracker" population that we saw seemed indigenous products of the starved soil. They suited their poverty-stricken surroundings as well as the gnarled and scrubby vegetation suited the sterile sand. Thin-chested, round-shouldered, scraggy-bearded, dull-eyed and open-mouthed, they all looked alike, all looked as ignorant, as stupid and as lazy, as they were poor and weak. They were "low-downers" in every respect and made our rough and simple-minded East Tennesseans look like models of elegant and cultured gentlemen in contrast. We looked on the poverty-stricken land with good-natured contempt, for we thought we were leaving it forever and would soon be in one which, compared to it, was as the fatness of Egypt to the leanness of the desert of Sinai.

The second day after leaving Andersonville, our train struggled across the swamps into Savannah and rolled slowly down the live-oak-shaded streets into the center of the city. It seemed like another Deserted Village, so vacant and noiseless the streets, and the buildings everywhere so overgrown with luxuriant vegetation. The limbs of the shade trees crashed along and broke upon the tops of the cars, as if no train had passed that way for years. Through the interstices between the trees and clumps of foliage could be seen the gleaming white marble of the monuments erected to Greene and Pulaski looking like giant tombstones in a City of the Dead. The unbroken stillness, so different from what we had expected on entering the metropolis of Georgia and a city that was an important port in Revolutionary days, became absolutely oppressive.

We could not understand it, but our thoughts were more intent upon the coming transfer to our flag than upon any speculation as to the cause of the remarkable somnolence of Savannah. Finally, some little boys straggled out to where our car was standing, and we opened conversation with them: "Say boys, are our vessels down in the harbor yet?"

The reply came in piercing treble shriek in which a boy of ten or twelve makes even his most confidential communications: "I don't know."

"Well," with our confidence in exchange somewhat dashed, "they intend to exchange us here, don't they?"

Another falsetto scream: "I don't know."

"Well," with something of a quaver in the questioner's voice, "what are they going to do with us, anyway?"

"Oh—" a treble shriek that became almost demoniac, "—they are fixing up a place over by the old jail for you!"

What a sinking of hearts there was then! Andrews and I would not give up hope so speedily as the others did and resolved to believe, for a while at least, that we were going to be exchanged. Ordered out of the cars, we were marched along the street. A crowd of small boys, full of the curiosity of the animal, gathered around us as we marched. Suddenly a door in a rather nice house opened. An angry-faced woman appeared on the steps and shouted: "Boys! Boys! Come away from them n-a-s-t-y things!" I will admit that we were not prepossessing in appearance, nor were we as cleanly as young gentlemen should habitually be. In fact, I may as well confess that I would not now, if I could help it, allow a tramp as dilapidated in raiment, as unwashed, unshorn, uncombed and populous with insects as we were, to come within several rods of me. Nevertheless, it was not pleasant to hear so accurate a description of our personal appearance set forth on the wings of the wind by a shrill-voiced rebel female.

A short march brought us to the place "they were fixing for us by the old jail." It was another pen, with high walls of thick pine plank which told us only too plainly how vain were our expectations of exchange. When we were turned inside and I realized that the gates of another prison had closed upon me, hope forsook me. I flung our odious little possessions—our can, chess-board, overcoat and blanket—upon the ground and, sitting down beside them, gave way to the bitterest despair. I wanted to die. Never in all my life had I desired anything in the world so much as I now did to get out of it. Had I had a pistol, knife, rope or poison, I would have ended my prison life then and there, and departed with the unceremoniousness of French leave. I remembered that I could get a quietus from a guard with very little trouble, but I would not give one of the bitterly hated rebels the triumph of shooting me. I longed to be another Samson, with the whole Southern Confederacy gathered in another Temple of Dagon, that I might pull down the supporting pillars and die happy in slaying thousands of my enemies.

While I was thus sinking deeper and deeper into the Slough of Despond, the firing of a musket and the shriek of a man who was struck attracted my attention. Looking towards the opposite end of the pen, I saw a guard bringing his still smoking musket to "receive arms" and, not fifteen feet from him, a prisoner lying on the ground in the agonies of death. The latter had a pipe in his mouth when he was shot and his teeth still clenched its stem. His legs and arms were drawn up convulsively and he was rocking backward and forward on his back. The charge had struck him above the hip bone. The rebel officer in command of the guard was sitting on his horse inside the pen at the time, and rode forward to see what the matter was.

Lieutenant Davis, who had come with us from Andersonville, was also sitting on his horse inside the prison and he called out in his usual harsh, disagreeable voice: "That's all right, Cunnel; the man's done just as I awdahed him to." I found that lying around inside were a number of bits of plank, each about five feet long, which had been sawed off by carpenters engaged in building the prison. The ground, being a bare common, was destitute of shelter and the pieces looked as if they would be quite useful in building a tent. There may have been an order issued forbidding the prisoners to touch them but if so, I had not heard it, and I imagine the first intimation to the prisoner just killed that the boards were not to be taken was the bullet which penetrated his vitals. Twenty-five cents would be a liberal appraisal of the value of the lumber for which the boy lost his life.

Half an hour afterward we thought we saw all the guards march out the front gate. There was still another pile of the same kind of pieces of board lying at the further side of the prison. The crowd around me noticed it and we all made a rush for it. In spite of my lame feet, I outstripped the rest and was just in the act of stooping down to pick up the boards when a loud yell from those behind startled me. Glancing to my left, I saw a guard cocking his gun and bringing it up to shoot me. With one frightened spring, quick as a flash and before he could cover me, I landed fully a rod back in the crowd and mixed with it. The fellow tried hard to draw a bead on me, but I was too quick for him and he finally lowered his gun with an oath expressive of disappointment in not being able to kill a Yankee. Walking back to my place, the full ludicrousness of the thing dawned on me so forcibly that I forgot all about my excitement and scare and laughed out loud.

Here, not an hour ago, I was murmuring because I could find no way to die.

I sighed for death as a bridegroom for the coming of his bride, and yet when a rebel had pointed his gun at me, it had nearly scared me out of a year's growth and made me jump farther than I could possibly do when my feet were well! I was in good condition otherwise.

The Idiotic Flute Player

CHAPTER XV

ESCAPING BY WHOLESALE——RECAPTURED EN MASSE

ANDREWS AND I did not let the the fate of the boy who was killed nor my own narrow escape from losing the top of my head deter us from further efforts to secure possession of those coveted boards. It was something like the story of the boy digging vigorously at a hole, who replied to the remark of a passing traveler that there was probably no groundhog there and even if there was "groundhog was mighty poor eatin' anyway," with "Mister, there's *got* to be a groundhog there—our family's out o' meat!"

That was whát actuated us. We were out of material for a tent. Our solitary blanket had rotted and was worn full of holes by its long double duty as bedclothes and tent at Andersonville and there was an imperative call for a substitute. Andrews and I flattered ourselves that when we matched our collective or individual wits against those of a "Johnny," his defeat was pretty certain, and with this cheerful estimate of our own powers to animate us, we set to work to steal the boards from under the guard's nose. The Johnny had malice in his heart and buck and ball in his musket, but his eyes were not sufficiently numerous to discharge adequately all the duties laid upon him. He had too many different things to watch at the same time.

I would approach a gap in the fence not yet closed as if I intended making a dash through it for liberty and when the Johnny had concentrated all his attention on letting me have the contents of his gun just as soon as he could have a reasonable excuse for doing so, Andrews would pick up a couple of boards and slip away with them. Then I would fall back in pretended (and some real) alarm and Andrews would come up and draw his attention by a similar feint, while I made off with a couple more pieces. After a few hours of this strategy, we found ourselves the possessors of some dozen planks with which we made a lean-to that formed a tolerable shelter for our heads and the upper portion of our bodies. As the boards were not over five feet long and the slope reduced the sheltered space to about four and a half feet, it left the *lower* part of our naked feet and legs to project "out of doors."

Andrews used to lament very touchingly the sunburning his toenails were receiving. He knew that his complexion was being ruined for life, and all the balm of all the flowers in the world would not restore his comely ankles to that condition of pristine loveliness which would admit of their introduction into good society again. Another defect was that, like the fun in a practical joke, it was all on one side—there was not enough of it to go clear round. It was very unpleasant, when a storm came up in a direction different from that we had calculated upon, to be compelled to get out in the midst of it and build our house over to face the other way. Still, we had a tent and were that much better off than three fourths of our comrades, who had no shelter at all. We were owners of a "brown stone front" on Fifth Avenue compared to the other fellows.

Our tent erected, we began a general survey of our new abiding place. The ground was a sandy common in the outskirts of Savannah. The sand was covered with a light sod. The rebels, who knew nothing of our burrowing propensities, had neglected to make the planks forming the walls of the prison project any distance below the surface of the ground, and had put up no "Dead Line" around the inside, so that it looked as if everything was arranged expressly to invite us to tunnel out. We were not the boys to neglect such an invitation. By noon about three thousand had been received from Andersonville and placed inside. When morning came it looked as if a colony of gigantic rats had been at work. There were tunnels every ten or fifteen feet, and at least twelve hundred of us had gone out through them during the night. I never understood why all in the pen did not follow our example and leave the guards watching a forsaken prison. There was nothing to prevent it. An hour's industrious work with a half-canteen would take anyone outside or, if a boy was too lazy to dig his own tunnel, he could have the use of one of the hundred others that had been dug.

But escaping was only begun when the Stockade was passed. The site of Savannah is virtually an island. On the north is the Savannah River; to the east, southeast and south are the two Ogeechee rivers and a chain of sounds and lagoons connecting with the Atlantic Ocean. To the west is a canal connecting the Savannah and Big Ogeechee rivers. We found ourselves headed off by water whichever way we went. All the bridges were guarded and all the boats destroyed. Early in the morning the rebels discovered our absence and the whole garrison of Savannah was sent out on patrol after us. They picked up the boys, in squads of from ten to thirty, lurking around the shores of the streams waiting for night to come to get across, or engaged in building rafts for transportation. By evening the whole mob of us were back in the pen again. As nobody was punished for running away, we treated the whole affair as a lark and those brought back first stood around the gate and yelled derisively as the others came in. That night big fires were built all around the Stockade and a line of guards placed on the ground inside of these. In spite of this precaution, quite a number escaped.

The next day a Dead Line was put up inside the prison, twenty feet from the Stockade walls.

This only increased the labor of burrowing by making us go farther. Instead of being able to tunnel out in an hour, it now took three or four hours. That night several hundred of us, rested from our previous performance and hopeful of better luck, brought our faithful half-canteens, now scoured very bright by constant use, into requisition again and before morning dawned we gained the high reeds of the swamps where we lay concealed until night. In this way we managed to evade the recapture that came to most of those who went out, but it was a fearful experience.

Having been raised in a country where venomous snakes abounded, I had that fear and horror of them that inhabitants of those districts feel and of which people living in sections free from such a scourge know little. I fancied that the southern swamps were filled with all forms of loathsome and poisonous reptiles, and it required all my courage to venture into them barefooted. Besides, the snags and roots hurt our feet fearfully. Our hope was to find a boat somewhere in which we could float out to sea and trust to being picked up by some of the blockading fleet. But we could find no boat with all our diligent and painful search. We learned afterward that the rebels made a practice of breaking up all the boats along the shore to prevent Negroes and their own deserters from escaping to the blockading fleet. We thought of making a raft of logs, but had we had the strength to do this, we would doubtless have thought it too risky since we dreaded missing the vessels and being carried out to sea to perish of hunger.

During the night we came to the railroad bridge across the Ogeechee. We had some slender hope that if we could reach this we might perhaps get across the river and find better opportunities for escape. But these last expectations were blasted by the discovery that it was guarded. There was a post and a fire on the shore next to us, and a single guard with a lantern was stationed on one of the middle spans. Almost famished with hunger and so weary and footsore that we could scarcely move another step, we went back to a cleared place on the high ground and lay down to sleep, entirely reckless as to what became of us. Late in the morning we were awakened by the rebel patrol and taken back to the prison.

Lieutenant Davis, disgusted with the perpetual attempts to escape, moved the Dead Line out forty feet from the Stockade wall; but this restricted our room greatly, since the number of prisoners in the pen had now risen to about six thousand and, besides, it offered little protection against tunneling. It was not much more difficult to dig fifty feet than it had been to dig thirty feet. Davis soon realized this and put the Dead Line back to twenty feet. His next device was a much more sensible one. A crowd of one hundred and fifty Negroes dug a trench twenty-five feet wide and five feet deep around the whole prison on the outside. This ditch was filled with water from the city water works. No one could cross this without attracting the attention of the guards. Still we were not discouraged, and Andrews and I joined a crowd that was constructing a large tunnel from near our quarters on the east side of the pen. We finished the burrow to within a few inches of the edge of the ditch and then ceased operations to await some stormy night when we could get across the ditch unnoticed. Orders were issued to the guards to fire without warning on men who were observed to be digging or carrying out dirt after nightfall. They occasionally did so, but the risk did not keep anyone from tunneling.

Our tunnel ran directly under a sentry box. When carrying dirt away, the bearer of a bucket had to turn his back on the guard and walk directly down the street in front of him, two or three hundred feet to the center of the camp, where he scattered the sand around so as to give no indication of where it came from. Though we always waited till the moon went down, it seemed as if, unless the guard were a fool both by nature and training, he could not help taking notice of what was going on under his eyes. I do not recall any more nervous promenades in my life than those when, taking my turn, I received my bucket of sand at the mouth of the tunnel and walked slowly away with it. The most disagreeable part was turning my back to the guard. Could I have faced him, I had sufficient confidence in my quickness of perception and talents as a dodger to imagine that I could make it difficult for him to hit me. But in walking with my back to him, I was wholly at his mercy. Fortune, however, favored us and we were allowed to go on with our work night after night without a shot.

Meanwhile another happy thought slowly gestated in Davis's alleged intellect. How he came to give birth to two ideas with no more than a week between them puzzled all who knew him, and it was still more of a puzzle that he survived this extraordinary strain upon the gray matter of his cerebrum. His new idea was to have a heavily laden mule cart driven around the inside of the Dead Line at least once a day. Either the wheels or the mule's feet broke through the thin sod covering the tunnels and exposed them. Our tunnel went with the rest, and those of our crowd who wore shoes had humiliation added to sorrow by being compelled to go in and spade the hole full of dirt. This put an end to the subterranean engineering. One day one of the boys watched his opportunity, got under the ration wagon and, clinging close to the coupling pole with hands and feet, was carried outside. He was detected, however, as he came from under the wagon and brought back.

One of the shrewdest and nearest successful attempts to escape that came under my notice was that of my friend, Sergeant Frank Beverstock of the 3rd West Virginia Cavalry. Frank, who was quite small and had a smooth boyish face, had converted to his own use a citizen's coat belonging to a young boy, a sutler's assistant, who had died in Andersonville. He had made himself a pair of bag pantaloons and a shirt from pieces of meal sacks which he had appropriated from day to day. He had also the sutler's assistant's shoes, and to crown all, he wore on his head one of those hideous-looking hats of quilted calico which the rebels had taken to wearing due to the lack of felt hats, which they could neither make nor buy. Altogether, Frank looked enough like a rebel to be dangerous to trust near a country store or a stable full of horses.

When we first arrived in the prison, quite a crowd of the Savannahians rushed in to inspect us. The guards had some difficulty in keeping them and us separate. While perplexed with this annoyance, one of them saw Frank standing in our crowd and, touching him with his bayonet, said with some sharpness, "See heah; you must stand back; you mustn't crowd on them prisoners so." Frank stood back. He did it promptly but calmly and then, as if his curiosity as to Yankees was fully satisfied, he walked slowly away up the street, deliberating as he went on a plan for getting out of the city. He hit upon an excellent one. Going to the engineer of a freight train making ready to start back to Macon, he told him that his father was working in the Confederate machine shops at Griswoldville near Macon, that he himself was also one of the machinists employed there, and that he desired to go there but lacked the necessary means to pay his passage. If the engineer would let him ride up on the engine, he would do work enough to pay his fare.

Frank told the story ingenuously. The engineer and fireman were won over and gave their consent. No more zealous assistant ever climbed upon a tender than Frank proved to be. He loaded wood with a nervous industry that stood him in place of great strength. He kept the tender in perfect order and anticipated, as far as possible, every want of the engineer and his assistant. They were delighted and treated him with great kindness, dividing their food with him and insisting that he should share their bed when they "laid by" for the night. Frank would have gladly declined this latter kindness with thanks, as he was conscious that the quantity of "graybacks" his clothing contained did not make him a very desirable sleeping companion for anyone, but his friends were so pressing that he was compelled to accede.

His greatest trouble was fear of recognition by some one of the prisoners continually passing by by the train-load on their way from Andersonville to other prisons. He had been one of the best known of the prisoners in Andersonville, bright, active, always cheerful and forever in motion during waking hours. Everyone in the prison speedily became familiar with him and all addressed him as "Sergeant Frankie." If anyone on the passing trains had caught a glimpse of him, that glimpse would have been followed almost inevitably with a shout of: "Hello, Sergeant Frankie! What are you doing there?" Then the whole game would have been up. Frank escaped this by persistent watchfulness and by busying himself on the opposite side of the engine, keeping his back to the passing trains.

At last—nearing Griswoldville—Frank, pointing to a large white house at some distance across the fields, said, "Now, right over there is where my uncle lives. I believe I'll just run over and see him and then walk to Griswoldville." He thanked his friends fervently for their kindness, promised to call and see them frequently, bade them good-by and jumped off the train. He walked towards the white house as long as he thought he could be seen, and then entered a large corn field and concealed himself in the center of a thicket until dark, when he made his way to the neighboring woods and began journeying northward as fast as his legs could carry him.

When morning broke, he had made good progress but was terribly tired. It was not prudent to travel by daylight, so he gathered himself some ears of corn and some berries, made his breakfast and, finding a suitable thicket, he crawled into it, fell asleep and did not wake up until late in the afternoon. After another meal of raw corn and berries, he resumed his journey and that night made still better progress. He repeated this for several days and nights, lying in the woods in the daytime, traveling by night through woods, fields and by-paths, avoiding all fords, bridges and main roads, and living on what he could glean from the fields, not taking even as much risk as was involved in going to the Negro cabins for food.

But there are always flaws in every man's armor of caution, even in so perfect an armor as Frank's. His complete success so far had the natural effect of inducing a growing carelessness which wrought his ruin. One evening he started off briskly after a refreshing rest and sleep. He knew that he must be very near Sherman's lines, and hope cheered him up with the belief that his freedom would soon be won. Descending from the hill in whose dense brushwood he had made his bed all day, he entered a large field of standing corn and made his way between the rows until on the other side he reached the fence that separated it from the main road across which was another corn field that Frank intended entering. But he neglected his usual precautions on approaching a road, and instead of coming up cautiously and carefully reconnoitering in all directions before he left cover, he sprang boldly over the fence and strode out for the other side.

As he reached the middle of the road, his ears were assailed with a sharp click of a musket being cocked and the harsh command: "Halt! Halt, dah, I say!" Turning with a start to his left, he saw not ten feet from him a mounted patrol, the sound of whose approach had been masked by the deep dust of the road into which his horse's hooves sank noiselessly. Frank, of course, yielded without a word. And when sent to the officer in command, he told a story about his being an employee of the Griswold-ville shops off on a leave of absence to make a visit to sick relatives. But unfortunately his captors, who belonged to that section themselves, speedily caught him in a maze of cross-questioning from which he could not extricate himself. It also became apparent from his language that he was a Yankee, and it was not far from this to the conclusion that he was a spy, a conclusion in which the proximity of Sherman's lines, then less than twenty miles distant, greatly assisted.

By the next morning this belief had become so firmly fixed in the minds of the rebels that Frank saw a halter dangling alarmingly near and he concluded the wisest plan was to confess who he really was. It was not the smallest of his griefs to realize by how slight a chance he had failed. Had he looked down the road before he climbed the fence or had he been ten minutes earlier or later, the patrol would not have been there; he could have gained the next field unseen, and two more nights of successful progress would have taken him into Sherman's lines at Sand Mountain. The patrol which caught him was on the look-out for deserters and shirking conscripts who had become unusually numerous since the fall of Atlanta. He was sent back to us at Savannah. As he came into the prison gate, Lieutenant Davis was standing near. He looked sternly at Frank and his rebel garments and muttering "By God, I'll stop this," caught the coat by the tails, tore it to the collar and took it and his hat away from Frank.

There was a strange sequel to this episode. A few weeks afterward a special exchange for ten thousand was made, and Frank succeeded in being included in this. He was given the usual furlough from the parole camp at Annapolis and went to his home in a little town near Mansfield, Ohio. One day while on the cars going, I think, to Newark, Ohio, he saw Lieutenant Davis on the train in citizen clothes. He had been sent by the rebel government to Canada with his dispatches relating to some of the raids then harassing our northern borders. Davis was the last man in the world to disguise himself successfully. He had a large, coarse mouth, that made him remembered by all who had ever seen him. Frank recognized him instantly and said: "You are Lieutenant Davis?"

"You are totally mistaken, sah, I am—" began Davis, somewhat discomfited. Frank insisted that he was right. Davis fumed and blustered but though Frank was small he was as game as a bantam rooster and he gave Davis to understand that there had been a vast change in their relative positions—that the one, while still the same insolent swaggerer, had not regiments of infantry or batteries of artillery to emphasize his insolence, and the other was no longer embarrassed in the discussion by the immense odds in favor of his jailer opponent. After a stormy scene, Frank called in the assistance of some other soldiers in the car, arrested Davis, and took him to Camp Chase near Columbus, Ohio, where he was fully identified by a number of paroled prisoners. He was searched, and documents showing the nature of his business beyond a doubt were found on his person. A court martial was immediately convened for his trial. This found him guilty and sentenced him to be hanged as a spy. At the conclusion of the trial, Frank stepped up to the prisoner and said quietly, "Mr. Davis, I believe we're even on that coat now."

Davis went to Johnson's Island for execution, but influences were immediately set at work to secure Executive clemency. What they were I do not know, but I am informed by the Reverend Robert McCune, then Chaplain of the 128th Ohio Infantry and the Post of Johnson's Island and the spiritual adviser appointed to prepare Davis for execution, that the sentence was hardly pronounced before Davis was visited by an emissary who told him to dismiss his fears, that he would not suffer punishment. It is likely that leading Baltimore Unionists were enlisted in his behalf through family connections, and as the border state Unionists were potent at Washington, they readily secured a commutation of his sentence to imprisonment during the war. It seems that the justice of this world is very unevenly dispensed when so much solicitude is shown for the life of such a man and none at all for the much better men whom he assisted to destroy.

The official notice of the commutation of the sentence was not published until the day set for the execution, but the certain knowledge that it would be forthcoming enabled Davis to display a great deal of bravado on approaching what was supposed to be his end. Davis was the man to improve to the utmost every opportunity to strut his little hour, and he did it in this instance. He posed and vapored, so that the camp and the country were filled with stories of the wonderful coolness with which he contemplated his approaching fate. Among other things, he said to his guard, as he washed himself elaborately the night before the day announced for his execution, "Well, you can be sure of one thing; tomorrow night there will certainly be *one* clean corpse on this island." Unfortunately for his braggadocio, he let it leak out in some way that he had been well aware all the time that he would not be executed. He was taken to Fort Delaware for confinement, and died there some time after.

Frank Beverstock went back to his regiment and served with it until the close of the war. He then returned home, and after a while became a banker in Bowling Green, Ohio. He was a fine business man and in time grew very prosperous. But though naturally healthy and vigorous, his system carried in it the seeds of death sown there by the hardships of captivity. He was one of the victims of the rebel vaccinations. The virus injected into his blood caused a large part of his right temple to slough off and left a ghastly cicatrix. Two years later he was taken suddenly ill and died before his friends had any idea that his condition was serious.

"He Crushed It All Out of Shape!"

CHAPTER XVI

WINDER, MAN WITH THE EVIL EYE

SAVANNAH WAS A WONDERFUL IMPROVEMENT on Andersonville. We got away from the pestilential swamp and that poisonous ground. Every mouthful of air was not laden with disease germs nor every cup of water polluted with the seeds of death. The earth did not breed gangrene nor the atmosphere promote fever. As only the more vigorous had come away, we were freed from the depressing spectacle of every third man dying. The keen disappointment prostrated many who had been of average health and, I imagine, several hundred died, but there were hospital arrangements of some kind and the sick were taken away from among us. Those of us who tunneled out had an opportunity of stretching our legs which we had not had for months in the overcrowded Stockade which we had left. The attempts to escape did all who engaged in them good even though they failed, since they aroused new ideas and hopes, set the blood into more rapid circulation and toned up the mind and system both.

I had come away from Andersonville with considerable scurvy manifesting itself in my gums and feet. Soon these signs almost wholly disappeared. We also got away from those murderous little brats of Reserves who guarded us at Andersonville and shot men down as they would stone apples out of a tree. Our guards were now mostly sailors from the rebel fleet in the harbor—Irishmen, Englishmen and Scandinavians, as free-hearted and kindly as sailors always are. I do not think they ever fired a shot at one of us. The only trouble we had was with that portion of the guard that was drawn from the infantry of the garrison. They had the same rattlesnake venom of the Home

Guard crowd wherever we met it, and shot us down at the least provocation. Fortunately, they formed only a small part of the sentinels. Best of all, we escaped for a while from the upas-like shadows of Winder and Wirz, in whose presence strong men sickened and died, as though near some malign genii in an Oriental story.

The peasantry of Italy believed firmly in the "evil eye." Had they ever known such men as Winder and Wirz, his satellite, I could comprehend how much foundation they might have for such a belief. Lieutenant Davis had many faults, but there was no comparison between him and the Andersonville commandant. He was a typical young Southern man, ignorant and bumptious as to the most common matters of schoolboy knowledge, inordinately vain of himself and his family, coarse in tastes and thoughts, violent in his prejudices, but after all with some streaks of honor and generosity that made the widest possible difference between him and Wirz, who never had any.

As one of my chums said to me, "Wirz is the most even-tempered man I ever saw—he's always foaming mad." This was nearly the truth. I never saw Wirz when he was not angry; if not violently abusive, he was cynical and sardonic. Never in my little experience with him did I detect a glint of kindly, generous humanity; if he ever was moved by any sight of suffering, its exhibition in his face escaped my eye. If he ever had even a wish to mitigate the pain or hardship of any man, the expression of such wish never fell on my ear. How a man could move daily through such misery as he encountered and never be moved by it except to scorn and mocking is beyond my limited understanding. Davis vapored a great deal, swearing big round oaths in the broadest Southern patois; he was perpetually threatening to "open on ye wid de ahtillery." But the only death that I knew him to cause directly or sanction was that which I have previously described. He would not put himself out of the way to annoy and oppress prisoners as Wirz would, but frequently showed a disposition to humor them in some little thing when it could be done without danger or trouble to himself. Later, however, he got an idea that there was some money to be made out of the prisoners, and he set his wits to work in this direction.

One day, standing at the gate, he gave one of his peculiar yells that he used to attract the attention of the camp with: "Wh-ah-ye!" We all came to "attention" and he announced: "Yesterday, while I wuz in the camps, some of you prisoners picked my pockets of seventy-five dollars in greenbacks. Now I give you notice that I'll not send in any more rations 'til the money's returned to me." This was a very stupid method of extortion, since no one believed that he had lost the money, and at all events he had no business to have the greenbacks as the rebel laws imposed severe penalties upon any citizen and still more upon any soldier dealing with, or having in his possession, any of "the money of the enemy." We did without rations until night when they were sent in.

There was a story that some of the boys in the prison had contributed to make up part of the sum and that Davis took it and was satisfied. I do not know how true the story was. At another time some of the boys stole the bridle and halter off an old horse that was driven in with a cart. The things were worth—at a liberal estimate— one dollar. Davis cut off the rations of the whole six thousand of us for one day for this. We always imagined that the proceeds went into his pocket.

A special exchange was arranged between our Navy Department and that of the rebels by which all seamen and marines among us were exchanged. Lists of these were sent to the different prisons and the men called for. About three fourths of them were dead, but many soldiers, divining the situation of affairs, answered to the dead men's names, went away with the squad and were exchanged. Much of this was done through the connivance of the rebel officers, who favored those who had ingratiated themselves with them. In many instances money was paid to secure this privilege, and I have been informed on good authority that Jack Huckleby of the 8th Tennessee and Ira Beverly of the 100th Ohio, who kept the big sutler shop on the North Side at Andersonville, paid Davis five hundred dollars each to be allowed to go with the sailors. As for Andrews and me, we had no friends among the rebels nor money to bribe them with, so we stood no show.

The rations issued to us for some time after our arrival seemed riotous luxury to what we had been getting at Andersonville. Each of us received daily a half-dozen rude and coarse imitations of our fondly remembered hardtack, and with these a small piece of meat or a few spoonfuls of molasses, a quart or so of vinegar and several plugs of tobacco for each hundred. How exquisite was the taste of the crackers and molasses! It was the first wheat bread I had eaten since my entry into Richmond months before, and molasses had been strange to me for years. After the corn bread we had so long lived upon, this was manna. It seems that the Commissary at Savannah labored under the delusion that he must issue to us the same rations as were served out to the rebel soldiers and sailors.

It was some little time before the fearful mistake came to the knowledge of Winder. I fancy the news almost threw him into an apoplectic fit. Nothing, save his being ordered to the front, could have caused him such poignant sorrow as the information that so much good food had been worse than wasted in undoing his work by building up the bodies of his hated enemies. Without being told, we knew that he had been heard from when the tobacco, vinegar and molasses failed to come in and the crackers gave way to corn meal. Still, this was a vast improvement on Andersonville, as the meal was fine and we each had a spoonful of salt issued to us regularly.

I am quite sure that I cannot make the reader who has not had an experience similar to ours comprehend the wonderful importance to us of that spoonful of salt. Whether or not the appetite for salt be, as some scientists claim, a purely artificial want, one thing is certain and that is that either the habit of countless generations or some other cause has so deeply ingrained this craving that it has come to be nearly as essential as food itself, and no amount of deprivation can accustom us to its absence. Rather, it seemed that the longer we did without it the more overpowering became our craving. I could get along today and tomorrow, perhaps the whole week, without salt in my food, since the lack would be supplied from the excess I had already swallowed. But at the end of that time Nature would begin to demand that I renew the supply of saline constituent of my tissues, and she would become more clamorous with every day that I neglected her bidding and finally summon Nausea to aid Longing.

The light artillery of the garrison at Savannah, four batteries of twenty-four pieces, was stationed around three sides of the prison—the guns unlimbered, planted at convenient distance and trained upon us ready for instant use. We could see all the grinning mouths through the cracks in the fence. There were enough of them to send us as high as the traditional kite flown by Gilderoy. The having at his beck this array of frowning metal lent Lieutenant Davis such an importance in his own eyes that his demeanor swelled to the grandiose. It became very amusing to see him puff up and vaunt over it as he did on every possible occasion. For instance, finding a crowd of several hundred lounging around the gate, he would throw open the wicket, stalk in with the air of a Jove threatening a rebellious world with the dread thunders of heaven, and shout, "W-h-a-a y-e-e! Prisoners, I give you jist two minutes to cleah away from this gate, aw I'll open on ye wid de ahtillery!"

One of the buglers in the artillery was a superb musician, evidently some old "regular" whom the Confederacy had seduced into its service, and his instrument was so sweet-toned that we imagined that it was made of silver. The calls he played were nearly the same as we used in the cavalry, and for the first few days we became bitterly homesick every time he sent ringing out the old familiar signals that to us were so closely associated with what now seemed the bright and happy days when we were in the field with the battalion. If we were only back in the valleys of Tennessee with what alacrity we would respond to that "assembly." No orderly's patience would be worn out in getting laggards and lazy ones to "fall in for roll call." How eagerly we would attend to "stable duty." How gladly we would mount our faithful horses and ride away to "water," and what bareback races going and coming. We would be even glad to hear "guard" and "drill" sounded; and there would be music in the disconsolate surgeon's call "Come—get—your—quinine. Come, get your quinine. It'll make you sad. It'll make you sick. Come, come." Oh! If we were only back, what admirable soldiers we would be!

One morning about three or four o'clock, we were awakened by the ground shaking and a series of heavy, dull thumps sounding off to seaward. Our silver-voiced bugler seemed to be awakened, too. He set the echoes ringing with a vigorously played "reveille." A minute later came an equally earnest "assembly" and when "boots and saddles" followed, we knew that all was not well in Denmark. The thumping and shaking now had a significance. It meant heavy Yankee guns somewhere near. We heard the gunners hitching up, the bugle signal "forward," the wheels roll off. And for a half hour afterward we caught the receding sound of the bugle commanding "right turn," "left turn," as the batteries marched away.

Of course, we became considerably wrought up over the matter as, knowing we were in Savannah, we fancied that our vessels were trying to pass up to the city and take it. The thumping and shaking continued until late in the afternoon. We subsequently learned that some of the blockaders, finding time hanging on their hands, had essayed a little diversion by knocking Forts Jackson and Bledsoe, two small forts defending the passage of the Savannah, about their defender's ears. After capturing the forts our folks desisted and came no farther.

Quite a number of the old Raider crowd had come with us from Andersonville, among them the shyster, Peter Bradley. They kept up their old tactics of hanging around the gates, currying favor with the rebels in every possible way, in hopes to get paroles outside or other favors. The great mass of prisoners was so bitter against the rebels as to feel that they would rather die than ask or accept a favor from their hands, and they had little else than contempt for these trucklers. The Raider crowd's favorite theme of conversation with the rebels was the strong discontent of the boys with the manner of their treatment by our Government.

The assertion that there was any such widespread feeling was utterly false. We all had confidence that our Government would do everything possible for us consistent with its honor and the success of military operations. Outside of the little squad of which I speak, not an admission could be extracted from anybody that blame could be attached to anyone except the rebels. It was regarded as unmanly and unsoldierlike to the last degree, as well as senseless, to revile our Government for the crimes committed by its foes. But the rebels were led to believe that we were ripe for revolt against our flag and ready to side with them. Imagine, if you can, the stupidity that mistook our bitter hatred of those who were our deadly enemies for any feeling that would lead us to join hands with those enemies!

One day we were surprised to see carpenters erect a rude stand in the center of the camp. When it was finished, Bradley appeared upon it in company with some rebel officers and guards. We gathered around in curiosity and Bradley began making a speech. He said that it had now become apparent to all that our Government had abandoned us; that it cared little or nothing for us, since it could hire as many more quite readily by offering a bounty equal to the pay which would be due us now; that it cost only a few hundred dollars to bring over a shipload of Irish, Dutch and French who were only too glad to agree to fight or do anything else to get to this country. The peculiar impudence of this consisted in Bradley himself being a foreigner who had only come out under one of the later calls and the influence of big bounty. Continuing in this strain, he repeated and dwelt upon the old lie, always in the mouths of his crowd, that Secretary Stanton and General Halleck had positively refused to enter upon negotiations for exchange because those in prison were "only a miserable lot of 'coffee boilers' and 'blackberry pickers' whom the Army was better off without." [38]

The terms "coffee boilers" and "blackberry pickers" were considered the worst terms of disgrace we had in prison. They were applied to that class of stragglers and skulkers who were only too ready to give themselves up to the enemy and who, on coming in, told some gauzy story about "just having stopped to boil coffee" or to do something else which they should not have done when they were gobbled up. It is not risking much to affirm the probability that Bradley and most of his crowd belonged to this dishonorable class. The assertion that either the Chief of Staff or the great War Secretary were even capable of applying such epithets to the mass of prisoners is too preposterous to need refutation or even denial. No person outside the Raider crowd ever gave the silly lie a moment's toleration. Bradley concluded his speech in some such language as this: "And now, fellow prisoners, I propose to you this: that we unite in informing our Government that unless we are exchanged in thirty days, we will be forced by self-preservation to join the Confederate Army."

For an instant his hearers seemed stunned at the fellow's audacity, and then there went up such a roar of denunciation and execration that the air trembled. The rebels thought that the whole camp was going to rush on Bradley and tear him to pieces, and they drew their revolvers and leveled muskets to defend him. The uproar only ceased when Bradley was hurried out of the prison, but for hours afterward everybody was savage and sullen and full of threatenings against him when opportunity served. We never saw him afterward. Angry as I was, I could not help being amused at the tempestuous rage of a tall, fine-looking and well-educated Irish sergeant of an Illinois regiment. He poured forth denunciations of the traitor and the rebels with the vivid fluency of his Hibernian nature, vowed he'd "give a year of me life, be Jasus, to have the handling of the dirty spalpeen for ten minutes, be God——" and finally in his rage, tore off his own shirt and threw it on the ground and trampled on it.

Imagine my astonishment, some time after getting out of prison, to find the Southern papers publishing as a defense against the charges in regard to Andersonville a document which they claimed to have been adopted by "a mass meeting of prisoners":

> At a mass meeting held September 28th, 1864, by the Federal prisoners confined at Savannah, Georgia, it was unanimously agreed that the following resolutions be sent to the President of the United States, in the hope that he might thereby take such steps as in his wisdom he may think necessary for our speedy exchange or parole.

Bradley had sponsored this spurious document which, in effect, resolved that while the prisoners declared "unbounded love for the Union and the graves of those we venerate" and that while the "Confederate authorities merited all due praise" for the attention paid to prisoners, great numbers of men had died "by force of circumstances." The document went on to state that, now that winter was approaching and the men were in need of clothes—many being almost naked—it would behoove the national Government to arrange for exchange or paroles for these prisoners; otherwise, it stated, "we are not willing to suffer further the ends of any party or clique to the detriment of our honor, our families and our country, and we beg that this affair be explained to us, that we may continue to hold the Government in that respect which is necessary to make a good citizen and soldier." The document was signed by Bradley.

I will simply say this, that while I cannot pretend to know all or even much that went on around me, I do not think it was possible for a mass meeting of prisoners to be held without my knowing about it and its essential features. Still less was it possible for a mass meeting to have been held which would have adopted any such document or anything else that a rebel would have found the least pleasure in republishing. The whole thing is a brazen falsehood.

One of Ferguson's Cavalry

CHAPTER XVII

FALL OF ATLANTA

THE REASON of our being hurried out of Andersonville under the false pretext of exchange dawned on us before we had been in Savannah long. If the reader will consult the map of Georgia he will understand this, too. Let him remember that several of the railroads which now appear were not built then. The railroad upon which Andersonville is situated was about one hundred and twenty miles long, reaching from Macon to Americus, Andersonville being about midway between these two. It had no connections anywhere except at Macon and it was hundreds of miles across the country from Andersonville to any other road. When Atlanta fell, it brought our folks to within sixty miles of Macon, and any day they were liable to make a forward movement which would capture that place and have us where we could be retaken with ease.

There was nothing left undone to rouse the apprehensions of the rebels in that direction. The humiliating surrender of General Stoneman at Macon in July showed them what our folks were thinking of and awakened their minds to the disastrous consequences of such a movement when executed by a bolder and abler commander. Two days of one of Kilpatrick's swift, silent marches would carry his hard-riding troopers around Hood's right flank and into the streets of Macon, where a half-hour's work with the torch on the bridge across the Ocmulgee and the creeks that enter it at that point would have cut all of the Confederate Army of the Tennessee's communications. Another day and night of easy marching would bring Kilpatrick's guidons fluttering through the woods about the Stockade at Andersonville, and give him a reinforcement of twelve or fifteen thousand able-bodied [39] soldiers with whom he could hold the whole Valley of the Chattahoochee and become the nether millstone against which Sherman could have ground Hood's Army to powder. Such a thing was not only possible but very probable, and doubtless would have occurred had we remained in Andersonville another week.

Hence the haste to get us away, and hence the lie about exchange, for had it not been for this, one quarter at least of those taken on the cars would have succeeded in getting off and attempting to reach Sherman's lines. The removal went on with such rapidity that by the end of September only eight thousand two hundred and eighteen men remained at Andersonville, and these were mostly too sick to be moved. Two thousand seven hundred died in September, fifteen hundred and sixty in October, and four hundred and eighty-five in November, so that at the beginning of December there were only thirteen hundred and fifty-nine remaining. The larger part of those taken out were sent on to Charleston and subsequently to Florence and Salisbury. About six or seven thousand of us, as near as I remember, were brought to Savannah.

We were all exceedingly anxious to know how the Atlanta campaign had ended. So far, our information only comprised the facts that a sharp battle had been fought and the result was the complete possession of our great objective point. The manner of accomplishing this glorious end, the magnitude of the engagement, the regiments, brigades and corps participating, the losses on both sides, the completeness of the victories, were all matters that we knew nothing of and thirsted to learn. The rebel papers said as little as possible about the capture, and the facts in that little were so largely diluted with fiction as to convey no real information. But few new prisoners were coming in, and none of these were from Sherman. However, toward the last of September, a handful of "fresh fish" were turned inside whom our experienced eyes instantly told us were western boys. There was never any difficulty in telling, as far as he could be seen, whether a boy belonged to the east or to the west.

First, no one in the Army of the Potomac was ever without his corps badge worn conspicuously; it was rare to see such a thing on one of Sherman's men. Then there was the dressy air about the Army of the Potomac that was wholly wanting in the soldiers serving west of the Alleghanies. The Army of the Potomac was always near to its base of supplies, always had its stores accessible, and the care of the clothing and equipments of the men was an essential part of its discipline. A ragged or shabbily dressed man was a rarity. Dress coats, paper collars, fresh woolen shirts, neat-fitting pantaloons, good comfortable shoes, and trim caps or hats, with all the blazing brass of company letters an inch long, regimental number, bugle and eagle, all according to regulations, were as common to eastern boys as they were rare among the westerners.

The latter wore blouses instead of dress coats, and as a rule their clothing had not been renewed since the opening of the campaign, and it showed this. Those who wore good boots or shoes generally had to submit to forcible exchanges by their captors and the same was true of headgear. The rebels were badly off in regard to hats. They did not have skill and ingenuity enough to make these out of felt or straw and the makeshifts they contrived of quilted calico and long-leaved pine were ugly enough to frighten horned cattle. I never blamed them much for wanting to get rid of these, even if they did have to commit a sort of highway robbery upon defenseless prisoners to do so. To be a traitor in arms was bad enough, but one never appreciated the entire magnitude of the crime until he saw a rebel wearing a calico or a pine-leaf hat. Then one felt as if it would be a great mistake to ever show such a man mercy. The Army of Northern Virginia seemed to have supplied themselves with headgear of Yankee manufacture of previous years, and they then quit taking the hats of their prisoners. Johnston's Army did not have such good luck, and had to keep plundering to the end of the war.

Another thing about the Army of the Potomac was the variety of the uniforms. There were members of Zouave regiments wearing baggy breeches of various hues, gaiters, crimson fezzes and profusely braided jackets. One of the most striking uniforms was that of the 14th Brooklyn. They wore scarlet pantaloons, a blue jacket handsomely braided and a red fez with a white cloth wrapped around the head, turban fashion. As a large number of them were captured, they formed quite a picturesque feature of every crowd. They were generally good soldiers and likeable fellows.

Another uniform that attracted much, though not so favorable, attention was that of the 3rd New Jersey Cavalry, or 1st New Jersey Hussars, as they preferred to call themselves. The designer of that uniform must have had an interest in a curcuma plantation or else he was a fanatical Orangeman. Each uniform would furnish occasion enough for a dozen New York riots on July 12th. Never was such an eruption of the yellows seen outside of the jaundiced livery of some Eastern potentate. Down each leg of the pantaloons ran a stripe of yellow braid one and a half inches wide. The jacket had enormous gilt buttons and was embellished with yellow braid until it was difficult to tell whether it was blue cloth trimmed with yellow or yellow adorned with blue. From the shoulders swung a little false hussar jacket lined with the same flaring yellow. The vizorless cap was similarly warmed up with the hue of the perfect sunflower. The saffron magnificence of the 1st Hussars was like the gorgeous gold of the lilies of the field and Solomon in all his glory could not have been arrayed like one of them. I hope he was not. I want to retain my respect for him. We dubbed these daffodil cavaliers "Butterflies," and the name stuck to them like a poor relation.

Still another distinction that was always noticeable between the two armies was in the bodily bearing of the men. The Army of the Potomac was drilled more rigidly than the western men and had comparatively few long marches. Its members had something of the stiffness and precision of German soldiery, while the western boys had the long "reachy" stride and easy swing that made forty miles a day a rather commonplace march for an infantry regiment. This was why we knew the new prisoners to be Sherman's boys as soon as they came inside and we started for them to hear the news. Inviting them over to our lean-to, we told them of our anxiety for the story of the decisive blow that gave us the "Central Gate" of the Confederacy and asked them to give it to us.

An intelligent, quick-eyed, sunburned boy, without an ounce of surplus flesh on face or limbs which had been reduced to greyhound condition by the labors and anxieties of the months of battling between Chattanooga and Atlanta, seemed to be the accepted talker of the crowd, and all the rest looked at him as if expecting him to answer for them.

"You want to know about how we got Atlanta at last, do you?" he said. "Well, if you don't know, I should think you *would* want to know. If I didn't, I'd want somebody to tell me all about it just as soon as he could get to me, for it was one of the neatest little bits of work that 'old Billy' and his boys ever did, and it got away with Hood so bad that he hardly knew what hurt him. Well, first I'll tell you that we belong to the old 14th Ohio Volunteers which, if you know anything about the Army of the Cumberland, you'll remember has just about as good a record as any that trains around old Pap Thomas, and he don't allow no slouches of any kind near him, either. You can bet $500 to a cent on that, and offer to give back the cent if you win.

"Ours is Jim Steedman's old regiment. You've all heard of old Chickamauga Jim who slashed his division of 7,000 fresh men into the rebel flank on the second day at Chickamauga in a way that made Longstreet wish he'd stayed on the Rappahannock and never tried to get up any little sociable with the Westerners——

"If I do say it myself, I believe we've got as good a crowd of square, stand-up, trust-'em-every-minute-in-your-life boys as ever chawed hardtack and sowbelly. We got all the grunters and weak sisters fanned out the first year, and since then we've been on a business basis all the time. We're in a mighty good brigade, too. Most of the regiments have been with us since we formed the first brigade Pap Thomas ever commanded, and waded with him through the mud of Kentucky, from Wild Cat to Mill

Springs, where he gave Zollicoffer just a little of the awfullest thrashing that a rebel General ever got.

"That, you know, was in January, 1862, and was the first victory gained by the western army, and our people felt so rejoiced over it that——

"Yes, yes. We've read all about that," we broke in, "and we'd like to hear it again some other time; but tell us about Atlanta."

"All right," he said, "let's see—where was I? Oh, yes, talking about our brigade. It is the 3rd Brigade of the 3rd Division of the 14th Corps, and is made up of the 14th and 38th Ohio, 10th Kentucky and 74th Indiana. Our old Colonel, George P. Este, commands it. We never liked him very well in camp, but I tell you he is a whole team in a fight, and he'll do so well there that all would take to him again, and he'd be real popular for a while."

"Now, isn't that strange," broke in Andrews, who was given to fits of speculation of psychological phenomena: "None of us yearn to die, but the surest way to gain the affection of the boys is to show zeal in leading them into scrapes where the chances of getting shot are the best. Courage in action, like charity, covers a multitude of sins. I have known it to make the most unpopular man in a battalion the most popular inside of half an hour. Now, Mac," he said, addressing himself to me, "you remember Lieutenant H—— of our battalion. You know—he was a very fancy young fellow, wore as 'snipsish' clothes as the tailor could make, had gold lace on his jacket wherever the regulations would allow it, decorated his shoulders with the stunningest pair of shoulder knots I ever saw. Well, he did not stay with us long after we went to the front. He went back on a detail for a court martial and stayed a good while. When he rejoined us, he was not in good odor at all, and the boys weren't at all careful in saying unpleasant things when he could hear them.

"A little while after he came back, we made that reconnaissance up on the Virginia Road. We stirred up the Johnnies with our skirmish line and while the firing was going on in front, we sat on our horses in line, waiting for the order to move forward and engage. You know how solemn such moments are. I looked down the line and saw Lieutenant H—— at the right of company in command of it. I had not seen him since he came back, and I sung out: 'Hello, Lieutenant, how do you feel?'

"The reply came back, promptly, and with boyish cheerfulness: 'Bully, by God; I'm going to lead seventy men of Company L into action today!' How his boys did cheer him. When the bugle sounded 'Forward, trot,' his company sailed in as if they meant it and swept the Johnnies off in short meter. You never heard anybody say anything against Lieutenant H—— after that."

"You know how it was with Captain G——, of our regiment," said one of the 14th

to another. "He was promoted from orderly sergeant to a second lieutenant and assigned to Company D. All the members of Company D went to Headquarters in a
body and protested against his being put in their company, and he was not. Well, he
behaved so well at Chickamauga that the boys saw that they had done him a great
injustice, and all those that still lived went again to Headquarters and asked to take
all back that they had said and to have him put into the company . . ."

"Well, that was doing the manly thing, sure; but go on about Atlanta."

"I was telling about our brigade," said the young narrator. "Of course, we think
our regiment's the best in the army by long odds—every feller thinks that of his regiment—but next to it come the other regiments of our brigade. There's not a cent of
discount on any of them.

"Sherman had stretched out his right of way to the south and west of Atlanta.
About the middle of August our Corps commanded by Jefferson C. Davis was lying
in the works at Utoy Creek,⁴⁰ a couple of miles from Atlanta. We could see the tall
steeples and the high buildings of the city quite plainly. Things had gone on dull and
quiet-like for about ten days. This was longer by a good deal than we had been at rest
since we left Resaca in the spring.

"We knew that something was brewing, and that it must come to a head soon.
I belong to Company C. Our little mess, now reduced to three by the loss of two of
our best soldiers and cooks—Disbrow and Sulier, killed in front of Atlanta by sharpshooters—had one fellow that we called 'Observer,' because he had such a faculty for
picking up news in his prowling around Headquarters. He brought us in so much of
this, and it was generally so reliable, that we frequently made up his absence from duty
by taking his place. He was never away from a fight, though.

"On the night of the twenty-fifth of August, Observer came in with the news that
something was in the wind. Sherman was getting awful restless, and we had found out
that this always meant lots of trouble to our friends on the other side. Sure enough,
orders came to get ready to move and the next night we all moved to the right and
rear, out of sight of the Johnnies. Our well-built works were left in charge of Garrard's
Cavalry, who concealed their horses in the rear and came up and took our places. The
whole army except the 20th Corps moved quietly off, and did it so nicely that we were
gone some time before the enemy suspected it. Then the 20th Corps pulled out
towards the north and fell back to the Chattahoochee, making quite a show of retreat.

"The rebels snapped up the bait greedily. They thought the siege was being
raised, and they poured over their works to hurry the 20th boys off. The 20th fellows
let them know that there was lots of sting in them yet, and the Johnnies were not long
in discovering that it would have been money in their pockets if they had let that

'moon-star'—that's the 20th's badge, you know—crowd alone. But the rebs thought the rest of us were gone for good and that Atlanta was saved. Naturally, they felt mighty happy over it, and resolved to have a big celebration, a ball, a sort of jubilee. Extra trains were run in with girls and women from the surrounding country, and they just had a high old time.

"In the meantime, we were going through so many different kinds of tactics that it looked as if Sherman was really crazy this time, sure. Finally we made a grand left wheel, and then went forward a long way in line of battle. It puzzled us a good deal, but we knew that Sherman couldn't get us into any scrape that Pap Thomas couldn't get us out of, and so it was all right. Along on the evening of the 31st, our right wing seemed to have run against a hornet's nest and we could hear the musketry and cannon speak out real spiteful, but nothing came down our way. We had struck the railroad leading south from Atlanta to Macon and began tearing it up.

"The jollity at Atlanta was stopped right in the middle by the appalling news that the Yankees hadn't retreated worth a cent, but had broken out in a new and much worse spot than ever. Then there was no end of trouble all around, and Hood started part of his army back after us. Part of Hardee's and Pat Cleburne's men went into position in front of us. We left them alone till Stanley could come up on our left and swing around so as to cut off their retreat, when we would bag every one of them. But Stanley was as slow as he always was and did not come up until it was too late, and the game was gone.

"The sun was just going down on the evening of the 1st of September, when we began to see we were in for it, sure. The 14th Corps wheeled into position near the railroad, and the sound of musketry and artillery became very loud and clear on our front and left. We turned a little and marched straight toward the racket, becoming more excited every minute. We saw the Carlin Brigade of Regulars, who were some distance ahead of us, pile knapsacks, form in line, fix bayonets and dash off with a rousing cheer. The rebels beat upon them like a summer rain storm, the ground shook with the noise, and just as we reached the edge of the cotton field, we saw the remnant of the brigade come flying back out of the awful blasting shower of bullets. The whole slope was covered with dead and wounded."

"Yes," interrupts one of the members of the 14th, "and they made that charge right gamely, too, I can tell you. They were good soldiers and well led. When we went over the works, I remember seeing the body of a little major of one of the regiments lying right on the top. If he hadn't been killed, he'd have been inside in a half a dozen steps more. There's no mistake about it—those Regulars will fight."

"When we saw this," continued the narrator, "it set our fellows fairly wild. They became just crying mad. I never saw them so before. The order came to strip for the charge and our knapsacks were piled in half a minute. A lieutenant of our company who was then on the staff of General Baird, our division commander, rode slowly down the line and gave us our instructions to load our guns, fix bayonets and hold fire until we were on top of the rebel works. Then Colonel Estes sang out clear and steady as a bugle signal: 'Brigade, forward! Guide center! March!' And we started.

"Heavens! How they let into us as we came up into range! They had ten pieces of artillery and more men behind the breastworks than we had in line, and the fire they poured on us was simply withering. We walked across the hundreds of dead and dying of the Regular Brigade, and at every step our own men fell down among them. General Baird's horse was shot down and the General thrown far over his head, but he jumped up and ran alongside of us. Major Wilson, our regimental commander, fell mortally wounded; Lieutenant Kirk was killed, and also Captain Stopfard, Adjutant-General of the brigade. Lieutenants Cobb and Mitchell dropped with wounds that proved fatal in a few days. Captain Ogan lost an arm, one third of the enlisted men fell. But we went straight ahead, the grape and the musketry becoming worse every step, until we gained the edge of the hill, where we were checked a minute by the brush which the rebels had fixed up in the shape of abatis.

"Just then a terrible fire from a new direction, our left, swept down the length of our whole line. The Colonel of the 17th New York, as gallant a man as ever lived, saw the new trouble, took his regiment in on the run and relieved us of this, but he was himself mortally wounded. If our boys were half crazy before, they were frantic now and as we got out of the brush we raised a fearful yell and ran at the works. We climbed the sides, fired right down into the defenders, and then began with the bayonet and sword. For a few minutes it was simply awful. On both sides men acted like infuriated devils. They dashed each other's brains out with clubbed muskets; bayonets were driven into men's bodies up to the muzzle of the gun; officers ran their swords through their opponents; and revolvers, after being emptied into the faces of the rebels, were thrown with desperate force into the ranks.

"In our regiment was a stout German butcher named Frank Fleck. He became so excited that he threw down his sword and rushed among the rebels with his bare fists, knocking down a swath of them. He yelled to the first rebel he met, 'Py Gott, I've no patience mit you,' and knocked him sprawling. He caught hold of the commander of the rebel brigade and snatched him back over the works by main strength. Wonderful to say, he escaped unhurt, but the boys will probably not soon let him hear the last of 'Py Gott, I've no patience mit you.'

"The 10th Kentucky, by the queerest luck in the world, was matched against the rebel 9th Kentucky. The commanders of the two regiments were brothers-in-law and the men were relatives, friends, acquaintances and schoolmates. They hated each other accordingly, and the fight between them was more bitter, if possible, than anywhere else on the line. The 38th Ohio and 74th Indiana put in some work that was just magnificent. We hadn't time to look at it then, but the dead and wounded piled up after the fight told the story. We gradually forced our way over the works, but the rebels were game to the last and we had to make them surrender almost one at a time. The artillerymen tried to fire on us when we were so close we could lay our hands on the guns.

"Finally nearly all in the works surrendered and were disarmed and marched back. Just then an aide came dashing up with the information that we must turn the works and get ready to receive Hardee, who was advancing to retake the position. We snatched up some shovels lying near and began work. We had no time to remove the dead and dying rebels on the works and the dirt we threw covered them up. It proved a false alarm. Hardee had as much as he could do to save his own hide, and the affair ended about dark.

"When we came to count up what we had gained, we found that we had actually taken more prisoners from behind breastworks than there were in our brigade when we started the charge. We had made the only really successful bayonet charge of the campaign. Every other time since we left Chattanooga, the party standing on the defensive had been successful. Here we had taken strong double lines, ten guns, seven battle flags and over two thousand prisoners. We had lost terribly—not less than one third of the brigade—and many of our best men. Our regiment went into the battle with fifteen officers; nine of these were either killed or wounded. The 38th Ohio and the other regiments of the brigade lost equally heavily. We thought Chickamauga awful, but Jonesboro discounted it."

"Do you know," said another member of the 14th, "I heard our surgeon telling about how that Colonel Grower of the 17th New York, who came in so splendidly on our left, died? They say he was a Wall Street broker before the war. He was hit shortly after he led his regiment in and, after the fight, was carried back to the hospital. While our surgeon was going the rounds, Colonel Grower called him, and said quietly, 'When you get through with the men, come and see me, please.' The doctor would have attended to him then, but Grower wouldn't let him. After he got through, he went back to Grower, examined his wound, and told him that he could live only a few hours. Grower received the news tranquilly, had the doctor write a letter to his wife, and gave him his things to send her; and grasping the doctor's hand, he said,

'Doctor, I've just one more favor to ask; will you grant it?' The doctor said, 'Certainly; what is it?'

" 'You say I can't live but a few hours?' asked the Colonel.

" 'Yes, that is true,' replied the doctor.

" 'And that I will likely be in great pain?'

" 'I am sorry to say so,' replied the doctor sadly.

" 'Well, then,' begged the Colonel, 'do give me morphia, enough to put me to sleep, so that I will wake up only in another world.' The doctor did so. Colonel Grower thanked him, wrung his hand, bade him good-by and went to sleep to wake no more."

"Do you believe in presentiments and superstitions?" said another of the 14th. "There was Fisher Pray, orderly sergeant of Company I. He came from Waterville, Ohio, where his folks are now living. The day before we started out he had a presentiment that we were going into a fight, and that he would be killed. He couldn't shake it off. He told the Lieutenant and some of the boys about it and they tried to ridicule him out of it, but it was no good. When the sharp fighting broke out in front, some of the boys said, 'Fisher, I do believe you are right,' and he nodded his head mournfully. When we were piling knapsacks for the charge, the Lieutenant, who was a great friend of Fisher's, said: 'Fisher, you stay here and guard the knapsacks.' Fisher's face blazed in an instant. 'No, sir,' said he, 'I never shirked a fight yet, and I won't begin now.' So he went into the fight and was killed, as he knew he would be. Now, that's what *I* call nerve."

"The same thing was true of Sergeant Arthur Tarbox of Company A," said the narrator. "He had a presentiment, too. He knew he was going to be killed if he went in, and he was offered an honorable chance to stay out, but he would not take it and went in and was killed. . . . Well, we stayed there the next day, buried our dead, took care of our wounded and gathered up the plunder we had taken from the Johnnies. The rest of the Army went off 'hotblocks' after Hardee and the rest of Hood's Army which, it was hoped, would be caught outside of entrenchments. But Hood had too much the start, and got into the works at Lovejoy ahead of our fellows.

"The night before we heard several very loud explosions up to the north. We guessed what that meant and so did the 20th Corps, who was lying back at the Chattahoochee, and the next morning the general commanding, Slocum, sent out a reconnaissance. It was met by the Mayor of Atlanta, who said that the rebels had blown up their stores and retreated. The 20th then came in and took possession of the city and the next day, the 3rd, Sherman came in and issued an order declaring the campaign at an end and that we were to rest awhile and refit. We laid around Atlanta a good while and things quieted down so that it seemed almost like peace, after the four months of continual fighting we had gone through. We had been under a strain so long that now we boys went in the other direction and became too careless, and that's how we got picked up.

"We went out about five miles one night after a lot of nice smoked hams that a nigger told us was stored in an old cotton press and which we knew would be darned sight better eating for Company C than the commissary pork we had lived on so long. We found the cotton press and the hams, just as the nigger told us, and we hitched up a team to take them into camp. As we hadn't seen any signs of Johnny anywhere, we set our guns down to help load the meat, and just as we all came stringing out to the wagon with as much meat as we could carry, a company of Ferguson's Cavalry popped out of the woods about one hundred yards in front of us and were on top of us before we could say 'scat.' . . . You see, they'd heard of the meat, too!"

A Hut Builded with Our Own Hands

CHAPTER XVIII

BACK TRACK TO ANDERSONVILLE

ON THE EVENING of the 11th of October there came an order for one thousand prisoners to fall in and march out for transfer to some other point. Of course Andrews and I "flanked" [41] into this crowd. That was our usual way of doing. Holding that the chances were strongly in favor of every movement of prisoners being towards our lines, we never failed to be numbered in the first squad of prisoners to be sent out. The seductive mirage of exchange was always luring us on. It must come some time, certainly, and it would be most likely to come to those who were most earnestly searching for it. At all events, we should leave no means untried to avail ourselves of whatever seeming chances there might be. There could be no other motive for this move, we argued, than exchange.

The Confederacy was not likely to be at the trouble and expense of hauling us about the country without some good reason, something better than a wish to make us acquainted with southern scenery and topography. It would hardly take us away from Savannah so soon after bringing us there for any other purpose than delivery to our people. The rebels encouraged this belief with direct assertions of its truth. They framed a plausible lie about there having arisen some difficulty concerning the admission of our vessels past the harbor defenses of Savannah, which made it necessary to take us elsewhere, probably to Charleston, for delivery to our men. Wishes are always the most powerful allies of belief. There is little difficulty in convincing a man of that which he wants to be convinced. We forgot the lie they told us when we were taken from Andersonville and believed the one which was told us now.

Andrews and I hastily snatched our worldly possessions, our overcoat, blanket, can, spoon, chess-board and men, yelled to some of our neighbors that they could have our hitherto much-treasured house and, running down to the gate, forced ourselves well up to the front of the crowd that was being assembled to go out. The usual scenes accompanying the departure of the first squads were being enacted tumultuously. Everyone in the camp wanted to be one of the supposed-to-be-favored few and, if not selected at first, tried to "flank in"—that is, slip into the place of someone else who had had better luck.[42] This one naturally resisted displacement *vi et armis,* and the fights would become so general as to cause a resemblance to the famed Fair of Donnybrook.[43] The cry would go up: "Look out for flankers!" The lines of the selected would "dress up" compactly, and outsiders trying to force themselves in would get mercilessly pounded.

We finally got out of the pen and into the cars, which soon rolled away to the westward. We were packed in too densely to be able to lie down. We could hardly sit down. Andrews and I took up our position in one corner, piled our little treasures under us and, trying to lean against each other in such a way as to afford mutual support and rest, dosed fitfully through a long, weary night. When morning came we found ourselves running northwest through a poor, pine-barren country which strongly resembled that we had traversed in coming to Savannah. The more we looked at it the more familiar it became, and soon there was no doubt we were going back to Andersonville. By noon we had reached Millen, eighty miles from Savannah and fifty-three from Augusta. It was the junction of the roads leading to Macon and to Augusta.

We halted a little while at the Y and to us the minutes were full of anxiety. If we turned off to the left, we were going back to Andersonville. If we took the right-hand road, we were on the way to Charleston or Richmond, with the chances in favor of exchange. At length we started and, to our joy, our engine took the right-hand track. We stopped again—after a run of five miles—in the midst of one of the open forests of long-leafed pine. We were ordered out of the cars and, marching a few rods, came in sight of another of those hateful stockades which seemed to be as natural products of the sterile sand of the dreary land as its desolate woods and its breed of boy murderers and gray-headed assassins. Again our hearts sank and death seemed more welcome than incarceration in those gloomy wooden walls. We marched despondently up to the gates of the prison and halted while a party of rebel clerks made a list of our names, rank, companies and regiments.

We learned that the place at which we had arrived was Camp Lawton, but we almost always spoke of it as "Millen"—the same as what we called "Camp Sumter" is universally known as Andersonville. Shortly after dark we were turned inside the stockade. Being the first that had entered, we found quite a quantity of wood, the offal from the timber used in constructing the stockade, lying on the ground. The night was chilly and we soon had a number of fires blazing. Green pitch-pine, when burned, gives off a peculiar pungent odor which is never forgotten by one who has once smelled it. I first became acquainted with it on entering Andersonville and to this day it is the most powerful remembrance I can have of the opening of my dreadful Iliad of woe. On my journeys to Washington of late years, the locomotives are invariably fed with pitch-pine as we near the Capital and as the well-remembered smell reaches me I grow sick at heart with the flood of saddening recollections indissolubly associated with it.

As our fires blazed up, the clinging, penetrating fumes diffused themselves everywhere. The night was as cool as the one when we arrived at Andersonville; the earth, meagerly sodded with sparse, hard, wiry grass, was the same; the same piney breezes blew in from the surrounding trees; the dismal owls hooted at us and the same mournful whippoorwill lamented God knows what in the gathering twilight. What we both felt in the gloomy recesses of our downcast hearts, Andrews expressed as he turned to me: "My God, Mac, this looks like Andersonville all over again."

A cupful of corn meal was issued to each of us. I hunted up some water. Andrews made a stiff dough and spread it about half an inch thick on the back of our chessboard. He propped this up before the fire and when the surface was neatly browned over, slipped it off the board and turned it over to brown the other side similarly. This done, we divided it carefully between us, swallowed it in silence, spread our old overcoat on the ground, tucked chess-board, can, and spoon under far enough to be out of the reach of thieves, adjusted the thin blanket so as to get the most possible warmth out of it, crawled in close together and went to sleep. This, thank heaven, we could do. We could still sleep, and so Nature had some opportunity to repair the waste of the day. We slept, and forgot where we were.

In the morning we took a survey of our new quarters and found that we were in a stockade resembling Andersonville in construction and dimensions. The principal difference was that here the upright logs were in their very rough state whereas they were hewed at Andersonville, and the brook running through the camp was not bordered by a swamp but had clean firm banks. Our next move was to make the best of the situation. We were divided into hundreds, each commanded by a sergeant. Ten hundreds constituted a division, the head of which was also a sergeant. I was elected by my comrades to the sergeancy of the second hundred of the first division.

As soon as we were assigned to our ground, we began constructing shelter. For the first and only time in my prison experience, we found a full supply of material for this purpose. The use we made of it showed how infinitely better we would have fared if in each prison the rebels had done even so slight a thing as to bring in a few logs from the surrounding woods and distribute them to us. A hundred or so of these would probably have saved thousands of lives at Andersonville and at Florence. A large tree lay on the ground assigned to our hundred. Andrews and I took possession of one side of the ten feet nearest the butt. Other boys occupied the rest in a similar manner. One of our boys had succeeded in smuggling an ax in with him, and we kept it in constant use day and night, each group borrowing it for an hour or so at a time. It was as dull as a hoe and we were very weak, so that it was slow work "niggering off" a cut of the log. It seemed as if beavers could have gnawed it off easier and more quickly. We only cut an inch or so off at a time and then passed the ax to the next users. Making little wedges with a dull knife, we drove them into the log with clubs and split off long, thin strips like the weatherboards of a house. By the time we had split off our share of the log in this slow and laborious way, we had a fine lot of these strips.

We were lucky enough to find four forked sticks, of which we made the corners of our dwelling which we roofed carefully with our strips held in place by sods torn up from the edge of the creek bank. The sides and ends were enclosed. We gathered enough pine tops to cover the ground to a depth of several inches; we banked up the outside and ditched around it, and then had the most comfortable abode we had during our prison career. It was truly a house built with our own hands, for we had no tools whatever save the occasional use of the aforementioned dull ax and equally dull knife. The rude little hut represented as much actual hard manual labor as would be required to build a comfortable little cottage in the North but we gladly performed it, as we would have any other work to better our condition. For a while, wood was quite plentiful and we had the daily luxury of warm fires which the increasing coolness of the weather made important accessories to our comfort.

Other prisoners kept coming in. Those we left behind at Savannah followed us, and the prison there was broken up. Quite a number also came from Andersonville, so that in a little while we had between six and seven thousand in the stockade. The last comers found all the material for tents and fuel used up and consequently did not fare so well as the earlier arrivals. The Commandant of the prison, Captain Bowes, was the best of his class it was my fortune to meet. Compared with the senseless brutality of Wirz, the reckless deviltry of Davis or the stupid malignance of Barret at Florence, his administration was mildness and wisdom itself. He enforced discipline better than any of those named and having what they all lacked, executive ability, he secured results that they could not possibly attain and without anything like the friction that attended their efforts. I do not remember that anyone was shot during our six weeks' stay at Millen, a circumstance simply remarkable since I do not recall a single week passed anywhere else without at least one murder by the guards.

One instance will illustrate the difference of his administration from that of other prison commandants. He came upon the grounds of our division one morning accompanied by a pleasant-faced, intelligent-appearing lad of about fifteen or sixteen. "Gentlemen," he said with polite designation, "this is my son who will hereafter call your roll. He will treat you as gentlemen and I know you will do the same to him." This understanding was observed to the letter on both sides. Young Bowes invariably spoke civilly to us and we obeyed his orders with a prompt cheerfulness that left him nothing to complain of. The only charge I have to make against Bowes is that he took money from well prisoners for giving them the first chance to go through on the Sick Exchange.

How culpable this was I must leave to the reader to decide for himself. I thought it very wrong at the time, but possibly my views might have been colored highly by my not having any money wherewith to procure my own inclusion in the happy lot of exchanged. Of one thing I am certain—that his acceptance of money to bias his official action was not unique. I am convinced that every commandant we had over us did except Wirz, and this is the sole good thing I can say of that fellow. Against this it may be said, however, that he plundered the boys' belongings so effectually on entering prison as to leave them little of the wherewithal to bribe anybody. Davis was probably the most unscrupulous bribe-taker of the lot. He actually received money for permitting prisoners to escape to our lines and got down to as low a figure as one hundred dollars for this sort of service. I never heard that any of the other commandants went this far.

The rations issued to us were somewhat better than those of Andersonville, as the meal was finer and better—though it was absurdly insufficient in quantity, and we received no salt. On several occasions fresh beef was dealt out to us and each time the excitement created among those who had not tasted fresh meat for weeks and months was wonderful. On the first occasion the meat was simply the heads of the cattle killed for the use of the guards. Several wagonloads of these were brought in and distributed. We broke them up so that every man got a piece of the bone which was boiled and reboiled as long as a single bubble of grease would rise to the surface of the water. Every vestige of meat was gnawed and scraped from the surface and then the bone was charred until it crumbled, when it was eaten. No one who has not experienced it can imagine the inordinate hunger for animal food of those who had eaten little else than corn bread for so long. Our exhausted bodies were perishing for lack of proper sustenance. Nature indicated fresh beef as the best medium to repair the great damage already done, and our longing for it became beyond description.

Our old antagonists, the Raiders, were present in strong force in Millen. Like ourselves, they had imagined the departure from Andersonville was for exchange, and their relations to the rebels were such that they were all given a chance to go with the first squad. A number had been allowed to go with the sailors on the Special Naval Exchange from Savannah in the place of sailors and marines who had died. On the way to Charleston a fight had taken place between them and the real sailors, during which one of their number, a curly-headed Irishman named Daly, who was in such high favor with the rebels that he was given the place of driving the ration wagon that came in the North Side at Andersonville, was killed and thrown under the wheels of the moving train, which passed over him.

After things began to settle into shape at Millen, they seemed to believe that they were in such ascendancy as to numbers and organization that they could put into execution their schemes of vengeance against those of us who had been active participants in the execution of their confederates at Andersonville. After some little preliminaries they settled upon Corporal Wat Payne of my Company as their first victim. The reader will remember Payne as one of the two corporals who triggered the scaffold at the time of the execution. Payne was a very good man physically and was still in fair condition. The Raiders came up one day with their best man, Pete Donnelly, and provoked a fight, intending in the course of it to kill Payne. We who knew Payne felt reasonably confident of his ability to handle even so redoubtable a pugilist as Donnelly, and we gathered together a little squad of our friends to see fair play.

The fight began after the usual amount of bad talk on both sides and we were pleased to see our man slowly get the better of the New York plug-ugly. After several sharp rounds they closed and still Payne was ahead, but in an evil moment he spied a pine knot at his feet, which he thought he could reach and end the fight by cracking Donnelly's head with it. Donnelly took instant advantage of the movement to get it, threw Payne heavily and fell upon him. His crowd rushed in to finish our man by clubbing him over the head. We sailed in to prevent this and, after a rattling exchange of blows all around, succeeded in getting Payne away. The issue of the fight seemed rather against us, however, and the Raiders were much emboldened. Payne kept close to his crowd after that and, as we had shown such an entire willingness to stand by him, the Raiders, with their accustomed prudence when real fighting was involved, did not attempt to molest him farther though they talked very savagely.

A few days after this, Sergeant Goody and Corporal Ned Carrigan, both of our battalion, came in. Sergeant Goody was one of the six hangmen who put the mealsacks over the heads and ropes around the necks of the condemned. Corporal Carrigan was the gigantic prizefighter who was universally acknowledged to be the best man physically among the whole thirty-four thousand in Andersonville. The Raiders knew that Goody had come in before we of his own battalion did. They resolved to kill him then and there and in broad daylight. He had secured in some way a shelter tent and was inside of it fixing it up. The Raider crowd, headed by Pete Donnelly and Dick Allen, went up to his tent and one of them called to him, "Sergeant, come out; I want to see you." Goody, supposing it was one of us, came crawling out on his hands and knees. As he did so, their heavy clubs crashed down upon his head. Neither killed nor stunned as they had reason to expect, he succeeded in raising himself to his feet and breaking through the crowd of assassins. He dashed down the side of the hill hotly pursued by them. Coming to the creek, he leaped it in his excitement, but his pursuers could not and so were checked.

One of the battalion boys who saw and comprehended the whole affair, ran over to us shouting: "Turn out! Turn out, for God's sake! The Raiders are killing Goody!" We snatched up our clubs and started after the Raiders but before we could reach them Ned Carrigan, who also comprehended what the trouble was, had run to the side of Goody, armed with a terrible-looking club. The sight of Ned and this evidence that he was thoroughly aroused was enough for the Raider crew, and they abandoned the field hastily. We did not feel ourselves strong enough to follow them on to their own dunghill and try conclusions with them, but we determined to report the matter to the rebel commandant, from whom we had reason to believe we could expect assistance.

We were right. He sent a squad of guards, arrested Dick Allen, Pete Donnelly and several other ringleaders, took them out and put them in the stocks in such a manner that they were compelled to lie upon their stomachs. A shallow tin vessel containing water was placed under their faces to furnish them drink. They stayed there a day and night, and when released they joined the rebel army, entering the artillery company that manned the guns in the fort covering the prison. I used to imagine with what zeal they would send us over a round of shell or grape if they could get anything like an excuse. This gave us good riddance of our dangerous enemies, and we had little further trouble with any of them.

The depression in the temperature made me very sensible of the deficiencies in my wardrobe. Unshod feet, a shirt like a fishing net and pantaloons as well-ventilated as a pale fence might do very well for the broiling sun at Andersonville and Savannah, but now with the thermometer nightly dipping a little nearer the frost line, it became unpleasantly evident that as garments their office was purely perfunctory—one might say ornamental, if he wanted to be very sarcastic. They were worn solely to afford convenient quarters for multitudes of lice and in deference to the prejudice which has existed since the Fall of Man against our mingling with our fellow creatures in the attire provided by Nature. Had I read Darwin then, I should have expected that my long exposure to the weather would start a fine suit of fur as Nature's effort to adapt me to my environment. But no more indication of this appeared than if I had been a hairless Mexican dog suddenly transplanted to more northern latitudes. Providence did not seem to be in the tempering-the-wind-to-the-shorn-lamb business as far as I was concerned. I still retained an almost unconquerable prejudice against stripping the dead to secure clothes, and so unless exchange or death came speedily I was in a bad fix.

One morning about daybreak Andrews, who had started to go to another part of the camp, came slipping back in a state of gleeful excitement. I thought at first he either had found a tunnel or had heard some good news about exchange. It was neither. He opened his jacket and handed me an infantryman's blouse which he had found in the main street where it had dropped from some fellow's bundle. We did not make any extra exertion to find the owner. Andrews was in sore need of clothes himself, but my necessities were so much greater that the generous fellow thought of my wants first. We examined the garment with as much interest as ever a belle bestowed on a new dress from Worth's. It was in fair preservation, but the owner had cut the buttons off to trade to the guard, doubtless for a few sticks of wood or a spoonful of salt. We supplied the place of these with little wooden pins, and I donned the garment as a shirt and coat, and vest, too, for that matter. The best suit I ever put on never gave me a hundredth part the satisfaction that this did. Shortly after, I managed to subdue my own aversion so far as to take a good shoe which a one-legged dead man had no further use for, and a little later a comrade gave me for the other foot a boot bottom from which he had cut the top to make a bucket.

The day of the Presidential election of 1864 approached. The rebels were naturally very much interested in the result, as they believed that the election of McClellan meant compromise and cessation of hostilities, while the re-election of Lincoln meant prosecution of the war to the bitter end. The toadying Raiders, who were perpetually hanging around the gate to get a chance to insinuate themselves into the favor of the rebel officers, persuaded them that we were also so bitterly hostile to our Government for not exchanging us that if we were allowed to vote we would cast an overwhelming majority in favor of McClellan.[44] The rebels thought that this might perhaps be used to advantage as political capital for their friends in the North. They gave orders that we might, if we chose, hold an election on the same day of the Presidential election. They sent in some ballot boxes and we elected judges of the election.

About noon of that day, Captain Bowes and a crowd of tight-booted, broad-hatted rebel officers strutted in with the peculiar "ef-yer-don't-believe-I'm-a-butcher-jest-smell-o'-me-butes" swagger characteristic of the class. They had come in to see us all voting for McClellan. Instead they found the polls surrounded with ticket peddlers, shouting: "Walk right up here, now, and get your Unconditional Union, Abraham Lincoln Tickets!"; "Here's your straight-haired prosecution-of-the-war ticket!"; "Vote the Lincoln Ticket. Vote to whip the rebels and make peace with them when they've laid down their arms!"; "Don't vote a McClellan Ticket and gratify long-rebels everywhere."

The rebel officers did not find the scene what their fancy painted it and, turning around, they strutted out. When the votes came to be counted, there were over seven thousand for Lincoln and not half that many hundred for McClellan. The latter got very few votes outside the Raider crowd. The same day a similar election was held in Florence with a like result. Of course, this did not indicate that there was any such a preponderance of Republicans among us. It meant simply that the Democratic boys, little as they might have liked Lincoln, would have voted for him a hundred times rather than do anything to please the rebels. I never heard that the rebels sent the result North!

Killing Lice

CHAPTER XIX

DREARY WEATHER

ONE DAY IN NOVEMBER some little time after the occurrences narrated in the last chapter, orders came in to make out rolls of all those who were born outside the United States and whose terms of service had expired. We held a little council among ourselves as to the meaning of this and concluded that some partial exchange had been agreed on, and the rebels were going to send back the class of boys whom they thought would be of least value to the Government.

Acting on this conclusion the great majority of us enrolled ourselves as foreigners and as having served out our terms of enlistment. I made out the roll of my hundred and managed to give every man a foreign nativity. Those whose names would bear it were assigned to England, Ireland, Scotland, France and Germany, and the balance were distributed through Canada and the West Indies. After finishing the roll and sending it out, I did not wonder that the rebels believed the battles for the Union were fought by foreign mercenaries. The other rolls were made out in the same way, and I do not suppose that they showed five hundred native Americans in the stockade.

The next day after sending out the rolls, there came an order that all those whose names appeared thereon should fall in. We did so promptly, and as nearly every man in camp was included, we fell in—as for other purposes—by hundreds and thousands. We were then marched outside and massed around a stump on which stood a rebel officer evidently waiting to make us a speech. We awaited his remarks with the greatest impatience, but he did not begin until the last division had marched out and came to a parade rest close to the stump. It was the same old story: "Prisoners, you can no longer have any doubt that your government has cruelly abandoned you; it makes no efforts to release you and refuses all our offers of exchange. We are anxious to get our men back and have made every effort to do so, but it refuses to meet us on any reasonable grounds. Your Secretary of War [45] has said that the Government can get along very well without you and General Halleck [46] has said that you were nothing but a set of 'blackberry pickers' and 'coffee boilers' anyhow. You've already endured much more than it could expect of you; you served faithfully during the term you enlisted for and now, when it is through with you, it throws you aside to starve and die. You also can have no doubt that the Southern Confederacy is certain to succeed in securing its independence. It will do this in a few months. It now offers you an opportunity to join its service, and if you serve it faithfully to the end, you will receive the same rewards as the rest of its soldiers. You will be taken out of here, be well-clothed and fed, given a good bounty and, at the conclusion of the war, receive a land warrant for a nice farm. If you——"

But we had heard enough. The sergeant of our division, a man with a stentorian voice, sprang out and shouted, "Attention, First Division!" We other sergeants of the "hundreds" repeated the command down the line: "First Division, about—"; "First hundred, about—"; "Second hundred, about—"; "Third hundred, about—"; "Fourth hundred, about—"; "Face!" Ten sergeants repeated the command, one after the other, and each man in the hundreds turned on his heel. Then our leader commanded: "First Division—Forward! march!" and we strode back into the stockade, followed immediately by all the other divisions, leaving the orator still standing on the stump.

The rebels were furious at this curt way of replying. We had scarcely reached our quarters when they came with several companies with loaded guns and fixed bayonets. They drove us out of our tents and huts into one corner under the pretense of hunting axes and spades but in reality to steal our blankets and whatever else they could find that they wanted and to break down and injure our huts, many of which, costing us days of patient labor, they destroyed in pure wantonness. We were burning with the bitterest indignation.

A tall, slender man named Lloyd, a member of the 61st Ohio, a rough, uneducated fellow but brimful of patriotism and manly common sense, jumped up on a stump and poured out his soul in rude but fiery eloquence. "Comrades," he shouted, "do not let the blowing of these rebel whelps discourage you; pay no attention to the lies they have told you today; you know well that our Government is too honorable and just to desert anyone who serves it; it has *not* deserted us; their hell-born Confederacy is *not* going to succeed. I tell you that as sure as there is a God who reigns and judges in Israel, before the spring breezes stir the tops of these blasted old pines, their damn Confederacy and all the lousy graybacks who support it will be so deep in Hell that nothing but a search warrant from the throne of God Almighty can ever find it again. And the glorious old Stars and Stripes——"

Here we began cheering tremendously. A rebel captain, running up, said to the guard who was leaning on his gun gazing curiously at Lloyd, "What in hell are you standing gaping there for? Why don't you shoot the Yankee son of a bitch?" Snatching the gun away from him, he cocked it and leveled at Lloyd, but the boys near him jerked the speaker down from the stump and saved his life. We became fearfully wrought up. Some of the more excitable shouted out to charge on the line of guards, snatch their guns away from them and force our way through the gates. The shouts were taken up by others and, as if in obedience to the suggestion, we instinctively formed in line of battle facing the guards. A glance down the line showed me an array of desperate tensely drawn faces such as one sees who looks at men when they are summoning up all their resolution for some deed of great peril.

The rebel officers hastily retreated behind the line of guards, whose faces blanched, but they leveled their muskets and prepared to receive us. Captain Bowes, who was overlooking the prison from an elevation, had, however, divined the trouble at the outset and was preparing to meet it. The gunners, who had shotted their pieces and trained them upon us when we came out to listen to the speech, had again covered us with them and were ready to sweep the prison with grape and canister at the instant of command. The long roll was summoning the infantry regiments back into line, and some of the cooler-headed among us pointed these facts out and succeeded in getting the line to dissolve again into groups of muttering sullen-faced men. When this was done, the guards marched out by a cautious indirect maneuver so as not to turn their backs to us.

It was believed that we had some among us who would like to avail themselves of the offer of the rebels and that they would try to inform the rebels of their desires by going to the gate during the night and speaking to the officer of the guard. A squad armed themselves with clubs and laid in wait for these. They succeeded in catching several, snatching some of them back even after they had told the guard their wishes in a tone so loud that all near could hear distinctly. The officer of the guard rushed in two or three times in a vain attempt to save the would-be deserter from the cruel hands that clutched him and bore him away to where he had a lesson in loyalty impressed upon the fleshiest part of his person by a long flexible strip of pine wielded by very willing hands.

After this was kept up for several nights, different ideas began to prevail. It was felt that if a man wanted to join the rebels, the best way was to let him go and get rid of him. He was of no benefit to the Government and would be of none to the rebels. After this, no restriction was put upon anyone who desired to go outside and take the oath. But very few did so and these were wholly confined to the Raider crowd.

As November wore away, long-continued, chill, searching rains desolated our days and nights. The great cold drops pelted down slowly, dismally and incessantly. Each seemed to beat through our emaciated frames against the very marrow of our bones and to be battering its way remorselessly into the citadel of life, like the cruel drops that fell from the basins of the Inquisitors upon the firmly fastened bodies of their victims until reason fled and the death-agonies cramped their hearts to stillness. The lagging, leaden hours were inexpressibly dreary. Compared with many others, we were quite comfortable, as our hut protected us from the actual beating of the rain upon our bodies. But we were much more miserable than under the sweltering heat of Andersonville as we lay almost naked upon our bed of pine leaves, shivering in the raw rasping air, and looked out over acres of wretches lying dumbly on the sodden sand, receiving the benumbing drench of the sullen skies without a groan or a motion.

It was enough to kill healthy vigorous men, active and resolute, with bodies well-nourished and well-clothed and with minds vivacious and hopeful, to stand these day-and-night-long cold drenchings. No one can imagine how fatal it was to boys whose vitality was sapped by long months in Andersonville, by the coarse, meager, changeless food, by the grovelling on the bare earth, and by the hopelessness as to any improvement of conditions. Fever, rheumatism, throat and lung diseases and despair now came to complete the work begun by scurvy, dysentery and gangrene in Andersonville. Hundreds, weary of the long struggle and, hoping against hope, laid themselves down and yielded to their fate. In the six weeks that we were at Millen, one man in every ten died. The ghostly pines there sigh over the unnoted graves of seven hundred boys for whom life's morning closed in the gloomiest shadows. As many as would form a splendid regiment, as many as constitute the first-born of a city populace, more than three times as many as were slain outright on our side in the bloody battle of Franklin[47] succumbed to this new hardship. The country for which they died does not even have record of their names. They were simply blotted out of existence; they became as though they had never been.

About the middle of the month, the rebels yielded to the importunities of our Government so far as to agree to exchange ten thousand sick.[48] The rebel surgeons took praiseworthy care that our Government should profit as little as possible from this by sending every hopeless case, every man whose lease of life was not likely to extend much beyond his reaching the parole boat. If he once reached our receiving officers, it was all that was necessary; he counted to them as much as if he had been a Goliath. A very large portion of these sent through died on the way to our lines or within a few hours after their transports at being once more under the old Stars and Stripes had moderated.

The sending of the sick through gave our commandant, Captain Bowes, a fine opportunity to fill his pockets by conniving at the passage of well men. There was still considerable money in the hands of a few prisoners. All this and more, too, were they willing to give for their lives. In the first batch that went away were two of the leading sutlers at Andersonville, who had accumulated perhaps one thousand dollars each by their shrewd and successful bartering. It was generally believed that they gave every cent to Bowes for the privilege of leaving. I know nothing of the truth of this, but I am reasonably certain that they paid him very handsomely. Soon we heard that one hundred and fifty dollars had been sufficient to buy some men out: then one hundred, seventy-five, fifty, thirty, twenty, ten and—at last—five dollars. Whether the upright Bowes drew the line at the latter figure and refused to sell his honor for less than the ruling rates of a street-walker's virtue, I know not. It was the lowest quotation that came to my knowledge, but he may have gone cheaper. I have always observed that when men or women begin to traffic in themselves, their price falls as rapidly as that of a piece of tainted meat in hot weather. If one could buy them at the rate they wind up with and sell them at their first price, there would be room for an enormous profit.

The cheapest I ever knew a rebel officer to be bought was some weeks after this at Florence. The sick exchange was still going on. I have before spoken of the rebel passion for bright gilt buttons. It used to be a proverbial comment upon the small treasons that were of daily occurrence on both sides that you could buy the soul of a mean man in our crowd for a pint of corn meal, and the soul of a rebel guard for a half-dozen brass buttons. A boy of the 54th Ohio, whose home was at or near Lima, wore a blue vest with the gilt bright-rimmed buttons of a staff officer. The rebel surgeon who was examining the sick for exchange saw the buttons and admired them very much. The boy stepped back, borrowed a knife from a comrade, cut the buttons off and handed them to the doctor. "All right, sir," said he as his itching palm closed over the coveted ornaments, "you can pass." And pass he did to home and friends.

Captain Bowes's merchandising in the matter of exchange was as open as the issuing of rations. His agent in conducting the bargaining was a Raider, a New York gambler and stool-pigeon whom we called "Matty." He dealt quite fairly. Several times when the exchange was interrupted, Bowes sent the money back to those who had paid him and received it again when the exchange was renewed. Had it been possible to buy our way out for five cents each, Andrews and I would have had to stay back, since we had not had that much money for months. All our friends were in an equally bad plight. Like almost everybody else, we had spent the few dollars we happened to have on entering the prison in a week or so and since then we had been entirely penniless. There was no hope left for us but to try to pass the surgeons as desperately sick, and we expended our energies in simulating this condition.

Rheumatism was our forte, and I flatter myself we got up two cases that were apparently bad enough to serve as illustrations for a patent medicine advertisement. But it would not do. Bad as we made our condition appear, there were so many more who were infinitely worse that we stood no show in the competitive examination. I doubt if we would have been given an average of "50" in a report. We had to stand back and see about one quarter of our number march out and away home. We could not complain at this, much as we wanted to go ourselves, since there could be no question that these poor fellows deserved precedence.

We did grumble savagely at Captain Bowes's banality in selling out our chances to moneyed men, since these were invariably those who were best prepared to withstand the hardships of imprisonment as they were mostly new men and all had good clothes and blankets. We did not blame the men, however, since it was not in human nature to resist an opportunity to get away, at any cost, from that accursed place. The sutlers had accumulated sufficient money to supply themselves with all the necessaries and some of the comforts of life during any probable term of imprisonment and still have a snug amount left, but they would rather give it all up and return to service with their regiments in the field than take the chances of any longer continuance in prison. I can only surmise how much Bowes realized out of the prisoners by his venality, but I feel sure that it could not have been less than three thousand dollars and I would not be astonished to learn that it was ten thousand dollars in greenbacks.

One night toward the end of November, there was a general alarm around the prison. A gun was fired from the fort, the long roll was beaten in the various camps of the guards, and the regiments answered by getting under arms in haste and forming near the prison gates. The reason for this—which we did not learn until weeks later— was that Sherman, who had cut loose from Atlanta and started on his famous "march to the sea," had taken such a course as rendered it probable that Millen was one of his objective points. It was therefore necessary that we should be hurried away with all possible speed. As we had had no news from Sherman since the end of the Atlanta campaign, we were ignorant of his having begun his great raid, and we were at an utter loss to account for the commotion among our keepers.

About three o'clock in the morning the rebel sergeants who called the roll came in and ordered us to turn out immediately and get ready to move. The morning was one of the most cheerless I had ever known. A cold rain poured relentlessly down upon us half-naked, shivering wretches as we groped around in the darkness for our pitiful little belongings of rags and cooking utensils and huddled together in groups, urged on continually by the curses and abuse of the rebel officers. Though we were roused at three o'clock, the cars were not ready to receive us till nearly noon.

In the meantime we stood in ranks numb, trembling and heartsick. The guards around us crouched over fires and shielded themselves as best they could with blankets and bits of tent cloth. We had nothing to build fires with and were not allowed to approach those of the guards. Around us everywhere was the dull, cold, gray, hopeless desolation of the approach of winter. The hard wiry grass that thinly covered the once arid sand, the occasional stunted weeds and the sparse foliage of the gnarled and dwarfish undergrowth, all were parched brown and seered by the fiery heat of the long summer and now rattled drearily under the pitiless cold rain streaming from the lowering clouds that seemed to have floated down to us from the cheerless summit of some great iceberg. The tall naked pines moaned and shivered: dead sapless leaves fell wearily to the sodden earth like withered hopes drifting down to deepen some Slough of Despond. Scores of our crowd found this the culmination of their misery. They laid down upon the ground and yielded to death as a welcome relief, and we left them lying there unburied when we moved to the cars.

As we passed through the rebel camp at dawn, on our way to the cars, Andrews and I noticed a nest of four large bright, new tin pans—a rare thing in the Confederacy at that time. We managed to snatch them without the guard's attention being attracted and in an instant had them wrapped up in our blanket. But the blanket was full of holes, and in spite of all our efforts it would slip at the most inconvenient times and would show a bit of the bright metal just when it seemed it could not help attracting the attention of the guards or their officers. A dozen times at least we were on the imminent brink of detection, but we finally got our treasures safely to the cars and sat down upon them.

The cars were open flats. The rains still beat unrelentingly. Andrews and I huddled ourselves together so as to make our bodies afford as much heat as possible, pulled our faithful old overcoat around us as far as it would go, and endured the inclemency as best we could. Our train headed back to Savannah, and again our hearts warmed with hopes of exchange. It seemed as if there could be no other purpose in taking us out of a prison so recently established—and at such cost—as Millen. As we approached the coast the rain ceased, but a piercing cold wind set in that threatened to convert our soaked rags into icicles.

Many died on the way. When we arrived at Savannah almost every car had on it one whom hunger no longer gnawed nor disease wasted, whom cold had pinched for the last time, and for whom the golden portals of the Beyond had opened for an exchange that neither Davis nor his despicable tool, Winder, could control. We did not sentimentalize over these. We could not mourn: the thousands that we had seen pass away made that emotion hackneyed and wearisome. With the death of some friend and comrade as regularly an event of each day as roll call and drawing rations, the sentiment of grief had become nearly obsolete. We were not hardened; we had simply come to look upon death as commonplace and ordinary. To have had no one dead or dying around us would have been regarded as singular. Besides, why should we feel any regret at the passing away of those whose condition would probably be better thereby. It was difficult to see where we who still lived were any better off than they who were gone before. Even if imprisonment was to continue only another month, we would rather be with them.

Arriving at Savannah we were ordered off the cars. A squad from each car carried the dead to a designated spot and laid them in a row, composing their limbs as well as possible but giving no other funeral rites, not even making a record of their names and regiments. Negro laborers came along afterwards with carts, took the bodies to some vacant ground and sunk them out of sight in the sand. We were given a few crackers each, the same rude imitation of "hardtack" that had been served out to us when we arrived at Savannah the first time, and then were marched over and put upon a train on the Atlantic and Gulf Railroad, running from Savannah along the seacoast toward Florida. What this meant we had little conception, but hope which sprang eternal in the prisoner's breast whispered that perhaps it was exchange; that there was some difficulty about our vessels coming to Savannah; and so we were being taken to some other more convenient seaport; probably to Florida to deliver us to our folks there.

We satisfied ourselves that we were running along the seacoast by tasting the water in the streams we crossed whenever we could get an opportunity to dip up some. As long as the water tasted salty we knew we were near the sea and hope burned brightly. The truth was, as we afterwards learned, the rebels were terribly puzzled as to what to do with us. We were brought to Savannah but that did not solve the problem, and we were sent down the Atlantic and Gulf Railroad as a temporary expedient.

The railroad was the worst of the many bad ones which it was my fortune to ride upon in my excursions while a guest of the Southern Confederacy. It had run down until it had nearly reached the worn-out condition of that western road of which an employee of a rival route once said that all there was left of it was two streaks of rust and the right of way. As it was one of the non-essential roads to the Southern Confederacy, it had been stripped of the best of its rolling-stock and machinery to supply the other more important lines.

There was a scarcity of grease in the South and difficulty in supplying the railroads with lubricants. Apparently there had been no oil on the Atlantic and Gulf since the beginning of the war, and the screeches of the dry axles revolving in the worn-out boxes were agonizing. Something would break on the cars or blow out on the engine every few miles, necessitating a long stop for repairs. Then there was no supply of fuel along the line. When the engine ran out of wood it would halt, and a couple of Negroes, riding on the tender, would assail a panel of fence or a fallen tree with their axes and, after an hour or such matter of hard chopping, would pile sufficient wood upon the tender to enable us to renew our journey.

Frequently the engine stopped as if from sheer fatigue or inanition. The rebel officers tried to get us to assist it up the grade by dismounting and pushing behind. We respectfully but firmly declined. We were gentlemen of leisure, we said, and decidedly averse to manual labor. We had been invited on this excursion by Mr. Jeff Davis and his friends who set themselves up as our entertainers, and it would be a gross breach of hospitality to reflect upon our host by working our passage. If this was insisted upon, we should certainly not visit them again. Besides, it made no difference to us whether the train got along or not. We were not losing anything by the delay; we were not anxious to go anywhere. One part of the Southern Confederacy was just as good as another to us. So not a finger could they persuade any of us to raise to help along the journey.

The country we were traversing was sterile and poor, worse even than that in the neighborhood of Andersonville. Farms and farm houses were scarce and of towns there were none. Not even a collection of houses big enough to justify a blacksmith shop or a store appeared along the whole route. But few fields of any kind were seen, and nowhere was there a farm which gave evidence of a determined effort on the part of its occupants to till the soil and to improve their condition. When the train stopped for wood or for repairs or from exhaustion, we were allowed to descend from the cars and stretch our numbed limbs.

It did us good in other ways also. It seemed almost happiness to be outside of those cursed stockades, to rest our eyes by looking away through the woods, by seeing birds and animals that were *free*. They must be happy, because to us to be free once more was the summit of earthly happiness. There was a chance too to pick up something green to eat, and we were famishing for this. The scurvy still lingered in our systems and we were hungry for an antidote. A plant grew rather plentifully along the track that looked very much as I imagine a palm-leaf fan does in its green state. The leaf was not so large as an ordinary palm leaf, and came directly out of the ground. The natives called it "bull-grass," but anything more unlike grass I never saw, so we rejected that nomenclature, and dubbed them "green fans." They were very hard to pull up, it being usually as much as the strongest of us could do to draw them out of the ground. When pulled up there was found the smallest bit of a stock—not as much as a joint of one's little finger—that was edible. It had no particular taste and probably little nutriment, still it was fresh and green, and we strained our weak muscles and enfeebled sinews at every opportunity, endeavoring to pull up a "green fan."

At one place where we stopped, there was a makeshift of a garden, one of those sorry "truck patches" which do poor duty about southern cabins for the kitchen gardens of the northern farmers and produce a few coarse cowpeas, a scanty lot of collards (a coarse kind of cabbage with a stalk about a yard long) and some onions to vary the usual sidemeat and corn pone diet of the Georgia "cracker." Scanning the patch's ruins of vine and stalk, Andrews espied a handful of onions which had remained ungathered. They tempted him as the apple did Eve. Without stopping to communicate his intention to me, he sprang from the car, snatched the onions from their bed, pulled up half a dozen collard stalks and was on his way back before the guard could make up his mind to fire upon him.

The swiftness of his motions saved his life, for had he been more deliberate the guard would have concluded he was trying to escape and shot him down. As it was, he was turning back before the guard could get his gun up.

The onions he had secured were to us more delicious than wine upon the lees. They seemed to find their way into every fiber of our bodies and invigorate every organ. The collard stalks he had snatched up in the expectation of finding in them something resembling the nutritious "heart" that we remembered as children seeking and finding in the stalks of cabbage. But we were disappointed. These stalks were as dry and rotten as the bones of Southern society. Even hunger could find no meat in them.

After some days of this leisurely journeying toward the south, we halted permanently about eighty-six miles from Savannah. There was no reason why we should stop there more than any place else where we had been or were likely to go. It seemed as if the rebels had simply tired of hauling us and so dumped us off. We had another lot of dead, accumulated since we left Savannah, and the scenes at that place were repeated. The train returned for another load of prisoners.

"The Goober-Grabber"

CHAPTER XX

A SHATTERING DISAPPOINTMENT

WE WERE INFORMED that we were at Blackshear, the county seat of Pierce County. Where they kept the Court House or "county seat" is beyond conjecture to me, since I could not see a half-dozen houses in the whole clearing and not one of them was a respectable dwelling, taking even so low a standard for respectable dwellings as that afforded by the majority of Georgia houses. Pierce County, as I have since learned by the census report, is one of the poorest counties of a poor section of a very poor state. A population of less than two thousand, thinly scattered over its five hundred square miles of territory, gains a meager subsistence by a weak simulation of cultivating patches of its sandy dunes and plains in "nubbin" corn and "dropsical" sweet potatoes.

A few "razor-back" hogs, a species so gaunt and thin that I heard a man once declare that he had stopped a lot belonging to a neighbor from crawling through the cracks of a tight board-fence by tying a knot in their tails, roam the woods and supply all the meat used. Andrews used to insist that some of the hogs which we saw were so thin that the connection between their fore and hind quarters was only a single thickness of skin with hair on both sides, but then Andrews sometimes had a tendency to exaggerate. The swine certainly did have proportions that strongly resembled those of the animals which children cut out of cardboard. They were like the geometrical definition of a superficies—all length and breadth and no thickness. A ham from them would look like a palm-leaf fan.

I never ceased to marvel at the delicate adjustments of the development of animal life to the soil in these lean sections of Georgia. The poor land would not maintain anything, but lank lazy men with few wants sought a maintenance from it. I may have tangled up cause and effect in this proposition, but if so the reader can disentangle them at his leisure. I was not astonished to learn that it took five hundred square miles of Pierce County land to maintain two thousand "crackers" even as poorly as they lived. I should fully want that much of it to support one fair-sized Northern family as it should be.

After leaving the cars we were marched off into the pine woods by the side of a considerable stream and told that this was to be our camp. A heavy guard was placed around us and a number of pieces of artillery mounted where they could command the whole camp. We started in to make ourselves comfortable, as at Millen, by building shanties. The prisoners we left behind followed us, and we soon had our crowd of five or six thousand, who had been our companions at Savannah and Millen, again with us. The place looked very favorable for escape. We knew we were still near the seacoast, really not more than forty miles away, and we felt that if we could once get there we should be safe. Andrews and I meditated plans of escape and toiled away at our cabin.

About a week after our arrival, we were startled by an order for one thousand of us who had first arrived to get ready to move out. In a few minutes we were taken outside the guard line, massed close together and informed in a few words by a rebel officer that we were about to be taken back to Savannah for exchange. The announcement took our breath away. For an instant the rush of emotion made us speechless, and when utterance returned, the first use we made of it was to join in one simultaneous outburst of acclamation. Those inside the guard line, understanding what our cheer meant, answered us with a loud shout of congratulation, the first real, genuine, hearty cheering that had been done since receiving the announcement of the exchange at Andersonville, three months before. As soon as the excitement subsided somewhat, the rebel proceeded to explain to us that we would all be required to sign a parole. This set us to thinking.

After our scornful rejection of the proposition to enlist in the rebel army, the rebels had felt around among us considerably as to how we were disposed toward taking what was called the "non-combatant's oath"—that is, swearing not to take up arms against the Southern Confederacy again during the war. To most of us this seemed only a little less dishonorable than joining the rebel army. We held that our oaths to our own Government placed us at its disposal until it chose to discharge us, and we could not make any engagements with its enemies that might come in contravention of that duty. In short, it looked very much like desertion, and this we did not feel at liberty to consider.

There were still many among us who, feeling certain that they could not survive imprisonment much longer, were disposed to look favorably upon the non-combatant's oath, thinking that the circumstances of the case would justify their apparent dereliction of duty. Whether it would or not, I must leave to more skilled casuists than myself to decide. It was a matter I believed every man must settle with his own conscience. The opinion that I then held and expressed was that if a boy felt that he was hopelessly sick, and that he could not live if he remained in prison, he was justified in taking the oath. In the absence of our own surgeons he would have to decide for himself whether he was sick enough to be warranted in resorting to this means of saving his life. If he was in good health—as the majority of us were—with a reasonable prospect of surviving some weeks longer, there was no excuse for taking the oath, for in that few weeks we might be exchanged, be recaptured or make our escape.

While the rebel was talking about our signing the parole, there flashed upon all of us at the same moment a suspicion that this was a trap to delude us into signing the non-combatant's oath. Instantly there went up a general shout: "Read the parole!" The rebel was handed a blank parole by a companion and he read over the printed conditions at the top, which was that those signing agreed "not to bear arms against the Confederacy in the field, in the garrison, not to man any works, assist in any expedition, do any sort of guard work, serve in any military constabulary, or perform any military service *until properly exchanged.*"

For a minute this was satisfactory; then our ingrained distrust of anything a rebel said or did burst out, and we shouted: "No! No! Let some of us read it. Let Illinoy read it!" The rebel looked around in a puzzled manner: "Who the hell is Illinoy? Where is he?" I saluted and said, "That's a nickname they give me." "Very well," he said, "get up on this stump and read this parole to these damn fools that won't believe me." I mounted the stump, took the blank from his hand and read it over carefully and slowly, giving as much emphasis as possible to the all-important clause at the end—*until properly exchanged.* "Boys, this seems all right to me," I said, and they answered with almost one voice, "Yes, that's all right. We'll sign that."

I never was so proud of the American soldier as at that moment. They all felt that signing that paper was to give them freedom and life. They knew too well from sad experience what the alternative was. Many felt that, unless they were released, another week would see them in their graves. All knew that every day's stay in rebel hands greatly lessened their chances for life. Yet in all that thousand there was not one voice in favor of yielding a tittle of honor to save life. They would secure their freedom honorably or die faithful. Remember that this was a miscellaneous crowd of boys gathered from all sections of the country, from many of whom no exalted conceptions of duty and honor were expected. I wish someone would point out to me on the brightest pages of knightly record some deed of fealty and truth that equals the simple fidelity of these unknown heroes. I do not think that one of them felt that he was doing anything especially meritorious. He only obeyed the natural promptings of his heart.

The business of signing the paroles was then begun in earnest. We were separated in squads according to the first letters of our names, all those whose names began with A being placed in one squad, those beginning with B in another, and so on. Blank paroles for each letter were spread out on boxes and planks at different places and the signing went on under the superintendence of a rebel sergeant and one of the prisoners. The squad of M's selected me to superintend the signing for us, and I stood by to direct the boys and sign for the very few who could not write. After this was done we fell into ranks again, called the roll of the signers, and carefully compared the number of men with the number of signatures so that nobody should pass unparoled. The oath was then administered to us and two days' rations of corn meal and fresh beef were issued. This formality removed the last lingering doubt that we had of the exchange being a reality, and we gave way to the happiest emotions.

We cheered ourselves hoarse and the fellows still inside followed our example, as they expected that they would share our good fortune in a day or two. Our next performance was to set to work, cook our two days' rations at once and eat them. This was not very difficult as the whole supply for two days would hardly make one square meal. This done, many of the boys went to the guard line and threw their blankets, clothing, and cooking utensils to their comrades who were still inside. No one thought that they would have any further use for such things.

"Tomorrow, at this time, thank Heaven," said a boy near me as he tossed his blanket and overcoat back to someone inside, "we'll be in God's country, and then I wouldn't touch them damn lousy old rags with a ten-foot pole."

One of the boys in M squad, a Maine infantryman who had been with me in the Pemberton Building in Richmond, had fashioned himself a little square pan out of a tin plate of a tobacco press. He had carried it with him ever since, and it was his sole vessel for all purposes—for cooking, carrying water and drawing rations. He had cherished it as if it were a farm or good situation. But now as he turned away from signing his name to the parole, he looked at his faithful servant for a minute in undisguised contempt. On the eve of restoration to happier and better things, it was a reminder of all the petty, inglorious, contemptible trials and sorrows he had endured. He actually loathed it for its remembrances and, flinging it on the ground, he crushed it all out of shape and usefulness with his feet, trampling upon it as he would like to trample on everything connected with his prison life.

Andrews and I flung the bright new tin pans we had stolen at Millen inside the line to be scrambled for. It was hard to tell who were the most surprised at their appearance—the rebels or our own boys, for few had any idea that there were such things in the whole Confederacy and certainly none looked for them in the possession of two such poverty-stricken specimens as we were. We thought it best to retain possession of our little can, spoon, chess-board, blanket and overcoat. As we marched down and boarded the train, the rebels confirmed their previous action by taking all the guards from around us. Only some eight or ten were sent to the train, and these quartered themselves in the caboose and paid us no further attention.

The train rolled away amid cheering by ourselves and those we left behind. One thousand happier boys than we never started on a journey. We were going home. The wintry sun had something of geniality and warmth. The landscape lost some of its repulsiveness. The dreary palmettos had less of that hideousness which made us regard them as very fitting emblems of treason. We even began to feel a little good-humored contempt for our hateful little brats of guards and to reflect how much vicious education and surroundings were to be held for their misdeeds. We laughed and sang as we rolled along toward Savannah, going back much faster than we came. We retold old stories and repeated old jokes that had become wearisome months and months ago but were now freshened up and given their olden pith by the joyousness of the occasion. We revived and talked over old schemes, gotten up in earlier days of prison life, of what "we would do when we got out," schemes almost forgotten in the general uncertainty of ever getting out. We exchanged addresses, and promised faithfully to write to each other and tell how we found everything at home.

So the afternoon and night passed. We were too excited to sleep and passed the hours watching the scenery, recalling the objects we had passed on the way to Blackshear and guessing how near we were to Savannah. Though we were running along within fifteen or twenty miles of the coast, with all our guards asleep in the caboose, no one thought of escape. We could step off the cars and walk over to the seashore as easily as a man steps out of his door and walks to a neighboring town. But why should we? Were we not going directly to our vessels in the harbor of Savannah, and was it not better to do this than to take chances of escaping and encounter the difficulties of reaching our blockaders? We thought so and we stayed on the cars.

A cold gray winter morning was just breaking as we reached Savannah. Our train ran down in the city and then whistled sharply and ran back a mile or so. It repeated this maneuver two or three times, the evident design being to keep us on the cars until the people were ready to receive us. Finally our engine ran with all the speed she was capable of, and as the train dashed into the street we found ourselves between two heavy lines of guards with bayonets fixed. The whole sickening reality was made apparent by one glance at the guard line. Our parole was a mockery, its only object to get us to Savannah as easily as possible and to prevent benefit from our recapture to any of Sherman's raiders who might make a dash for the railroad while we were in transit. There had been no intention of exchanging us. There was no exchange going on at Savannah.

After all, I do not think we felt the disappointment as keenly as the first time we were brought to Savannah. Imprisonment had stupefied us; we were duller and more hopeless. Ordered down out of the cars, we were formed in line in the street. A rebel officer spoke up. "Now, any of you fellers that ah too sick to go to Chahlston, step foh-wahd one pace." We looked at each other an instant, and then the whole line stepped forward. We all felt too sick to go to Charleston or to do anything else in the world.

As the train left the northern suburbs of Savannah, we came upon a scene of busy activity strongly contrasting with the somnolent lethargy that seemed to be the normal condition of the city and its inhabitants. Long lines of earthworks were being constructed, gangs of Negroes were felling trees, building forts and batteries, making abatis, and toiling with numbers of huge guns which were being moved out and placed in position. As we had had no new prisoners nor any papers for some weeks—the papers doubtless designedly being kept away from us—we were at a loss to know what this meant. We could not understand this erection of fortifications on that side because, knowing as we did how well the flanks of the city were protected by the Savannah and Ogeechee rivers, we could not see how a force from the coast, whence we supposed an attack must come, could hope to reach the city's rear, especially as we had just come up on the right flank of the city and saw no sign of our folks in that direction.

Our train stopped for a few minutes at the edge of this line of works, and an old citizen who had been surveying the scene with senile interest tottered over to our car to take a look at us. He was a type of the old man of the South, one of the scanty middle-class small farmer. Long white hair and beard, spectacles with great, round, staring glasses, a broad-brimmed hat of ante-revolutionary pattern, clothes that had apparently descended to him from some ancestor who had come over with Oglethorpe, and a two-handed staff with a head of buckhorn, upon which he leaned as old peasants do in plays, formed such an image as recalled to me the picture of the old man in the illustrations in *The Dairyman's Daughter*.[49] He was as garrulous as a magpie and as opinionated as a Southern white always is. Halting in front of our car, he steadied himself by planting his staff, clasping it with both lean and skinny hands. Then leaned forward upon it, his jaws addressed themselves to motion, thus: "Boys," he said, "who mout these be that ye got?"

One of the guards answered, "Oh, these is some Yanks that we've bin hivin' down at Camp Sumter."

"Yes?" said the old man with an upward inflection of the voice followed by a close scrutiny of us through the goggle-eyed glasses, "Wall, they're a powerful ornery lookin' lot, I'll declah." It will be seen that the old gentleman's perceptive powers were much more highly developed than his politeness.

"Wall, they ain't what ye mout call perty," squeaked the old man.

"That's a fack," said the guard.

"So yer Yanks, air ye?" said the venerable "goober-grabber"—the nickname in the South for Georgians—directing his conversation to me. "Wall, I'm powerful pleased to see ye, an' 'specially whar ye can't do no harm. I've wanted to see some Yankees ever sence the beginnin' of the war, but nevah had no chance. Whar did ye come from?"

I seemed called upon to answer and said, "I came from Illinois. Most of the boys in this car are from there, Ohio, Indiana, Michigan and Iowa."

" 'Deed! All westerners, air ye? Wall, do ye know I alluz liked the westerners a heap sight better than them blue-bellied New England Yankees." No discussion with a rebel ever proceeded very far without the making of an assertion like this. It was a favorite declaration of theirs, but its absurdity was comical when one remembered that the majority of these rebels could not for their lives tell the names of the New England states and could no more distinguish a Downeaster from an Illinoisan than they could tell a Saxon from a Bavarian.

One day while I was holding a conversation similar to the above with an old man on guard, another guard, who had been stationed near a squad of Germans that talked altogether in the language of the Fatherland, broke in with, "Out there by post numbah foahteen where I wuz yesterday, there's a lot of Yanks who jest jabbered away all the hull time, and I hope I may nevah see the back of my neck ef I could understand airy a word they said. Are them the Regular blue-belly kind?"

The old gentleman entered upon the next stage of the invariable routine of discussion with a rebel: "Wall, what air you'uns down heah a-fightin' we'uns foah?"

As I had answered this question several hundred times, I had found the most extinguishing reply to be to ask in return: "What are you'uns coming up into our country to fight we'uns for?"

Disdaining to notice this return in kind, the old man passed on to the next stage:

"What air you'uns takin' ouah niggahs away from us foah?" Now, if Negroes had been as cheap as oroide watches, it is doubtful whether the speaker had ever had money enough in his possession at one time to buy one, and yet he talked of taking away "ouah niggahs" as if they were as common about his place as hills of corn. As a rule, the more abjectly poor a Southerner was, the more readily he worked himself into a rage over the idea of "takin' away ouah niggahs."

I replied in burlesque of his assumption of ownership: "What are you coming up North to burn my rolling mills and rob my comrade here's bank and plunder my brother's store and burn down my uncle's factories?" No reply to this counter thrust.

The old man passed to the third inevitable proposition: "What air you'uns puttin' ouah niggahs in the field to fight we'uns for?"

The whole carload shouted back at him at once, "What are you'uns putting blood-hounds on our trails to hunt us down, for?"

"Waal, ye don't think ye kin evah lick us," said the old man savagely, "leastways sick fellers as ye air?"

"Well, we warmed it to you pretty lively," I replied, "until you caught us. There were none of us but what were doing about as good work as any stock you fellows could turn out. No rebels in our neighborhood had much to brag on. We are not a drop in the bucket either. There's millions more and better men than we are where we came from, and they are all determined to stamp out your miserable Confederacy. We've got to come to it, sooner or later. You must knock under, sure as white blossoms make little apples. You'd better make up your mind to it."

"No sah, nevah," said the old man heatedly, "ye nevah kin conquer us! We're the bravest people and the best fighters on airth.[50] Ye nevah kin whip any people that's a-fightin' fur their liberty an' their right; an' ye nevah can whip the South, sah, anyway. We'll fight ye until all the men air kilt, and then the wimmen'll fight ye, sah."

"Well, you may think so or you may not," I replied. "From the way our boys are snatching the Confederacy's real estate away, it begins to look as if you'd not have enough to fight anybody on pretty soon. What's the meaning of all this fortifying?"

"Why, don't you know?" asked the old man. "Ouah folks air fixin' up a place foah Bill Sherman to butt his brains out agin."

"Bill Sherman!" we all shouted in surprise. "Why, he ain't within two hundred miles of this place, is he?"

"Yas, but he is though," said the old man. "He thinks he's played a sharp Yankee trick on Hood. He found out he couldn't lick him in a squar' fight nohow—he tried that 'un too often—so he just sneaked 'round behind him and made a break for the center of the State [51] where he thought there was lots of good stealin' to be done. But we'll show him. We'll soon hev him just whar we want him, an' we'll learn him how to go traipsin' 'round the country, stealin' niggahs, burnin' cotton, an' runnin' off folkses' beef critters. He sees now the scrape he's got into, an' he's tryin' to get to the coast, whar the gun-boats'll help him out. But he'll nevah git thar, sah. No sah, nevah! He's mouty nigh the end of his rope, sah, an' we'll perty soon hev him jist whar you fellers air, sah."

"Well, if you fellows intended stopping him," I replied, "why didn't you do it up about Atlanta? Why did you let him come clear through the State, burning and stealing as you say? It was money in your pockets to head him off as soon as possible."

"Oh, we didn't set nothin' afore him up thar except Joe Brown's Pets.[52] Those sorry little Reserves—they're powerful little account; no stand-up to 'em at all; they'd break their necks runnin' away if ye so much as bust a cap near to 'em."

Our guards who belonged to Brown's Reserves instantly felt that the conversation had progressed farther than was profitable and one of them spoke up roughly: "See heah, old man, you must go off. I can't hev ye talkin' to these prisoners. Hit's agin my ordahs. Go 'way now!"

The old fellow moved off, but as he did he flung this Parthian arrow: "When Sherman gits down heah, he'll find somethin' different from the little snots of Reserves he ran over up about Milledgeville. He'll find he's got to fight real soldiers!" We could not help enjoying the rage of the guards over this low estimate of the fighting ability of themselves and comrades, and as they raved around about what they would do if they were only given an opportunity to go into a line of battle against Sherman, we added fuel to the flames of their anger by confiding to each other that we always "knew that little brats whose highest ambition was to murder a defenseless prisoner could be nothing else than cowards and skulkers in the field."

A little later a paper which someone had gotten hold of in some mysterious manner was secretly passed to me. I read it as I could find opportunity and communicated its contents to the rest of the boys. The most important of these was a flaming proclamation by Governor Joe Brown [53] setting forth that General Sherman was now traversing the state, committing all sorts of depredations; that he had prepared the way for his own destruction; and the Governor called upon all good citizens to rise en masse and assist in crushing the audacious invader. Bridges must be burned before and behind him, roads obstructed and every inch of soil resolutely disputed. We enjoyed this. It showed that the rebels were terribly alarmed, and we began to feel some of that confidence that Sherman would come out all right which so marvelously animated all under his command.

The train started a few minutes after the close of the conversation with the old

Georgian and we soon came to and crossed the Savannah River into South Carolina. The river was wide and apparently deep; the tide was setting back in a swift muddy current; the crazy old bridge creaked and shook, and the grinding axles shrieked in their dry journals as we pulled across. It looked very much at times as if we were all to crash down into the turbid flood. We did not care very much if we did if we were not going to be exchanged.

The road lay through the tide-swamp region of South Carolina, a peculiar and interesting country. Though swamps and fens stretched in all directions as far as the eye could reach, the landscape was more grateful to the eye than the famine-stricken pine-barrens of Georgia, which had become weary to the sight. The soil, where it appeared, was rich; vegetation was luxuriant; great clumps of laurel showed a glossy richness in the greenness of its verdure that reminded us by its fresh color of the vegetation of our northern homes, so different from the parched and impoverished look of Georgia's foliage. Immense blocks of wildfowl fluttered around us. The Georgian woods were almost destitute of living creatures. The evergreen live oak with its queer festoons of Spanish moss and the ugly and useless palmettos gave novelty and interest to the view. The rice swamps through which we were passing were the princely possessions of the few nabobs who before the war stood at the head of South Carolina's aristocracy.

They were South Carolina in fact, as absolutely as Louis XIV was France. In their hands, only a few score in number, was concentrated about all there was of South Carolina's education, wealth, culture and breeding. They represented a pinchbeck imitation of that regime in France which was happily swept out of existence by the French Revolution, and the destruction of which more than compensated for every drop of blood shed in those terrible days. Like the provincial Grand Seigneurs of Louis XIV's reign, they were gay, dissipated and turbulent; accomplished in the superficial acquirements that made the "gentlemen" of one hundred years ago but are grotesquely out of place in this sensible, solid age which demands that a man shall be of use and not merely for show. They ran horses and fought cocks, dawdled through society when young, and intrigued in politics the rest of their lives, with frequent spice-work of duels.

Esteeming personal courage as a supreme human virtue and never wearying of prating their devotion to the highest standard of intrepidity, they never produced a general [53] who was even mediocre. Nor did anyone ever hear of a South Carolina regiment gaining distinction.[54] Regarding politics and the art of government as, equally with arms, their natural vocations, they have never given the nation a statesman, and their greatest politicians achieved eminence by advocating ideas which only attracted by their balefulness. Still further resembling the French Grand Seigneurs of the eighteenth century, they rolled in wealth wrung from the laborer by reducing the rewards of his toil to the last fraction that would support his life and strength. The rice culture was immensely profitable, because they had found the secret for raising it more cheaply than even the pauper laborer of the Old World could.[55]

Their lands had cost them nothing originally, the improvements of dykes and ditches were comparatively inexpensive, the taxes were nominal, and their slaves were not so expensive as good horses in the North. Thousands of the acres along the road belonged to the Rhetts, thousands to the Haywards, thousands to the Manigaults, the Lowneses, the Middletons, the Hugers, the Barnwells, and the Elliotts—all names too well known in the history of our country's sorrows.[56] Occasionally one of their stately mansions could be seen on some distant elevation, surrounded by noble old trees and superb grounds. Here they lived during the healthy part of the year but fled thence to summer resorts in the highlands as the miasmatic season approached.

The people we saw at the stations along our route were melancholy illustrations of the evils of the rule of such an oligarchy. There was no middle class visible anywhere, nothing but the two extremes. A man was either a "gentleman" and wore a white shirt and city-made clothes, or he was a loutish hind, clad in near apologies for garments. We thought we had found in the Georgia "cracker" the lowest substratum of human society, but he was bright intelligence compared to the South Carolina "clayeater" and "sand-hiller." The "cracker" always gave hopes that, if he had the advantage of common schools and could be made to understand that laziness was dishonorable, he might develop into something.

There was little foundation for such hope in the average low South Carolinian. His mind was a shaking quagmire which did not admit of the erection of any superstructure of education upon it. The South Carolina guards about us did not know the name of the next town though they had been raised in that section. They did not know how far it was to there or to any place else, and they did not care to learn. They had no conception of what the war was being waged for and did not want to find out; they did not know where their regiment was going and did not remember where it had been. They could not tell how long they had been in service nor the time they had enlisted for. They only remembered that sometimes they had "sorter good times" and sometimes "they had been powerful bad," and they hoped there would be plenty to eat wherever they went and not too much hard marching. Then they wondered "whar a feller'd be likely to make a raise of a canteen of good whiskey."

Bad as the whites were, the rice plantation slaves were even worse, if that were possible. Brought to the country centuries ago as brutal savages from Africa, they had learned nothing of Christian civilization except that it meant endless toil in malarial swamps under the lash of the task master. They wore possibly a little more clothing than their Senegambian ancestors did; they ate corn meal, yams and rice instead of bananas, yams and rice as their forefathers did, and they had learned a bastard, almost unintelligible, English. These were the sole blessings acquired by a transfer from a life of freedom in the jungles of the Gold Coast to one of slavery in the swamps of the Combahee. I could not then, nor can I now, regret the downfall of a system of society which bore such fruits.

Towards night a distressingly cold breeze, laden with a penetrating mist, set in from the sea and put an end to future observations by making us too uncomfortable to care for scenery or social conditions. We wanted most to devise a way to keep warm. Andrews and I pulled our overcoat and blanket closely about us, snuggled together so as to make each one's meager body afford the other as much heat as possible, and endured. We became fearfully hungry. It will be recollected that we ate the whole of the two days' rations issued to us at Blackshear at once, and we had received nothing since. We had reached the sullen, fainting stage of great hunger, and for hours nothing was said by anyone except an occasional bitter execration on rebels and rebel practices.

It was late at night when we reached Charleston. The lights of the city and the apparent warmth and comfort there cheered us up somewhat with the hopes that we might have some share in them. Leaving the train, we were marched some distance through well-lighted streets in which were plenty of people walking to and fro. There were many stores, apparently stocked with goods, and the citizens seemed to be going about their business very much as was the custom up North. At length our head of column made a "right turn," and we marched away from the lighted portion of the city to a part which, I could see through the shadows, was filled with ruins. An almost insupportable odor of gas escaping, I suppose, from the ruptured pipes mingled with the cold, rasping air from the sea to make every breath intensely disagreeable.

As I saw the ruins, it flashed upon me that this was the burnt district of the city and they were putting us under the fire of our own guns. At first I felt much alarmed. Little relish as I had on general principles for being shot, I had much less for being killed by our own men. Then I reflected that if they put me there and kept me, a guard would have to be placed around us who would necessarily be in as much danger as we were. I knew I could stand any fire that a rebel could. We were halted in a vacant lot and sat down, only to jump up the next instant as someone shouted, "There comes one of 'em!" It was a great shell from the "Swamp Angel" Battery.[57]

Starting from a point miles away, where seemingly the sky came down to the sea, was a narrow ribbon of fire which slowly unrolled itself against the star-lit vault over our heads. On, on it came, apparently following the sky down to the horizon behind us. As it reached the zenith, there came to our ears a prolonged but now sharp "Whish-ish-ish-ish!" We watched it breathlessly, and it seemed to be long minutes in running its course; then a thump upon the ground and a vibration told that it had struck. For a moment there was a dead silence. Then came a loud roar and the crash of breaking timber and crushing walls. The shell had burst. Ten minutes later, another shell followed with like results.

For a while we forgot all about hunger in the excitement of watching the messengers from "God's Country." What happiness to be where those shells came from! Soon a rebel battery of heavy guns somewhere near and in front of us waked up and began answering with dull, slow thumps that made the ground shudder. This continued about an hour, when it quieted down again, but our shells kept coming over at regular intervals with the same slow deliberation, the same prolonged warning, and the same dreadful crash when they struck. They had already gone on this way for over a year and were to keep it up months longer until the city was captured.

The routine was the same from day to day, month in and month out, from early in August 1863 to the middle of April 1865. Every few minutes during the day, our folks would hurl a great shell into the beleaguered city, and twice a day, for perhaps an hour each time, the rebel batteries would talk back. It must have been a lesson to the Charlestonians as to the persistent, methodical spirit of the North. They prided themselves on the length of the time they were holding against the enemy, and the papers each day had a column headed: 390th DAY OF THE SIEGE——or 391st or 393rd, as the number might be since our people opened fire upon the city. The part where we lay was a mass of ruins. Many large buildings had been knocked down; very many more were riddled with shot-holes and tottering to their fall.

One night a shell passed through a large building about a quarter of a mile from us. It had already been struck several times and was shaky. The shell went through with a deafening crash. All was still for an instant; then it exploded with a dull roar, followed by more crashing of timbers and walls. The sound died away and was succeeded by a moment of silence. Finally the great building fell, a shapeless heap of ruins, with a noise like that of a dozen field pieces. We wanted to cheer but restrained ourselves. This was the nearest to us that any shell came. There was only one section of the city in reach of our guns and this was nearly destroyed. Fires had come to complete the work begun by the shells.

Outside of the boundaries of this region, the people felt themselves as safe as in one of our Northern cities today. They had an abiding faith that they were clear out of reach of any artillery that we could mount. I learned afterwards from some of the prisoners who went into Charleston ahead of us, and were camped on the racecourse outside of the city, that one day our fellows threw a shell clear over the city to this racecourse.[58] There was an immediate and terrible panic among the citizens. They thought we had mounted some new guns of increased range and now the whole city must go. But the next shell fell inside the established limits and those following were equally well-behaved, so that the panic abated.

I have never heard any explanation of the matter. It may have been some freak of the gun-squad, trying the effect of an extra charge of powder. Had our people but known of its signal effect, they could have depopulated the place in a few hours. The whole matter impressed me queerly. The only artillery I had seen at any time in action were field pieces. They made an ear-splitting crash when they were discharged, and there was likely to be oceans of trouble for everybody in that neighborhood about that time. I reasoned from this that bigger guns made a proportionally greater amount of noise and bred an infinitely larger quantity of trouble.

Now I was hearing the giants of the world's ordnance and they were not so impressive as a lively battery of three-inch rifles. Their reports did not threaten to shatter everything, but had a dull resonance something like that produced by striking an empty barrel with a wooden maul. Their shells did not come at one in that wildly ferocious way with which a missile from a six-pounder convinces every fellow in a long line of battle that he is the identical one it is meant for, but they meandered over in a lazy, leisurely manner, as if time was no object and no person would feel put out at having to wait for them. Then too the idea of firing every quarter of an hour for a year, "fixing up a job for a lifetime" as Andrews expressed it; of being fired back at for an hour at nine o'clock every morning and evening; of fifty thousand people going on buying and selling, eating, drinking and sleeping; of their having dances, drives and balls, marrying and giving in marriage—all within a few hundred yards of where the shells were falling—struck me as a most singular method of conducting warfare.

We received no rations until the day after our arrival, and then they were scanty, though fair in quality. We were by this time so hungry and faint that we could hardly move. We did nothing for hours but lie around on the ground and try to forget how famished we were. At the announcement of rations, many acted as if crazy, and it was all that the sergeants could do to restrain the impatient mob from tearing the food away and devouring it when they were trying to divide it up. Very many, perhaps thirty, died during the night and morning. No blame for this is attached to the Charlestonians. They distinguished themselves from the citizens of every other place in the Southern Confederacy where we had been by making efforts to relieve our condition. They sent quite a quantity of food to us, seeking and ministering to the sick. I believe our experience was the usual one. The prisoners who passed through Charleston before us all spoke very highly of the kindness shown them by the citizens there.

We remained in Charleston but a few days. One night we were marched down to a rickety depot and put aboard a still more rickety train. When morning came, we found ourselves running northward through a pine-barren country that resembled somewhat that in Georgia, except that the pine was short-leafed, there was more oak and other hard woods, and the vegetation generally assumed a more northern look. We had been put into closed box cars, with guards at the doors and on top. During the night quite a number of the boys, who had fabricated little saws out of case knives and fragments of hoop iron, cut holes through the bottoms of the cars through which they dropped to the ground and escaped, but they were mostly recaptured after several days. There was no hole cut in our car, and so Andrews and I stayed in.

Just at dusk we came to the insignificant village of Florence, the junction of the road leading from Charleston to Cheraw with that running from Wilmington to Kingsville. It was about one hundred and twenty miles from Charleston and the same distance from Wilmington. As our train ran through a cut near the junction, a darky stood by the track gazing at us curiously. When the train had nearly passed him, he started to run up the bank. In the imperfect light the guards mistook him for one of us who had jumped from the train. They all fired, and the unlucky Negro fell pierced by a score of bullets. That night we camped in the open field. When morning came we saw, a few hundred yards from us, a stockade of rough logs with guards stationed around it.

It was another prison pen. They were just bringing the dead out and two men were tossing the bodies up into the four-horse wagon which hauled them away for burial. The men were going about their business as coolly as if loading slaughtered hogs. One of them would catch the body by the feet and the other by the arms. They would give it a swing and up it would go into the wagon. This was filled to heaping with corpses; a Negro mounted the wheel horse, grasped the lines and shouted to his animals, "Now, walk off on your tails, boys." The horses strained, the wagon moved, and its load of what were once gallant devoted soldiers was carted off to nameless graves. This was a part of the daily morning routine. As we stood looking at the sickeningly familiar architecture of the prison pen, a 7th Indianian near me said in tones of wearisome disgust, "Well, this Southern Confederacy is the damnedest country to stand logs on end on God Almighty's footstool."

A Lucky Find

CHAPTER XXI

THE RED-HEADED KEEPER

IT DID NOT REQUIRE a very acute comprehension to understand that the stockade at which we were gazing was likely to be our abiding place for some indefinite period in the future. As usual, this discovery was the death-warrant of many whose lives had only been prolonged by the hoping against hope that this last movement would terminate inside our lines. When the portentous palisades showed, a fatal certainty that the word of promise had been broken struck home to their hearts, and they gave up the struggle wearily, lay back on the frozen ground and died.

Andrews and I were not in the humor for dying just then. The long imprisonment, the privations of hunger, the scourging by the elements, the deaths of four out of every five of our number, had indeed dulled and stupefied us, bred an indifference to our own suffering and a seeming callosity to that of others. But there still burned in our hearts and in the hearts of every one about us, a dull, sullen, smoldering fire of hate and defiance toward everything rebel and a lust for revenge upon those who had showered woes upon our heads.

There was little fear of death. Even the King of Terrors loses most of his awful character upon tolerably close acquaintance, and we had been on very intimate terms with him for a year now. He was a constant visitor who dropped in upon us at all hours of the day and night and would not be denied to anyone. Since my entry into prison, fully fifteen thousand boys had died around me, and in no one of them had I seen the least dread or reluctance to go. I believe this is generally true of death by disease everywhere. Our ever kindly Mother Nature only makes us dread death when she desires us to preserve life. When she summons us hence, she tenderly provides that we shall willingly obey the call.

More than for anything else we wanted to live now to triumph over the rebels. Simply to die would be of little importance, but to die unrevenged would be fearful. If we, the despised, the condemned, the insulted, the starved and maltreated, could live to come back to our oppressors as the armed ministers of retribution, terrible in the remembrance of the wrongs to ourselves and comrades, irresistible as the agents of heavenly justice, and mete out to them that Biblical return of seven-fold of what they had measured out to us, then we would be content to go to death afterwards. Had the thrice-accursed Confederacy and our malignant jailers had millions of lives, our great desire for revenge would have had stomach for them all.

The December morning was gray and leaden; dull, somber, snow-laden clouds swept across the sky before the sloughing wind. The ground, frozen hard and stiff, cut and hurt our bare feet at every step. An icy breeze drove in through the holes in our rags and smote our bodies like blows from sticks. The trees and shrubbery around were as naked and forlorn as in the north in the days of early winter before the snow comes. Over and around us hung like a cold miasma the sickening odor peculiar to southern forests in winter time.

Out of the naked, repelling, unlovely earth rose the stockade in hideous ugliness. At the gate the two men continued at their monotonous labor of tossing the dead of the previous day into the wagon, heaving into the rude hearse the inanimate remains that had once templed gallant manly hearts glowing with patriotism and devotion to country, piling up listlessly and wearily a mass of nameless emaciated corpses fluttering with rags and swarming with vermin, the pride and the joy of a hundred fair Northern homes whose light had now gone out forever. Around the prison walls shambled the guards, blanketed like Indians and with faces and hearts of wolves. Other rebels, also clad in dingy butternut, slouched around lazily, crouched over diminutive fires and talked idle gossip in the broadest of "nigger" dialect. Officers swelled and strutted hither and thither, and Negro servants loitered around, striving to spread the least amount of work over the greatest amount of time.

While I stood gazing in gloomy silence at the depressing surroundings, Andrews, less speculative and more practical, saw a good-sized pine stump nearby, which had so much of the earth washed away from it that it looked as if it could be readily pulled up. We had had bitter experience in other prisons as to the value of wood and Andrews reasoned that, as we would be likely to have a repetition of this in the stockade we were about to enter, we should make an effort to secure the stump. We both attacked it and, after a great deal of hard work, succeeded in uprooting it. It was very lucky that we did, since it was the greatest help in preserving our lives through the three long months that we remained at Florence.

While we were arranging our stump so as to carry it to the best advantage, a vulgar-factd man with fiery red hair, and wearing on his collar the yellow bars of a lieutenant, approached. This was Lieutenant Barret, commandant of the interior of the prison and a more inhuman wretch even than Captain Wirz because he had a little more brains than the commandant at Andersonville. This extra intellect was wholly devoted to cruelty. As he came near he commanded, in loud, brutal tones, "Attention, prisoners!" We all stood up and fell in in two ranks. "By companies," he shouted, "right wheel, march!" This was simply preposterous. As every soldier knows, wheeling by companies is one of the most difficult of maneuvers and requires some preparation of a battalion before attempting to execute it.

Our thousand was made up of infantry, cavalry and artillery, representing, perhaps, one hundred different regiments. We had not been divided off into companies and were encumbered with blankets, tents, cooking utensils and wood, which prevented our moving with such freedom as to make a company wheel even had we been divided up into companies and drilled for the maneuver. The attempt to obey the command was, of course, a ludicrous failure. The rebel officers standing near Barret laughed openly at his stupidity in giving such an order, but he was furious. He hurled at us a torrent of the vilest abuse the most corrupt imagination of man can conceive, and swore until he was fairly black in the face. He fired his revolver off over our heads and shrieked and shouted until he had to stop from sheer exhaustion. Another officer took command then and marched us into prison.

We found this a small copy of Andersonville. There was a stream running north and south, on either side of which was a swamp. A stockade of rough logs with the bark still on enclosed several acres. The front of the prison was toward the west. A piece of artillery stood before the gate and a platform at each corner bore a gun, elevated high enough to rake the whole inside of the prison. A man stood behind each of these guns continually, so as to open with them at any moment. The earth was thrown against the outside of the palisades in a high embankment along the top of which the guards on duty walked, it being high enough to elevate their head, shoulders and breasts above the tops of the logs. Inside the inevitable Dead Line was traced by running a furrow around the prison, twenty feet from the stockade, with a plow.

In one respect it was an improvement on Andersonville. Regular streets were laid off, so that motion about the camp was possible and cleanliness was promoted. Also, the crowd inside was not so dense as at Andersonville. The prisoners were divided into hundreds and thousands, with sergeants at the heads of the divisions. A very good police force, organized and officered by the prisoners, maintained order and prevented crime. Thefts and other offenses were punished, as at Andersonville, by the chief of police sentencing the offenders to be spanked or tied up.

We found very many of our Andersonville acquaintances inside, and for several days comparisons of experience were in order. They had left Andersonville a few days after us, but were taken to Charleston instead of Savannah. The same story of exchange was dinned into their ears until they arrived at Charleston, when the truth was told them—that no exchange was contemplated and that they had been deceived for the purpose of getting them safely out of reach of Sherman. Still, they were treated well in Charleston, better than they had been anywhere else. Intelligent physicians had visited the sick, prescribed for them, furnished them with proper medicines and admitted the worst cases to the hospital where they were given something of the care that one would expect in such an institution.

Wheat bread, molasses and rice were issued to them, and also a few spoonfuls of vinegar daily, which were very grateful to them in their scorbutic condition. The citizens sent in clothing, food and vegetables. Altogether, their recollections of the place were quite pleasant. Despite the disagreeable prominence which the city had in the secession movement, there was a very strong Union element there and many who found opportunity to do favors for the prisoners revealed to them how much they abhorred secession.

After they had been in Charleston a fortnight or more, the yellow fever [59] broke out in the city and soon extended its ravages to the prisoners, quite a number dying from it. Early in October they had been sent away from the city to their present location, which was a piece of forest land. There was no stockade or other enclosure about them, and one night they forced the guard-line, about fifteen hundred escaping under a pretty sharp fire from the guards. After getting out they scattered, each group taking a different route, some seeking Beaufort and other places along the seaboard, and the rest trying to gain the mountains.

The whole state was thrown into the greatest excitement by the occurrence. The papers magnified the proportion of the outbreak and lauded the guards' gallantry in endeavoring to withstand the desperate assaults of the frenzied Yankees. The people were wrought up into the highest alarm as to outrages and excesses that these flying desperadoes might be expected to commit. One would think that another Grecian horse, introduced into the heart of the Confederate Troy, had let out its fatal band of armed men. All good citizens were enjoined to turn out and assist in arresting the runaways. The vigilance of all patrolling was redoubled and such was the effectiveness of the measures taken that before a month nearly every one of the fugitives had been retaken and sent back to Florence. Few of these complained of any special ill treatment by their captors, while many reported frequent acts of kindness, especially when their captors belonged to the middle and upper classes. The low-down class, the "clay-eaters," on the other hand, almost always abused their prisoners and sometimes, it is pretty certain, murdered them in cold blood.

About this time, Winder came on from Andersonville, and then everything changed immediately in the complexion of that place. He began the erection of the stockade, and made it very strong. The Dead Line was established, but instead of being a strip of plank upon the top of low posts as at Andersonville, it was simply a shallow trench which was sometimes plainly visible and sometimes not. The guards always resolved matters of doubt against the prisoners and fired on them when they supposed them to be near where the Dead Line ought to be. Fifteen acres of ground were enclosed by the palisades, of which five were taken up by the creek and swamp, and three or four more by the Dead Line, leaving about seven or eight for the actual use of the prisoners, whose numbers had been swelled to fifteen thousand by the arrivals from Andersonville. This made the crowding together nearly as bad as at the latter place, and for a while the same fatal results followed. The mortality and the sending away of several thousand on the Sick Exchange reduced the aggregate number at the time of our arrival to about eleven thousand, which gave more room to all; but there was still not one twentieth of the space which that number should have had.

No shelter nor material for constructing any was furnished. The ground was rather thickly wooded and covered with undergrowth when the stockade was built, and certainly no bit of soil was ever as thoroughly cleared as this was. The trees and brush were cut down and worked up into hut-building materials by the same slow and laborious process that I have already described. Then the stumps were attacked for fuel, and with such persistent thoroughness that after some weeks there was certainly not enough woody material left in that whole fifteen acres of ground to kindle a small kitchen fire. The men would begin work on the stump of a good-sized tree and would chip and split it off painfully and slowly until they had followed it to the extremity of the tap root ten or fifteen feet below the surface. The lateral roots would be followed with equal determination, and trenches thirty feet long and two or three feet deep were dug with case knives and half-canteens, to get a root as thick as one's wrist. The roots and shrubs and vines were followed up and gathered with similar industry. The cold weather and the scanty issues of wood forced men to do this.

The huts constructed were as various as the materials and the tastes of the builders. Those who were fortunate enough to get plenty of timber built cabins like those

Andrews and I had at Millen. Those who had less eked out their materials in various ways. Most frequently all that a squad of three or four could get would be a few slender poles and some brush. They would dig a hole in the ground two feet deep and large enough for them all to lie in. Then putting up a stick at each end and laying a ridge pole across, they would adjust the rest of their material so as to form sloping sides capable of supporting earth enough to make a water-tight roof.

The great majority were not so well off as these and had absolutely nothing of which to build. They had recourse to the clay of the swamp, from which they fashioned rude sun-dried bricks and made adobe houses shaped like beehives which lasted very well until a hard rain came, when they dissolved into red mire about the bodies of their miserable inmates. Remember that all these makeshifts were practiced within a half mile of an almost boundless forest from which in a day's time the camp could have been supplied with material enough to give every man a comfortable hut.

Winder had found in Barret an even better tool for his cruel purposes than Wirz. The two resembled each other in many respects. Both were absolutely destitute of any talent for commanding men. They could no more handle a thousand men properly than a cabin boy could navigate an ocean steamer. Both were given to the same senseless fits of insane rage, coming and going without apparent cause, during which they fired revolvers and guns or threw clubs into crowds of prisoners or knocked down such as were within reach of their fists. These exhibitions were such as an overgrown child might be expected to make. They did not secure any result except to increase the prisoners' wonder that such ill-tempered idiots could be given positions of responsibility.

A short time previous to our entry, Barret thought he had reason to suspect a tunnel. He immediately announced that no more rations should be issued until its whereabouts was revealed and the ringleaders in the attempt to escape delivered up to him. The rations at that time were very scanty, so that the first day they were cut off the sufferings were fearful. The boys thought that he would surely relent the next day, but they did not know their man. He was not suffering in any way, so why should he relax his severity? He strolled out leisurely from his dinner table, picking his teeth with his penknife in the comfortable self-satisfied way of a coarse man who has just filled his stomach, an attitude and an air that was simply maddening to the famishing wretches whom he tantalized with: "Air ye're hungry enough to give up them goddam sons o' bitches yet?"

That night thirteen thousand men, crazy and fainting with hunger, walked hither and thither until exhaustion forced them to become quiet, then sat on the ground and pressed their bowels in by leaning against sticks of wood laid across their thighs; or trooped to the creek and drank water until their gorges rose and they could swallow no more. They did everything in fact that imagination could suggest to assuage the pangs of the deadly gnawing that was consuming their vitals. All the cruelties of the terrible Spanish Inquisition, if heaped together, would not sum up a greater aggregate of anguish than was endured by them.

The third day came, and still no signs of yielding by Barret. Something had to be done. The sergeants counseled together. Barret would starve the whole camp to death with as little compunction as one drowns blind puppies. It was necessary to get up a tunnel to show Barret and to get boys who would confess to being leaders in the work. A number of gallant fellows volunteered to brave his wrath and save the rest of their comrades. It required high courage to do this, as there was no question but that the punishment meted out would be as fearful as the cruel mind of Barret could devise. The sergeants decided that four would be sufficient to answer the purpose. They selected these by lot, marched them to the gate and delivered them over to Barret, who thereupon ordered rations to be sent in. He was considerate enough, too, to feed the men he was going to torture.

The starving men in the stockade could not wait after the rations were issued to cook them, but in many instances mixed the meal up with water and swallowed it raw. Frequently their stomachs, irritated by the long fast, rejected the mess, and very many had reached the stage where they loathed food. A burning fever was consuming them and seething their brains with delirium. Hundreds died within a few days, and hundreds more were so debilitated by the terrible strain that they did not linger long afterward.

The boys who had offered themselves as a sacrifice for the rest were put into a guard house and kept overnight that Barret might make a day of the amusement of torturing them. After he had laid in a hearty breakfast and doubtless fortified himself with some of the villainous sorghum whiskey which the rebels were now reduced to drinking, he set about his entertainment. The devoted four were brought out, one by one, and their hands tied together behind their backs. Then a noose of a strong, slender hemp rope was slipped over the first one's thumbs and drawn tight, after which the rope was thrown over a log projecting from the roof of the guard house and two or three rebels hauled upon it until the miserable Yankee was lifted from the ground and hung suspended by the thumbs, while his weight seemed to be tearing his limbs from his shoulder blades.

The other three were treated in the same manner. The agony was simply excruciating. The boys were brave and had resolved to stand their punishment without a groan, but this was too much for human endurance. Their will was strong, but Nature could not be denied and they shrieked aloud so pitifully that a young Reserve stand-ing near fainted. Each one screamed, "For God's sake, kill me! Kill me! Shoot me if you want to, but let me down from here!"

The only effect of this upon Barret was to light up his brutal face with a leer of fiendish satisfaction. He said to the guards with a gleeful wink, "By God, I'll learn these Yanks to be more a-feared uv me than of the old devil himself. They'll soon un-derstand that I'm not the man to fool with. I'm ol' pizen, I am, when I git started. Jest hear 'em squeal, won't yer?" Then, walking from prisoner to prisoner, he said, "Damn yer skins, ye'll dig tunnels, will ye? Ye'll try to git out an' run through the country, stealin' and carryin' off niggers, an' makin' more trouble than yer goddam necks are worth. I'll learn ye all about that. If I ketch ye at this sort o' work agin, goddam ye, ef I don't kill ye ez soon ez I ketch ye!" And so on ad infinitum. How long the boys were kept up there undergoing this torture cannot be said. Perhaps it was an hour or more. To the looker-on, it seemed long hours; to the poor fellows themselves, it was ages. When they were at last let down, all fainted and were carried away to the hospital, where they were weeks in recovering from the effects. Some of them were crippled for life.

When we came into the prison there were about eleven thousand there. More uniformly wretched creatures I have never before seen. Up to the time of our de-parture from Andersonville, the constant influx of new prisoners had prevented the misery and wasting away of life from becoming fully realized. Though thousands were continually dying, thousands more of healthy, clean, well-clothed men were as con-tinually coming from the front, so that a large portion of these inside looked in fairly good condition. But here no new prisoners had come in for months; the money which made such a show about the sutler shops of Andersonville had been spent; and there was in every face the same look of ghastly emaciation, the same shrunken muscles and feeble limbs, the same lack-luster eyes and hopeless countenances. One of the common-est of sights was to see men whose hands and feet were simply rotting off.

The nights were frequently so cold that ice a quarter of an inch thick formed on the water. The naked frames of starving men were poorly calculated to withstand this frosty rigor, and thousands had their extremities so badly frozen as to destroy the life in those parts and induce a rotting of the tissues by a dry gangrene. The rotted flesh frequently remained in its place for a long time, a loathsome but painless mass that gradually sloughed off, leaving the sinews that passed through it to stand out like shining white cords. While this was in some respects less terrible than the hospital gangrene at Andersonville, it was more generally diffused and dreadful to the last de-gree. The rebel surgeons at Florence did not follow the habit of those at Andersonville who tried to check the disease by wholesale amputation, but simply let it run its course, and thousands finally carried their putrefied limbs through our lines to be treated by our surgeons when the Confederacy broke up in the spring.

I had been in the prison but a little while when a voice called out from a hole in the ground as I was passing: "Say, sergeant! Won't you please take these shears and cut my toes off?"

"What?" I said in amazement, stopping in front of the dugout.

"Just take these shears, won't you, and cut my toes off?" answered the poor fellow, an Indiana infantryman, holding up a pair of dull shears in his hand and elevating a foot for me to look at. I examined the latter carefully. All the flesh of the toes, except little pads at the ends, had rotted off, leaving the bones as clean as if scraped. The little tendons still remained and held the bones to their places, but this seemed to hurt the rest of the feet and annoy the man.

"You'd better let one of the rebel doctors see this," I said after finishing my survey, "before you conclude to have them off. Maybe they can be saved."

"No!" he exclaimed emphatically. "Damned if I'm going to have any of them rebel butchers fooling around me. I'd die first, and then I wouldn't. You can do it better than they can. It's just a little snip. Just try it."

"I don't like to," I replied. "I might lame you for life and make you lots of trouble."

"Oh, bother!" exclaimed. "What business is that of yours? They're *my* toes, and I want 'em off. They hurt me so I can't sleep. Come, now, take the shears and cut 'em off."

I yielded and, taking the shears, snipped one tendon after another close to the feet, and in a few seconds had the whole ten toes lying in a heap at the bottom of the dugout. I picked them up and handed them to their owner, who gazed at them complacently and remarked, "Well, I'm durned glad they're off. I won't be bothered with corns any more, I flatter myself!"

We were put into the old squads to fill the places of those who had recently died, being assigned to these vacancies according to the initials of our surnames, the same rolls being used that we had signed as parolees. This separated Andrews and me, for the A's were taken to fill up the first hundreds of the first thousand, while the M's to which I belonged went into the next thousand. I was put into the second hundred of the second thousand, and its sergeant dying shortly after, I was given his place and commanded the hundred, drew its rations, made out its rolls and looked for its sick during the rest of our stay there.

Andrews and I got together again and began fixing up what little we could to protect ourselves against the weather. Cold as this was we decided that it was safer to endure it and risk frost-biting every night than to build one of the mud-walled and mud-covered holes that so many lived in. These were much warmer than lying out on the frozen ground, but we believed that they were very unhealthy and that no one lived long who inhabited them. So we set about repairing our faithful old blanket, now full of great holes. We watched for the dead men, to get pieces of cloth from their garments to make patches which we sewed on with yarn raveled from other fragments of woolen cloth. Some of our company whom we found in the prison donated us the three sticks necessary to make tent-poles, wonderful generosity when the preciousness of firewood is remembered. We hoisted our blanket upon these, built a wall of mud bricks at one end, and in it a little fireplace to economize our scanty fuel to the last degree, and were once more at home and much better off than most of our neighbors.

One of these, the proprietor of a hole in the ground covered with an arch of adobe bricks, had absolutely no bedclothes except a couple of short pieces of board, and very little other clothing. He dug a trench in the bottom of what was by courtesy called his tent, sufficiently large to contain his body below his neck. At nightfall he would crawl into this, put his two bits of board so that they joined over his breast and then say, "Now, boys, cover me over." Whereupon his friends would cover him up with dry sand from the sides of his domicile and he would slumber quietly till morning, when he would rise, shake the sand from his garments and declare that he felt as well refreshed as if he had slept on a spring mattress. There has been much talk of earth baths of late years in scientific and medical circles. I have been sorry that our Florence comrade, if he still lives, did not contribute the results of his experience.

The pinching cold cured my repugnance toward wearing dead men's clothes, or rather it made my nakedness so painful that I was glad to cover it as best I could, and I began foraging among the corpses for garments. For a while my efforts to set myself up in the mortuary second-hand clothing business were not all successful. I found that dying men with good clothes were as carefully watched over by sets of fellows who constituted themselves their residuary legatees as if they were men of fortune dying in the midst of a circle of expectant nephews and nieces. Before one was fairly cold, his clothes would be appropriated and divided, and I have seen many sharp fights between contesting claimants. I soon perceived that my best chance was to get up very early in the morning and do my hunting. The nights were so cold that many could not sleep and they would walk up and down the streets, trying to keep warm by exercise. Towards morning, becoming exhausted, they would lie down on the ground almost anywhere and die. I have frequently seen as many as fifty of these.

My first find of any importance was a young Pennsylvania Zouave who was lying dead near the bridge that crossed the creek. His clothes were all badly worn except his baggy dark trousers which were nearly new. I removed these, scraped out from each of the dozens of great folds in the legs about a half-pint of lice, and drew the garments over my own half-frozen limbs, the first real covering those members had had for four or five months. The pantaloons only came down about halfway between my knees and feet, but were wonderfully comfortable compared to what I had been—or rather not been—wearing. I had picked up a pair of boot bottoms which answered me for shoes, and now I began a hunt for socks. This took several morning expeditions, but on one of them I was rewarded with finding a corpse with a good brown one, army make, and a few days later I got another, a good thick genuine one, knit at home of blue yarn by some patient, careful housewife. Almost the next morning I had the good fortune to find a dead man with a warm, whole infantry dress coat, a most serviceable garment. As I still had for a shirt the blouse Andrews had given me at Millen, I now considered my wardrobe complete and left the rest of the clothes to those who were more needy.

Those who used tobacco seemed to suffer more from a deprivation of the weed than from lack of food. There were no sacrifices they would not make to obtain it, and it was no uncommon thing for boys to trade off half their rations for a chew of "Navy Plug." As long as one had anything—especially buttons—to trade, tobacco could be procured from the guards who were plentifully supplied with it. When means of barter were gone, chewers frequently became so desperate as to beg the guards to throw them a bit of the precious nicotine. Shortly after our arrival at Florence, a prisoner on the east side approached one of the Reserves with the request: "Say, guard, can't you give a fellow a chew of tobacco?" To which the guard replied, "Yes, come right across the line there and I'll drop you down a bit." The unsuspecting prisoner stepped across the Dead Line and the guard, a boy of sixteen, raised his gun and killed him.

At the north side of the prison, the path down to the creek lay right alongside of the Dead Line, which was a mere furrow in the ground. At night the guards, in their zeal to kill somebody, were very likely to imagine that anyone going along the path for water was across the Dead Line and fire upon him. It was as bad as going up on the skirmish line to go for water after nightfall. Yet every night a group of boys would be found standing at the head of the path crying out: "Fill your buckets for a chew of tobacco." That is, they were willing to take all the risk of running that gauntlet for this moderate compensation.

The rations of wood grew smaller as the weather grew colder until at last they settled down to a piece about the size of a kitchen rolling-pin a day for each man. This had to serve for all purposes, cooking as well as warming. We split the rations up into slips about the size of a carpenter's lead pencil and used them parsimoniously, never building a fire so big that it could not be covered with a half-peck measure. We hovered closely over this, covering it, in fact, with our hands and bodies so that not a particle of heat was lost. Remembering the Indian's sage remark that "the white man built a big fire and sat away off from it while the Indian made a little fire and got up close to it," we let nothing in the way of caloric heat be wasted by distance. The pitch-pine produced great quantities of soot which, on cold and rainy days when we hung over the fires all the time, blackened our faces until we were beyond the recognition of intimate friends.

There was the same economy of fuel in cooking. Less than half as much as is contained in a penny bunch of kindling was made to suffice in preparing our daily meal. If we cooked mush, we elevated our little pan an inch from the ground upon a chunk of clay and piled the little sticks around it so carefully that none should burn without yielding all its heat to the vessel, and not one more was burned than absolutely necessary. If we baked bread, we spread the dough upon our chess-board, propped it up before the little fireplace and used every particle of heat that emanated from it. We had to pinch and starve ourselves thus, while within a five minute walk from the prison gate stood enough timber to build a great city. The stump Andrews and I had had the foresight to secure now did us excellent service. It was pitch-pine, very fat with resin, and a little split off each day added much to our fires and our comfort.

One morning, upon examining the pockets of an infantryman of my hundred who had just died, I had the wonderful luck to find a silver quarter. I hurried off to tell Andrews of our unexpected good fortune. By an effort he succeeded in calming himself to the point of receiving the news with philosophic coolness, and we went into committee upon the state of our stomachs to consider how the money could be spent to the best advantage.

At the south side of the stockade, on the outside of the timbers, was a sutler's shop kept by a rebel, and communicating with the prison by a hole two or three feet square cut through the logs. The Dead Line was broken at this point so as to permit prisoners to come up to the hole to trade. The articles for sale were corn meal and bread, flour and wheat bread, meat, beans, molasses, honey, and sweet potatoes. I went down to the place, carefully inspected the stock, priced everything there and studied the relative food value of each. I came back, reported my observations and conclusions to Andrews, and then stayed at the tent while he went on a similar errand. The consideration of the matter was continued during the day and night, and the next morning we determined upon investing our twenty-five cents in sweet potatoes, as we could get nearly a half-bushel of them, which was "more fillin' at the price," to use the words of Dickens' fat boy, than anything else offered us. We bought the potatoes, carried them home in our blanket, buried them in the bottom of our tent to keep them from being stolen, and restricted ourselves to two per day until we had eaten them all.

The rebels did something more towards properly caring for the sick than at Andersonville. A hospital was established in the northwestern corner of the stockade and separated from the rest of the camp by a line of police composed of our own men. In this space several large sheds were erected of that rude architecture common to the coarser sort of buildings in the South. There was not a nail or a bolt used in their entire construction. Forked posts at the ends and sides supported poles, upon which were laid long "shakes" or split shingles forming the roofs. These were held in place by other poles laid upon them. The sides and ends were enclosed by similar "shakes," and altogether they formed quite a fair protection against the weather. Beds of pine leaves were provided for the sick, and some coverlets which our Sanitary Commission had been allowed to send through.

But nothing was done to bathe or cleanse the bedridden or to exchange their lice-infested garments for others less full of torture. The long-tangled hair and whiskers were not cut, nor indeed were any of the commonest suggestions for the improvement of the condition of the sick put into execution. Men who had lain in their mud hovels until they had become helpless and hopeless were admitted to the hospital, usually only to die.

The diseases were different in character from those which swept off the prisoners at Andersonville. There they were mostly of the digestive organs; here of the respiratory system. The filthy, putrid, speedily fatal gangrene of Andersonville became here a dry, slow wasting away of the parts, which continued for weeks, even months, without being necessarily fatal. Men's feet and legs and less frequently their hands and arms decayed and sloughed off. The parts became so dead that a knife could be run through them without causing a particle of pain. The dead flesh hung onto the bones and tendons long after the nerves and veins had ceased to perform their functions, and sometimes startled one by dropping off in a lump without causing pain or hemorrhage. The appearance of these was, of course, frightful, or would have been had we not become accustomed to them. The spectacle of men with their feet and legs a mass of dry ulceration, which had reduced the flesh to putrescent deadness and left the tendons standing out like cords, was too common to excite remark or even attention. Unless the victim was a comrade, no one specially heeded his condition.

Lung diseases and lung fevers ravaged the camp, existing all the time in a more or less virulent condition, according to the changes of the weather, and occasional raging

in destructive epidemics. I am unable to speak with any degree of definiteness as to the
death rate, since I had ceased to interest myself about the number dying each day.
I had now been a prisoner over a year, and had become so torpid and stupefied mentally and physically that I cared comparatively little for anything save the rations of
food and of fuel. The difference of a few spoonfuls of meal or a large splinter of wood
in the daily issues to me were of more actual importance than the increase or decrease
of the death rate. At Andersonville I frequently took the trouble to count the number
of dead and living, but all curiosity of this kind had now died out.

The medicines furnished the sick were quite simple in nature and mainly composed of indigenous substances. For diarrhea, red pepper and decoctions of blackberry
root and of pine leaves were given. For coughs and lung diseases, a decoction of wild
cherry bark was administered. Chills and fever were treated with dogwood bark, and
fever patients who craved something sour were given a weak acid drink, made by
fermenting a small quantity of meal in a barrel of water.

All these remedies were quite good in their way, and would have benefited the
patients had they been accompanied by proper shelter, food and clothing. But it was
idle to attempt to arrest the diarrhea with blackberry root, or with wild cherry bark
the consumption of a man lying in a cold, damp, mud hovel, devoured by vermin and
struggling to maintain himself upon less than a pint of unsalted corn meal per day.
Finding that the doctors issued red pepper for diarrhea and an imitation of sweet oil
made from peanuts for the gangrenous sores, I reported to them an imaginary comrade in my tent, whose symptoms indicated those remedies, and succeeded in drawing
a small quantity of each two or three times a week. The red pepper I used to warm up
our bread and mush and give some different taste to the corn meal, which had now become so loathsome to us. The peanut oil served to give a hint of the animal food we
hungered for. It was greasy and, as we did not have any meat for three months, even
this flimsy substitute was inexpressibly grateful to palate and stomach. But one morning the hospital steward made a mistake and gave me castor oil instead, and the consequences were unpleasant.

A more agreeable remembrance is that of two small apples about the size of wal-
nuts, given me by a boy named Henry Clay Montague Porter of the 16th Connecticut.
He had relatives in North Carolina, who sent him a small package of edibles out of
which, in the fullness of his generous heart, he gave me this share, enough to make me
always remember him with kindness. Speaking of edibles reminds me of an incident.
Joe Darling of the 1st Maine, our chief of police, had a sister living at Augusta, Georgia, who occasionally came to Florence with a basket of food and other necessaries for

her brother. On one of these journeys, while sitting in Colonel Iverson's tent waiting for her brother to be brought out of prison, she picked out of her basket a nicely browned doughnut and handed it to the guard pacing in front of the tent: "Here, guard, wouldn't you like a genuine Yankee doughnut?"

The guard, a lank, loose-jointed Georgia cracker who had in all his life seen very little more inviting food than the hog, hominy and molasses upon which he had been raised, took the cake, turned it over and inspected it curiously for some time without apparently getting the least idea of what it was or was for, and then handed it back to the girl, saying, "Really, mum, I don't believe I've got any use for it."

"Andrews Managed to Pass Me Three Roasted Chickens"

CHAPTER XXII

DULL WINTER DAYS

THE REBELS CONTINUED THEIR EFFORTS to induce prisoners to enlist in their army, and with much better success than at any previous time. Many men had become so desperate that they were reckless as to what they did. Home, relatives, friends, happiness—all they had remembered or looked forward to, all that had nerved them up to endure the present and brave the future, now seemed separated from them forever by a yawning and impassable chasm. For many weeks no new prisoners had come in to rouse their drooping courage with news of the progress of our arms toward final victory or refresh their remembrances of home and the gladsomeness of "God's Country." Before them they saw nothing but weeks of slow and painful progress toward bitter death. The other alternative was enlistment in the rebel army.

Another class went out and joined with no other intention than to escape at the first opportunity. They justified their bad faith to the rebels by recalling the numberless instances of the rebels' bad faith to us, and usually closed their arguments in defense of their course with: "No oath administered by a rebel can have any binding obligation. These men are outlaws who have not only broken their oaths to the Government but who have deserted from its service, and turned its arms against it. They are perjurers and traitors and, in addition, the oath they administer to us is under compulsion and for that reason is of no account." Still another class, mostly made up from the old Raider crowd, enlisted from natural depravity. They went out more than for anything else because their hearts were prone to evil and they did that which was wrong in preference to what was right. By far the largest portion of those the rebels obtained were of this class, and a more worthless crowd of soldiers has not been seen since Falstaff mustered his famous recruits.

After all, however, the number who deserted their flag was astonishingly small considering the circumstances. The official report says three hundred and twenty-six, but I imagine this is under the truth since quite a number were turned back in after their utter uselessness had been demonstrated. I suppose that five hundred "galvanized" [60] as we termed it, but this was very few when the hopelessness of exchange, the despair of life and the wretchedness of the condition of the eleven or twelve thousand inside the Stockade is remembered. The motives actuating men to desert were not closely analyzed by us, but we held all who did so despicable scoundrels too vile to be adequately described in words. It was not safe for a man to announce his intention of "galvanizing" for he incurred much danger of being beaten until he was physically unable to reach the gate. Those who went over to the enemy had to use great discretion in letting the rebel officers know so much of their wishes as would secure their being taken outside. Men were frequently knocked down and dragged away while telling the officers they wanted to go out.

On one occasion, several of the Raider crowd, who had "galvanized" were stopped for a few hours in some little town on their way to the front. They lost no time in stealing everything they could lay their hands upon, and the disgusted rebel commander ordered them to be returned to the stockade. They came in in the evening, all well rigged out in rebel uniforms and carrying blankets. We chose to consider their good clothes and equipments an aggravation of their offense and an insult to ourselves. We had at that time quite a squad of Negro soldiers inside with us. Among them was a gigantic fellow with fists like wooden mallets. Some of the white boys resolved to use these to wreck the camp's displeasure on the "galvanized." The plan was carried out capitally. The big darky, followed by a crowd of smaller, nimbler "shades," would approach one of the leaders among them with, "Is you a galvanized?" The surly reply would be, "Yes, you black bastard. What the hell business is that of yours?" At that instant a bony fist of the darky, descending like a pile driver, would catch the recreant under the ear and lift him about a rod. As he fell, the smaller darkies would pounce upon him and in an instant despoil him of his blanket and perhaps the larger portion of his warm clothing. The operation was a success and repeated with a dozen or more. The whole camp enjoyed it as rare fun, and it was the only time that I saw nearly everybody at Florence laugh.

A few prisoners were brought in in December who had been taken in Foster's attempt to cut the Charleston & Savannah Railroad at Pocataligo. Among them we were astonished to find Charley Hirsch, a member of Company K of our battalion. He had had a strange experience. He was originally a member of a Texas regiment and was captured at Arkansas Post. He then took an oath of allegiance and enlisted with us. While we were at Savannah he approached a guard one day to trade for tobacco. The moment he spoke to the man he recognized him as a former comrade in the Texas regiment. The latter knew him also, and sang out, "I know you, you're Charley Hirsch that used to be in my company!" Charley backed into the crowd as quickly as possible to elude the fellow's eyes, but the latter called for the Corporal of the Guard, had himself relieved and in a few minutes came in with an officer in search of the deserter. He found him with little difficulty and took him out. The luckless Charley was tried by court martial, found guilty and sentenced to be shot. While waiting execution he was confined in the jail.

But before the sentence could be carried out, Sherman came so close to the city that it was thought best to remove the prisoners. In the confusion Charley managed to escape and at the moment the battle of Pocataligo opened was lying concealed between the two lines of battle without knowing, of course, that he was in such a dangerous locality. After the firing opened, he thought it better to lie still than run the risk from the fire of both sides, especially as he momentarily expected our folks to advance and drive the rebels away. But the reverse happened. The Johnnies drove our fellows, and finding Charley in his place of concealment, took him for one of Foster's men and sent him to Florence where he stayed until we went through our lines.

Our days went by as stupidly and eventlessly as can be conceived. We had grown too spiritless and lethargic to dig tunnels or plan escapes. We had nothing to read, nothing to make or destroy, nothing to work with, nothing to play with, and even no desire to contrive anything for amusement. All the cards in the prison were worn out long ago. Some of the boys had made dominoes from bones and Andrews and I still had our chessmen, but we were too listless to play. The mind, enfeebled by the long disuse of it except in a few limited channels, was unfitted for even so much effort as was involved in a game for pastime. Nor were there any physical exercises such as that a crowd of young men would have delighted in under other circumstances. There was no running, boxing, jumping, wrestling or leaping. All were too weak or too hungry to make any exertion beyond that absolutely necessary.

On cold days everybody seemed totally benumbed. The camp would be silent and still. Little groups everywhere hovered for hours, moody and sullen, over diminutive flickering fires made with one poor handful of splinters. When the sun shone, more activity was visible. Boys wandered around and hunted up their friends and saw what

gaps death, always busiest during the cold spells, had made in the ranks of their acquaintances. During the warmest part of the day everybody disrobed and spent an
hour or more killing lice that had waxed and multiplied to grievous proportions during the few periods of comparative immunity.

Besides the whipping of the "galvanized" by the darkies, I remember but two
other bits of amusement we had while at Florence. One of these was in hearing the
colored soldiers sing patriotic songs, which they did with great gusto when the weather
became mild. The other was the antics of a circus clown, a member, I believe, of a
Connecticut or New York regiment. On rare occasions when we were feeling not exactly too well, he would give an hour or two of recitations of the drolleries with which
he entertained the crowds under canvas. One of his happiest efforts, I remember, was
a stilted paraphrase of "Old Uncle Ned," a song very popular sometime ago. The
actual words were:

> There was an old darky, an' his name was Uncle Ned.
> But he died long ago, long ago.
> He had no wool on the top of his head,
> De place whar de wool ought to grow.
> Den lay down de shubbel, lay down de hoe,
> Den hang up de fiddle and de bow;
> For dere's no more hard work for poor Uncle Ned;
> He's gone whar de good niggahs go.

But in the hands of our artist friend, the song became;

> There was an aged and indigent African whose cognomen was Uncle Edward
> But he is deceased since a remote period, a very remote period;
> He possessed no capillary substance on the substance of his cranium,
> The place designated by kind Nature for the capillary substance to vegetate.

These rare flashes of fun only served to throw the underlying misery out in
greater relief. It was like lightning playing across the surface of a dreary morass. I have
alluded several times to the general inability of the rebels to count accurately, even in
low numbers. One continually met phases of this that seemed simply incomprehen-
sible to us who had taken the multiplication tables almost with our mother's milk and
knew the "rule of three" as well as a Presbyterian boy does the Shorter Catechism.

A cadet, an undergraduate of the South Carolina Military Institute, called our
roll at Florence and, though an inborn young aristocrat who believed himself made of
finer clay than most mortals, he was not a bad fellow at all. He thought South Carolina

aristocracy the finest gentry and the South Carolina Military Institute the greatest institution of learning in the world. One day he came in so full of some matter of rare importance that we became somewhat excited as to its nature. Dismissing our hundred after roll call, he unburdened his mind. "Now you fellers are so damned peart on mathematics and sure things," he said with a knowing smile, "that you always want to snap me up on every opportunity, but I guess I've got something this time that'll settle you. It's something that a feller gave out yesterday, and Colonel Iverson and all the officers out there have been figuring on it ever since and none have got the right answer. I'm powerful sure that none of you, smart as you think you are, can do it."

"Well, let's hear this wonderful problem," we all said at once.

"Well," he said smugly, "what is the length of a pole standing in a river, one fifth of which is in the mud, two thirds in the water, and one eighth above the water while one foot and three inches of the top is broken off?"

In a minute a dozen answered loudly, "One hundred and fifty feet!" The young cadet could only look his amazement at the possession of such an amount of learning by a crowd of mudsills, and one of our fellows said contemptuously, "Why, if you South Carolina Institute fellows couldn't answer such questions as that they wouldn't allow you in the infant class up north." The young cadet, amazement and chagrin written all over his face, turned and walked away.

Lieutenant Barret, our red-headed tormentor, could not for the life of him count those inside in hundreds and thousands in such a manner as to be reasonably certain of correctness. As it would have cankered his soul to feel that he was being beaten out of half a dozen rations by the superior cunning of the Yankees, he adopted a plan which he must have learned at some period of his life when he was a hog or sheep drover. Every Sunday morning all in the camp were driven across the Creek to the East Side and then made to file back slowly, one at a time, between two guards stationed on a little bridge that spanned the Creek. By this means, if he was able to count up to a hundred, he could get our number correctly.

The first time this was done after our arrival he gave us a display of his wanton malevolence. We were nearly all assembled on the East Side and were standing in ranks at the edge of the swamp, facing the West. Barret was walking along the opposite edge of the swamp and, coming to a little gully, jumped it. He was very awkward and came very near falling into the mud. We all yelled derisively. He turned toward us in a fury, shook his fist, and shouted curses and imprecations. We yelled still louder. He snatched out his revolver and began firing at our line. The distance was considerable, say four or five hundred feet, and the bullets struck in the mud in advance of the line. We still yelled. Then he jerked a gun from a guard and fired, but his aim was bad and the bullet sang over our heads, striking the bank above us. He posted off to get another gun but his fit subsided before he obtained it.

Christmas, with its swelling flood of happy memories, memories now bitter because they marked the high tide whence our fortunes had receded to this despicable state, came but brought no change to mark its coming. It is true that we had expected no change. We had not looked forward to the day and hardly knew when it arrived, so indifferent were we to the lapse of time. When reminded that the day was one that in all Christendom was sacred to good cheer and joyful meetings; that wherever the upraised Cross proclaimed followers of Him who preached Peace on earth and good will to men, parents and children, brothers and sisters, long-time friends and all congenial spirits were gathering around hospitable boards to delight in each other's society and strengthen the bonds of unity between them, we listened as if hearing of a remote land from which we had parted forever more. It seemed years since we had known anything of the kind. The experience we had had of it belonged to the dim and irrevocable past. It could not come to us again nor we go to it. Squalor, hunger, cold and wasting disease had become the ordinary conditions of an existence from which there was little hope that we would ever be exempt. Perhaps it was well to a certain degree that we felt so. It softened the poignancy of our reflections over the difference in the conditions of ourselves and our happier comrades who were elsewhere.

The weather was in harmony with our feelings. The dull, gray, leaden sky was as sharp a contrast with the crisp, bracing sharpness of a Northern Christmas morning as our beggarly little ration of saltless corn meal was to the sumptuous cheer that loaded the dinner tables of Northern homes. We turned out languidly in the morning to roll-call, endured silently the raving abuse of the cowardly brute, Barret, hung stupidly over the flickering little fires, until the gates opened to admit the rations. For an hour there was bustle and animation. All stood around and counted each sack of meal to get an idea of the rations we were likely to receive.

This was the daily custom. The number intended for the day's issue was brought in and piled up in the street. Then there was a division of the sacks to the thousands, the sergeant of each being called in turn and allowed to pick out and carry away one until all were taken. When we entered the prison each thousand received an average of ten or eleven sacks a day. Every week saw a reduction in the number, until by midwinter the daily issue to a thousand averaged four sacks. In short, one thousand men received two hundred and fifty-six quarts, or less than a half pint each.

We thought we had sounded the depths of misery at Andersonville, but Florence showed a much lower depth. Bad as it was parching under the burning sun, whose fiery rays bred miasma and putrefaction, it was still not so bad as having one's life chilled out by exposure in nakedness upon the frozen ground to biting winds and freezing sleet. Wretched as the rusty bacon and coarse maggot-filled bread of Andersonville was, it would still go much farther towards supporting life than the handful of saltless meal at Florence. While I believed it possible for any young man with the forces of life strong within him and healthy in every way to survive—by taking due precautions—such treatment as we received in Andersonville, I cannot understand how anybody could live a month in Florence. That many did live is only an astonishing illustration of the tenacity of life in some individuals.

Let the reader imagine a fifteen acre field with a stream running through the center. Let him imagine this enclosed by a stockade eighteen feet high, made by standing logs on end. Let him conceive of ten thousand feeble men debilitated by months of imprisonment turned inside this enclosure without a yard of covering given them and told to make their homes there. One quarter of them, two thousand five hundred, pick up brush, pieces of rail, splits from logs sufficient to make huts that will turn the rain tolerably. The huts are in no case as good shelter as an ordinarily careful farmer provides for his swine. Half of the prisoners—five thousand—who cannot do so well, work the mud up into rude bricks with which they build shelters that wash down at every hard rain. The remaining two thousand five hundred do not even do this, but lie around on the ground on old blankets and overcoats and in daytime prop these up on sticks as shelter from the rain and wind. Let them be given rations not to exceed a pint of corn meal a day and a piece of wood about the size of an ordinary stick for a cooking stove to cook with. Then let such weather prevail as we ordinarily have in the North in November, freezing cold rains with frequent days and nights when the ice forms as thick as a pane of glass.

How long does he think men could live through that? He will probably say that a week, or at most a fortnight, would see the last and strongest of these ten thousand lying dead in the frozen mire where he wallowed. He will be astonished to learn that probably not more than four or five thousand of those who underwent this at Florence died there. How many died after release in Washington, on the vessels coming to Annapolis, in the hospital and camp at Annapolis or after they reached home, none but the Recording Angel can tell. All that I know is that we left a trail of dead behind us wherever we moved so long as I was with the doleful caravan.

Looking back after this lapse of years, the salient characteristic seems to be the ease with which men died. There was little of the violence of dissolution as at Andersonville. The machinery of life in all of us was running slowly and feebly; it would simply grow still slower and feebler in some and then stop without a jar, without a sensation to manifest it. Nightly one of two or three comrades sleeping together would die. The survivors would not know it until they tried to get him to "spoon" over, when they would find him rigid and motionless. As they could not spare even so little heat as was still contained in his body, they would not remove it, but would lie up the closer until morning. Such a thing as a boy making an outcry when he discovered his comrade dead or manifesting any desire to get away from the corpse was unknown.

I remember one who, as Charles II said of himself, was "an unconscionable long time in dying." His name was Bickford; he belonged to the 21st Ohio Volunteer Infantry and lived, I think, near Findlay, Ohio, and was in my hundred. His partner and he were both in a very bad condition, and I was not surprised on making my rounds one morning to find them apparently quite dead. I called help and took his partner to the gate. When we picked up Bickford, we found he still lived and had strength enough to gasp out, "You fellers had better let me alone." We laid him back to die, as we supposed, in an hour or so. When the rebel surgeon came in on his rounds, I showed him Bickford, lying there with his eyes closed and limbs motionless. The surgeon said, "Oh, that man's dead; why don't you have him taken out?" I replied: "No, he isn't. Just see." Stooping, I shook the boy and said, "Bickford! Bickford, how do you feel?" The eyes did not unclose, but the lips opened slowly and said with a painful effort, "First rate!" It ended one morning by his inability to make his usual answer, and then he was carried out to join the two score others being loaded into the wagon.

On New Year's Day we were startled by the information that our old-time enemy, General John H. Winder, was dead. It seemed that the rebel sutler of the post had prepared in his tent a grand New Year's dinner to which all the officers were invited. Just as Winder bent his head to enter the tent he fell and expired shortly after. The boys said it was a clear case of "death by visitation of the Devil." It was always insisted that his last words were, "My faith is in Christ; I expect to be saved. Be sure and cut down the prisoners' rations."

Thus passed away the chief evil genius of the prisoners of war. American history has no other character approaching Winder's in vileness. I doubt if the history of the world can show another man so insignificant in abilities and position at whose door can be laid such a terrible load of human misery. There have been many great conquerors and warriors who have "Waded through slaughter to a throne and shut the gates of mercy on mankind." But they were great men, with great objects, with grand plans to carry out, whose benefits they thought would be more than an equivalent for the suffering they caused. The misery they inflicted was not the motive of their schemes, but an unpleasant incident, and usually the sufferers were men of other races and religions, for whom sympathy had been dulled by long antagonism.

From the time Winder assumed command of all the prisons east of the Mississippi sometime in the Fall of 1863 until death removed him, January 1, 1865, certainly not less than twenty-five thousand incarcerated men died in the most horrible manner that the mind can conceive. He cannot be accused of exaggeration when, surveying the thousands of new graves at Andersonville, he could say with a quiet chuckle that he was "doing more to kill off the Yankees than twenty regiments at the front." No twenty regiments in the rebel army ever succeeded in slaying any like thirteen thousand Yankees in six months or in any other time. His cold-blooded cruelty was such as to disgust even the rebel officers.

Colonel D. T. Chandler of the rebel War Department sent on a tour of inspection to Andersonville reported back under the date of August 5th, 1864:

My duty requires me respectfully to recommend a change in the officer in command of the post, Brigadier General John H. Winder, and the substitution in his place of someone who unites both energy and good judgment with some feelings of humanity and consideration for the welfare and comfort, as far as is consistent with their safe keeping, of the vast number of unfortunates placed under his control; someone who, at least, will not advocate *deliberately and in cold blood*, the propriety of leaving them in their present condition until their number is sufficiently reduced by death to make the present arrangements suffice for their accommodation, and who will not consider it a matter of self-laudation and boasting that he has never been inside of the Stockade, a place the horrors of which it is difficult to describe and which is a disgrace to civilization, the condition of which he might, by the exercise of a little energy and judgment, even with the limited means at his command, have considerably improved.

In his examination touching this report, Colonel Chandler says: "I noticed that General Winder seemed very indifferent to the welfare of the prisoners, indisposed to do anything, or to do as much as I thought he ought to do to alleviate their sufferings. I remonstrated with him as well as I could, and he used that language which I reported to the Department with the reference to it, the language stated in the report. When I spoke of the great mortality existing among the prisoners, and pointed out to him that the sickly season was coming on, and that it must necessarily increase unless something was done for their relief—the swamp, for instance, drained, proper food furnished, and in better quantity, and other sanitary suggestions which I made to him—he replied to me that he thought it was better to see half of them die than to take care of the men."

It was Winder who could issue such an order as this when it was supposed that General Stoneman was approaching Andersonville:

Headquarters, Military Prison
Andersonville, Georgia.
July 27th, 1863.

The officers on duty and in charge of the battery of Florida Artillery at the time will, upon receiving notice that the enemy has approached within seven miles of this post, open upon the Stockade with grape-shot, without reference to the situation beyond these lines of defense.

Signed
John H. Winder
Brigadier General Commanding

This man was not only unpunished, but the Government is today supporting his children in luxury by the rent it pays for the use of his property, the well-known Winder Building which is occupied by one of the Departments at Washington.

I confess that all my attempts to satisfactorily analyze Winder's character and discover a sufficient motive for his monstrous conduct have been futile. Even if we imagine him inspired by a hatred of the people of the North that rose to fiendishness, we cannot understand him. It seems impossible for the mind of any man to cherish so deep and insatiable an enmity against his fellow-creatures that it could not be quenched and turned to pity by the sight of even one day's misery at Andersonville or Florence. No one man could possess such a grievous sense of private or national wrongs as to be proof against the daily spectacle of thousands of his own fellow citizens—inhabitants of the same country, associates in the same institutions, educated in the same principles, speaking the same language, his brethren and race, creed, and all that unite men into great communities—starving, rotting and freezing to death. There is many a man who has a hatred so intense that nothing but the death of the detested one will satisfy it. A still fewer number thirst for a more comprehensive retribution who would slay perhaps a half dozen persons; and there may be such gluttons of revenge as would not be satisfied with the sacrifice of less than a score or two. But such would be monsters of whom there have been very few even in fiction. How must they all bow their diminished heads before a man who fed his animosity fat with tens of thousands of lives.

But what also militates greatly against the presumption that either revenge or an abnormal predisposition to cruelty could have animated Winder is that the possession of any two such mental traits so strongly marked would presuppose a corresponding activity of other intellectual faculties, which was not true of him, as from all I can learn of him his mind was in no respect extraordinary. It does not seem possible that he had either the brain to conceive or the firmness of purpose to carry out so gigantic and long-enduring a career of cruelty, because that would imply superhuman qualities in a man who had previously held his own very poorly in the competition with other men.

The probability is that neither Winder nor his direct superiors, Howell Cobb and Jefferson Davis, conceived in all its proportions the gigantic engine of torture and death they were organizing, nor did they comprehend the enormity of the crime they were committing. But they were willing to do much wrong to gain their end, and the smaller crimes of today prepared them for greater ones tomorrow and still greater ones the day following. Killing ten men a day by starvation and hardship at Belle Isle in January led very easily to killing one hundred men a day in Andersonville in July, August and September. Probably at the beginning of the war they would have felt uneasy at slaying one man per day by such means, but as retribution came not and as their appetite for slaughter grew with feeding and as their sympathy with human misery atrophied from long suppression, they ventured upon ever widening ranges of destructiveness. Had the war lasted another year and they lived, five hundred deaths a day would doubtless have been insufficient to disturb them.

Winder doubtless went about his part of the task of slaughter coolly, leisurely, almost perfunctorily. His training in the regular army was against the likelihood of his displaying zeal in anything. He instituted certain measures, and let things take their course. That course was a rapid transition from bad to worse, but it was still in the direction of his wishes, and what little of his own energy was infused into it was in the direction of impetuousness, not of controlling or improving the course. To have done things better would have involved some personal discomfort. He was not likely to incur personal discomfort to mitigate evils that were only afflicting someone else. By an effort of one hour a day for two weeks, he could have had every man in Andersonville and Florence given good shelter through his own exertions. He was not only too indifferent and too lazy to do this, he was too malignant. This neglect to allow—simply *allow*, remember—the prisoners to protect their lives by providing their own shelter, gives the key to his whole disposition and would stamp his memory within infamy even if there were no other charges against him.

"They Removed Every Trace of Prison Grime"

CHAPTER XXIII

UNBOUNDED LUXURY IN GOD'S COUNTRY

A<small>S JANUARY DRAGGED SLOWLY INTO FEBRUARY</small>, rumors of the astonishing success of Sherman began to be so definite and well authenticated as to induce belief. We knew that the western chieftain had marched almost unresisted through Georgia and had captured Savannah with comparatively little difficulty. We did not understand it nor did the rebels around us, for neither of us comprehended the Confederacy's near approach to dissolution, and we could not explain why a desperate attempt was not made somewhere to arrest the onward sweep of the conquering armies of the West. It seemed that if there was any vitality left in rebel-dom, it would deal a blow that would at least cause the presumptuous invader to pause. As we knew nothing of the battles of Franklin and Nashville, we were ignorant of the destruction of Hood's Army and so were at a loss to account for its failure to contest Sherman's progress. The last we had heard of Hood, he had been flanked out of Atlanta, but we did not understand that the strength or morale of his force had been seriously reduced in consequence.

Soon it drifted in to us that Sherman had cut loose from Savannah, as from Atlanta, and had entered South Carolina, to repeat there the march through her sister state. Our sources of information now were confined to the gossip which our men, working outside on parole, could overhear from the rebels and communicate to us as occasion served. These occasions were not frequent, as the men outside were not allowed to come in except rarely or stay long then. Still we managed to know reasonably soon that Sherman was sweeping resistlessly across the State, with Hardee, Dick

Taylor, Beauregard and others vainly trying to make head against him. It seemed impossible to us that they should not stop him soon, for if each of all these leaders had any command worthy the name, the aggregate must make an army that, standing on the defensive, would give Sherman a great deal of trouble. That he would be able to penetrate into the State as far as we were never entered into our minds.

By and by we were astonished at the number of trains that we could hear passing north on the Charleston and Cheraw Railroad. Day and night for two weeks there did not seem to be more than half an hour's interval at any time between the rumble and whistles of the trains as they passed Florence Junction, and sped away towards Cheraw, thirty-five miles north of us. We at length discovered that Sherman had reached Branchville, and was swinging around toward Columbia, and other important points to the north. That Charleston was being evacuated and its garrison, munitions and stores were being removed to Cheraw which the rebel generals intended to make their new base, was a certainty. As this news was so well confirmed as to leave no doubt of it, it began to wake up and encourage all the more hopeful of us. We thought we could see some premonitions of the glorious end. We were getting a vicarious satisfaction at the hands of our friends under the command of "Uncle Billy" [Sherman].

One morning orders came for one thousand men to get ready to move. Andrews and I held a council of war on the situation, the question before the house being whether we would go with that crowd or stay behind. The conclusion we came to was thus stated by Andrews: "Now, Mac, we flanked ahead every time, and see how we've come out. We flanked into the first squad that left Richmond, and we were consequently in the first that got into Andersonville. Maybe if we'd stayed back, we'd have got into that squad that was exchanged. We were in the first squad that left Andersonville. We were the first to leave Savannah and enter Millen. Maybe if we'd stayed back, we'd have got exchanged with ten thousand sick. We were the first to leave Millen, and the first to reach Blackshear. We were again the first to leave Blackshear. Perhaps those fellows we left behind there are exchanged. Now, as we've played ahead every time with such infernal luck, let's play *backwards* this time and try what that brings us."

"But, Lale," I said, "we made something by going ahead every time, that is—if we were not going to be exchanged. By getting into those places first, we picked out the best spots to stay and got tent-building stuff that those who came after us could not. And certainly we can never again get into as bad a place as this is. The chances are that if this does not mean exchange, it means transfer to a better prison." But we concluded to reverse our usual order of procedure and flank back in hopes that something would favor our escape to Sherman. Accordingly we let the first squad go off without us and the next and so on, till there were only eleven hundred, mostly those sick in the hospital, remaining behind. Those who went away, we afterward learned, were run down on the cars to Wilmington and afterward up to Goldsboro, North Carolina.

For a week or more we eleven hundred tenanted the stockade and, by burning up the tents of those who had gone, had the only decent, comfortable fires we had while in Florence. In hunting around through the tents for fuel we found many bodies of those who had died as their comrades were leaving. As the larger portion of us could barely walk, the rebels paroled us to remain inside the Stockade or within a few hundred yards of the front of it and took the guards off.

While these were marching down, a dozen or more of us, exulting in even so much freedom as we had obtained, climbed on the hospital shed to see what the outlook was and perched ourselves on the ridgepole. Lieutenant Barret came along, at a distance of two hundred yards, with a squad of guards. Observing us, he halted his men, faced them toward us and they leveled their guns as if to fire. He expected to see us tumble down in ludicrous alarm to avoid the bullets. But we hated him and them so bad that we could not give them the poor satisfaction of scaring us. Only one of our party attempted to slide down, but the moment we swore at him he came back and took his seat with folded arms alongside of us. Barret gave the order to fire, and the bullets shrieked over our heads, fortunately not hitting anbody. We responded with yells of derision and the worst abuse we could think of. Coming down after a while, I walked to the now open gate and looked through it over the barren fields to the dense woods a mile away, and a wild desire to run off took possession of me. It seemed as if I could not resist it. The woods appeared full of enticing shapes beckoning me to come to them and the winds whispered in my ears to run. But the words in my parole were still fresh in my mind, and I stilled my frenzy to escape by turning back into the Stockade and looking away from the tempting view.

Once five new prisoners, the first we had seen in a long time, were brought in from Sherman's Army. They were plump, well-conditioned, well-dressed, healthy devil-may-care young fellows whose confidence in themselves and in Sherman was simply limitless and their contempt for all rebels, and especially those who terrorized over us, enormous.

"Come up here to Headquarters," said one of the rebel officers to them as they stood talking to us, "and we'll parole you."

"Oh, go to hell with your parole," said the spokesman of the crowd with nonchalant contempt. "We don't want none of your paroles. Old Billy'll parole us before Saturday."

To us they said, "Now boys, you want to cheer right up; keep a stiff upper lip. This thing's workin' all right. Their goddam old Confederacy's goin' to pieces like a house afire. Sherman's promenadin' through it just as it suits him, and he's liable to pay us a visit at any hour. We're expectin' him all the time, because it was generally understood all through the Army that we were to take the prison pen here on our way." I mentioned my distrust of the concentration of rebels at Cheraw and their faces took on a look of supreme disdain. "Now, don't let that worry you a minute," said the confident spokesman. "All the rebels between here and Lee's Army can't prevent Sherman from going just where he pleases. Why, we've quit fightin' 'em except with the 'bummers' in advance. We haven't had to go into regular line of battle against them for I don't know how long. Sherman wouldn't like anything better than to have 'em make a stand somewhere so that he could get a good fair whack at 'em."

No one can imagine the effect of all this upon us. It was better than a carload of medicine and trainload of provisions would have been. From the depths of despondency we sprang at once to tiptoe on the mountain tops of expectation. We did little day and night but listen for the sound of Sherman's guns and discuss what we would do when he came. We planned schemes of terrible vengeance on Barret and Iverson, but those worthies had mysteriously disappeared, whither no one knew. There was hardly an hour of any night passed without some one of us fancying that he heard the welcome sound of distant firing.

As everybody knows, by listening intently at night one can hear just exactly what he is intent upon hearing, and so it was with us. In the middle of the night, boys listening awhile with strained ears would say, "Now, if ever I heard musketry firing in my life, that's a heavy skirmish line at work, and sharply too, and not more than three miles away, neither." Then another would say, "I don't want to ever get out of here if that don't sound just as the skirmishing at Chancellorsville did the first day to us. We were lying down about four miles off, when it began pattering just as that is doing now." One night about nine or ten, there came two short sharp peals of thunder that sounded precisely like the reports of rifled field pieces. We sprang up in a frenzy of excitement and shouted as if our throats would split. But the next peal went off in the usual rumble and our excitement had to subside.

For more than a week during the middle of February, every waking hour was spent in anxious expectancy of Sherman, listening for the far-off rattle of his guns, straining our ears to catch the sullen boom of his artillery, scanning the distant woods to see the rebels falling back in hopeless confusion before the pursuit of his dashing advance. Though we became as impatient as those ancient sentinels who for ten long years stood upon the Grecian hills to catch the first glimpse of the flames of burning Troy, Sherman came not. We afterward learned that two expeditions were sent down from Cheraw, but they met with unexpected resistance and were turned back.

It was now plain to us that the Confederacy was tottering to its fall, and we were only troubled by occasional misgivings that we might in some way be caught and crushed under the toppling ruins. It did not seem possible that after the cruel tenacity with which the rebels had clung to us, they would be willing to let us go free at last but would be tempted, in the rage of their final defeat, to commit some unparalleled atrocity upon us.

One day all of us who were able to walk were made to fall in and march over to the railroad where we were loaded into box cars. The sick, except those who were manifestly dying, were loaded into wagons and hauled over. The dying were left to their fate without any companions or nurses. The train started off in a northeasterly direction and, as we went through Florence, the skies were crimson with great fires burning in all directions. We were told these were cotton and military stores being destroyed in anticipation of a visit from a part of Sherman's forces. When morning came we were still running in the same direction that we started.

In the confusion of loading us upon the cars the previous evening, I had been allowed to approach near to a rebel officer's stock of rations, and the result was his being the loser—and myself the gainer—of a canteen filled with fairly good molasses. Andrews and I had some corn bread, and we breakfasted sumptuously upon it and the molasses which was certainly nonetheless sweet from having been stolen. Our meal over, we began reconnoitering, as much for employment as anything else. We were in the front end of a box car. With a saw made on the back of a case knife, we cut a hole through the boards big enough to permit us to pass out and perhaps escape. We found that we were on the foremost box car of the train, the next vehicle to us being a passenger coach in which were the rebel officers. On the rear platform of this car was seated one of their servants, a trusty old slave, well-dressed for a Negro and as respectful as his class usually was. "Well, uncle," I said to him, "where are they taking us?"

"Well, suh, I couldn't rightly say," he replied politely. "But you could guess, if you'd tried, couldn't you? Yas suh." He gave a quick look around to see if the door behind him was so securely shut that he could not be overheard by the rebels inside the car, his dull, stolid face lighted up as a Negro's always does in the excitement of doing something cunning, and he said in a loud whisper, "Dey's a gwine to take you to Wilmington if dey can git you dar!"

"Can get us there!" said I in astonishment. "Is there anything to prevent them taking us there?" The dark face filled with inexpressible meaning. "It isn't possible that there are any Yankees down there to interfere, is it?"

The great eyes flamed up with intelligence to tell me that I guessed aright. Again he glanced nervously around to assure himself that no one was eavesdropping, and then he said in a whisper just loud enough to be heard above the noise of the moving train, "De Yankees took Wilmington yesterday mawnin'."

The news startled me, but it was true, our troops having driven out the rebel troops and entered Wilmington on the preceding day, the 22nd of February, 1865, as I learned afterward. How this Negro came to know more of what was going on than his masters puzzled me much. That he did know more was beyond question, since if the rebels in whose charge we were had known of Wilmington's fall, they would not have gone to the trouble of loading us upon the cars and hauling us one hundred miles in the direction of a city which had come into the hands of our men.

It has been asserted by many writers that the Negroes had some occult means of diffusing important news among the mass of their people, probably by relays of swift runners who traveled at night, going twenty-five or thirty miles and back before morning. The rebels believed something of it, too. In spite of their rigorous patrol— an institution dating long before the war—and the severe punishments visited upon Negroes found off their masters' premises without a pass, none of them ever entertained a doubt that the young Negro men were in the habit of making long, mysterious journeys at night, which had other motives than love-making or chicken-stealing.

The country we were running through, if such straining, toilsome progress as our engine was making could be called running, was a rich turpentine district. We passed by forests where all the trees were marked with long scores through the bark and extended up to a height of twenty feet or more. Into these, the turpentine and rosin running down, were caught and conveyed by Negroes to stills nearby, where it was prepared for market. As we approached the coast the country became swampier and our old acquaintances, the cypresses with their malformed "knees," became more and more numerous.

About the middle of the afternoon our train suddenly stopped. Looking out to ascertain the cause, we were electrified to see a rebel line of battle stretched across the track about a half mile ahead of the engine, with its rear toward us. It was as real a line as was ever seen on any field. The double ranks of "Butternuts" with arms gleaming in the afternoon sun stretched away out through the open pine woods, farther than we could see. Close behind the motionless line stood the company officers leaning on their drawn swords. Behind these were the regimental officers on their horses. On a slight rise of the ground a group of horsemen, to whom other horsemen momentarily dashed up to or sped away from, showed the station of the general in command. On another knoll at a little distance were several field pieces standing "in battery," the cannoneers at the guns, the postilions dismounted and holding their horses by the bits, the caisson men standing in readiness to serve out ammunition. Our men were evidently close at hand in strong force and the engagement was likely to open at any instant.

For a minute we were speechless with astonishment. Then came a surge of excitement. What should we do? What could we do? Obviously nothing. Eleven hundred sick and feeble prisoners could not even overpower their guards, let alone make such a diversion in the rear of a line of battle as would assist our folks to gain a victory. But while we debated, the engine whistled sharply—a frightened shriek, it sounded to us—and began pushing our train rapidly backward over the rough and wretched track. Back, back we went as fast as rosin and pine knots could force the engine to move us. The cars swayed continually back and forth, momentarily threatening to fly off the crazy roadway and roll over the embankment or into one of the adjacent swamps. We would have hailed such a catastrophe as it would probably have killed more of the guards than of us and the confusion would have given many of the survivors opportunity to escape.

But no such accident happened, and toward midnight we reached the bridge across the great Peedee River where our train was stopped by a squad of rebel cavalrymen who brought the intelligence that as Kilpatrick was expected into Florence every hour, it would not do to take us there. We were ordered off the cars, and laid down on the banks of the Peedee, our guards and the cavalry forming a line around us and taking precautions to defend the bridge against Kilpatrick, should he find out our whereabouts and come after us.[61]

"Well, Mac," said Andrews as we adjusted our old overcoat and blanket on the ground for a bed, "I guess we needn't care whether school keeps or not. Our fellows have evidently got both ends of the road and are coming towards us from each way. There's no road, not even a wagon road, for the Johnnies to run us off on, and I guess all we've got to do is to stand still and see the salvation of the Lord. Bad as these hounds are, I don't believe they will shoot us down rather than let our folks retake us. At least, they won't since old Winder's dead. If he was alive, he'd order our throats cut, one by one, with the guards' pocket knives rather than give us up. I'm only afraid we'll be allowed to starve before our folks reach us."

I concurred in this view.

But Kilpatrick, like Sherman, came not. Perhaps he knew that all the prisoner had been removed from the stockade; perhaps he had other business of more impor tance on hand; probably his movement was only a feint. At all events it was definitely known the next day that he had withdrawn so far as to render it wholly unlikely that he intended attacking Florence, so we were brought back and returned to our old quarters. For a week or more we loitered about the nearly abandoned prison; skulked and crawled around the dismal mud tents like the ghostly denizens of some Potter's Field who, for some reason, had been allowed to return to earth and for a while to creep painfully around the little hillocks beneath which they had been entombed. A few score whose vital powers were strained to the last degree of tension gave up the ghost and sank to dreamless rest. It mattered now little to these when Sherman came or when Kilpatrick's guidons should flutter through the forest of sighing pines.

One day the order came for us to be loaded on the cars, and over to the railroad we went again in the same fashion as before. The comparatively few of us who were still able to walk at all well loaded ourselves down with the bundles and blankets of our less fortunate companions who hobbled and limped, many even crawling on their hands and knees over the hard frozen ground by our sides. Those not able to crawl even were taken in wagons, for the orders were imperative not to leave a living prisoner behind. At the railroad we found two trains awaiting us. On the front of each engine were two crude white flags, made by fastening the halves of meal sacks to short sticks. The sight of these gave us some hope, but our belief that rebels were constitutional liars and deceivers was so firm and fixed that we persuaded ourselves that the flags meant nothing more than some willful delusion for us.

Again we started off in the direction of Wilmington and traversed the same country. Again Andrews and I found ourselves in the next box car to the passenger coach containing the rebel officers. Again we cut a hole through the end with our saw, and again found a darky servant sitting on the car platform. Andrews went out and sat down alongside of him and found that he was seated upon a large gunnysack containing the cooked rations of the rebel officers. The intelligence that there was something there worth taking, Andrews communicated to me by an expressive signal such as soldiers campaigning together as long as he and I had, always have an extensive and well understood supply.

I took a seat in the hole we had made in the end of the car in reach of Andrews. Andrews called the attention of the Negro to some feature of the country nearby, and asked him a question in regard to it. As he looked in the direction indicated, Andrews slipped his hand into the mouth of the bag and pulled out a small sack of wheat biscuits which he passed to me and I concealed. The darky turned and told Andrews all about the matter in regard to which the interrogation had been made. Andrews became so much interested in what was being told him that he sat up closer and closer to the darky who in turn moved farther away from the sack. Next we ran through a turpentine plantation, and as the darky was pointing out where the still, the master's place and the "quarters" were, Andrews managed to fish out of the bag and pass to me three roasted chickens. Then a great swamp called for description, and before we were through it, I had about a peck of boiled sweet potatoes. Andrews emptied the bag as the darky was showing him a great peanut plantation, taking from it a small frying pan, a canteen of molasses and a half-gallon tin bucket which had been used to make coffee in. We divided up our wealth of edibles with the rest of the boys in the car, not forgetting to keep enough to give ourselves a magnificent meal.

As we ran along, we searched carefully for the place where we had seen the line of battle, expecting that it would now be marked with signs of a terrible conflict, but we could see nothing. We could not even fix the locality where the line stood. As it became apparent that we were going directly toward Wilmington, as fast as our engines could pull us, the excitement rose. We had many misgivings as to whether our folks still retained possession of Wilmington and whether, if they did, the rebels could not stop at a point outside of our lines and transfer us to some other road.

For hours we had seen nobody in the country through which we were passing. What few houses were visible were apparently deserted, and there were no towns or stations anywhere. We were very anxious to see someone, in hopes of getting a hint of what the state of affairs was in the direction we were going. At length we saw a young man, apparently a scout on horseback, but his clothes were so equally divided between the blue and the butternut as to give no clue to which side he belonged. An hour later we saw two infantrymen who were evidently out foraging. They had sacks of something on their backs and wore blue clothes. This was a very hopeful sign of a near approach to our lines, but bitter experience in the past warned us against being too sanguine.

About four o'clock in the afternoon, the trains stopped and whistled long and loud. Looking out I could see—perhaps half a mile away—a line of rifle pits running at right angles with the track. Guards whose guns flashed as they turned were pacing up and down, but they were too far away for me to distinguish their uniforms. The suspense became fearful. But I received much encouragement from the singular conduct of our guards. First I noticed a captain who had been especially mean to us at Florence. He was walking on the ground by the train. His face was pale, his teeth set, and his eyes shone with excitement. He called out in a strange, forced voice to his men and boys on the roof of the cars: "Here, you fellers, git down off'n thar an' form a line." The fellows did so in a slow, constrained, frightened way and huddled together in the most unsoldierly manner. The whole thing reminded me of a scene I once saw in our

lines, where a weak-kneed captain was ordered to take a party of rather chicken-
hearted recruits out on the skirmish line.

We immediately divined what was the matter. The lines in front of us were really
those of our people, and the idiots of guards, not knowing their entire safety was protected by a flag of truce, were scared half out of their small wits at approaching so
near to armed Yankees. We showered taunts and jeers upon them. An Irishman in my
car yelled, "Och, ye dirty spalpeens; it's not shootin' prisoners ye are now; it's comin'
where the Yankee b'ys hev the guns; an' the minit ye see thim, ye're white livers show
themselves in ye're pale faces. Bad luck to the blatherin' bastards that yez are and to
the mothers that bore ye!"

At length our train moved up so near to the line that I could see it was the grand
old loyal blue that clothed the forms of the men who were pacing up and down. And
certainly the world rarely sees as superb-looking men as these appeared to me. Finely
formed, stalwart, full-fed and well-clothed, they formed the most delightful contrast
with the scrawny, shambling, villain-visaged little clay-eaters and white trash who had
looked down upon us from the sentry boxes for many long months.

I sprang out of the cars and began washing my face and hands in the ditch at the
side of the road. The rebel captain, noticing me, said in the old hateful, brutal, impe-
rious tone: "Git back in dat cah, dah." An hour before I would have scrambled back as
quickly as possible, knowing that an instant's hesitation would be followed by a bullet. Now, I looked him in the face and said, as irritatingly as possible, "Oh, you go to
hell, you bastard rebel! I'm going into Uncle Sam's lines with as little rebel filth on
me as possible." He passed me without replying. His day of shooting was past.

Descending from the cars, we passed through the guards into our lines, a rebel
and a Union clerk checking us off as we passed. By the time it was dark, we were all
under our flag again. The place where we came through was several miles west of Wilmington where the railroad crossed a branch of the Cape Fear River. The point was
held by a brigade of Schofield's Army, the XXIII Army Corps. The boys lavished un-
stinted kindness upon us. All of the brigade off duty crowded around, offering blankets, shirts, shoes, pantaloons and other articles of clothing, and similar things that we
were obviously in the greatest need of. The sick were carried by hundreds of willing
hands to a sheltered spot and laid upon good comfortable beds improvised with leaves
and blankets. A great line of huge, generous fires was built around which every one of
us had plenty of place.

By and by a line of wagons came over from Wilmington laden with rations, and
they were dispensed to us with what seemed prodigality. The lid of a box of hardtack
would be knocked off and the contents handed to us as we filed past, with absolute dis-

regard as to quantity. If a prisoner looked wistful after receiving one handful of crackers, another was handed to him; if his long-famished eyes still lingered as if enchained by the rare display of food, the men who were issuing said, "Here, old fellow, there's plenty of it, take just as much as you can carry in your arms."

So it was also with the pickled pork, the coffee, the sugar. We had been stinted and starved so long that we could not comprehend that there was anywhere actually "enough" of anything. The kind-hearted boys who were acting as our hosts began preparing food for the sick, but the surgeons who had arrived in the meantime were compelled to repress them, as it was plain that while it was a dangerous experiment to give any of us all we could or would eat, it would never do to give the sick such a temptation to kill themselves. Only a limited amount of food was allowed to be given those who were unable to walk.

Andrews and I hungered for coffee, the delightful fumes of which filled the air and intoxicated our senses. We procured enough to make our half-gallon bucket full and very strong. We drank so much of this that Andrews became positively drunk and fell helplessly into some brush. I pulled him out and dragged him away to a place where he had made our rude bed. I was dazed. I could not comprehend that the long looked-for, often despaired-of, event had actually happened. I feared that it was one of those tantalizing dreams that had so often haunted my sleep, only to be followed by a wretched awakening.

Then I became seized with a sudden fear lest the rebels attempt to retake me. The line of guards around seemed very slight. It might be forced in the night and all of us recaptured. Shivering at this thought, absurd though it was, I arose from our bed and taking Andrews with me, crawled two or three hundred yards into a dense undergrowth where in the event of our lines being forced, we would be overlooked. After a sound sleep, Andrews and I awoke to the enjoyment of our first day of freedom and existence in God's country. The sun had already risen, bright and warm, consonant with the happiness of the new life now opening for us. But to nearly a score of our party, the sun's beams brought no awakening gladness. They fell upon stony, staring eyes from out of which the light of life had now faded as the light of hope had done long ago. The dead lay there upon the rude beds of fallen leaves, scraped together by thoughtful comrades the night before, their clenched teeth showing through parted lips, faces fleshless and pinched, long, unkempt and ragged hair and whiskers just stirred by the lazy breeze, the rotting feet and limbs drawn up, the skinny hands clenched in the last agonies. Their fate seemed harder than that of any who had died before them. It was doubtful if many of them knew that they were at last inside of our lines. Again the kind-hearted boys of the brigade crowded around us with proffers of service.

From an Ohio boy who directed his kind tenders to Andrews and me, we procured a chunk of coarse rosin soap about as big as a pack of cards and a towel. Never was there as great a quantity of solid comfort got out of that much soap as that we obtained. It was the first that we had since that which I stole in Wirz' headquarters in June, months before. We felt that the dirt which had accumulated upon us since then would subject us to assessment as real estate if we were in the North. Hurrying off to a little creek, we began our ablutions, and it was not long until Andrews declared that there was a perceptible sandbar forming in the stream from what we washed off. Dirt deposits of the Pliocene era rolled off feet and legs. Eocene incrustations let loose reluctantly from neck and ears. Our hair was such a mass of tangled locks matted with the months' accumulation of pitch-pine tar, rosin soot and South Carolina sand that we did not think we had better start in upon it until we either had the shock cut off or had a whole ocean and a vat of soap to wash it out with. After scrubbing until we were exhausted, we got off the first few outer layers—the post-tertiary formation, a geologist would term it—and the smell of many breakfasts cooking coming down over the hill set our stomachs in a mutiny against any longer fasting. We went back, rosy, panting, glowing but happy, to get ourselves some breakfast.

Should Providence for some inscrutable reason vouchsafe me the years of Methuselah, one of the pleasantest recollections that will abide with me to the close of the nine hundred and sixty-ninth year will be of that delightful odor of cooking food which regaled our senses as we came back. From the boiling coffee and the meat frying in the pan rose an incense sweeter to the senses a thousand times than all the perfumes of far Arabia. It differed from the loathsome odor of cooking corn meal as much as it did from the effluvia of a sewer. Our noses were the first of our senses to bear testimony that we had passed from the land of starvation to that of plenty. Andrews and I hastened off to get our own breakfast, and soon had a half-gallon of strong coffee and a frying pan full of meat cooking over the fire—not one of the beggarly skimpy little fires we had crouched over during our months of imprisonment but a royal, generous fire fed with logs instead of shavings and splinters giving out heat enough to warm a regiment.

Having eaten all that we could swallow, those of us who could walk were ordered to fall in and march over to Wilmington. We crossed the branch of the river on a pontoon bridge and took the road that led across the narrow sandy island between the two branches, Wilmington being situated on the opposite bank of the further one. When about half way, a shout from someone in advance caused us to look up and then we saw, flying from a tall steeple in Wilmington, the glorious old Stars and Stripes, resplendent in the morning sun. We stopped with one accord and shouted and cheered until every throat was sore. It seemed as if our cup of happiness would certainly run over if any more additions were made to it.

When we arrived at the bank of the river opposite Wilmington, a whole world of new and interesting sights opened up before us. Wilmington during the last year and a half of the war, next to Richmond, was the most important place in the Southern Confederacy. It was the only port to which blockade-running was safe enough to be lucrative. The rebels held the strong forts of Caswell and Fisher at the mouth of the Cape Fear River. And outside, the Frying Pan Shoals, which extended along the coast forty or fifty miles, kept our blockading fleet so far off and made the line so weak and scattered that there was comparatively little risk to the small, swift, sailing vessels employed by the blockade-runners in running through it. Before the war, Wilmington was a dull, sleepy North Carolina town, with as little animation of any kind as a Breton village. The only business was the handling of the tar, turpentine, rosin and peanuts produced in the surrounding country, a business never lively enough to excite more than a lazy ripple in the sluggish lagoons of trade.

But very new wine was being poured in this old bottle when blockade-running began to develop in importance. Then this Sleepy Hollow of a place took on the appearance of San Francisco at the height of the gold fever. The English houses engaged in blockade-running established branches there conducted by young men who lived like princes. They literally clothed themselves in purple and fine linen and fared sumptuously every day, with their fine wines and imported delicacies and retinue of servants to wait upon them. Fast young rebel officers, eager for a season of dissipation, could imagine nothing better than a leave of absence to go to Wilmington. Money flowed like water. The money obtained so recklessly was squandered as recklessly and all sorts of debauchery ran riot.

Almost as gratifying as the sight of the old flag flying in triumph was the exhibition of our naval power in the river before us. The larger part of the great North Atlantic Squadron which had done such excellent service in the reduction of the defenses of Wilmington was lying at anchor, with the hundreds of huge guns yawning as if ardent for more great forts to beat down, more vessels to sink, more heavy artillery to crush, more rebels to conquer.

While we were standing, contemplating all the interesting sights within view, a small steamer about the size of a canal boat and carrying several light brass guns, ran swiftly and noiselessly up to the dock nearby and a young pale-faced officer, slender of build and nervous in manner, stepped ashore. Some of the blue jackets who were talking to us looked at him and the vessel with an expression of greatest interest and said: "Hello! there's the *Monticello* and Lieutenant Cushing." This then was the naval boy hero with whose exploits the whole country was ringing. Our sailor friends proceeded to tell us of his achievements of which they were justly proud. They told us of his perilous scouts and his hairbreadth escapes, of his wonderful audacity and still more wonderful success. He had come prominently into notice in the preceding autumn when he had, by one of the most daring performances in naval history, destroyed the formidable ram, *Albemarle*. We were ferried across the river into Wilmington and marched up the streets to some vacant ground near the railroad depot where we found most of our old Florence comrades already assembled.

It was now nearly noon and we were ordered to fall in and draw rations, a bewildering order to us who had been so long in the habit of drawing food but once a day. We fell in in single rank and marched up, one at a time, past where a group of employees of the Commissary Department dealt out the food. One handed each prisoner as he passed a large slice of meat; another gave him a handful of ground coffee; a third gave him a handful of sugar; a fourth gave him a pickle; while a fifth and sixth handed him an onion and a loaf of fresh bread. This filled the horn of plenty to full. To have all these in one day—meat, coffee, sugar, onions and soft bread—was simply a riot of undreamed of luxury. Many of the boys, poor fellows, could not yet realize that there was *enough* for all, nor could they give up their old "flanking" tactics. They stole around and, falling into the rear, came up again for another share. We laughed at them, as did the Commissary men who nevertheless duplicated the rations already received, and sent them away happy and content.

We stayed in Wilmington a few days of almost purely animal enjoyment, the joy of having as much to eat as we could possibly swallow and no one to molest us or make us afraid in any way. How we did eat—and fill up! The wrinkles in our skin filled out under the stretching and we began to feel as if we were returning to our old plumpness, though so far the plumpness was wholly abdominal. One morning we were told that the transports would begin going back with us that afternoon, the first that left taking the sick. Andrews and I, true to our old prison practices, resolved to be among those on the first boat. We slipped through the guards and, going uptown, went straight to Major General Schofield's headquarters and solicited a pass to go on the very first boat, the steamer *Thorn*. General Schofield treated us very kindly, but declined to let anybody but the helplessly sick go on the *Thorn*.

Defeated here, we went down to where the vessel was lying at the dock and tried to smuggle ourselves aboard, but the guard was too strong and too vigilant and we were driven away. Going along the dock, angry and discouraged by our failure, we saw a surgeon at a little distance, who was examining and sending the sick who could walk aboard another vessel, the *General Lyon*. We took our cue, and a little shamming secured from him tickets which permitted us to take passage in her. The larger portion of those on board were in the hold, a few were on deck. Andrews and I found a snug place under the forecastle by the anchor chains.

Both vessels speedily received their complements and leaving their docks started down the river. The *Thorn* steamed ahead of us and disappeared. Shortly after we got underway, the colonel who was put in command of the boat, himself a released prisoner, came around on a tour of inspection. He found about a thousand of us aboard, and singling me out made me the non-commissioned officer in command. I was put in charge of issuing the rations and of a barrel of milk punch which the Sanitary Commission had sent down to be dealt out on the voyage to such as needed it. I went to work and arranged the boys the best way I could and returned to the deck to view the scenery.

Wilmington is thirty-four miles from the sea and the river for that distance is a calm, broad estuary. At this time, the resources of rebel engineering had been exhausted in the defense against its passage by a hostile fleet, and undoubtedly the best work of the kind in the Southern Confederacy was done upon it. At its mouth were Forts Fisher and Caswell, the strongest seacoast forts in the Confederacy. Fort Caswell was an old United States fort much enlarged and strengthened. Fort Fisher was a new work begun immediately after the beginning of the war and labored at incessantly until captured. Behind these, every one of the thirty-four miles to Wilmington was covered by the fire of the best guns English arsenals could produce, mounted on forts built at every advantageous spot. Lines of piles running out into the water forced incoming vessels to wind back and forth across the stream under the point-blank range of massive Armstrong rifles. As if this were not sufficient, the channel was thickly studded with torpedoes that would explode at the touch of a keel of a passing vessel.

We passed hundreds of sailors fishing for torpedoes and saw many of the dangerous monsters which they had hauled out of the water. We caught up with the *Thorn*, when about halfway to the sea, passed her to our great delight and soon left a gap between us of nearly half a mile. We ran through an opening in the piling, holding up close to the left side, and she apparently followed our course exactly. Suddenly there was a dull roar. A column of water bearing with it fragments of timbers, planking and human bodies, rose up through one side of the vessel and, as it fell, she lurched forward and sank. She had struck a torpedo. I never learned the number lost, but it must have been very great.

When we reached the mouth of the Cape Fear River, the wind was blowing so hard that our captain did not think it best to venture out, so he cast anchor. The cabin of the vessel was filled with officers who had been released from prison about the same time we were. I also got a berth in the cabin in consideration of my being the non-commissioned officer in charge of the men, and I found the associations quite pleasant. The wind at length calmed sufficiently to encourage our captain to venture out and we were soon battling with the rolling waves far out of sight of land. For a while the novelty of the scene fascinated me. I was at last on the ocean of which I had heard, read and imagined much. The creaking cordage, the straining engine, the plunging ship, the wild haste of tumbling billows—every one apparently racing to where our tossing bark was struggling to maintain herself—all had an entrancing interest for me.

Just then my reverie was broken by the strong hand of the gruff captain of the vessel descending upon my shoulder. "See here, youngster!" he said gruffly, "Ain't you the fellow that was put in command of these men?" I acknowledged such to be the case. "Well," said the captain, "I want you to 'tend to your business and straighten them around, so that we can clean off the decks." I turned from the bulwark over which I had been contemplating the vast deep, and saw the sorriest, most woebegone lot that the imagination can conceive. They were paying the penalty of their over-feeding in Wilmington, and every face looked as if its owner was discovering for the first time what the real lower depths of human misery was. Every mother's son was wretchedly seasick. They all seemed afraid they would not die and as if they were praying for death, but feeling certain that He was going back on them in a most shameful way. We straightened them out a little, washed them and the decks off with a hose, and then I started down in the hold to see how matters were with the six hundred down there. The boys there were much sicker than those on deck.

As I lifted the hatch there rose an odor which appeared strong enough to raise the plank itself. I recoiled, and leaned against the bulwark, but soon summoned up courage enough to go halfway down the ladder and shout out in as stern a tone as I could command: "Here, now! I want you fellows to straighten up around here, right off, and help clean up!"

They were as angry and cross as they were sick. They wanted nothing in the world so much as the opportunity I had given them to swear at and abuse somebody. Every one of them raised on his elbow and shaking his fist at me, yelled out, "Oh, you go to hell, you damn fool! Just come down another step, and I'll knock the whole head off'n you!" I did not go down any farther.

Coming back on the deck, my stomach began to feel squeamish. Some wretched idiot—whose grandfather's grave I hope the jackasses have defiled, as the Turks would say—told me that the best preventive of seasickness was to drink as much of the milk punch as I could swallow. Like another idiot, I did so. I went to the side of the vessel, but now the fascination of the scene had all faded out. The restless billows were dreary, savage, hungry and dizzying. They seemed to claw at and tear and wrench the struggling ship as a group of huge lions would tease and worry a captive dog. They distressed her and all on board by dealing a blow which would send her reeling in one direction, then, before she had swung the full length that impulse would have sent her, catching her on the opposite side with a stunning shock that sent her another way, only to meet another rude buffet from still another angle.

I think we could all have stood it if the motion had been like that of a swing, backward and forward, or even if the to-and-fro motion had been complicated with a sidewise swing, but to be put through every possible bewildering motion in the briefest space of time was more than heads of iron and stomachs of brass could stand. Mine was not made of such stuff. They commenced mutinous demonstrations in regard to the milk punch. I began wondering whether the milk punch was not the horrible beer swill, the "stumptail" kind of which I had heard so much. And the whiskey in it! To use a vigorous westernism descriptive of mean whiskey, it seemed to me that I could smell the boy's feet who plowed the corn from which it was distilled. I became so utterly wretched that life had no further attractions.

After this misery had lasted about two days, we got past Cape Hatteras, and out of reach of its malign influence, we recovered as rapidly as we had prostrated. We gained spirits and appetites with amazing swiftness. The sun came out warm and cheerful. During the remainder of the voyage we were as blithe and cheerful as so many crickets. The fun in the cabin was rollicking. The officers had been as sick as the men, but were wonderfully vivacious when the mal de mer passed off.

In the party was a fine Glee Club, which had been organized at Camp Sorghum, the officers' prison at Columbia. Its leader was a major of the 5th Iowa Cavalry, who possessed a marvelously sweet tenor voice and well developed musical powers. While we were at Wilmington he sang "When Sherman Marched Down To The Sea" to an audience of soldiers that packed the Opera House. The enthusiasm he aroused there was simply indescribable. Men shouted and tears ran down their faces. He was recalled time and again, each time with an increase in the furore. The audience would have stayed there all night to listen to him sing. Poor fellow, he only went home to die. An attack of pneumonia carried him off within a fortnight after we separated at Annapolis.

The next day our vessel ran alongside of the dock at the Naval Academy at Annapolis, that institution now being used as a hospital for paroled prisoners. The musicians of the Post band came down with stretchers to carry the sick to the hospital, while those of us who were able to walk were ordered to fall in and march up. The distance was but a few hundred yards. On reaching the building we marched up on a little balcony where each one of us was seized by a hospital attendant who, with the quick dexterity attained by long practice, snatched every one of our filthy, lousy rags off in the twinkling of an eye and flung them over the railing to the ground to be loaded on a wagon by a man with a pitchfork.

With them went our faithful little black can, our hoop-iron spoon, and our chessboard and men. Entirely denuded, each boy was then given a shove which sent him into a little room where a barber pressed him down upon a stool and, almost before he understood what was being done, had his hair and beard cut off as close as shears would do it. Another tap on the back sent the shorn lamb into a room furnished with great tubs of water with about six inches of soap suds on the zinc-covered floor. In another minute two men with sponges had removed every trace of prison grime from his body and passed him on to two more men who wiped him dry and moved him on to where a man handed him a new shirt, a pair each of drawers, socks, pantaloons, slippers, and a hospital gown, and motioned him to go into the large room and array himself in his new garments.

Like everything else about the hospital this performance was reduced to a perfect system. Not a word was spoken by anybody, not a moment's time was lost, and it seemed to me that it was not ten minutes after I marched up the balcony, covered with dirt, rags, vermin and a matted shock of hair, until I marched out of the room, clean and well-clothed. Now I began to feel as if I was really a man again. The next thing done was to register our names, rank, regiment, when and where captured, when and where released and other significant details. After this we were shown to our rooms.

And such rooms as they were. All the old maids in the country could not have improved the spic-and-span neatness. The floors were as white as pine plank could be scoured; the sheets and bedding as clean as cotton and linen and woolen could be washed. Nothing in any home in the land was any more daintily, wholesomely, unqualifiedly clean than were these little chambers, each containing two beds, one for each man assigned to their occupancy. Andrews doubted if we could stand all this radical change in our habits. He feared that it was rushing things too fast. We might have had all our hair cut one week and taken a bath all over a week later, and so progress down to sleeping between white sheets in the course of six months. But to do it all in one day seemed like tempting fate.

Every turn showed us some new feature of the marvelous order of this wonderful institution. Shortly after we were sent to our rooms, a surgeon entered with a clerk. After answering the usual questions as to name, rank, company and regiment, the surgeon examined our tongues, eyes, limbs and general appearance and communicated his conclusions to the clerk who filled out a blank card. The card was stuck into a little tin holder at the head of my bed. Andrews' card was the same, except the name. The surgeon was followed by a sergeant who was chief of the dining room and his clerk who made a minute record of the diet ordered for us, and moved off.

Andrews and I immediately became very solicitous to know what species of diet No. 1 was. After our seasickness left us, our appetites had become as ravenous as a buzz-saw and unless Diet No. 1 was more than just a name, it would not fill the bill. We had not long to remain in suspense, for soon another commissioned officer passed through at the head of a train of attendants bearing trays. Consulting the list in his hand, he said to one of his followers, "Two No. 1's," and that satellite set down two large trays, upon each of which were a cup of coffee, a shred of meat, two boiled eggs and rolls.

"Well," said Andrews as the procession moved away, "I want to know where this thing's going to stop. I am trying hard to get used to wearing a shirt without any lice in it and to sitting down on a chair and to sleeping in a clean bed, but when it comes to having meals sent to my room, I'm afraid I'll degenerate into a child of luxury."

"It seems like years, Lale," I said. "But for heaven's sake let's try to forget it as soon as possible. We will always remember much of it."

The days that followed were happy ones. The Paymaster came around and paid us each two months' pay and twenty-five cents a day "ration money" for every day we had been in prison. This gave Andrews and me about one hundred and sixty dollars apiece, an abundance of spending money. Uncle Sam was very kind and considerate to his soldier-nephews, and the hospital authorities neglected nothing that would add to our comfort. The superbly kept grounds of the Naval Academy were renewing the freshness of their loveliness under the tender wooing of the advancing spring, and every step one sauntered through them was a new delight. A magnificent band gave us sweet music morning and evening. Every dispatch from the South told of the victorious progress of our arms and the rapid approach of the close of the struggle. All we had to do was to enjoy the goods the gods were showering on us, and we did so with appreciative hearts.

After a while, all able to travel were given furloughs of thirty days to visit their homes with instructions to report, at the expiration of their leaves of absence, to the camps of rendezvous nearest their homes, and we separated, nearly every man going in a different direction.

"I Want to Know Where this Thing's Going to Stop"

CHAPTER XXIV

FIRST TRIAL OF A WAR CRIMINAL

OF ALL THOSE more or less concerned in the barbarities practiced upon our prisoners, only Captain Henri Wirz was punished. The Turners at Richmond, Lieutenant Boisseux of Belle Isle, Major Gee of Salisbury, Colonel Iverson and Lieutenant Barret of Florence and the many brutal miscreants about Andersonville escaped scot-free. What became of them no one knows. They were never heard of after the close of the war. They had sense enough to retire into obscurity and stay there. This saved their lives for each one of them had made such deadly enemies among those whom they had maltreated that, had they known where they were, they would have walked every step of the way to kill them.

When the Confederacy went to pieces in April, 1865, Wirz was still at Andersonville. General Wilson commanding our cavalry forces, who had established his headquarters at Macon, Georgia, learned of this and sent one of his staff, Captain H. E. Noyes of the 4th Regular Cavalry with a squad of men to arrest him. This was done on the 7th of May. Wirz protested against his arrest, claiming that he was protected by the terms of Johnston's surrender, and addressed the following letter to General Wilson:

Andersonville, Georgia, May 7, 1865.

General:

It is with great reluctance that I address you these lines, being fully aware how little time is left you to attend to such matters as I now have the honor to lay before you, and if I could see any other way to accomplish my object I would not intrude upon you. I am a native of Switzerland, and was before the war a citizen of Louisiana, and by profession a physician. Like hundreds and thousands of others, I was carried away by the maelstrom of excitement and joined the Southern army. I was very severely wounded at the battle of Seven Pines, near Richmond, Virginia, and have nearly lost the use of my right arm. Unfit for field duty, I was ordered to report to Brevet Major General John H. Winder, in charge of the Federal prisoners of war, who ordered me to take charge of a prison in Tuscaloosa, Ala. My health failing me, I applied for a furlough and went to Europe, from whence I returned in February, 1864. I was then ordered to report to the commandant of the military prison at Andersonville, Georgia, who assigned me to the command of the interior of the prison. I now bear the odium, and men who were prisoners have seemed disposed to wreak their vengeance upon me for what they have suffered. I, who was only the medium, or, I may better say, the tool in the hands of my superiors. This is my condition. I am a man with a family. I lost all my property when the Federal army besieged Vicksburg. I have no money at present to go to any place, and, even if I had, I know of no place where I can go. My life is in danger, and I most respectfully ask of you help and relief. If you will be so generous as to give me some sort of a safe conduct, or what I should greatly prefer, a guard to protect myself and family against violence, I should be thankful to you: and you may rest assured that your protection will not be given to one who is unworthy of it. My intention is to return with my family to Europe, as soon as I can make the arrangements. In the meantime I have the honor, General, to remain, very respectfully, your obedient servant,

Henri Wirz, Captain C.S.A.

Major General James Harrison Wilson
    Commanding, Macon, Ga.

Wirz was kept at Macon under guard until May 20 when Captain Noyes was ordered to take him and the hospital records of Andersonville to Washington. Between Macon and Cincinnati, the journey was a perfect gauntlet. Our men were stationed all along the road, and among them everywhere were ex-prisoners, who recognized Wirz, and made such determined efforts to kill him that it was all that Captain Noyes, backed by a strong guard, could do to frustrate them. At Chattanooga and Nashville the struggle between his guards and his would-be slayers, was quite sharp. At Louisville, Noyes had Wirz clean-shaved and dressed in a complete suit of black, with a beaver hat which so altered his appearance that no one recognized him and the rest of the journey was made unmolested.

The authorities at Washington ordered that he be tried immediately, by a court-martial composed of Generals Lewis Wallace,[62] Mott, Geary, L. Thomas, Fessenden, Bragg and Baller, Colonel Allcock, and Lieutenant-Colonel Stibbs. Colonel Chipman was Judge Advocate.

The trial began August 23, 1865. The prisoner was arraigned on a formidable list of charges and specifications which accused him of "combining, confederating, and conspiring together with John H. Winder, Richard B. Winder, Isaiah H. White, W. S. Winder, R. R. Stevenson and others unknown, to injure the health and destroy the lives of soldiers in the military service of the United States, there held, and being prisoners of war within the lines of the so-called Confederate States, and in the military prisons thereof, to the end that the armies of the United States might be weakened and impaired, in violation of the laws and customs of war."

The main facts of the dense over-crowding, the lack of sufficient shelter, the hideous mortality were cited, and to these were added a long list of such specific acts of brutality—hunting men down with hounds, robbing them, confining them in the stocks, cruelly beating and murdering them—of which Wirz was personally guilty.

When the defendant was called upon to plead, he claimed that his case was covered by the terms of Johnston's surrender and furthermore that the country now being at peace, he could not be lawfully tried by a court-martial. These objections being overruled, he entered a plea of not guilty to all the charges and specifications. He had two lawyers for counsel.

The prosecution called Captain Noyes first, who detailed the circumstances of Wirz' arrest and denied that he had given any promises of protection. The next witness was Colonel George C. Gibbs who commanded the troops of the post at Andersonville. He testified that Wirz was the commandant of the prison and had sole authority under Winder over all the prisoners; that there was a Dead Line there and orders to shoot any one who crossed it; that dogs were kept to hunt down escaping prisoners; that the dogs were the ordinary plantation dogs, mixture of hound and cur.

Dr. J. C. Bates who was a surgeon in the prison hospital, testified that the condition of things in his division was horrible. Nearly naked men, covered with lice, were dying on all sides. Many were lying in the filthy sand and mud. He went on to describe the terrible condition of men, dying from scurvy, diarrhea, gangrenous sores and lice. He wanted to carry in fresh vegetables for the sick but did not dare, the orders being very strict against such things.[63] He thought the prison authorities might easily have sent in enough green corn to have stopped the scurvy; the miasmatic effluvia from the prison was exceedingly offensive and poisonous, so much so that when the surgeons received a slight scratch on their persons, they carefully covered it up with court plaster before venturing near the prison. A number of other Confederate surgeons testified to substantially the same facts. Several residents of that section of the state testified to the plentifulness of the crops there in 1864.

Dr. R. Randolph Stevenson, Surgeon in the Army of the Confederate States of America and Chief Surgeon of the Confederate States Military Prison Hospital at Andersonville, Georgia, gave the following testimony:

> From the sameness of the food, and from the action of the poisonous gases in the densely crowded and filthy Stockade and Hospital, the blood was altered in its constitution, even before the manifestation of actual disease.
>
> In almost all cases which I examined after death, even in the most emaciated, there was more or less serious effusion into the abdominal cavity. In cases of hospital gangrene of the extremities and in cases of gangrene of the intestines, heart-clots and firm coagula were universally present. The presence of these clots in the cases of hospital gangrene, whilst they were absent in the cases in which there were no inflammatory symptoms, appears to sustain the conclusion that hospital gangrene is a species of inflammation (imperfect and irregular though it may be in its progress), in which the fibrinous element and coagulability of the blood are increased, even in those who are suffering from such a condition of the blood and from such diseases as are naturally accompanied with a decrease in the fibrinous constituent.
>
> The mental condition connected with long confinement, with the most miserable surroundings, and with no hope for the future, also depressed all the nervous and vital actions, and was especially active in destroying the appetite. The effects of mental depression, and of defective nutrition, were manifested not only in the slow, feeble motions of the wasted, skeleton-like forms, but also in such lethargy, listlessness, and torpor of the mental faculties as rendered these unfortunate men oblivious and indifferent to their afflicted condition. In many cases, even of the greatest apparent suffering and distress, instead of showing any anxiety to communicate the causes of their distress, or to relate their privations, and their longings for their homes and their friends and relatives, they lay in a listless, lethargic, uncomplaining state, taking no notice either of their own distressed condition, or of the gigantic mass of human misery by which they were surrounded. Nothing ap-

palled and depressed me so much as this silent, uncomplaining misery. It is a fact of great interest, that notwithstanding this defective nutrition in men subjected to crowding and filth, contagious fevers were rare; and typhus fever, which is supposed to be generated in just such a state of things as existed at Andersonville, was unknown.

The fact that hospital gangrene appeared in the Stockade first, and originated spontaneously, without any previous contagion, and occurred sporadically all over the Stockade and Prison Hospital, was proof positive that this disease will arise whenever the conditions of crowding, filth, foul air, and bad diet are present.

The exhalations from the Hospital and Stockade appeared to exert their effects to a considerable distance outside of these localities. The origin of gangrene among these prisoners appeared clearly to depend in great measure upon the state of the general system, induced by diet, exposure, neglect of personal cleanliness, and by various external noxious influences. The rapidity of the appearance and action of the gangrene depended upon the powers and state of the constitution, as well as upon the intensity of the poison in the atmosphere, or upon the direct application of poisonous matter to the wounded surface. This was further illustrated by the important fact, that hospital gangrene, or a disease resembling this form of gangrene, attacked the intestinal canal of patients laboring under ulceration of the bowels, although there were no local manifestations of gangrene upon the surface of the body. This mode of termination in cases of dysentery was quite common in the foul atmosphere of the Confederate States Military Prison Hospital; and in the depressed, depraved condition of the system of these Federal prisoners, death ensued very rapidly after the gangrenous state of the intestines was established.

Thus ended Dr. Stevenson's testimony.

In addition to these, about one hundred and fifty Union prisoners were examined who testified to all manner of barbarities which had come under their personal observation. They had all seen Wirz shoot men. They had seen him knock sick and crippled men down; stamp upon them. They had seen men run down by him with hounds. Their testimony occupied about two thousand pages of manuscript and is, without doubt, the most terrible record of crime ever laid to the account of any man.

Dr. Joseph Jones, of the Medical Department of the Confederacy, was then called to the stand to give testimony for the prosecution.

Dr. Joseph Jones for the prosecution:

By the Judge Advocate:

Q. Where do you reside?

A. In Augusta, Georgia.

Q. Are you a graduate of any medical college?

A. Of the University of Pennsylvania.

Q. How long have you been engaged in the practice of medicine?

A. Eight years.

Q. Has your experience been as a practitioner, or rather as an investigator of medicine as a science?

A. Both.

Q. What position do you now hold?

A. That of Medical Chemist in the Medical College of Georgia.

Q. How long have you held that position in that college?

A. Since 1858.

Q. How were you employed during the rebellion?

A. I served six months in the early part of it as a private in the ranks, and the rest of the time in the medical department.

Q. Under the direction of whom?

A. Under the direction of Dr. George Moore, Surgeon General.

Q. Did you, while acting under his direction, visit Andersonville professionally?

A. Yes, sir.

Q. For the purpose of making investigations there?

A. For the purpose of prosecuting investigations ordered by the Surgeon General.

Q. You went there in obedience to a letter of instructions?

A. In obedience to orders which I received.

Q. Did you reduce the results of your investigations to the shape of a report?

A. I was engaged in that work when General Johnston surrendered.

(A document being handed to the witness)

Q. Have you examined this extract from your report and compared it with the original?

A. Yes, sir, I have.

Q. Is it accurate?

A. So far as my examination extended, it is accurate.

(The document just examined by witness was offered in evidence)

Dr. Jones described the Stockade in detail. He told of the terrible condition of the soil and of the boggy condition of the sink, and of the causes of various diseases rampant among the soldiers which he had determined by post mortem investigations. He testified that the Stockade had originally been intended to accommodate only ten thousand prisoners, but by August of 1864 there were 39,899 prisoners, each man allotted to a space measuring 35.7 square feet, and that the dense crowding contributed to the high mortality rate.

The taking of this testimony lasted until October 18, when the Government decided to close the case, as any further evidence would be simply cumulative.

The prisoner then presented a statement in which he denied that he had been an accomplice in a conspiracy between John H. Winder and others to destroy the lives of United States soldiers. He also denied that there had been such a conspiracy and made the pertinent inquiry why he alone, of all those who were charged with the conspiracy, was brought to trial. He said that "Winder has gone to the Great Judgment Seat to answer for all his thoughts, words and deeds, and surely I am not to be held culpable for them. General Howell Cobb has received the pardon of the President of the United States." He further claimed that there was no principle of law which would sanction the holding of him, a mere subordinate, guilty for simply obeying as literally as possible the orders of his superiors.

Wirz denied all the specific acts of cruelty alleged against him, such as maltreating and killing prisoners with his own hands. The prisoners killed for crossing the Dead Line, he claimed, should not be charged against him, since they were simply punished for the violation of a known order which formed part of the discipline, so he believed, of all military prisons. The statement that soldiers were given a furlough for killing a Yankee prisoner was declared to be "a mere idle, absurd camp rumor." As to the lack of shelter, room and rations for so many prisoners, he claimed that the sole responsibility rested upon the Confederate Government. There never were but two prisoners whipped by his order and these were for sufficient cause. He asked the Court to consider favorably two important items in his defense: first, that he had of his own accord taken the drummer boys from the Stockade and placed them where they could get purer air and better food; second, that no property taken from prisoners was retained by him but was turned over to the Prison Quartermaster.

The Court, after due deliberation, declared the prisoner guilty on all the charges and specifications save two unimportant ones and sentenced him to be hanged by the neck until dead at such time and place as the President of the United States should direct. On November 3, President Andrew Johnson approved of the sentence and ordered Major General C. C. Augur to carry the same into effect on Friday, November 10, which was done.

Wirz made frantic appeals against the sentence; he wrote imploring letters to President Johnson, and lying ones to the *New York News,* a paper sympathetic to the south. It is said that his wife attempted to convey poison to him that he might commit suicide and avoid the ignominy of being hanged. When all hope was gone, he nerved himself up to meet his fate, and died with calmness. His body was buried in the grounds of the Old Capitol Prison alongside that of Atzerodt, one of the accomplices in the assassination of President Lincoln.

There is much circumstantial evidence connecting the rebel authorities with the premeditated plan for destroying the prisoners. Let us examine the direct evidence. The first feature is the assignment to the command of the prisons of "General" John H. Winder, the confidential friend of Jefferson Davis, and a man so unscrupulous, cruel and blood-thirsty that, at the time of his appointment, he was the most hated and feared man in the Confederacy. His loathsome administration of the odious office of Provost Marshal General [64] showed him to be fittest tool for their purpose. Their selection, considering the end in view, was eminently wise. Baron Haynau was made eternally infamous by a fraction of the wanton cruelties which load the memory of Winder. But it can be said in extenuation of Haynau's offenses that he was a brave, skillful and energetic soldier who overthrew on the field the enemies he maltreated. If Winder at any time during the war was nearer the front than Richmond, history does not mention it. Haynau was the bastard son of a German Elector and the daughter of a village druggist. Winder was the son of a sham aristocrat whose cowardice and incompetence in the War of 1812 delivered Washington into the hands of the British.

It is sufficient indication of this man's character that he could look unmoved upon the terrible suffering that prevailed in Andersonville in June, July, and August; that he could see three thousand men die horribly each month without lifting a finger; that he could call attention in a self-boastful way to the fact that he was "killing off more Yankees than twenty regiments in Lee's Army."

History has no parallel to John H. Winder, save among the blood-reveling kings of Dahomey or those sanguinary Asiatic chieftains who built pyramids of human skulls and paved roads with men's bones. How a man bred an American came to display such a Timour-like thirst for human life, such an Oriental contempt for the sufferings of others is one of the mysteries that perplexes me the more I study it.

They who lie in the shallow graves of Andersonville, Belle Isle, Florence and Salisbury, lie there in obedience to the precepts and maxims inculcated into their minds in the churches and common schools of the North—precepts which impressed upon them the duty of manliness and honor in all the relations and exigencies of life; not the "chivalric" prate of their enemies but the calm steadfastness which endureth to the end. The highest tribute that can be paid them is to say they did full credit to their teachings and they died as every American should when duty bids him. No richer heritage was ever bequeathed to posterity.

APPENDIX

The Trial of Captain Henri Wirz

McElroy, in his narrative, quotes portions of the trial testimony. In order to give a fuller picture of this amazing trial, the following is a transcript from the *Official Records,* November 1865, of the prosecution's case against Captain Wirz, namely, the use of hounds, vaccinations, Wirz' ability to use his arms, the findings of the court, the sentence, the execution order and the report.

Special Order, No. 453.

War Department,
Adjutant General's Office,
Washington, D. C., Aug. 23, 1865.

A special Military Commission is hereby appointed to meet in this city at 11 o'clock A. M. on the 23d day of August, 1865, or as soon thereafter as practicable, for the trial of Henry Wirz, and such other prisoners as may be brought before it.
Detail of the commission:

Maj.-Gen. L. Wallace, U. S. Volunteers.
Brev't Maj.-Gen. L. Thomas, Adjutant Gen., U. S. A.
Brev't Maj.-Gen. G. Mott, U. S. Volunteers.
Brig.-Gen. Francis Fessenden, U. S. Volunteers.
Brig.-Gen. A. S. Bragg, U. S. Volunteers.

Brev't Brig.-Gen. John F. Ballior, U. S. Volunteers.

Brev't Col. T. Allcock, 4th N. Y. Artillery.

Lieut.-Col. J. H. Stibbs, 12th Iowa Volunteers.

Col. N. P. Chipman, Additional Aide-de-Camp, Judge-Advocate of the Commission, with such assistants as he may select, with the approval of the Judge-Advocate-General.

The Commission will sit without regard to hours.

By order of the President of the United States.

E. D. TOWNSEND,
Assistant Adjutant-Gen.

*   *   *

USE OF HOUNDS

In this connection, as further illustrating the barbarous treatment of our soldiers and the cruelty of the prisoner at the bar, as well as systematic violation of the laws of war at Andersonville, it seems proper to notice the method adopted for recapturing prisoners.

The court will remember that the counsel for the prisoner laid great stress on the fact that a law existed in the State of Georgia authorizing the use of dogs for the capture of fugitive slaves, and attempt was made to prove by Judge Hall, the witness who testified to this fact, that a justice of the supreme court of that State had made a decision sustaining the law. The court very properly excluded the evidence, but I will give the prisoner the benefit of the decision. It was made by Justice Lumpkin, and is another evidence of the extent to which a naturally strong mind may be warped and turned from a strict view of justice when compelled to square it with a system of slavery. The case referred to is "Moran *vs.* Davis," (18 vol. Ga. Reports.) The facts were substantially these: A negro ran away, was pursued by dogs, and in trying to escape from them plunged into a creek and was drowned. The slave had been hired to the man who pursued him, and the owner brought suit for the value of the negro. The court below held "that the hirer or overseer had no right to chase the slaves with such dogs as may lacerate or materially injure the slave; should he do so he will be responsible to the owner for all damage that may ensue to the slave." Exceptions were taken to the rulings of the court, and on appeal Justice Lumpkin reversed the decision, remarking, "The South has already lost 60,000 slaves, worth between 25 and 30 millions of dollars. Instead, therefore, of relaxing the means allowed by law for the security and enjoyment of this species of property, the facilities afforded for its escape, and the temptation and encouragement held out to induce it, constrain us willingly or otherwise to redouble our vigilance and to tighten the cords that bind the negro to his condition of servitude, a condition," he adds with a flourish of rhetoric and a shameful distortion of scripture, "which is to last, if the apocalypse be inspired, to the end of time."

Unfortunately for the argument of counsel, prisoners of war are not property, neither are they slaves, and with all his adroitness he can hardly torture this case to his purpose, especially in view of the fact that the decision was given in support of a relic of the dark ages now happily passed away.

When two nations are at war, neither has a right to prescribe a code of laws for the other; a moment's reflection will show the injustice of such a thing; but both are governed by a higher law than that prescribed by either—that is, the law governing civilized nations; and it seems to me that no refinement of reasoning is necessary to show that Judge Lumpkin's decision, given in the interest of barbarism, is plainly in violation of the rules of enlightened civilization. Dogs were kept at Andersonville from the organization to the close of the prison, and of this the rebel government had notice from several sources. Dr. Eldridge reported it, as we learn from Exhibit No. 15, A. The prisoner also reported it, as we learn from Exhibit No. 13. Mr. Benjamin Harris and a man named W. W. Turner were employed and paid for this despicable business. The first named, a citizen, was a professional negro catcher who kept a pack of hounds for that purpose; the other was a detailed soldier, detailed by order of General Winder, and paid as an extra duty man. These hounds were fed with provisions taken from the cook-house and furnished the prisoners of war, taken, too, from the scanty supply issued by the commissary for those prisoners. They were mustered into the military service of the rebel government the same as cavalry horses. They were of two kinds, "tracking hounds" and "catch dogs," and if anything were wanting to show the deliberate purpose to injure prisoners by resorting to this means of capture it would be found in the presence in these packs of hounds of "catch dogs," which are described by many as fierce and bloodthirsty. If there had been no desire to injure, why were they used at all? They have none of those qualities peculiar to the tracking; they run only by sight, and, as has been testified to, always remained with the pursuer until approaching a prisoner. The tracking hounds would have been sufficient to discover the prisoners, and as they are usually harmless, would have served the purpose of the pursuer and at the same time inflicted no injury upon the pursued. The evidence, however, convinces one that this was only another means of putting prisoners of war out of the way. The prisoner at the bar frequently accompanied Harris and Turner in their chases after prisoners, and, as we shall see hereafter, gloated over the pain inflicted by those bloodthirsty beasts. Cannot we safely stop here and ask that the prisoner at the bar be recorded as one of the conspirators? I know that it is urged that during all this time he was acting under General Winder's orders, and for the purpose of argument I will concede that he was so acting. A superior officer cannot order a subordinate to do an illegal act, and if a subordinate obey such an order and disastrous consequences result, both the superior and the subordinate must answer for it. General Winder could no more command the prisoner to violate the laws of war than could the prisoner do so without orders. The conclusion is plain, that where such orders exist both are guilty, and *a fortiori* where the prisoner at the bar acted upon his own motion he was guilty. You cannot conclude that this prisoner was not one of the conspirators because he is not shown to have been present and to have acted in concert with all the conspirators. If he was one of the conspiracy to do an illegal thing, it matters not whether he knew all his co-conspirators or participated in all that they did. It is not necessary to prove any direct concert or even meeting of the conspirators. A concert may be proved by evidence of a concurrence of the acts of the prisoner with those of others, convicted together by a correspondence in point of time and in their manifest adaptation to effect the same object. These rules of law place beyond doubt the guilt of the prisoner, for in every respect there is plainly discoverable "a correspondence of time and a manifest adaptation to effect the same object," in all that he did; and these principles apply not only to the prisoner, but to all others on duty at Andersonville, whose acts concurred with those of others of the conspiracy and were adapted to effect the same object.

The prisoner at the bar appeals to you through his letter of May 7, directed to General Wilson, and asks, "Shall I now bear the odium (and men who were prisoners here have seemed disposed wreak their vengeance upon me for what they have suffered) who was only the medium or I may better say the tool in the hands of my superiors." Strongly as it may strike you that strict justice would require the punishment of the arch-conspirator himself; strongly as this wreck of a man, with body tortured by disease and over whom already gather the shadows of death, may appeal to your sympathies, you cannot stop the course of justice or refuse to brand his guilt as the law and evidence direct. While I would not dignify the chief conspirators in this crime without a name by associating with them the prisoner at the bar, yet he and they, so closely connected as they are, must share the same fate before the bar of a righteously indignant people. Nothing can ever separate them, and nothing should prevent their names going down to history in common infamy.

I have said that Phillip II had his Alva, that Jefferson Davis had his Winder, I might add that the Duke of Alva had his De Vargas, and Winder his Wirz. As the Duke of Alva rises out of the mists of history the agent of a powerful prince, so Winder stands out with fearful distinctness no less perfect for his willing obedience to the government he served than for his skill to devise and ability to select agents as capable to execute the refinements of cruelty. Nor does the parallel cease here; has not history repeated itself in making Wirz a man cast in the same mould as the infamous De Vargas, a hand to execute with horrible enthusiasm what his superior had the genius to suggest?

Motley tells us in his "Rise of the Dutch Republic," vol. II, p. 140, of these men Alva and De Vargas, whose spirits, after the Pythagorean theory, seemed to have centuries afterwards infused themselves into the bodies of this prisoner and his immediate superior, Winder. He says of the subordinates of Alva:

Del Rio was a man without character or talent, a mere fool in the hands of his superior; but Juan de Vargas was a terrible reality—no better man could have been found in Europe for the post to which he was thus elevated. To shed human blood was in his opinion the only important business, and the only exhilarating pastime of life.

He executed the bloody work with an industry which was almost superhuman and with a merriment which would have shamed a demon; his execrable jests ringing through the blood and smoke and death cries of those days of perpetual sacrifice. There could be no collision where the subaltern was only anxious to surpass an incomparable superior.

There are other conspirators in this crime whom we must notice further than has yet been done, before coming to charge second; these are Surgeon Isaiah H. White and Surgeon R. R. Stevenson. Surgeon White, as we have already seen, went to Andersonville under orders from the rebel war department, and was there at its organization. It is he who was responsible for the erection, management and condition of the hospital there, which Dr. Jones said did not deserve the name, and to enter which as a patient was almost certain death. It is he to whose account stands recorded the deaths of over 9,000 prisoners; whose neglect, malpractice and prostitution of his abilities as a surgeon make him no less a criminal in the light of testimony showing a criminal intent than if he had deliberately killed those who were placed in his charge; and of his criminal intent there can scarcely be any doubt, when it is remembered that in his house, and in his presence, letters directed to Union prisoners were opened, rifled of their contents, and their messages of love turned into "merrymakings," as we learn from the evidence of Lewis Dyer. It was he who often spoke of the mortality with shocking levity, and who uniformly neglected to take any notice of the suggestions made by the surgeons in their morning reports to him. It was he who drove Major Boyle out of the hospital in the stockade, and refused to allow his wound to be dressed because he was an officer of a colored regiment. It was he who established the system, and enforced it by orders, of practicing by formulas and numbers, which, in the opinion of Drs. Rice, Head, and Thornburgh was the sheerest empiricism. It was he who kept in his employment as hospital steward, one Dr. Kerr, who in the disguise of a federal soldier robbed the patients in the hospital, and was a man of a notoriously cruel and brutal nature; and it was he with regard to whom Surgeon General Moore remarks in his indorsements, "not having supplies is his own fault; he should have anticipated the wants of the sick by timely requisitions;" and who, upon the recommendation and by the order of this same surgeon general, in the face of the fact of his incompetency, was less than two months afterwards assigned to duty as surgeon-in-chief of all the military hospitals east of the Mississippi, and who departed from Andersonville in company with and on the staff of General Winder, rewarded rather than punished, as was this general, for his faithfulness in carrying out this conspiracy.

With all Dr. White's incompetency, and, as we learn from Dr. Bates's testimony, stepping into the shoes of his predecessor without instituting a single reform or showing himself in any way his superior, was Surgeon R. R. Stevenson. Further than this, indeed, he showed himself not only willing to perpetrate the evils that existed under Dr. White, but he showed himself also wanting in the principles of honesty. It is not necessary to enter into the details of his administration. We learn enough of him through the witnesses, Drs. Bates, Roy, Flewellen, Thornburgh, and Rice.

The evidence of these witnesses and others show that he refused to distribute bed-sacks and bedding to the suffering patients for the alleged reason that they would be destroyed; that he refused to allow Dr. Rice to go home and bring vegetables that were rotting in his garden for the use of the sick, or to send a person for them; that he constantly converted to his own use and loaded his own private table with viands sent for distribution among the sick; that he misappropriated the hospital fund, which accumulated by commuting in money a ration for each patient, at the rate under his administration of about two dollars per ration, and to increase which we learn, from the evidence of Dr. Thornburgh, he caused to be entered upon the hospital register the names of hundreds of persons as having been treated in the hospital who really died in the stockade without any medical treatment whatever; and that for his glaring malfeasances and crime he was compelled to leave that post.

VACCINATION

The record so far presented cannot fail to excite a feeling of horror and disgust; but there is still another and a very important feature of the case yet to be brought out, namely, the inoculating of prisoners of war with poisonous vaccine matter.

This, I believe, is the only allegation set out in the charge not yet noticed, but which, when compared with other specific acts of cruelty, seems to me the most revolting in the whole catalogue.

Before speaking particularly of the effects of this alleged precautionary action on the part of the surgeons in charge, who it seems acted under orders from the rebel authorities through Winder and the prisoner, I would call your attention to the evidence, so that no man may say that this averment is false.

This evidence on this point proves distinctly one of two propositions, either of which fixes on the persons responsible a most atrocious crime; these are, 1. That the vaccine matter used was poison and known to be such; or 2d. That it was knowingly and purposely applied under circumstances which made it almost certain that death would ensue.

The defence has set up that impure vaccine matter was used throughout the south, with similar consequences, and several medical gentlemen of the rebel army were called to prove that fact, among others Dr. Flewellen and Dr. Castlen. But it will be remembered that their experience and their knowledge was limited to observations in the year 1863, and they distinctly told you that orders were issued directing the surgeons upon the discovery of these fatal consequences to cease the use of the virus. How then can the counsel presume to use this circumstance as a defence to the injurious results arising from the use of this spurious matter, as late as 1864, with the full knowledge of a year's practice and year's experience before them?

I would rather think that the Andersonville prisoners were made the victims of this experience, not, it may be, with the knowledge of many of the surgeons on duty at that place —for some of them seem to have been conscientious men—but doubtless with the knowledge of the surgeons in charge, their chief at Richmond, the prisoner at the bar, and his immediate chief.

This evidence of the soldiers on this point is homely and blunt, but it enables one to determine with some certainty that the effects described by them were by no means the ordinary results of vaccination.

Oliver B. Fairbanks says:

Large sores originated from the effects of poisonous matter: they were the size of my hand and were on the outside of the arms and also underneath in the arm-pits. I have seen holes eaten under the arms, where I could put my fist in; these cases were in the stockade.

In reply to the question, "State the circumstances under which you were vaccinated," he replies:

I was at the south gate one morning when the operation was being performed. While I was standing there looking on, one of the surgeons came to me and requested me to roll up my sleeves, that he was going to perform the operation on me. I told him I could not consent to such an operation. He called for a file of guards and I was taken to Captain Wirz' headquarters. Arriving there one of the guard went in and directly Captain Wirz came out of his office saying he wanted to know where that God-damned Yankee son of a bitch was. I was pointed out to him as being the person; he drew his revolver and presented it within three inches of my face, and wanted to know why I refused to obey his orders.

The witness proceeds to narrate his interview with the prisoner and says:

I told him, "Captain, you are aware that the matter with which I would be vaccinated is poisonous, and therefore I cannot consent to an operation which I know will prove fatal to my life." The prisoner flourished his revolver around and stated that it would serve me right: the sooner I would die, the sooner he would get rid of me.

The witness still refusing, he was kept in chains, and after a punishment of two weeks finally consented to the operation. He says:

As soon as it was performed, I went immediately to the brook, and took a piece of soap and rubbed the spot, and wrung it, and thereby saved myself.

As confirmatory of Fairbanks' statement, that the prisoner interfered in this matter of vaccination, and as tending to show that there was criminal design, I quote the evidence of Frank Maddox. In reply to a question whether he ever heard the prisoner give orders in regard to vaccination, he says:

I heard him tell the doctor at the gate to vaccinate all those men: they were talking about having the small-pox there; the doctor told him that according to his orders he would do it.

The same witness, being asked whether he saw the prisoner and any of the surgeons at the graveyard and heard them speak of vaccination, replied:

They were laughing over it one day; the doctors had been examining and had cut some bodies open, had sawed some heads open; in some cases a green streak from the arms had extended to the bodies; they were laughing about it killing the men so.

George W. Gray says:

It affected their arms; the sores began just to rot around and to eat in until it got to the bone; they generally lost their arms; a great many of the men who had been vaccinated had their arms amputated.

John L. Yonker, who was engaged in burying the dead, in speaking of the amputated arms which were constantly sent to the graveyard to be buried, says:

I noticed it daily; the great part of it originated from vaccination; the sores were mostly right here, (on the outer part of the arm near the shoulder,) and under the arms; you could look into the ribs and see the bone; it looked all black, and green, and blue.

Lewis Dyer says:

I have seen men going around who had been vaccinated, and two or three days after all their arms would be eaten out, and their arms would have to be taken off.

Charles E. Tibbles, who was also engaged in burying the dead, says:

I saw a great many extra arms at the graveyard, that were not cut, but were disjointed at the shoulder; they would be brought out with the dead, and almost always the next day; the bodies would be brought out belonging to them; they were generally eaten up with vaccination.

William Crouse says:

I saw men get vaccinated there; it broke out; I saw about twenty of them die, and I saw five of them get their arms amputated.

Doran H. Stearns, speaking of amputation, says:

The result was almost invariably death; I do not remember a single case of recovery after an operation.

This witness was on duty at the hospital and is a man of much intelligence and candor.

To the same purport is the testimony of Charles E. Smith, who also speaks of the orders with regard to vaccination, and says:

He (the prisoner) said, any one who would refuse to obey his orders would have a ball and chain put on. There was a man named Shields belonging to the 2d Iowa infantry, who refused to be vaccinated; they took him out and put a ball and chain on him until he consented to have the matter put in his arm.

Several of the surgeons on duty at Andersonville have also testified to the fatal result of vaccination. You will remember that the surgeons who have testified through their reports, and upon the witness stand, have spoken largely of hospital gangrene that prevailed at Andersonville as a consequence of vaccination; and indeed, as they have universally testified, as a consequence of even the slightest abrasion of the skin, in cases of vaccination, however, resulting in appalling mortality.

Vaccination with genuine virus has never before resulted in such frightful mortality. The records of medicine and pathology nowhere, in no country and no age, afford or approach a parallel to Andersonville; and it is eminently important that an explanation be reached if possible, and if criminality attach to any one, let its just consequences be upon him. The best medical and pathological authorities agree in describing hospital gangrene as a variety of mortification and ulceration with rapid contamination of the whole system, depression and exhaustion of the vital powers. All of the conditions necessary to produce this terrible disease, we learn from many sources in this record, were abundantly supplied at Andersonville, and that there was scarcely a prisoner who was not more or less affected by it, or in a scorbutic condition to a greater or less degree. Now we all know what is the normal effect of pure vaccine virus properly introduced into a healthy system—one not previously vaccinated. A local inflammation is set up, a fever ensues, attended with a general disturbance of the constitution, and the insertion of the virus is the centre and source of it all, with which the whole system sympathizes more or less, and from which, under the most careful circumstances and attention, alarming and sometimes fatal results follow.

This is so well understood by the profession—as all of us have experienced who have submitted to the operation—that they always counsel a preparatory process by sanitary observances.

These facts, drawn from reliable and recognized medical sources, will enable the court and the world to appreciate in some degree the heartlessness and implacable cruelty of the rebel authorities at Andersonville, in persistently compelling prisoners of war to be vaccinated, in the condition they are shown to have been in. It will not do to say that this was resorted to as a preventive or precautionary measure. The record shows but few cases of death by small-pox, while the evidence establishes beyond doubt the fact that of many hundred prisoners vaccinated, few recovered. No one will pretend, after a perusal of this record, that the course of the rebel surgeons in this particular can in the slightest degree be excused; and with the fair inference of evil intent and wicked purpose on the part of the chief surgeons, Drs. White and Stevenson, and the prisoner at the bar, who with pistol in hand stood ready to enforce their direction, which can be drawn from the evidence, can you hesitate to find them "guilty" as laid in the charge?

The court cannot fail to observe that after having drawn from the record this long black catalogue of crimes, these tortures unparalleled, these murders by starvation, implacable as could have been perpetrated had the spirit of darkness controlled them, there are yet many, very many, phases of Andersonville prison life that I must leave unnoticed.

Has there been any defence made to these horrors? Is there any palliation for their perpetrators? Lives there a witness who has denied or can deny them? The counsel for the prisoner has had unlimited control of the strong arm of the government; he has had days and weeks for preparation; he has, as all must admit, labored sedulously and untiringly for his client, constituting himself at the same time counsel for his co-conspirators, yet, with all his efforts, so earnestly put forth, he has utterly, signally failed. The special acts of cruelty committed by the prisoner at the bar he has sought to explain; with what success I leave to you to judge. The general management and discipline, and his responsibility for the same while at Andersonville, he has sought to deny by showing the presence at that place of a superior officer, General Winder, who, he alleges, had chief control. All this is swept away by the fact that before General Winder's arrival the fearful rigors of that prison began; they continued during his stay, from June till October, and they subsided only in proportion as the number of prisoners became less, after General Winder's departure. And notwithstanding his earnest appeal, made to you in his final statement, begging that he, a poor subaltern, acting only in obedience to his superior, should not bear the odium and the punishment deserved, with whatever force these cries of a desperate man, in a desperate and terrible strait may come to you, there is no law, no sympathy, no code of morals, that can warrant you in refusing to let him have all justice, because the lesser and not the greater criminal is on trial.

To the charge of suffering and death by starvation something excusatory could be urged in the fact that supplies were not to be obtained, had this been established; but here, as elsewhere, the defence has wholly failed. While the burden of proof rested upon the defence to show that the sufferings at Andersonville were unavoidable, it will be remembered it was part of the elements of the case made by the prosecution to show not only the fact of starvation, but also that it occurred in a region of plenty, and in view of this fact, so clearly proven, we find reason for concluding beyond all doubt that this crime against nature was the work of a deliberate, malicious, traitorous, and hellish conspiracy to aid a most treasonable rebellion.

I desire now to present to the court the evidence which supports me in the belief just declared. Here, as always, I desire that the witnesses may speak, that no man shall gainsay the facts.

Major General J. H. Wilson, of our army, who, perhaps, can speak as advisedly upon this point as any witness who has been upon the stand, for reasons shown in his testimony, says:

After passing through the mountainous region of northern Alabama, I found supplies in great abundance on our lines of march: in sufficient abundance to supply a command of 17,000 men, without going off our lines of march for them.

His lines of march, he says, were—

From the northwest corner of Alabama, to a point called Monte Bello, and from thence south to Selma; from Selma, southward to Montgomery; from Montgomery, two lines, one to Columbus,

Georgia, and the other to West Point, Georgia, and thence, by two converging lines, to Macon, Georgia; and then, all over the State of Georgia; from there to the Gulf.

In reply to the question if the rebel government drew supplies from that part of the country, he says:

Yes, from central Alabama to southwestern Georgia, for the wants of their armies operating in the field; that was their grand region of supplies.

And speaking with regard to railroad communication by which these supplies could reach Andersonville, he says:

We found lines of railway running very nearly in the direction of the march from Monte Bello, and between the parts of country spoken of, and Macon and Andersonville.

Ambrose Spencer, a resident of Georgia for many years, says:

Southwestern Georgia, I believe, is termed the garden of America. It was termed the garden of the confederacy, as having supplied the greater part of the provisions of the rebel army. Our section of Georgia, Sumter county, is perhaps not as rich as the counties immediately contiguous, * * * but still it produces heavily. I suppose that the average of that land would be one bale of cotton to the acre; the wheat would average about six bushels to the acre; the average of corn about eight bushels.

And the court will recollect that he says he is stating the "general average," and not what one cultivated acre will produce; and adds:

We have land in that county that will produce 35 bushels of corn to the acre.

Speaking of the subject of vegetables in 1864, he says:

It struck me that there was an uncommon supply of vegetables. Heretofore at the south there has been but little attention paid to gardens on a large scale; but last year a very large supply of vegetables was raised, as I understood, for the purpose of being disposed of at Andersonville.

James Van Valkenburgh, of Bibb county, near Macon, Georgia, says he has resided in that section for nineteen years, and that in the year 1864, speaking of the crops—

I should suppose, as to provisions, it was more than an average crop, inasmuch as no cotton was planted, and all the ground was pretty well planted in provisions; I should think the provision crop was larger than before the war.

This witness says that at Macon, which is about sixty-five miles by rail from Andersonville—

There were a great many storehouses, where provisions of various kinds were stored—sugar, rice, molasses, meat, (bacon) corn, wheat, flour, &c.

At Americus, he says:

There seemed to be very large quantities. I saw a great deal of stores in various warehouses.

Americus, it will be remembered, is only about nine or ten miles from Andersonville. The court will remember that of this "more than ordinary crop of provisions" the farmers were compelled by law to pay to the rebel government one-tenth. I make a few extracts from the evidence of one of the agents of that government—a tithe gatherer.

W. T. Davenport says:

I was tithe agent from April, 1864, till the surrender, for Sumter county. The amount of bacon received at that depot from Sumter county, and from the counties of Schley, Webster, and Marion, of which my depot, being on the railroad, was the receiving depot, for the year 1864, was 247,768 pounds; we received of corn, 38,900 bushels; of wheat, 3,567 bushels; we received 3,420 pounds of rice in the rough; of peas, we received 817 bushels; of sirup of West India cane and sorghum, 3,700 gallons; of sugar, 1,166 pounds.

This was all in the year 1864. In 1865, he says:

From the 1st of January till the 19th of April, which was the time of the surrender, I received from those same counties 155,726 pounds of bacon, 13,591 bushels of corn, and 86 bushels of wheat. This was the remnant due on the old crop, the new crop not having been gathered. I received of rice, (rough, 2,077 pounds; of peas, 854 bushels; of sirup, 5,082 gallons.

And these, he says, were not the only tithes gathered. In these counties there were, besides his depot, others from which he has no account. He says:

There was a depot at Andersonville. Some portion of the tithes were delivered there, and some portions were delivered to travelling companies that received tithes, and were not reported to me.

He says, referring to the counties named:

Two of them, Schley and Webster, were quite small. Sumter and Marion are fair average counties.

This immense amount of provisions is but a small portion received by the rebel government through their tithe-gatherers, it being brought to the depots by the farmers themselves, and was only *one-tenth* of the amount produced by them. These stores were turned over to W. B. Harrold, who was commissary agent for those counties, and who was also purchasing agent.

W. B. Harrold says:

For the last three years I have been purchasing and shipping supplies for the commissary department of the rebel government for a district embracing from four to six counties in southwestern Georgia; one of the counties being that in which Andersonville is located. I was ordered at all times to hold all supplies which I had at Americus, after May or June, I think, subject, first, to Andersonville, in case they should get out of provisions there at any time. My provisions were rather reserved for Andersonville, to be called on in case of an emergency. I was 10 miles distant. Such provisions as I had there—bacon and meal—I don't think they were ever out of at Andersonville.

He continues:

I don't think I was ever called on for provisions that I did not furnish, with the exception of meal. In the early part of 1864, they depended on my arrangements for meal altogether. During the first two or three months of the prison, say February, March, and April, before the crowded condition of the prison, the orders were to issue five day's rations at a time, on requisition. I kept up very well until they began to crowd the prisoners in, and then I could not furnish sufficient meal, and other arrangements were made. The meal was afterwards obtained in large quantities from the Palace mills, in Columbus.

When asked, "Was there ever a time when there need to have been suffering at Andersonville because of the inability to get supplies there?" he answers, "Not so far as corn-bread and meal were concerned."

I quote further from the record:

Q. Was there any difficulty with regard to supplies?
A. No, sir.
Q. Was there no time when transportation could not have been procured?
A. At all times I think they could have procured transportation, and did procure it.

On cross-examination, he says:

The same provisions were furnished to Andersonville that were furnished to the army, and the same were furnished there as were furnished to the hospital.

But we have the evidence of scores of witnesses that they were never received by our starving prisoners.

James W. Armstrong was commissary at Andersonville from the 31st of March, 1864, until August 1, 1864, and from the 10th of December, 1864, until the close of the war.

Until the 14th of July all the rations were delivered to R. B. Winder, or to his sergeant for him, and after that time to Captain Wirz' sergeant. He says he doesn't pretend to know whether the rations issued by him were actually delivered to the prisoners or not.

Q. You never were at any time so short that you could not issue to the prisoners?
A. No, sir. In three or four instances I issued rice instead of corn-meal; but I always made up the rations.
Q. You never found it necessary to diminish the rations, except by substituting one thing for another?
A. That is all.
Q. You always had plenty to issue?
A. Yes, sir.

Colonel Ruffin, who was in the commissary department at Richmond, and who was called for the defence to show that Lee's army suffered for the want of provisions, says that at that time the prisoners were consuming General Lee's reserve of 30,000 barrels of flour; the removal of prisoners from Richmond *to the seat of plenty* was urged by the commissary department. "After awhile," he says, "the prisoners were sent to the place of comparative plenty, or to the place of supply." He further says, that in sending the prisoners to Georgia the only object of his department was to get them to what was considered a good region of country; that they were drawing supplies from Georgia to feed General Lee. He says that the armies of the southwest fared better than General Lee's army, "because they were in Georgia, where there was more abundance." And in the same connection, on cross-examination, says that General Lee's army suffered because it was cut off from the southwest by federal raids, which destroyed their railroad communication.

Ambrose Spencer says:

That section of southwestern Georgia is well supplied with mills—both grist-mills, flour-mills, and saw-mills. Between Andersonville and Albany—about fifty miles—there are five saw-mills, one of them a large one. There is one at a distance of six miles from Andersonville that goes by steam. There is another about five miles from Andersonville that goes by water. There are saw-mills on the road above Andersonville.

And in this connection, as touching the question of shelter and the facilities with which it could have been furnished the prisoners, the witness says further:

It is a very heavily timbered country, especially in the region adjoining Andersonville; it may be termed one of the most densely timbered countries in the United States.

I was there (Andersonville) during June and July very frequently, at the time Governor Brown had called out the militia of the State. Their tents were all floored with good lumber, and a good many shelters of lumber were put up by the soldiers. I noticed a good many tents that were protected from the sun by boards. There seemed to be no want of lumber at that time among the confederate soldiers.

Colonel Persons says, "That about five train loads, perhaps fifty car loads in all," came to Andersonville while he was there. This, he says, would have covered two, three, four, or five acres with barracks.

Thus we have shown from evidence of the highest character, that the defence based upon want of supplies within the reach of the rebel authorities, and which is popularly believed to have been the real cause of the sufferings of Andersonville, is entirely overthrown, and without foundation in fact; and the same may be said of every question entering into the defence incident to the matter of supplies. With whatever truth the straitened circumstances of the South may be urged to exculpate those in charge of other prisons, certainly, so far as Andersonville is concerned, no one will hereafter with seriousness dare to urge it.

Having shown with certainty that supplies were abundant and available, I cannot omit to mention what amount was actually issued as the only means of sustenance to the prisoners. I quote Dr. Bates, whose acknowledged credibility on the part of the accused in his statement to the court makes it unnecessary to support him by the many witnesses who testify to the same point; but the court will remember that his estimate is several ounces more than the prisoners themselves testify to having received. He says,

I wish to be entirely safe and well guarded on this point. There might have been less than 20 ounces to the 24 hours; but I do not think it could have exceeded that.

The ration, it will also be remembered, consisted of one unvarying diet of cornbread and salt meat, with an occasional issue of peas, and with no vegetables whatever. In comparison with this scanty allowance which the concurrent testimony of all the witnesses shows was the immediate cause of the great mortality at that prison, I desire to call your attention to some interesting and instructive facts, showing the amount of food necessary to sustain life. I quote from a work on the economy of armies, by medical inspector Lieutenant Colonel A. C. Hamlin, United States Army:

The data of French's show that 18 ounces of properly selected food will be sufficient, and the observations of Sir John Sinclair are to the same effect, yet Dr. Christison maintains that 36 ounces are required to preserve the athletic condition of prisoners confined for a long term. To preserve the athletic condition with these small quantities, the nutrient substance must be of known value.

In the public establishments of England the following quantities are given:

British soldier, 45 ounces; seaman, royal navy, 44 ounces; convict, 57 ounces; male pauper, 29 ounces; male lunatic, 31 ounces.

The full diets of the hospitals of London give, Guy, 29 ounces, with one pint of beer; Bartholomew, 31 ounces, with 4 pints of beer or tea; St. Thomas, 25 ounces, with 3 pints of beer or tea; St. George, 27 ounces, with 4 pints of beer or tea; Kings, 25 ounces.

The Russian soldier has bread 16 ounces, meat 16 ounces; Turkish soldier has bread 33 ounces, meat 13 ounces; French soldier has bread 26 ounces, meat 11 ounces; Hessian soldier has bread 36 ounces, meat 6 ounces; English sailor has bread 20 ounces, meat 16 ounces.

The United States soldier receives ¾ pound of bacon, or 1¼ pound of fresh or salt beef; 18 ounces of bread or flour, or ¾ pound of hard bread, or 1¼ ound of corn-meal; with rice, beans, vegetables, coffee, sugar, tea, &c., in proportion.

When we remember that there seems to have been no difference made in the rations issued to the sick in the hospital and prisoners confined in the stockade; that, as we have seen by the testimony of Dr. Jones, the mortality was proportionately the same in both places, and all the surroundings so prolific of disease, added to the fact that for months the prisoners had barely room to stand upon, we are prepared to comprehend the force of the illustrations above given and those which I shall now give. The number of patients treated in the hospital at Andersonville is shown by the hospital register to have been something less than 18,000, the number of deaths a little short of 13,000, and to this number must be added 2,000 more, who, as we have shown with reasonable certainty, died before reaching their homes, making in all 15,000, and this falls far short of the maximum number, giving, as we see, the frightful ratio of mortality of over 83 per cent.

Quoting from the same learned author we find that "the average mortality of the London hospitals is nine per cent; in the French hospitals in the Crimea, for a period of twenty-two months, the mortality was 14 per cent. The city of Milan received during the campaign in Italy 34,000 sick and wounded, of whom 1,400, or four per cent., died. The city of Nashville, Tennessee, received during the year 1864 65,157 sick and wounded, of whom 2,635, or four per cent., died. During the year 1863 Washington received 68,884, and of these but 2,671, or less than 4 per cent., died; and in 1864 her hospitals received 96,705 sick and wounded (49,455 sick, 47,250 wounded) of whom 6,283, or 6⁴⁄₁₀ per cent., died. The mortality of the rebel prisoners at Fort Delaware for eleven months was two per cent.; at Johnson's island during twenty-one months 134 deaths out of 6,000 prisoners."

This is the record of history, against the charnel-house of Andersonville. Let the mouths of those who would defend these atrocities by recrimination, charging the United States government with like cruelty, forever hereafter be closed.

Fort Delaware and Johnson's island, with their two per cent. of dead. Andersonville with its 83 per cent.! "Look upon this picture and then upon this," and tell me there was no design to slay! Let no mind, be it warped never so much by treason and treasonable sympathies, doubt this record, for "If damned custom have not brazed its soul—that it be proof and bulwark against sense," it must believe; it cannot deny these things.

May it please the court, I have done with the argument under charge first. I leave it with you to answer by your verdict whether this charge of conspiracy, solemnly and seriously preferred, can be frittered away and disposed of without a single explanatory line in defence. I place before you, gentlemen, on the one hand the protestations of this accused, who speaks for himself and his co-conspirators; on the other the testimony of Dr. Bates, where he declared, as you well remember, with faltering tone and feelings overpowered, "I feel myself safe in saying that 75 per cent. of those who died might have been saved had those unfortunate men been properly cared for."

I leave it with you to say whether the prisoner at the bar can acquit himself and his associates in crime by declaring the charge here laid to be, as he has told you, "a myth," "a phantasy of the brain," "a wild chimera, as unsubstantial as the baseless fabric of a vision."

(At this point, the court on the suggestion of the judge advocate, adjourned until tomorrow morning at 10 o'clock.)

UNITED STATES MILITARY COMMISSION,
Washington, D. C., Saturday, October 21, 1865.

The commission met pursuant to adjournment. Present, all the members and the judge advocate.

The prisoner and his counsel were also present.

The proceedings of the last meeting were read and approved.

The judge advocate continued his argument as follows:

May it please the court, we now come to notice charge second, alleging "murder in violation of the laws of war," under which there are laid numerous specifications, alleging, with all the particularity that was possible, the circumstances in each case.

In presenting the evidence under this charge, I shall try to do so in the briefest and simplest manner. I shall not endeavor to torture the evidence to support any preconceived theory, nor ingeniously dovetail scattered scraps of testimony to make out a case. I am content to leave the court to reach its own conclusions; and therefore I shall (except in two cases which have been particularly referred to in the defence) do little more than simply recite the evidence of the witnesses. My simple purpose is to aid the court in the discharge of the arduous task upon which it is about to enter, in making up a verdict on this voluminous record.

The various cases of death which are justly to be laid to the charge of this prisoner as murders, may be considered under four heads:

1. The cases of death resulting from mutilation by the hounds.

2. The instances of death resulting from confinement in the stocks and the chain-gang.

3. The cases of killing of prisoners by the guards, pursuant to the direct order of the accused given at the time; and

4. The cases of killing by the prisoner's own hand.

This classification does not embrace those very numerous cases (which it is not deemed necessary to recount in detail) where prisoners at or near the dead-line were shot by the guards when the accused was not present.

The responsibility of the prisoner for these murders (for such wanton, unprovoked and unjustifiable destruction of human life was nothing less) has been treated of in a previous branch of the argument. Without repeating that argument, I will say in addition that there is no truth in the assumption put forth as a defence in the written statement of the accused, that the prisoners within the stockade had ample notice of the dead-line regulation, and that, if any were shot in crossing that line, he was not responsible. The evidence of the defence failed to show (although I believe it was attempted) that the dead-line regulation was posted up within the stockade.

Besides, many of the witnesses on this stand testified that, going to Andersonville, as new prisoners, they received no authoritative notice of the dead-line regulation, but accidentally or casually acquired that knowledge from their companions; and some have told us of their hair-breadth escapes from being shot soon after entering the stockade, in consequence of their ignorance of that regulation; and a number of witnesses have described how their comrades lost their lives in consequence of similar ignorance. After all the evidence on this subject, I was astonished, as I doubt not was the court, when the prisoner, in his statement, inquired with singular effrontery,

Is it within the range of probability that there was a single prisoner within the stockade who did not know the penalty for encroaching upon the dead-line.

Before proceeding to refer to the evidence as to the deaths from mutilation by the hounds and from confinement in the stocks and chain-gang, it may be proper to say a few words as to the criminal responsibility of the prisoner for these deaths. In the first place, I need hardly remind the court of that fundamental principle of law that "a sane man is conclusively presumed to contemplate the natural and probable consequences of his own acts." (1 Greenleaf on Evidence, sec. 18.). This principle, I submit, applies in this case with great force. I maintain that the deaths resulting from the use of the stocks and the chain-gang as an indiscriminate punishment for the healthy and the sick, the strong and the feeble, and the deaths consequent upon the pursuit of escaping prisoners with ferocious hounds, were but the "natural and probable consequences" of the act of the prisoner in maintaining and carrying out this barbarous system of discipline. What more "natural and probable" than that a prisoner, emaciated by disease and starvation, should, when confined in the chain-gang or the stocks, die from such confinement? What more "natural and probable" than that a ferocious dog, when pursuing an escaping prisoner, should tear and mortally mutilate such prisoner, particularly if he were in the debilitated condition which characterized most of the prisoners at Andersonville? And when death results under such circumstances and from the adoption of such methods of treatment, an intention to kill on the part of him who adopts them is the necessary and rightful presumption of the law, just as "an intent to murder is conclusively inferred from the deliberate use of a deadly weapon." (1 Greenleaf on Evidence, sec. 18.)

Again, it has been laid down that the crime of murder is consummated "whensoever any one *wilfully endangers the life of another by any act or omission likely to kill, and which does kill.*" (2 Starkie on Evidence, 710, note.) It has also been declared by high legal authority that—

It is not essential that the hand of the party should immediately occasion the death; it is sufficient if he be proved to have used any mechanical means *likely to occasion death and which do ultimately occasion it;* as if a man lay poison for another with intent that he should take it by mistake for medicine, or *expose him against his will in a severe season, by means of which he dies.* (2 Starkie on Evidence, 710, note.)

As illustrative of the same legal principle, allow me to quote from Wharton's Criminal Law, 435:

If a person breaking in an unruly horse wilfully ride him among a crowd of persons, the probable danger being great and apparent, and death ensue from the viciousness of the animal, it is murder. For how can it be supposed that a person wilfully doing an act so manifestly attended with danger, especially if he showed any consciousness of such danger himself, should intend any other than mischief to those who might be encountered by him? So if a man maliciously throw from a roof into a crowded street, where passengers are constantly passing and repassing, a heavy piece of timber, calculated to produce death on such as it might fall, and death ensue, the offence is murder at common law.

From these principles, it follows that when we show the prisoner's responsibility for the use of the chain-gang and the stocks, and for the employment of the hounds, we show that every death resulting from these was a murder for which he is to be held accountable.

In this connection, allow me to refer hastily to some of the evidence showing the responsibility of the prisoner for the use of the stocks and the chain-gang, and for the employment of the hounds.

Robert Tait, George W. Gray, Col. Gibbs, Charles F. Williams, J. H. Goldsmith, J. H. Burns, and numerous other witnesses, testify as to the prisoner ordering men into the stocks and the chain-gang. In some cases the men subjected to this treatment were very greatly debilitated, and in other cases they had just been brought back wounded by the hounds.

Several of the witnesses testify that the accused would go round the stockade every morning in company with the hounds to get the track of prisoners who had escaped. A. W. Barrows, P. V. Halley, and many others, testify that the accused gave orders for starting the dogs in pursuit of prisoners who had escaped. J. D. Keyser states that he heard him tell Turner to get the dogs. James Mohan, a rebel officer who was on duty at Andersonville, testifies that when "Frenchy" escaped the prisoner gave orders to get the dogs after him, and he was captured, the prisoner going with the dogs; and this, the court will remember, is admitted in the statement submitted by him. Boston Corbett testifies that after being captured by the dogs, he was brought before the accused, who said to the captor: "Why did you not make the dogs bite him?"

J. H. Davidson saw a prisoner torn by the dogs, the accused being present.

Dr. F. G. Castlen, who was a surgeon in the rebel service, relates an instance where a man was ordered down from a tree and bitten by the hounds, the prisoner being present. John F. Heath, a rebel officer who was on duty at Andersonville, testifies that when "Frenchy" was pursued the prisoner ordered him down from the tree and the dogs rushed at him and bit him, the prisoner not trying to keep the dogs off. This rebel witness, it will be observed, contradicts the allegation made by the prisoner in his written statement, that he endeavored to keep the dogs off. James P. Stone says that the dogs were fed with rations drawn from the bakery, most frequently by a young man who assisted Turner, and that the prisoner signed an order once "to give this man all the bread and meat he wants for the dogs." Joseph Adler testifies that on one occasion Dr. White and the prisoner were looking at a man who was so mangled by the dogs as to be almost dead, when the prisoner said, "it was perfectly right, that it served the man right; that he had no business to make his escape, and that he would not care if all the damned Yankees in the stockade could be served in the same way as that, as he wanted to get rid of them." The prisoner himself, in his consolidated return for August, 1864, speaks of 25 prisoners who escaped during the month, but were taken up by the dogs.

These citations, which might be multiplied, are sufficient to show the responsibility of the accused for the punishment of the prisoners by the stocks and the chain-gang, and for the pursuit of prisoners by the hounds; and according to the principles already referred to, every death resulting from such punishment and such pursuits must justly be considered as having been murderously caused by him, remembering also that the use of the means resorted to and the means themselves were a gross and wicked violation of the laws of war.

I will now proceed to recite the evidence as to the cases where death resulted from the pursuit of prisoners by the hounds.

William Henry Jennings testifies that a month or two after he was whipped, which was in the month of March, he being in the hospital, saw a man come in who was torn by the dogs—bitten from his feet up to his head and all round his neck, and that the man died shortly afterwards.

Bernard Corrigan states that in May he saw a prisoner who was badly bitten by the dogs in both legs, and he had a piece of his ear cut off. The man was carried to the hospital the day following, and the witness never saw him afterwards.

James E. Marshall testifies that in May he saw a man whose leg was torn by the hounds, and who afterwards died in the hospital.

John L. Yonker testifies that just before the raiders were hung, which was about the 11th of July, a man belonging to an Indiana regiment tried to make his escape from the hospital, was recaptured by the hounds and sent back to the stockade in the evening; that his right ear was almost off, and that he was bitten in several places in the legs and had hardly any clothing on him; that witness gave him a piece of his shirt and helped to tie up his wounds; that the wounded man gave his friend a picture to give to his mother if he should never recover, because he believed he would die; that the next morning he was dead; that the man stated that he had tried to climb a tree, but the dogs pulled him down.

In connection with the incident just narrated, it may be pertinent to adduce the evidence of Joseph Adler and George Conway, apparently having reference to the same transaction.

George Conway testifies that on one occasion that he saw a man who had been caught by the hounds, while making his escape from the hospital; the man was bitten on his legs and in his cheek.

Joseph Adler states that in the latter part of June or the beginning of July, Dr. White and the prisoner were looking at a man who had been mangled by the dogs; the prisoner said it was perfectly right.

George W. Gray states that on one occasion he saw a young man who had just been brought into the stockade, after having been caught by the hounds. Part of his cheek was torn off; his arms, hands and legs were bitten, so that he only lived about 24 hours after having been brought into the stockade.

Thomas N. Way states that in the latter part of August he and two others, with whom he escaped, were pursued by the hounds, and that one of his comrades was caught by the foot as he was climbing a tree and was torn all to pieces.

A. W. Barrows states that about the end of August, a man who had been bitten by the dogs when trying to escape was brought into his ward and died about five days afterwards.

Jas. P. Stone states that in July or August he saw a man who had made his escape, who had been caught and badly torn by the dogs; that he was bitten badly in the legs and also a great deal about the neck and shoulders; that he had made his escape and climbed a tree; that the accused and Harris shook him down and allowed the dogs to tear him.

Frank Maddox testifies that when he was burying a man who had been bitten by the dogs, had afterwards been placed in the stocks by order of the prisoner, and who had died, Turner, who had charge of the hounds, came to the grave-yard and said that there had been two men bitten by the hounds, and that they let the dogs tear up the other one in the woods, and that they left him there.

W. W. Crandall testifies that on one occasion (he does not give the date) he saw a man with his legs badly torn by the dogs; that a ball was put upon his foot, and that he was kept that way for several weeks; that witness went to the prisoner and pleaded with him to take the balls off. The prisoner said he could not do it. Witness asked the surgeon to do it. The surgeon examined the man and said that he could not conscientiously take off but one. The man's leg became badly swollen, and witness believes the man died, as he three weeks afterwards buried a man whom he thought he recognized as the same.

I have thus hastily passed over the evidence touching this class of murders. I shall presently endeavor to individualize the instances mentioned and to reconcile and unite the separated, and in some instances apparently complicated, circumstances. But, before doing so, let me suggest that on the review of this evidence, while the testimony must be and ought to be subjected to the closest criticism and scrutiny, and while the court should be convinced, beyond a reasonable doubt, of the guilt of this accused, still I submit it as worthy of grave consideration that there are many circumstances peculiar to prison life, as it was at Andersonville, which make the ordinary test applied in tribunals of law for the verification of testimony altogether inappropriate in this case. The court will not forget that there existed at Andersonville a condition of affairs for which it would be impossible to find a precedent. The prisoners were deprived, to a great measure, of facilities for ordinary intelligence or for communication with each other and the outer world. They were subjected to the closest and most cruel confinement and discipline. Most of them were constantly racked with the pangs of hunger or disease, or engrossed from hour to hour in a struggle with death in which the odds were fearfully against them. Their companions were constantly dying around them, either from emaciation, disease, or acts of violence, so that, as the prisoners themselves have declared in the presence of the court, they became so habituated to these horrible surroundings, that the death of a comrade, under what would ordinarily seem the most frightful circumstances, made in many cases but a slight impression upon their minds; and certainly they would not charge their memory with dates or circumstances, even should they be able to fix the time, and it will be remembered that many of them state that they lost all knowledge of the days of the week and the month. Besides, they never expected to emerge from that scene alive, and never hoped that a day would come when their persecutor should be arraigned before a tribunal of justice, and they themselves be summoned as witnesses to his iniquitous acts. It is not to be expected that, under these circumstances, witnesses should evince such precision as to dates and minute particulars as might be expected in an ordinary trial for the investigation of offences disturbing but rarely the tranquillity of civilized society. A court of justice never requires higher evidence than the best of which the case will admit; for, as has well been remarked by a distinguished legal writer:

The rules of evidence are adopted for practical purposes in the administration of justice, and must be so applied as to promote the end for which they were designed. (1st Greenleaf's Evidence, sec. 83.)

But I have no apology to offer, no defence to make, for the testimony upon which the prosecution relies for the conviction of this accused under the charge now being examined.

In every case where you are asked to hold the prisoner responsible for the death of any one of those in his custody, you will find the evidence direct, positive, and clear; you are not asked to find this prisoner guilty upon vague, uncertain, doubtful testimony, but you are asked to apply the rules of evidence properly applicable to cases occurring under the peculiar circumstances to which we have alluded, always remembering that your duty is to arrive at the truth in the most direct manner possible.

Without pretending to make an argument in this connection, desiring only to aid the court in determining the fact, I will try to arrange the evidence under this branch of charge second in chronological order.

The first proof of injury by the dogs, where death resulted, was some time in the month of May, 1864. I have already cited, at some length, the testimony of the witnesses bearing upon this point, and will not recapitulate, but will merely refer the court to the witnesses. They are, William Henry Jennings, Bernard Corrigan, and James E. Marshall.

Another case which is clearly defined in the evidence occurred about the 11th of July, and is stated with some particularity of time, place, and circumstances, by a witness whom the court must remember as one of intelligence and candor. To his testimony I call especial attention. It has already been briefly cited, but I will give his language, at greater length.

John L. Yonker, after having related the circumstances as I have before given them, goes on to narrate the death scene of his murdered comrade, and what occurred at the time, and from all the circumstances, together with the dying declarations of the unfortunate victim, we have presented a clear case of murder.

Q. Did he (the dying man) in that same conversation say anything as to how he had been injured?

A. Yes, sir.

Q. State what he said.

A. We questioned him, and he replied, in a feeble voice, that he had got about 35 or 40 miles, and was strongly pursued by the hounds; that as he was very weak, coming out of the hospital, he tried to climb up a bush, but was pulled down by one of the hounds, and so disabled that he could proceed no further. We had to stir him up once in a while, give him a regular shaking, so that he might answer a few more questions, because he was expiring. I saw him after he was dead.

Q. When was that?

A. Just a few days before the six raiders were hung, which was on the 11th of July.

The testimony of Joseph Adler and George Conway, heretofore cited, corroborates, if that be necessary, the testimony of William Yonker.

Another case which stands out clearly in the evidence is that related by Thomas W. Way. This witness, in company with two comrades, had made his escape. They were overtaken by the dogs. This is his testimony on that point:

Q. Do you remember anything about a soldier being torn to pieces by hounds?

A. Yes, sir; he was a young fellow, whose name I don't know; I knew him by the name of Fred. He was about 17 years old. When he heard the dogs coming, I and another prisoner who was with me, being old hands, climbed a tree. He tried to do so, but he had not got up when the hounds caught him by the foot and pulled him down; and in less than three minutes he was torn all to atoms.

Q. Was Turner there?

A. Turner was close behind; he got up just as the man was torn to pieces and secured the hounds, and we came down.

Q. Did "Fred" die?

A. Yes, sir; I should think so, he was all torn to pieces.

Q. Was any other of your number torn at the same time?

A. No, sir.

Q. When was that occurrence?

A. In the latter part of August, 1864, just before we were moved from Andersonville, which was on the 24th of August.

Q. What did Turner say at the time?

A. He said, "It is good for the son of a bitch; I wish they had torn you all three to pieces."

It would seem impossible to doubt a statement so clearly made and under circumstances calculated to impress the incident indelibly upon the mind of the witness. Corroborative of Mr. Way, however, is the testimony of Samuel [Frank] Maddox, who says that Turner told him one day at the graveyard that he had let the dogs tear a man to pieces in the woods, which, from coincidence of time and circumstances, seems to be the same incident as that given by Way.

The next case of murder by dogs, and as clearly defined as any previously given, is the one related by Dr. A. W. Barrows, who was on duty in the hospital. He says:

I remember a man making his escape from the hospital in July, and being overtaken by the hounds. A large portion of his ear was torn off, and his face mangled, and he was afterwards brought into the hospital. That man got well. This was in July or August, 1864. I do not remember the exact date. I remember also, that at the end of August, or in September, 1864, a man who had been bitten badly by the dogs, in trying to make his escape, was brought into my ward and died. The wound took on gangrene and he died. He was a Union prisoner.

Q. Was he trying to escape from the stockade, or from the hospital?

A. I am not certain.

Q. When did he die?

A. I cannot state the exact date. It was either the last of August or the fore part of September.

Q. How many days after he was torn by the dogs did he die?

A. Well, if my memory serves me right, I should say four or five days after. I know the wound took on gangrene and he died.

Q. Did he die from the effects of the wound?

A. Indirectly I think; he did not directly; it was from the effects of the gangrene.

Q. Was the gangrene manifested in the wound or elsewhere?

A. In the wound; in no other part. He was bitten through the throat, on the side of the neck, and gangrene set in and he died.

Q. Was the gangrene the result of the bite, in your opinion?

A. Yes, sir; it was.

This is confirmed by the testimony of James P. Stone, already cited. Of the facts as presented by Dr. Barrows' testimony there can be no doubt. He was an officer on duty in the rebel hospital, and is a gentleman whose credibility has in no way been doubted. It might perhaps be urged on the part of the defence that as the witness states that the death of the prisoner occurred from gangrene directly, and from the wound indirectly, the benefit of the doubt thus raised must be given to the accused. Let me remind the court of the law governing in such cases. It is laid down in 2 Starkie's Evidence, 711, that—

It is sufficient in law to prove that the death of the party was *accelerated* by the malicious act of the prisoner, although the former labored under a mortal disease at the time of the act. And it is sufficient to constitute murder that the party die of *the wound* given by the prisoner, although the wound was not *originally mortal,* but because so in consequence of negligence or unskilful treatment.

The evidence shows in this case that the patient died of gangrene; that the gangrenous affection was confined to the wound; that he was not so affected before the wound, but was affected immediately afterwards; that he did not die of any other disease or malady.

The fact, therefore, being clear that the death was occasioned or certainly accelerated by the wound, there is no other course left you but to find that the case stands in the same position as if the man had been killed on the spot by the dogs.

We have thus presented a classified analysis of the evidence bearing upon the charge of murder by the use of the hounds. The only defence set up under this charge is given in the statement made by the accused to the court, and is an attempt to confound the prisoner "Frenchy" with all the instances given by different witnesses; and as it was shown in the evidence of the defence that "Frenchy" did not die, you are asked to conclude that this prisoner must be acquitted of this branch of the charges.

Now, it has not been assumed at any time by the prosecution, nor was an attempt made to prove it, that the man "Frenchy," so called, was killed. The incident referred to by the defence was one occurring within plain sight of the post.

The witnesses, Heath, Castlen, and Mohan, rebel officers, testified with regard to it early in the prosecution, and made the facts so clear that it is somewhat surprising that counsel would attempt to raise a reasonable doubt in behalf of their client, by an attempt to confound this case with the numerous others so clearly and distinctly defined in the testimony. The court will bear with me a moment while I give, in this connection, a part of the prisoner's own statement of the "Frenchy" occurrence; and I give it for the reason that it discloses a fact which has been persistently denied, that the hounds used were ferocious and dangerous to human life; and for the additional reason, that it shows, from the prisoner's own admission his control over the dogs and his responsibility for whatever injury resulted from their use. The language of his statement is this:

"Frenchy" again effected his escape by jumping into a thicket near the creek. The matter was reported to me. *I had the dogs sent for.* They soon came on his track; he took to a tree; one of the pursuing party (not I) fired a pistol close to him to induce him to come down. He was not hurt, but he dropped or fell from the tree into a mud hole, and when the *dogs rushed upon him.* I jumped on the dogs and drove them off.

Here, as elsewhere, it would have been safer and wiser for the accused to have rested his case upon the evidence without attempting explanations.

In the next place, I will proceed to recite the evidence, as to cases of death from confinement in the stocks and in the chain-gang.

William Crouse states that a few days before the raiders were hung, which was the 11th of July, a man died in the tent next to the one occupied by witness; that the death occurred the next day after being relieved from the stocks, in which he had been confined about two weeks without intermission.

George W. Gray testifies that he was in stocks the last of August or the first of September, and that the third man from him—a sick man—died while in them; that the negroes took him out of the stocks after he was dead and hauled him away.

Nazareth Allen states that in August, 1864, he saw a man who died in the chain-gang or stocks; he thinks it was the stocks.

Alex. Kennell testifies that in February, 1865, a man was taken out of the stockade in the evening and put in the stocks and kept there all night, and that he died in eight hours after being released; that the man said he was chilled till he was insensible.

James P. Stone testifies that he saw (he thinks it was some time in June) a man in the chain-gang, sick with chronic diarrhœa; that he was kept in the gang until it was impossible for him to move; that he was taken out and left at the guard-house near the stocks; the band was left on his neck and the ball on his leg, and he died with these on him.

James Culver testifies that he saw twelve men in the chain-gang almost every day for a month or six weeks; one of them was very poorly, and looked as though he could hardly carry himself. Those in the gang complained about his being sick; he caused them a great deal of trouble by reason of his having diarrhœa. Witness afterwards saw the man out of the gang, but he still had the ball upon his legs and the band around his neck. He afterwards died in the guard-house. Witness saw the irons taken from him after he was dead. He died in three or four days after being taken out of the chain-gang. The witness thinks he died some time in July.

In connection with this some testimony given by Heath, Dillard, and Honeycutt, rebel soldiers, who were on duty at Andersonville, may be pertinently introduced.

John F. Heath testifies that in the month of August, 1864, a man was sick in the chain-gang and the gang objected to his being in it, because of his condition, that there were twelve men in the chain-gang.

William Dillard testifies that in August he guarded the chain-gang one day and night, when twelve men were in it; one of them was very low, and had to go out every five or ten minutes; that the others of the chain-gang wanted him taken out; that when the man was taken out, he could just stand up.

Calvin Honeycutt states that he guarded the chain-gang for one or two days and nights; that one of the men was sick and the rest wanted him taken out.

John Pasque states that some time in July he saw a man put in the chain-gang, and saw his dead body after he was taken out.

Robert Tait testifies that on one occasion (he does not know the date) one man was put in the chain-gang when very sick; that he remained in it for about two days; that the surgeon told the prisoner that he had better take the man out; that the prisoner gave orders to have him released; and the next morning he saw him hauled away to the graveyard.

The evidence here briefly recited presents two distinct murders by the use of the stocks and one by the chain-gang. The cases presented by William Crouse and George W. Gray (cases of death by the stocks) come directly within the general principles of law before cited. The witness Crouse, after narrating the circumstances, as heretofore briefly given, testifies as follows on cross-examination:

Q. Was there anything the matter with him besides being in the stocks?
A. No, sir; he was a hearty man before he went there.
Q. You did not see him in the stocks, outside?
A. Yes, sir; when I went out to get some medicine.
Q. How many times did you get out in that way?
A. I used to go out nearly every other day to get medicine.

Q. Was not the doctor's place close to the gate?

A. Yes, sir; about twenty feet from it, at the upper end, the southwest end.

Q. Could you see the stocks from there?

A. I could.

Q. How far was it from where you got the medicine to Captain Wirz's headquarters.

A. About three hundred feet.

Q. With nothing to obstruct the view?

A. No, sir.

Q. And you saw the men in the stocks for two weeks, when you went out in that way?

A. Yes, sir.

Q. How was that man injured who died?

A. Weakness; he was starved.

Q. Was he not starved instead of being hurt by the stocks?

A. That was one thing that killed him.

Q. Was it not the principal thing?

A. Yes.

This occurred, as the witness states, about the time the raiders were hung. The evidence, it is true, does not present a case of death directly attributable to the stocks; but it is clear that death resulted from a conjunction of circumstances, of which the stocks was one important element, all being the result of the orders of the accused. It is immaterial whether the man died from the injuries inflicted by the stocks alone; the circumstances fully bring the case within the principle already cited, that "it is sufficient in law to prove that the death of the party was *accelerated* by the malicious act of the prisoner." The second case of this class is presented by the testimony of George W. Gray. The witness had made his escape, was caught by the dogs and returned to the prison. He testifies:

I was brought back to Andersonville prison and taken to Wirz' quarters. I was ordered by him to be put in the stocks, where I remained for four days, with my feet in a block, and a lever placed over my legs, with my arms thrown back, and a chain running across the arms. I remained four days there in the sun. That was my punishment for trying to get away from the prison.

Q. Do you know anything about a person dying in the stocks?

A. I do. At the same time a young man was placed in the stocks, the third man from me. He died there. He was a little sick when he went in and he died there.

Q. Do you know his name?

A. I do not; if I heard it, I have forgotten it.

Q. When did this occur?

A. That was about the last of August or the 1st of September, 1864.

Q. Are you certain he died?

A. I am. The negroes took him out of the stocks after he was dead, threw him into the wagon and hauled him away.

This witness is strongly corroborated by the rebel soldier, Nazareth Allen, who testifies:

Q. Do you know anything about a prisoner having died in the stocks?

A. Yes, sir; one died in the chain-gang or stocks, I won't be certain which, but I think in the stocks.

Q. When was it?

A. I think some time in August, 1864.

Q. Do you know what was the state of his health when he was put in?

A. I do not know what his sickness was.

Q. What was his appearance?

A. He appeared to be sick when I saw him. I saw him only once or twice; and afterwards I saw him dead.

Q. How long was this man confined in the stocks?

A. I cannot say; there were several in the stocks.

Q. Do you know for what this man was placed in the stocks?

A. I do not; I think it was for trying to escape.

Q. Where were these stocks or this chain-gang with reference to Captain Wirz' headquarters?

A. They were between Captain Wirz' headquarters and the stockade.

Q. On the road you would take in going to the stockade?

A. Yes, sir.

In reference to this occurrence, Gray is so strongly corroborated by Allen that I do not deem it necessary to comment on the evidence more particularly.

There is still another case of death by the use of the stocks, to which I ask your attention, as giving, besides the fact itself, proof that these punishments were continued until almost the time of breaking up of the prison. This is the case mentioned by Alex. Kennell, who says:

I have seen them (the prisoners) put in the stocks. One special act which I know of occurred last February. In that case a man was taken out of the stockade in the evening, about 4 o'clock, and kept in the stocks all night. He was turned into the stockade the next morning at 9 o'clock, and he died in less than eight hours. He died in the stockade.

Q. What was the condition of the man when taken from the stockade?

A. He was apparently as healthy as any prisoner in the stockade.

Q. What was done with him during the night?

A. He was kept all night in the stocks, which were outside the stockade.

Q. Did he die from the effects of the stocks?

A. That was his supposition; it was a very cold night.

Q. Did you talk with that man during his dying moments?

A. Yes, sir; I talked with him an hour before he died.

Q. With what belief was he impressed?

A. He was impressed with the belief that he was chilled to death that night in the stocks.

Q. Did he expect to die?

A. He did not expect to live, from his conversation; he did not eat anything after he came into the stockade.

Q. What did he tell you?

A. He told me that he was kept in the stocks from the time he was taken out until about 8 o'clock in the morning. He was chilled so thoroughly that night that he was insensible.

Q. Did you see him after he died?

A. I helped to carry him to the gate.

Q. Did you know his name?

A. No, sir; I did not know his name; I never inquired it; he belonged to a Pennsylvania regiment.

Q. You are certain about the time?

A. I am certain that it occurred about the 15th of February, 1865.

I come now to notice the deaths resulting from confinement in the chain-gang. There is some evidence of more than one death having occurred by these means; but aside from one instance the testimony is so vague and unsatisfactory that I do not ask the court to consider it. There is one case, however, so clearly defined, so fully proved, as to admit of no doubt. This is the case, the court will readily remember, as occurring in the chain-gang of twelve. The facts in this case are given so clearly and by so many witnesses (a synopsis of whose testimony I have already presented) that the circumstances, I have no doubt, are fresh in the memory of the court; and I will therefore consume no further time by quoting particularly the evidence. The eye-witnesses of this occurrence, which seems to have been one of the most sad and cruel of the whole list, present an array of testimony which cannot be overthrown, and which there has been no attempt on the part of the defence to explain away. The witnesses fix this this occurrence about the time the raiders were hung. The testimony is given by James P. Stone, James [Jasper] Culver, John F. Heath, a rebel soldier, William Dillard, a rebel soldier, Calvin Honeycutt, a rebel soldier, John Pascol, [Pasque,] Robert Tait, and James H. Davidson.

Before proceeding to notice the evidence as to the acts of murder committed immediately under the prisoner's orders or by his own hand, allow me to remark that the court, in considering these specific acts, will hardly overlook the confirmatory evidence embraced in the testimony as to the general language and conduct of the accused towards the prisoners. I submit that his language and conduct, as exhibited in the testimony, furnish such evidence of malice as to raise a strong presumption of guilt.

Wharton, in his Criminal Law, speaks of the "presumption of guilt from *declarations of intentions and threats, from which the presumption of guilt may be drawn with great strength,* when there is preliminary ground laid."

On this principle, I maintain, the numerous well-proven declarations and threats of the accused, evincing his utter indifference whether the prisoners lived or died; nay, his desire that they should die, and his ambition to compete with rebel generals in the field by killing off as many Union soldiers as possible, are justly to be viewed as confirmatory of the evidence in regard to the specific acts of murder laid to his charge. And as similar proof of malice on his part, raising a presumption of guilt against him in reference to specific murderous acts alleged, the court will not, I think, disregard the general evidence of his brutal treatment of prisoners, exhibiting toward them a malignity of temper of which murder would be but the natural outgrowth. The conduct and the expressions of the accused, as proved throughout the whole evidence, show a vindictively malicious feeling towards the prisoners, and this general malice is sufficient to furnish probable cause for the special acts of killing testified to by the witnesses, particularly as in almost every instance of killing the act itself was accompanied by declarations indicating strongly a malicious and wilful intent.

In discussing the murders alleged to have been committed under the prisoner's direct orders, the first case that claims attention is that in which the victim was a one-legged soldier, known among the prisoners as "Chickamauga." The court will pardon me for dwelling somewhat at length on this case, as it is one of those two which the prisoner has singled out as the only cases worthy of a serious attempt at defence in connection with the charge of murder. Some of the witnesses who narrate the facts of this occurrence are S. D. Brown, O. S. Belcher, J. R. Achiff, Th. Hall, J. Adler, Gottfried Brunner, O. B. Fairbanks, E. L.

Kellogg, A. J. Spring, C. E. Tibbles, J. E. Marshall, A. A. Kellogg, A. Henshaw, Thomas N. Way.

The accounts of this occurrence, given by these different witnesses with greater or less particularity, are entirely consistent as to the main facts, while as to unimportant particulars there is doubtless that slight variation which always characterizes accounts given by different eye-witnesses of the same occurrence, and which, as it excludes the idea of concerted falsification, is the strongest voucher for the good faith and veracity of those who testify.

The essential facts which stand out clearly in this mass of testimony, so clearly that the prisoner himself, as I shall presently show, has been driven to a substantial admission of them, are, that a poor, demented cripple, whose imbecile condition was notorious in the stockade and among the guards, sought to be taken from the stockade that he might be protected from the indignation of some of his comrades, who charged that he had reported tunnels to the accused; that after some parleying on the part of Chickamauga with the guard, the prisoner made his appearance, when Chickamauga asked him to be taken out of the stockade, stating the reason for his request; that the prisoner refused to take him out, and ordered the guard (who had shown an unwillingness to treat the poor cripple harshly) to shoot him if he crossed the dead-line; that he did subsequently cross the dead-line, and the sentry, acting under the direct orders of the prisoner, shot him. Here, I submit, is a clear case of murder.

Before going further, it is proper to remark contradictions in the testimony of the witnesses to the Chickamauga affair appear only in the statement of the prisoner, and cannot be discovered by the closest scrutiny of the record. It is *not* a fact that two of the government witnesses represent the prisoner as having shot Chickamauga with his own hand; yet the prisoner's version of the evidence would make us believe this; and the supposed conflict of testimony is urged as an illustration of what he terms "the murky, foggy, indefinite and contradictory testimony" of the prosecution.

I will give the prisoner's ingenious version of the testimony, and then, as contrasting romance with reality, I will present the evidence as given in the record.

The prisoner says:

One witness, whom for his own sake I will not name, inasmuch as his statements must have been and were recognized by every one who heard him as undeserving the least belief, describes him ("Chickamauga") as a kind of weakly man, who, when I entered the stockade one day, wormed around me, saying that he wanted to go out in the air; whereupon Captain Wirz wheeled again, pulled out a revolver and shot him down.

Now, the sober fact is, that this witness, in describing and characterizing the prisoner who was shot, mentions no circumstance which can warrant the supposition that he intended to testify as to the Chickamauga affair. I read the continuation of the same narrative:

Q. Do you know who the man was that the prisoner shot?

A. He belonged to the 8th Missouri; they called him "Red" in the regiment. I knew him at Memphis.

Again I quote the prisoner's statement:

A still different version of this transaction is given in a more laconic and reckless style by another witness. I will quote it:

Q. Did you ever see Captain Wirz shoot any man?

A. Yes, sir.

Q. When?

A. About the first day of April, I think; shortly after he took command there.

Q. State the circumstances of the shooting.

A. Captain Wirz was coming in the south gate one day. A sick man, as I took him to be—a lame man—asked Captain Wirz something, and Captain Wirz turned round and shot him.

Here again no one has ever pretended that the case is identical with that of Chickamauga, the latter occurring in June and the former in April. When the evidence of the record is treated in this manner, no wonder that it becomes, in the language of the prisoner's statement, "murky, foggy, indefinite and contradictory."

It is a little remarkable, too, that after having introduced one of these witnesses as being "reckless" in his style of narration and the other as "undeserving the least belief," the prisoner in a later part of his statement dismisses them both with a concession that they were sincere in their testimony, for he says:

The two men who swore they saw me shoot the prisoner with my own hand were probably led to make that statement from having seen me draw my revolver in the manner I have described.

Let me now notice the prisoner's own version of this Chickamauga affair—a version which he gives us as the solution of the so-called irreconcilable testimony of the prosecution. The facts, as the prisoner would have the court believe them, and believing, accept as his exculpation, are given in his own language in this remarkable paragraph:

Will the court permit me to make a statement which may serve to explain all these conflicting accounts of the death of poor Chickamauga? On the evening in question, the sergeant or the officer of the guard came to my quarters and stated that there was a man within the dead-line jawing with the sentry and refusing to go outside, and that there was a crowd of prisoners around him and a good deal of disturbance. I rode my horse down to the stockade, dismounted outside, and went in. There I found things as they had been described to me. I went up to Chickamauga and asked him, in a rough tone of voice, what the hell he was doing there? He said he wanted to be killed. I took my revolver in my hand, and said in a menacing manner that if that was all he wanted I would accommodate him. I scared him somewhat and he was taken outside by some of the prisoners. I then in his presence, and solely as a menace, told the sentry to shoot him if he came in again. I little thought that he would come back or that his comrades would permit him, after their hearing the order, to go once more across the forbidden line. I left the stockade, remounted my horse, and was on my way back to my quarters, when I heard the report of a musket. I hastened back and ran up to the sentry-box from which the shot had been fired. There is the simple history of the case, without any reserve or misrepresentation. The court, I am sure, will recognize all the marks and evidences of truth in it. It is consistent with itself and consistent with the average line of the testimony.

I confess that I was greatly surprised when this startling declaration was read for the first time in my hearing and in the presence of the court, three days ago. This explanation seems to me to admit so fully the guilt of the prisoner that if it were the mere hypothesis of counsel, adopted as the last resort of a desperate defence, I would decline to hold the prisoner responsible for such damning admissions, which I would be bound to believe his counsel had no authority to make. But here we have the solemn statement of the prisoner, submitted without solicitation and after due deliberation. Charged with the gravest criminality in reference to an occurrence which is attested by a score of witnesses, he volunteers his own explanation, which is taken down from his lips, revised and signed by his own hand, and read before the court in his presence, with no attempt on his part at disavowal, when the impulse which prompted such self-criminating candor had had time to give place to a circumspect reserve. Under these circumstances, I believe I am treating the prisoner with entire fairness when I ask the court to hold him responsible for his own words and let him be the witness of his own guilt. I submit that his explanation of this occurrence, so far from exculpating him, exhibits his guilt scarcely less effectively than the evidence of the prosecution.

The main fact upon which the government insists is that the prisoner ordered the guard to shoot Chickamauga if he should cross the dead-line, and that in the act of crossing it, or immediately afterwards, this wretched imbecile was shot by the sentry in obedience to the prisoner's order. This is not denied in the statement of the prisoner, but is there fully admitted. It is admitted that the prisoner (I quote his own language) "told the sentry to shoot him if he came in again;" it is admitted that this order was obeyed by the sentry, and that thus Chickamauga was killed. While conceding all this the prisoner seeks to shield himself under the allegation that the order was given "solely as a menace."

Yet he does not pretend that he gave the sentry any reason to suppose that the order was not to be obeyed; he does not pretend that the act of the sentinel in shooting was anything else than the natural obedience of a subordinate to his superior's order, which had every appearance of being imperative. When the guilty and murderous act is thus admitted, the criminal cannot seek refuge under his own allegation of an innocent intent, particularly when he acknowledges that that intent was hidden within the recesses of his own mind and found no shadowing forth at the time in words or acts, but was contradicted by both. The prisoner's allegation of an innocent intent cannot overcome the conclusive presumption of the law, that "a sane man contemplates the natural and probable consequences of his own acts." When the motive of a man arraigned for crime shall be taken from his own lips, in contradiction of the obvious tendency of his acts, courts of justice will have become obsolete. It is admitted that the order to shoot was given by the prisoner; it is admitted that that order was obeyed, and that thus "Chickamauga" lost his life. The obedience of the sentry and the death which resulted were the "natural and probable consequences" of the prisoner's self-confessed act, and as I believe that the order for the shooting of "Chickamauga" was unjustifiable and cruel, I see not how this court can do otherwise than declare that the prisoner, in this melancholy affair, incurred the guilt of murder.

Before leaving this subject, I cannot refrain from making a passing remark on the picture of the prisoner's brutality, as painted by his own hand; a picture in singular contrast with another self-portraiture embraced in the same statement. In recounting the "Chickamauga" affair, the prisoner says:

I went up to "Chickamauga" and I asked him, in a rough tone of voice, "what the hell he was doing there?" He said he wanted to be killed. I took my revolver in my hand and said, in a menacing manner, that if that was all he wanted I would accommodate him. I scared him somewhat, and he was taken outside by some of the prisoners.

How startlingly in contrast with this has the prisoner portrayed himself in another part of his statement. This is his language:

I do trust that this enlightened court will bear with me in my humble effort to convince it that while commandant of the prison at Andersonville I was not the monster that I have been depicted as being; that I did not cause or delight in the spectacle of the sufferings, woes and deaths of the Union prisoners; that I did not contribute to their sufferings; but that, on the contrary, I did what little lay in my power to diminish or alleviate them, and to prove that, although I have been represented as little less than a fiend, "Heaven left some remnant of the angel still in that poor jailer's nature."

We are asked to believe that these two portraitures represent one and the same person. If it be so, then unfortunate was it for poor "Chickamauga" that his untutored mind did not comprehend that that fierce seeming man, who asked him in a rough tone of voice, "What the hell are you doing here," was at that very moment yearning with compassion for his wretched condition. The poor crazy cripple little dreamed that the stern-spoken man, who, revolver in hand, said to him, "If you want to be killed I will accommodate you," was a "poor jailer," in whom the remnant of the angel was struggling to exhibit itself under great difficulties, a lover of mankind, in a very embarrassing position, but doing, as he says, "what little lay in his power to diminish or alleviate the sufferings of those around him;" a John Howard, forsooth, whose compassionate heart prompted him, as he tells you, to take out of the stockade all the drummer boys, in order that the little fellows might, in the enjoyment of purer air and healthful exercise, have a better chance of being restored to their yearning mothers and sisters at home. Alas for poor "Chickamauga," that he did not whisper in the ear of this rough-mannered philanthropist that he, too, crippled and insane though he was, had a yearning mother or sister at home. Who knows but that the suggestion might have won for "Chickamauga" a happier fate.

But the subject is too serious for satire. I submit that in the many features of this trial, showing with what abandon the prisoner gave rein to his malicious passions, the killing of poor "Chickamauga" is one of the most despicable and indefensible. The insane cripple had subjected himself to the wrath of his comrades, being led, by the promises of this accused, to turn traitor to them and disclose their means of escape. He had thrown himself upon the protection of his murderer. He had alienated himself from all his companions, while he had done everything to commend him in the sight of the accused. Yet when fleeing from the just indignation of his comrades, which was so great that he even dared to trust his life in the hands of the guards, with death staring him in the face from the sentinel and from his outraged companions, he appeals to this accused, the only man who had the power to aid him in this terrible strait—the one of all others who was under an obligation so to do—and is rudely rebuffed by the man to whom he had rendered a service—brutally repulsed with a violence of manner and language which appears as vividly in the prisoner's own version of the transaction, as in that given by the witnesses for the prosecution—and is told to go back to this mob which is crying for his blood; or that if he did not do this, but remained within the dead-line, the sentry would shoot him. It was death to "Chickamauga" whichever way he went, and this accused must have known it, and must have intended it, else he would have led him out of that horrible place. With what conscience, then, can he ask you to believe him when he tells you he did not intend the death of "Chickamauga?" This court, I submit, in view of the evidence, must hold the prisoner responsible for the death of that miserable creature.

Having presented one of these cases at some length, one which I think will admit of no doubt, I will pass hastily over the evidence bearing upon similar cases, giving a brief analysis and reference to the testimony, leaving the court to arrive at its own conclusions.

William Bull testifies that on the 3d of June, at the north gate, he saw a man shot; that the prisoner came in at the head of a detachment, put three guards on the stoop, and ordered them to fire at the crowd to make them fall back; that one of the guards fired, and that the ball struck the man in the stomach, who was about 15 feet distant from the witness.

W. W. Crandall [Patrick Bradley] states that on one occasion, he thinks it was in June, 1864, when the men were crowding around the south gate, the prisoner was there and thought they crowded too much. He ordered the sentry on the outside of the gate to fire, and repeated the order three or four distinct times. The sentry fired and killed a man who was about five feet from the dead-line.

Jacob D. Brown testifies that on the 27th of July he saw the prisoner in the sentry-box near the brook; some of the prisoners were there getting water, and men would accidentally reach under the dead-line. The prisoner told the sentry if any man reached through the dead-line to get water to shoot him down. He had barely said the words when a prisoner reached through, and the sentry fired; the ball taking effect in the head, killing him instantly. Witness was close to him.

Joseph Adler testifies that some time in July the prisoner was standing in the sentry-box, when two or three men were at the brook after water; some got their hands beyond the dead-line, and the prisoner asked the sentry why he did not shoot, as it was no matter whether the man's whole body was over the dead-line or only a part of it; that if he did not shoot he would have him punished. The sentry thereupon shot the man in the right breast. He fell into the creek.

Bernard Corrigan testifies that a few days after the raiders were hung (which was on the 11th of July) a man was shot at the south gate. "We were going," he says, "for medicine; the man had two tin cups in his hands. Wirz told the guard if he did not keep the men back he would take him off and punish him. He repeated it, saying he had a gun. Wirz turned his back and started off, and the guard fired right among the crowd and shot this man."

Joseph R. Achuff states that in July they were carrying sick men to the gate; there was a great crowd there. The prisoner told the sentry if the men did not keep back to blow them through. The sentinel had his musket against a man's stomach, and drew back and fired, and killed a man from Pennsylvania.

Jacob D. Brown testifies that about the middle of August the prisoner ordered the sentinel to shoot men who were getting water from the brook, the men being much crowded. The sentry fired and a man was shot in the breast, the wound being fatal.

Prescott Tracey states that in the month of August, 1864, he heard the prisoner order the shooting of a man who had just come in and did not know the rules and regulations; that he went to get a drink, and slipped and fell with his head about six inches over the dead-line; that the prisoner at the bar called to the sentry, "God damn your soul, why don't you shoot that Yankee son of a bitch?" The guard fired, the ball striking the man in the head and coming out at the back of his neck. He died in the creek.

We come now to notice that class of murders committed with the prisoner's own hands. I shall here, as elsewhere, avoid all argumentation and present as briefly as possible the evidence of the witnesses, leaving the court to determine, in the light of the principles of law before mentioned, what amount of guilt attaches to this prisoner.

Your attention is called, first, to the death of a Union prisoner by beating with a pistol over the head, as given by the witness William Willis Scott. His evidence is as follows:

In one case, I was coming down after a bucket of water. I belonged way up in what they called the new stockade, on the north side. Captain Wirz was coming in; a sick man was sitting on the side of the bank; he asked Captain Wirz if he could get out. Captain Wirz turned around, gave him a kind of a sour look, and said, "Yes, God damn it; I will let you out," and with the revolver he struck the fellow over the head and shoulders several times. The fellow went to his tent then. On the third morning, I think, I made it my business to go down and see him; he was dead; he had died the night before.

Q. Did you see him?

A. Yes, sir.

Q. Did he die from the effects of the beating with the pistol?

A. I suppose so. He was pretty badly bruised around the head and face.

Q. With what did Captain Wirz beat him?

A. I think it was the butt of the revolver which he had in his hand.

Q. Which hand did he use?

A. I don't remember.

Q. Did he knock the man down?

A. Yes, sir; he knocked him down the first blow.

Q. When was that?

A. I think it was about the 25th or 26th of August, 1864.

Q. Can you give the man's name?

A. No, sir; I did not inquire about that: I just came down to see if he was much the worse for his treatment; and I did not inquire any further.

This witness is uncorroborated by any testimony presented, unless the evidence given by Patrick Bradley may refer to the same circumstance.

I leave it for the court to determine whether the accused shall be found guilty under this testimony. There are given, with certainty, time, place, and circumstance. The beating is shown to have been wanton, cruel, and malicious, and wholly unprovoked. The only element necessary to make the crime complete is the proof that death was the result of the wounds inflicted. Whether this may or may not be inferred from the circumstances as narrated by the witness, the court must be the sole judge.

The prisoner is also charged with the murder of a soldier, by stamping upon and kicking him so as to cause his death. The evidence in support of this allegation is given by Martin E. Hogan:

I saw Captain Wirz, at the time the prisoners were being moved from Andersonville to Millen, take a man by the coat-collar because he could not walk faster. The man was so worn out with hunger and disease, that if he had got the whole world I do not think he could move faster than he was moving. Captain Wirz wrenched him back, and stamped upon him with his boot. The man was borne past me, bleeding from his mouth or nose, I cannot say which, and he died a short time afterwards.

Q. When you speak of Captain Wirz, you mean the prisoner there?

A. I mean the man sitting there, (pointing to the prisoner.)

Q. Have you any doubt of his identity?

A. Not at all, sir; I should know him anywhere.

Q. About what month was that?

A. The prisoners commenced to move from there from the 5th to the 8th of September, 1864, and it was inside of a week from that time; it was some time in the early part of September; I cannot say within two or three days what date it was.

The character of this witness, his intelligence and his facilities for observation, must impress the court with the fact that his testimony is entitled to more than ordinary weight. It requires no exercise of imagination, nor a resort to improbabilities, to justify the conclusion of guilt, remembering the character of the accused and his many acts of cruelty, which furnish confirmatory evidence not to be overlooked.

Another murder laid to the charge of this prisoner, as perpetrated by his own hand, is described by George Conway, who testifies:

A. I saw a man shot one day: he came down after water; no one was allowed to put their head or any part of their body under the dead-line. This man, probably not being acquainted with the rules, as many of them were not, who came in there after the rules were read, put his hand in under the dead-line to get a cup of water, and the cup dropped from his hand. He put his hand in under the dead-line to raise it up again, and Captain Wirz shot him, the ball taking effect in his head; he died almost instantly. (To the court.) Captain Wirz shot him; he was standing in the sentry-box.

Q. When did this occur?

A. Well, it was about the time the raiders were hung; I could not say whether it was before or after.

Q. It was about that time?

A. Yes, sir.

Q. Are you certain you recognize Captain Wirz?

A. Yes, sir.

Q. You knew him well at that time?

A. Yes, sir.

Q. Do you know what kind of a gun he had in his hand?

A. He had a revolver, I believe.

Q. You state that Captain Wirz shot him; tell the court the circumstances.

A. Those were the circumstances. He was getting a cup of water out of the brook, when the cup dropped from his hand.

Q. Do you know the name of that man?

A. I do not; I never saw the man before till I saw him that time.

Q. Did he die?

A. Yes, sir, he died.

The testimony of this witness on other points, as upon this, is clear and distinct, so much so that the counsel on cross-examination seemed to think it unnecessary to interrogate the witness with regard to this very important part of his testimony. He is uncontradicted, and must be believed.

The next instance of this kind to which your attention is called is given in the testimony of Felix De la Baum, I do not desire to discriminate among witnesses, as it might imply that some are entitled to greater credit than others. Disclaiming any such intention, I still must remind the court of the character of this witness, his manner of testifying, and the air of truth and candor with which he told his story. Upon this point I give his testimony entire and without comment.

A. On the 8th of July I arrived at Andersonville, with 300 or 400 other prisoners, most of them sick and wounded. We were brought up to Captain Wirz' headquarters; were drawn up in line, four ranks deep, and kept there for a considerable length of time, without any business being transacted. The guards had orders to let none of us go to the water. One of the prisoners was attacked with epilepsy or fits; he fell down; some of his friends or neighbors standing near him ran down to the creek after water.

Q. By permission of the guard?

A. I don't know; I suppose so; because the guard was tied up by the thumbs for permitting them to do so. First I heard a shot fired, without seeing who fired it. After hearing that shot fired, I looked down to the left, and I saw Captain Wirz fire two more shots, wounding two men. One of them was carried up near his headquarters, and in my opinion he was in a dying condition.

Q. What became of the other?

A. He was wounded too; but I did not see him again.

Q. Did you ever see him afterwards?

A. No, sir.

Q. How were the men wounded?

A. The one who was carried up near the headquarters was wounded somewhere in the breast.

Q. What kind of a weapon had Captain Wirz in his hand?

A. A revolver.

Q. How near were you to him?

A. I was perhaps 20 paces distant from him; I am not positive about the distance.

Q. How far was the prisoner when he shot?

A. Not very far.

Q. You are certain you saw Captain Wirz discharge the pistol in his hand?

A. Yes, sir.

Q. Did the man who was brought up to the headquarters die?

A. I did not, myself, see him die; but he was evidently in a dying condition, judging by his appearance. I never saw him again; we were not allowed to speak to the guard, and I could not make any inquiries.

Q. Do you remember any language used by Captain Wirz on that occasion?

A. He asked the lieutenant of the guard, "Where is the guard who allowed this man to fall out of the ranks?" The guard was pointed out, and Captain Wirz ordered him to be tied up by the thumbs for two hours. After this, Captain Wirz pointed out the man, and said, "That is the way I get rid of you damned sons of bitches."

Q. Was anything said as to the purpose for which the men left the ranks and went towards the brook?

A. I myself saw the man fall down; he had epileptic fits, and I was informed that the men ran after water for him. We had not received any water all night; they kept us all night in the cars; on the way down from Macon to Andersonville we had no water. When we passed the creek we wished to get some water, but we were not allowed to have any. We were kept at the headquarters of Captain Wirz for about two hours, without receiving a drink. We were then divided into squads and transported into the stockade.

Q. When you were ordered into the stockade, was the man who had been shot still lying there, or had he been carried out?

A. I was taken out with four other men to be put into the 71st detachment, and was shortly afterwards taken away from the headquarters into the stockade.

Q. State whether you have any means of judging whether the man died from that gunshot wound.

A. All that I can state is, that he was, in my opinion, in a dying condition. I judged so from his heaving up and down, and from his gasping for breath. I have seen many men on the battle-field in the same condition, and they always died shortly afterwards.

Q. Where was the wound?

A. The blood was running out from his breast, or the middle of his body, somewhere.

Q. Did you hear anything about it afterwards?

A. All I heard of it was from a rebel sergeant—I think his name was Colby—he said the man died.

Q. When did he tell you that?

A. Some time after I was in the stockade.

There is evidence given by Hugh R. Snee of a double murder committed outside the stockade, on the way from the stockade to the depot, and which occurred a little after dark, the victims being Union prisoners, who were attempting to make their escape among those going out for exchange.

The circumstances, as given by this witness, are, that in September, 1864, when some men were going out for special exchange, there were two men belonging to an Iowa regi-ment who fainted between the prisoner's headquarters and the depot; they fell out of the ranks, and a man ran back and wanted to know why they came out. They said they wanted to get out of prison. A man said, "I will help you out damned soon." The witness heard six discharges from a pistol, and heard a cry as if some one was hurt. Presently a rebel officer, he thinks a lieutenant, coming along, remarked, "It was a brutal act." Some one asked him who it was, and he said, "The captain." He also said, "One of them is dead." Witness thought it was Captain Wirz' voice which he heard through the crowd, but could not state positively.

There is still other testimony of murders committed by the hand of this prisoner, as given in the testimony of Willis Van Buren and James H. Davidson. I desire only to call the attention of the court to the testimony of the witness Snee, and the two first named, as bearing upon this branch of the case, without venturing to express an opinion as to the guilt of the prisoner.

There is still one other case of deliberate murder by the hand of this accused. It is that related by George W. Gray. The court will remember that during the examination of this witness there occurred one of the most impressive episodes of this trial, which must not be overlooked or forgotten in judging of the truth or falsehood of George W. Gray's narration. He has been severely attacked by the prisoner in his statement to the court, although no contradicting evidence was introduced and no circumstances given which could raise a reasonable doubt for the benefit of this accused. I call the attention of the court to the entire evidence of this witness in relation to the occurrence. He testifies:

Q. Do you know anything about the prisoner having shot a prisoner of war there at any time?

A. He shot a young fellow named William Stewart, a private belonging to the 9th Minnesota infantry. He and I went out of the stockade with a dead body, and after laying the dead body in the dead-house, Captain Wirz rode up to us and asked by what authority we were out there. Stewart said we were there by proper authority. Wirz said no more, but drew a revolver and shot the man. After he was killed the guard took from his body about $20 or $30, and Wirz took the money from the guard and rode off, telling the guard to take me to prison.

Q. Are you sure about that?

A. If I was not I would not speak it.

Q. By whose orders did you come out with the dead body?

A. It was my determination, I don't know whether it was Stewart's or not, to get away again. For that reason we went out; we begged for the body.

Q. Do you know whether that was the time that Lieutenant Davis had something to do with the prison?

A. I recollect now that Lieutenant Davis ordered the sergeants of each detachment to detail men to carry out of the stockade the dead bodies of men belonging to that detachment.

Q. State what Captain Wirz had in his hand when he shot that soldier.

A. He had a revolver, whether a navy pistol or not I don't know; it was a large pistol.

Q. How near was he to him?

A. About eight feet from him, I think.

Q. Where did the ball take effect in your comrade?

A. In the breast. He died right there where he was shot.

Q. Were you at the time attempting to make your escape?

A. No, sir; but it was my intention to do so if I could. I was not attempting it at that time, nor was Stewart.

Q. How far were you from the dead-house?

A. About 50 yards—about half the distance from the stockade to the dead-house, a little off and to one side of it.

Q. You do not know whether Lieutenant Davis had a partial command there?

A. I think that in September Captain Wirz was relieved temporarily by Lieutenant Davis on account of ill-health, for about two weeks, probably.

Q. Of the fact of Wirz committing this particular offence you are certain?

A. I am, sir.

Q. When testifying with reference to the man on the white horse, you said something about not being able to identify him; had you any difficulty afterwards in identifying Captain Wirz?

A. The first time I knew such a man in the prison I heard Lieutenant Davis call his name at the gate. He said, "Captain Wirz come down this way." I looked at the man and asked the boys if he was not the commander of the Andersonville prison.

The judge advocate called upon the prisoner to stand up for identification.

The prisoner, who was lying on a lounge, partly raised himself, turning his face to the witness.

Q. Do you recognize that man as the person who shot your comrade?

A. That is the man.

The prisoner attempted to say something in contradiction of the witness, but was not permitted by the court. The judge advocate requested the prisoner to stand upon his feet.

The prisoner having complied with the judge advocate's request, the witness looked at him and said, "I think that is the man."

Q. The prisoner whom you have been talking about, you were in the habit of recognizing in the prison as Captain Wirz?

A. Yes.

Q. Do you recollect whether the man who shot your comrade had a foreign accent?

A. I took him to be a German or a foreigner by his talk, for this reason, when I was put in the stocks he said to me, "Gott tam you, I fix you." For that reason I took him to be a foreigner, or a Dutchman.

This impression of the scene, (one of the most remarkable occurring during the trial,) as the witness Gray confronted the murderer of his companion, was such as this court and all who were present will never forget. The witness was cautioned to be careful, and told that it was a very serious matter about which he was to speak; but there was no trepidation, no hesitation, no doubt discoverable in his manner, and I think all who heard him must have felt that he spoke only the truth when he said, "that is the man." You are told on the part of the defence that this witness is not to be believed, and among the reasons it is urged that on cross-examination he said that he thought the prisoner rode a roan horse, while the general testimony is to the effect that the prisoner usually rode a gray mare, and that he afterwards saw him on a sorrel horse. I would remind the court that Mr. Gray is not the only person who describes the prisoner as riding a roan horse, and I need hardly remind counsel so prolific of negative evidence, that men who usually ride gray horses have been known to ride sorrel horses.

Another reason urged why Gray's story is not to be believed is, that it is improbable. A complete answer to this is found in the conduct of this accused towards the prisoners of war in his custody. No act of brutality was improbable with him, no provocation was needed, but, like the infamous Vargas, killing with him was but a pleasant recreation, and seemed the business of the hour.

Again you are told that Gray is not to be believed because he mentioned a circumstance of cruelty (the bayoneting of soldiers) which was brought out by no other witness. Is this so surprising a fact that this court must reject the whole evidence of a witness otherwise supported? This whole record has been made up, not by calling a few witnesses who narrate all that occurred at Andersonville, but by calling very many, each of whom brings with him the knowledge of facts which, from the very necessities of their surroundings, were not always in the possession of others. Gray's statement of the cruel bayoneting of our soldiers at Andersonville is entirely consistent with the treatment they met from the beginning to the end of that horrible prison.

I insist, gentlemen, that the evidence of George W. Gray is entitled to your highest consideration, and although it alone fixes upon the prisoner at the bar guilt which can only be expiated by the highest punishment known to the law, you cannot resist the proof.

I have thus, without regard to the evidence under charge first, presented the evidence under charge second, as spread upon the record, showing that this accused, while acting as commandant of the prison at Andersonville, deliberately, wantonly, and maliciously destroyed the lives of 18 prisoners of war in his custody. I confess myself too much overcome with the melancholy details of this trial and the frightful disclosures to dwell longer on so sad a theme. If this accused still answer that, admitting the facts charged, he did these things in the exercise of authority lawfully conferred upon him, and that what he did was necessary to the discipline and safety of the prisoners, I answer him in the language of Lord Mansfield, given in an important case:

In trying the legality of acts done by military officers in the exercise of their duty, particularly beyond the seas, where cases may occur without the possibility of application for proper advice, great latitude ought to be allowed, and they ought not to suffer for a slip of form, if their intention appears, by the evidence, to have been upright. It is the same as when complaints are brought against inferior civil magistrates, such as justices of the peace, for acts done by them in the exercise of their civil duty. There the principal inquiry to be made by a court of justice is, how the heart stood, and if there appear to be nothing wrong there, great latitude will be allowed for misapprehension or mistake. But, on the other hand, if the heart is wrong, if cruelty, malice and oppression appear to have occasioned or aggravated the imprisonment, or other injury complained of, they shall not cover themselves with the thin veil of legal forms, or escape, under the cover of a justification the most technically regular, from that punishment which it is your province and your duty to inflict on so scandalous an abuse of public trust. (Wall *vs.* MacNamara.)

May it please the court, I have hastily analyzed and presented the evidence under charge second. If we have not travelled through the history of those long weary months of suffering, torture, starvation, and death, and become familiar with each day's roll of those who passed away, the mind could not contemplate this last though briefer roster of the dead without feelings of utmost horror. Mortal man has never been called to answer before a legal tribunal to a catalogue of crime like this. One shudders at the fact, and almost doubts the age we live in. I would not harrow up your minds by dwelling further upon this woeful record. The obligation you have taken constitutes you the sole judge of both law and fact. I pray you administer the one, and decide the other, meting out to those involved in this crime of the universe all justice, without fear, favor, or partiality, and without regard to position, high or low, of those proved guilty.

N. P. CHIPMAN,
Col. and Additional Aide-de-Camp, Judge Advocate.

WIRZ' ABILITY TO USE BOTH HIS ARMS

OCTOBER 24, 1865.

At the request of counsel for the accused, Dr. C. M. Ford and Dr. John C. Bates made, in the presence of the court, an examination of the physical condition of the prisoner.

By consent of the judge advocate,

Dr. C. M. FORD was called as a witness for the defence, and being duly sworn, was examined as follows:

By COUNSEL:

Q. State what is your position.

A. I am acting assistant surgeon in the army of the United States, in charge of the hospital at the Old Capitol.

Q. Have you, during some time past, been in the habit of seeing the prisoner?

A. Yes, sir; since June, I believe, ever since his imprisonment, he has been under my care when sick.

Q. Have you during that time examined his right arm, and have you examined it today?

A. Yes, sir.

Q. What do you find to be the present condition of his arm?

A. It is swollen and inflamed, ulcerated in three places; and it has the appearance of having been broken. In addition to that, I believe that portions of both bones of the arm are dead.

Q. State your professional opinion as to the strength of his arm in its present condition? Would he be capable with that arm of pushing or knocking down a person, or using any heavy or even a light instrument in doing so?

A. I don't know that I can answer that question entirely. I don't know how much strength he has in the arm; but I should think him incapable of knocking a man down, or lifting a very heavy instrument of any kind, without doing great injury to the arm.

Q. Have you examined also the prisoner's left shoulder?

A. Yes, sir.

Q. State what you found to be its condition.

A. There is a very large scar on the left shoulder, and a portion—about half, I should suppose—the outer half of the muscle of the shoulder. The deltoid muscle is entirely gone—I suppose from the wound; it has been carried away, only the front part of the muscle of the shoulder remaining.

Q. How does that influence the strength of the arm?

A. It prevents in a great measure the action of the deltoid muscle, the use of which is to elevate the arm. It would prevent the perfect elevation of the arm. It has no influence at all on the flexion of the arm at the elbow, or striking out with the fore-arm from the elbow; it does not have any material effect as to that.

Q. How do you find the fingers of the prisoner's right hand?

A. I believe that two fingers, the little finger and the next, are slightly contracted; not permanently so, I believe. I am not positive, but I think I could straighten them. The contraction is due to the injury of the nerve leading down to the fingers.

Q. Have you examined the legs of the prisoner?

A. I have.

Q. What do you find to be their condition?

A. I find both of them covered with dark brown scars, as if they had been ulcerated at one time.

Q. Do you find traces of his having had the scurvy?

A. Yes, sir.

Q. State your professional opinion as to the bodily strength of the prisoner, so far as regards his ability to do any injury to any one?

A. He is now in a very prostrated condition; and I should not think him now capable of doing much violence to any one in the present condition of his system.

Q. Taking into consideration the general condition of his arms, legs, and bodily frame, do you think him capable of exerting himself to any extent in doing injury to anybody, pushing a man down, or anything of that kind?

A. I believe that he might push a person down, but I do not think he would be apt to exert himself to do any act of violence, because in doing that he would be very apt to do injury to himself.

By the JUDGE ADVOCATE:

Q. In what you have said, you speak of the prisoner's present condition?

A. Yes, sir.

Q. The opinion which you give has no reference to the condition in which he was a year ago?

A. No, sir.

Q. From the symptoms presented, can you reason back and tell us what was his condition in 1864?

A. I should not think the right arm was any better in 1864 than it is now. The scurvy, if he was suffering from it then, might make the wound worse. Scurvy or similar disease will often cause fractures to open again after being reunited.

Q. Can you say with certainty what was the prisoner's condition a year ago?

A. I cannot; but the external appearances would indicate that there had been a very extensive injury to the bones and the tissues.

By the COURT:

Q. Can you say whether the wound has ever healed, and this is the second breaking out of it?

A. No, sir; I do not know; I first met the prisoner in June, when he came to the prison. The wound was then in very nearly the same condition as now.

The PRISONER. In 1863, my health failing, I asked a furlough to go to Europe, and received it after an examination by the chief surgeon at the hospital at Richmond. I went to Europe and had my wound operated upon at Paris. The doctor there thought that all the dead bone had come out. After spending several months in Switzerland, I returned to England, and from there to the Confederate States. On shipboard, three or four months afterwards, the wound broke open again, and has been in its present condition since February, 1864.

By consent of the judge advocate,
Dr. JOHN C. BATES, being recalled, was examined as a witness for the defence.

By COUNSEL:

Q. You have heard the opinion just given by Dr. Ford; give us your general opinion about the state of the prisoner's health.

A. I have the advantage of Dr. Ford in having seen the prisoner at Andersonville; but while there I never examined him professionally. I noticed on several occasions that he had difficulty in using his right arm. I never inquired what was the matter. As I stated some time since, he was feeble in September, 1864, and did not look like a man enjoying the best of health. The impression of some of the medical gentlemen at Andersonville (you can take it for what it is worth) was, that there was in his system a constitutional syphilitic taint. For that reason, I asked him to let me examine his shanks. There is, it seems to me, an intermingling of the scorbutic and syphilitic taint. When this first manifested itself I do not know. I agree with Dr. Ford in all that he has said; there is nothing from which I would dissent. I concur in his opinion in reference to the left shoulder, the destruction of a portion of the deltoid muscle, and also in his opinion in reference to the right arm, the inability to use it with any considerable degree of force in lifting or striking. He could not use the right arm very extensively, without injury to the bones, which are partially destroyed.

By the JUDGE ADVOCATE:

Q. May not a man disabled in the arm so that he cannot strike out straight, without danger of injury to himself, be still able to use a pistol with great effect by exercising the wrist?

A. In the case of injury or partial destruction of the main muscle of the shoulder, he might use the arm from the elbow; but the upper portion of the arm would remain partially inactive.

By COUNSEL:

Q. Would it cause the prisoner any pain if he should use a pistol or any instrument, by striking from the elbow with his right arm?

A. I should think so; considering the condition of the bones and the ulceration, it might be a serious injury to them.

FINDINGS AND SENTENCE

The court, being cleared for deliberation, and having maturely considered the evidence adduced, find the accused, Henry Wirz, as follows:

Of the specification to charge I, "guilty," after amending said specification to read as follows:

In this, that he, the said Henry Wirz, did combine, confederate, and conspire with them, the said Jefferson Davis, James A. Seddon, Howell Cobb, John H. Winder, Richard B. Winder, Isaiah H. White, W. S. Winder, W. Shelby Reed, R. R. Stevenson, S. P. Moore, ———— Kerr, late hospital steward at Andersonville, James Duncan, Wesley W. Turner, Benjamin Harris, and others whose names are unknown, citizens of the United States aforesaid, and who were then engaged in armed rebellion against the United States, maliciously, traitorously, and in violation of the laws of war, to impair and injure the health and to destroy the lives, by subjecting to torture and great suffering, by confining in unhealthy and unwholesome quarters, by exposing to the inclemency of winter and to the dews and burning suns of summer, by compelling the use of impure water, and by furnishing insufficient and unwholesome food, of large numbers of federal prisoners, to wit, the number of about forty-five thousand soldiers in the military service of the United States of America, held as prisoners of war at Andersonville, in the State of Georgia, within the lines of the so-called Confederate States, on or before the 27th day of March, A. D. 1864, and at divers times between that day and the 10th day of April, A. D. 1865, to the end that the armies of the United States might be weakened and impaired, and the insurgents engaged in armed rebellion against the United States might be aided and comforted; and he, the said Henry Wirz, an officer in the military service of the so-called Confederate States, being then and there commandant of a military prison at Andersonville, in the State of Georgia, located by authority of the so-called Confederate States, for the confinement of prisoners of war, and, as such commandant, fully clothed with authority, and in duty bound, to treat, care, and provide for such prisoners, held as aforesaid, as were or might be placed in his custody, according to the law of war, did, in furtherance of such combination, confederation, and conspiracy, maliciously, wickedly and traitorously confine a large number of prisoners of war, soldiers in the military service of the United States, to the number of about forty-five thousand men, in unhealthy and unwholesome quarters, in a close and small area of ground, wholly inadequate to their wants and destructive to their health, which he well knew and intended; and while there so confined, during the time aforesaid, did, in furtherance of his evil design and in aid of the said conspiracy, wilfully and maliciously neglect to furnish tents, barracks, or other shelter, sufficient for their protection from the inclemency of winter and the dews and burning sun of summer; and with such evil intent did take and cause to be taken from them their clothing, blankets, camp equipage and other property of which they were possessed at the time of being placed in his custody; and with like malice and evil intent did refuse to furnish or cause to be furnished food either of a quality or quantity sufficient to preserve health and sustain life; and did refuse and neglect to furnish wood sufficient for cooking in summer and to keep the said prisoners warm in winter, and did compel the said prisoners to subsist upon unwholesome food, and that in limited quantities, entirely inadequate to sustain health, which he well knew; and did compel the said prisoners to use unwholesome water, reeking with the filth and garbage of the prison and prison-guard, and the offal and drainage of the cook-house of said prison; whereby the prisoners became greatly reduced in their bodily strength and emaciated and injured in their bodily health; their minds impaired and their intellects broken; and many of them, to wit, about the number of ten thousand, whose names are unknown, sickened and died by reason thereof, which he, the said Henry Wirz, then and there well knew and intended; and so knowing and evilly intending, did refuse and neglect to provide proper lodgings, food, or nourishment for the sick, and necessary medicine and medical attendance for the restoration of their health, and did knowingly, wilfully and maliciously, in furtherance of his evil designs, permit them to languish and die from want of care and proper treatment; and the said Henry Wirz, still pursuing his evil purposes, did permit to remain in the said prison, among the emaciated sick and languishing living, the bodies of the dead, until they became corrupt and loathsome, and filled the air with fetid and noxious exhalations, and thereby greatly increased the unwholesomeness of the prison, insomuch that great numbers of said prisoners, whose names are unknown, sickened and died by reason thereof. And the said Henry Wirz, still pursuing his wicked and cruel purpose, wholly disregarding the usages of civilized warfare, did at the time and place aforesaid maliciously and wilfully subject the prisoners aforesaid to cruel, unusual and infamous punishment, upon slight, trivial and fictitious pretences, by fastening large balls of iron to their feet, and binding numbers of the prisoners aforesaid closely together with large chains around their necks and feet, so that they walked with the greatest difficulty; and being so confined, were subjected to the burning rays of the sun, often without food or drink, for hours and even days, from which said cruel treatment numbers whose names are unknown sickened, fainted, and died; and he, the said Wirz, did further cruelly treat and injure said prisoners by maliciously tying them up by the thumbs, and wilfully confining them within an instrument of torture called the stocks, thus depriving them of the use of their limbs, and forcing them to lie, sit, and stand for many hours without the power of changing position, and being without food or drink, in consequence of which many, whose names are unknown, sickened and died; and he, the said Wirz, still wickedly pursuing his evil purpose, did establish and cause to be designated, within the prison enclosure containing said prisoners, a "dead-line," being a line around the inner face of the stockade or wall, enclosing said prison, and about 25 feet distant from and within said stockade; and having so established said dead-line, which was in some places an imaginary line, and in other places marked by insecure and shifting strips of boards, nailed upon the top of small and insecure stakes or posts, he, the said Wirz, instructed the prison guards stationed around the top of said stockade to fire upon and kill any of the prisoners aforesaid who might fall upon, pass over or under or cross the said dead-line, pursuant to which said orders and instructions, maliciously and needlessly given by said Wirz, the said prison guard did fire upon and kill a number of said prisoners; and the said Wirz, still pursuing his evil purpose, did keep and use ferocious and blood-thirsty dogs, dangerous to human life, to hunt down prisoners of war aforesaid who made their escape from his custody; and did, then and there, wilfully and maliciously suffer, incite and encourage the said dogs to seize, tear, mangle, and maim the bodies and limbs of said fugitive prisoners of war, which the said dogs, incited as aforesaid, then and there did, whereby a number of said prisoners of war who, during the time aforesaid, made their escape and were recaptured, died; and the said Wirz, still pursuing his wicked purpose, and still aiding in carrying out said conspiracy, did cause to be used for the pretended purposes of vaccination impure and poisonous vaccine matter, which said impure and poisonous matter was then and there, by the direction and order of said Wirz, maliciously, cruelly, and wickedly, deposited in the arms of many of said prisoners, by reason of which large numbers of them lost the use of their arms, and many of them were so injured that they soon thereafter died; all of which he, the said Henry Wirz, well knew and maliciously intended, and, in aid of the then existing rebellion against the United States, with the view to assist in weakening and impairing the armies of the United States, and in furtherance of the said conspiracy, and with the full knowledge, consent, and connivance of his co-conspirators aforesaid, he, the said Wirz, then and there did.

Of charge I, "guilty," after amending said charge to read as follows:

Maliciously, wilfully and traitorously, and in aid of the then existing armed rebellion against the United States of America, on or before the 27th day of March A. D. 1864, and on divers other days between that day and the tenth day of April, 1865, combining, confederating and conspiring together with Jefferson Davis, James A. Seddon, Howell Cobb, John H. Winder, Richard B. Winder, Isaiah H. White, W. S. Winder, W. Shelby Reed, R. R. Stevenson, S. P. Moore, —— Kerr, late hospital steward at Andersonville, James Duncan, Wesley W. Turner, Benjamin Harris and others unknown, to injure the health and destroy the lives of soldiers in the military service of the United States, then held and being prisoners of war within the lines of the so-called Confederate States and in the military prisons thereof, to the end that the armies of the United States might be weakened and impaired; in violation of the laws and customs of war.

Of specification first to the charge II, "guilty," adding the words "or about" immediately before the phrase "the ninth day of July."

Of specification second to charge II, "guilty."

Of specification third to charge II, "guilty," after striking out "June," and inserting instead "September."

Of specification four to charge II, "not guilty."

Of specification five to charge II, "guilty," after striking out the phrase "on the thirtieth day," and inserting instead the phrase, "on or about the twenty-fifth day."

Of specification six to charge II, "guilty," after striking out the word "first," and inserting "fifteenth," and also striking out the phrase "on the sixth day," and inserting instead the phrase "on or about the sixteenth day."

Of specification seven to charge II, "guilty," after striking out the word "twentieth," and inserting instead the word "first," and also after inserting "or about" immediately before the phrase "the twenty-fifth day."

Of specification eight to charge II, "guilty."

Of specification nine to charge II, "guilty."

Of specification ten to charge II, "not guilty."

Of specification eleven to charge II, "guilty," after striking out the word "first," and inserting instead the word "sixth;" after striking out also the phrase "incite and urge" and the phrase "encouragement and instigation," and by adding the words "or about" after the word "on," where it last occurs in the specification; and also after striking out the phrase "animals called bloodhounds," and inserting the word "dogs;" and also striking out the word "bloodhounds" where it afterwards occurs, and inserting the word "dogs;" and also striking out the words "given by him."

Of specification twelve to charge II, "guilty."

Of specification thirteen to charge II, "not guilty."

Of the second charge, "guilty."

And the court do therefore sentence him, the said Henry Wirz, to be hanged by the neck till he be dead, at such time and place as the President of the United States may direct, two-thirds of the members of the court concurring herein.

LEW. WALLACE,
Major General and President of Com.

N. P. CHIPMAN,
Col. and Add. A. D. C., Judge Advocate.

And the court also find the prisoner, Henry Wirz, guilty of having caused the death, in manner as alleged in specification eleven to charge II, by means of dogs, of three prisoners of war in his custody and soldiers of the United States, one occurring on or about the 15th day of May, 1864; another occurring on or about the 11th day of July, 1864; another occurring on or about the 1st day of September, 1864, but which finding as here expressed has not and did not enter into the sentence of the court as before given.

LEW. WALLACE,
Major General and President of Com.

N. P. CHIPMAN,
Col. and Add. A. D. C., Judge Advocate.

————

REPORT OF THE JUDGE ADVOCATE GENERAL

WAR DEPARTMENT, BUREAU OF MILITARY JUSTICE,
October 31, 1865.

To the PRESIDENT:

Henry Wirz was tried by a military commission, convened at Washington, D. C., on the 23d day of August, 1865, by order of the President of the United States, on the following charges and specifications.

[Here follow the charges and specifications.]

Upon being arraigned, the prisoner's counsel submitted the following pleas: 1st. That he ought not to be held or tried, for any cause, by the government of the United States, because, according to the terms of the surrender of the rebel General Johnson, under whose command he was serving at the time, it was agreed that all officers and men should be permitted to return to their homes, not to be disturbed by the United States authorities so long as they observed their obligations and the laws in force where they resided. 2d. That he should not be held to trial, or in custody, because, at the time of his arrest he was in the enjoyment of his liberty, and was promised by Captain Noyes, of Major General Wilson's staff, that he should not be held as a prisoner, but that after giving such verbal information to General Wilson as he was able, he should have a safe conduct to his home, which promise was violated. 3d. That the commission had no jurisdiction to try him for the offences charged; also, that he had been on the 21st of August arraigned and put on trial before the same tribunal on the same charges, and could not be tried or "put to answer" a second time therefor. Also, that the charges and specifications were too vague and indefinite, and did not make out an offence, punishable by the laws of war.

All these pleas were discussed at length on both sides, and were, after deliberation, properly overruled by the commission.

A plea of "not guilty" to both charges and specifications thereto was then made by the prisoner.

The investigation of the matters alleged against the prisoner then commenced, and continued until the 21st day of October, during which time 148 witnesses for the prosecution and defence were examined, and a large amount of documentary evidence found in the official papers captured at Andersonville, and among the rebel archives at Richmond, was introduced.

One of the counsel for the defence then asked for an adjournment of two weeks at least to enable him to prepare an argument.

The commission first decided to adjourn ten days, and upon his further petition, twelve days, for this purpose. He, however, declared that it was insufficient time, and thereupon announced that he would submit the case without remark. After an adjournment of four days, an elaborate statement of the prisoner was submitted, which was prepared by him, with the aid of an able assistant, (the chief reporter of the trial, who shows himself familiar with all the material facts) which goes over the whole case in explanation of certain acts averred, and in denial of the proof or truth of all the others.

The closing address of the judge advocate immediately followed; and thereafter the court, it appears, having maturely considered the evidence adduced, found the accused, Henry Wirz, as follows:

[Here follow the findings and sentence of the court.]

It is not necessary for the purposes of this review to go into an elaborate discussion of the question involved in the findings on the first charge. From the document of the proceedings, containing more than 500 pages, presenting a mass of evidence bearing upon these questions, no brief summary can be made which would do justice to the subject. The argument of the judge advocate sets forth an able and exhaustive examination of the material legal points raised and proof established by the trial, and forms a part of the record. It may be relied on as giving a full and just exposition of the matters which entered into the deliberations of the court, and, as particularly applicable to this branch of the case, reference is respectfully invited to pages 4838 to 5148. The opinion is expressed that the conspiracy, as described in the findings above recited, was clearly made out, and that the conclusions arrived at by the court could not, in the light of the evidence this records contains, have been avoided.

Language fails in an attempt to denounce, even in faint terrors, the diabolical combination for the destruction and death, by cruel and fiendishly ingenious processes, of helpless prisoners of war who might fall into their hands, which this record shows was plotted and deliberately entered upon, and, as far as time permitted, accomplished by the rebel authorities and their brutal underlings at Andersonville prison. Criminal history presents no parallel to this monstrous conspiracy, and from the whole catalogue of infamous devices within reach of human hands, a system for the murder of men more revolting in its details could not have been planned. Upon the heads of those named by the court in its findings the guilt of this immeasurable crime is fixed, a guilt so fearfully black and horrible, that the civilized world must be appalled by the spectacle.

There remains yet to be noticed the matter involved in the second charge. The homicides alleged to have been committed under this charge, and which the court found were committed, are of four classes: First. Those cases of death which resulted from the biting of dogs. (Specification II.) Second. Cases of death which resulted from confinement in the stocks and chain-gang. (Specifications 5, 6, 7.) Third. Cases of prisoners killed by guards, pursuant to *direct* orders of Wirz, given at the time, (Specifications 8, 9, 12.) Fourth. Cases of prisoners killed by Wirz' own hand. (Specifications 1, 2, 3.)

That all the deaths embraced in these four classes resulted from the causes and in the manner set forth in the specifications, is conceived to be very clearly established by the evidence adduced by the prosecution, and it is not deemed necessary, in the absence of any contradictory testimony directly bearing on these instances, to recite the evidence applicable to each, except, it may be, briefly, that relating to the fourth class, (Specifications 1, 2, 3,) and some acts of a similar character.

The testimony supporting the first specification is that of Felix de la Baume, a Union soldier, who states, that on or about the 8th of July, 1864, he was one of a detachment of prisoners taken to Wirz' headquarters to be enrolled, before being sent into the prison; that one of his comrades was attacked with epilepsy, and some of his companions, by permission of the guard, ran to the creek for water; that he, the witness, heard a shot fired, and, on turning, saw Wirz fire two more, wounding two prisoners, one of whom the witness never saw nor heard of afterwards; and the other of whom he saw carried up to Wirz' headquarters, in a dying condition, the wound being in the breast.

There is also the testimony of George Conway, who states, that on or about the 11th of July, 1864, he saw Wirz shoot a Union prisoner within the stockade as he was stooping to pick up his cup, which had fallen under the dead-line, and that the man died almost instantly.

Which of these two cases (either being, it is conceived, sufficient to sustain the allegation) the court relied on, does not, of course, appear.

In support of the second specification, Martin E. Hogan testifies that some time in September, when the prisoners were being removed from Andersonville to Millen, he saw Wirz take a prisoner, who was worn out with hunger and disease, by the coat-collar, and, because he could not walk faster, wrench him back and stamp upon him with his boots; that the man was borne past him (witness) bleeding from his mouth and nose, and died in a short time.

The third specification is supported by the testimony of George W. Gray, who states, that about the middle of September, 1864, he and a comrade named William Stewart, a private belonging to a Minnesota regiment, went out of the stockade, in charge of a guard, to carry a dead body, and that after laying it in the dead-house they were on their way back to the stockade, when Wirz rode up to them and asked, "by what authority they were out there;" that Stewart replied, they were out there by proper authority; whereupon Wirz drew his revolver and shot Stewart, the ball taking effect in his breast and killing him instantly; and that the guard then took from his body some twenty or thirty dollars, which Wirz received and rode away.

Further evidence in regard to Wirz killing certain prisoners was presented, but the dates given by the witnesses show the murders to have been other than those alleged in the specifications. They will be referred to as illustrating the character of the prisoner, and establishing a frequency and repetition of like crimes.

James H. Davidson, testified, that in April, as he remembered, Wirz came into the stockade one day, and a lame man went up to him and asked him a question, whereupon Wirz *"turned around" and shot him,* and he died.

Thomas C. Alcoke states that one day (the witness seems to have no knowledge or recollection of dates) Wirz came into the stockade and man asked of him permission to go out and get some fresh air; that Wirz asked him what he meant, and that after a few more words had passed between them, Wirz *"wheeled around,"* pulled out a revolver *and shot him down,* the ball taking effect in his breast, and death occurring about three hours afterwards. It also appears by this witness, that when he remonstrated, Wirz told him he "had better look out, or he would be put in the same place," and that soon after Wirz came in with a guard and put him in irons.

Hugh R. Snee testified, that some time in September, 1864, a party of Union prisoners were to be exchanged under an arrangement between General Sherman and the rebel Hood; that they were taken from the stockade after dark, as the heat in the day was so great that the men would have fainted; that none but able-bodied men were selected, it being stated when they were called out, that any one who could not walk 18 miles a day would be shot; that notwithstanding this, the men were so anxious to escape imprisonment that some too weak to perform the day's travel came out. The witness states that three, who belonged to some western regiments, were able to go but a short distance, before they fainted and fell out of the ranks, and were pushed one side by the guard; that thereupon a man ran back, and speaking in a voice he *thought at the time to be that of Captain Wirz,* wanted to know why they were there; that they replied, they wished to get out of prison; whereupon this man said, "I'll help you out, God damn you." Witness then heard six pistol-shots, followed by a cry as if some one was hurt, "and immediately after, a rebel lieutenant came past remarking that it was a brutal act;" "that one of them was dead," and when asked "who did it," replied, "the *captain.*"

The most prominent features of the defence under this second charge will now be considered:

An attempt was made to prove that during the whole of August and parts of July and September the prisoner was sick and confined to his bed, and could not have committed the crimes charged to him in those months. In his statement to the court, however, he made no reference to his absence—doubtless for the reason that the testimony was of too general and loose a character to set up as contradictory to the explicit statements of numerous witnesses as to the dates when the crimes recorded in the finding were committed, corroborated as those statements were, by official papers, bearing his signature, showing that at different times during those months he was in the performance of his ordinary functions as commandant of the prison.

It was claimed that deaths resulting from the use of dogs, in the capture of escaped prisoners, were not crimes fastened upon Wirz, he not being present at the pursuit and therefore not responsible. But it appears to have been the fact that this use of dogs was under Wirz' special direction; that the pursuit of prisoners was in many instances initiated under his immediate orders, and in some cases captures were made under his personal supervision. It was also clearly proved that a part of each pack were ferocious dogs, dangerous to life, so as to make it probable that the men on whose track they were sent would be killed. A man overtaken by these beasts, and desiring to surrender, could not, by coming to a stand, save his life; the instinct of the dogs was for human blood, and to surrender to them was death. A most shocking illustration will be given. Two soldiers had escaped, but were overtaken; the party who captured them returned with but one, (who was so mangled that he died) and the chief of the party, known as Turner, exulted in accounting for the other, stating that they allowed the dogs to tear him in pieces, and left him in the woods.

As applying to the question of criminal responsibility involved in this class of homicides, the judge advocate referred the court to the well settled principle of law, that it is not essential that the hand of the party should be the immediate occasion of the death, but that if it be shown that means were used likely to occasion death, and which did so occasion it, the party using such means is to be held responsible for the consequences.

There is but one of this class of homicides which enters into the findings of "guilty," under this charge. A discussion of the legal points involved is conceived to be needless, inasmuch as the charge is sustained by a conviction on nine other distinct allegations of murder.

As to the deaths resulting from the use of stocks and chain-gangs, the defence urged that the men were placed therein for the purposes of discipline; that they were commonly used for such purposes, and that their use at this place was attributed to those higher in authority than Wirz, to whose orders he was subject. Upon this point it is to be observed that prisoners were put in these instruments of torture as punishment for having escaped, or having made attempts to escape from their captors, which attempts, whether successful or not, it was their right and duty as prisoners of war to make. Any punishment inflicted upon them, therefore, by their captors was a violation of the laws of war, and deaths resulting from such unlawful punishment are murders. This would be the judgment of the law apart from some of the peculiar circumstances which surround these crimes, and which so decidedly indicate their true character, prominent among which is the often declared animus of the prisoner, showing conclusively that in these and kindred barbarities he was deliberately seeking to sacrifice the lives of his victims. It was shown that these stocks and chain-gangs were under Wirz' immediate and direct control; that he exercised full authority in committing prisoners to both. While it may be and probably is the fact that his action in this matter was sanctioned by the rebel Winder when he was on duty at that place, it does not relieve the prisoner of responsibility for the result.

Relating to the three homicides embraced in the third class, the prisoner makes no special defence, except as to the killing of the man known as Chickamauga. He urges in his final statement, that his order to the guard to shoot this man was only intended as a menace. It is clear, however, from the testimony, that his order in this case, as in the others, was peremptory, and, according to his own version, it was not a command that could be construed by any subordinate as merely a menace; moreover, it was distinctly proved to have been accompanied by a threat that he would shoot the guard if the guard did not shoot this crippled soldier. He states further, and it is so found by the record, that this poor man desired to be killed, it would seem, because he was suspected by his comrades of having given information to the prison-keepers of some attempts of prisoners to escape from the stockade. This fact, however, in no degree palliates his murderous guilt.

Of the homicides embraced in the fourth class (those committed directly by his own hands) the prisoner's statement notices but one, that of Stewart, sworn to by the witness Gray. It is asserted that the testimony of this witness is a pure fabrication. There is nothing found in the examination of the record which casts a doubt on his veracity, and the court seems to have discovered nothing in his manner on the stand to raise the question of his credibility.

As to all those cases not heretofore specially mentioned, the defence insists that the allegations were too vague and indefinite, and that the testimony is insufficient to sustain them, and also that it is altogether improbable that such murders could have been committed without coming to the knowledge of various witnesses, who stated that they had never heard of such crimes at Andersonville. No evidence being submitted which contradicts the concurrent and explicit statements of the witnesses who gave positive testimony of their perpetration, these murders are fastened to Wirz' hands.

Many points were raised by both sides relating to the admission of evidence as the trial progressed. These were fully debated at the time. No discussion of them here is deemed necessary, it not being found that competent proof material to the prisoner's defence on the specific offences of which the court pronounced him guilty was excluded.

Much latitude seems to have been given him. He was allowed to show special acts of kindness to prisoners, and to introduce declarations made by himself in explanation of his acts. Letters and official reports, and oral testimony of his personal efforts, offered as indicating his interest in, and a care for, the comfort of the prisoners, were also admitted. It is shown that every witness asked for by the defence was subpœnaed, except certain rebel functionaries, who, for reasons stated at the time, did not appear on the stand. But the judge advocate proposed that if the counsel for the defence would set forth, according to the common rule by affidavit, *what* he expected and *had reason to believe* any witness who did not so appear *would* testify, it would be admitted of record that such witness would so testify. This proposition was not accepted. One hundred and six witnesses were subpœnaed for the defence, of whom 68 reported, but 39 of these, many of them soldiers of our army, and sufferers at Andersonville, were discharged by the prisoner's counsel without being put upon the stand.

A review of the proceedings leads to the opinion that no prejudice to the legal rights of the prisoner can be successfully claimed to have resulted from any decision which excluded testimony he desired to introduce. The trial is believed to have been conducted in accordance with the regulations governing military courts, and the record presents no error which can be held to invalidate the proceedings.

The annals of our race present nowhere and at no time a darker field of crime than that of Andersonville, and it is fortunate for the interests alike of public justice and of historic truth, that from this field the veil has been so faithfully and so completely lifted. All the horrors of this pandemonium of the rebellion are laid bare to us in the broad, steady light of the testimony of some 150 witnesses who spoke what they had seen and heard and suffered, and whose evidence, given under oath and subjected to cross-examination and to every other test which human experience has devised for the ascertainment of truth, must be accepted as affording an immovable foundation for the sentence pronounced.

The proof under the second charge shows that some of our soldiers, for mere attempts to escape from their oppressors, were given to ferocious dogs to be torn in pieces; that others were confined in stocks and chains till life yielded to the torture, and that others were wantonly shot down at Wirz' bidding or by his own hand. Here in the presence of these pitiless murders of unarmed and helpless men, so distinctly alleged and proved, justice might well claim the prisoner's life. There remain, however, to be contemplated crimes yet more revolting, for which he and his co-conspirators must be held responsible. The Andersonville prison records (made exhibits in this case) contain a roster of over thirteen thousand (13,000) dead, buried naked, maimed, and putrid, in one vast sepulchre. Of these, a surgeon of the rebel army who was on duty at this prison, testifies that at least three-fourths died of the treatment inflicted on them while in confinement; and a surgeon of our own army, who was a prisoner there, states that four-fifths died from this cause. Under this proof, which has not been assailed, nearly 10,000, if not more, of these deaths must be charged directly to the account of Wirz and his associates. This widespread sacrifice of life was not made suddenly or under the influence of wild, ungovernable passion, but was accomplished slowly and deliberately, by packing upwards of 30,000 men, like cattle, in a fetid pen—a mere cesspool, there to die for need of air to breathe, for want of ground on which to lie, from lack of shelter from sun and rain, and from the slow, agonizing processes of starvation; when air and space and shelter and food were all within the ready gift of their tormentors. This work of death seems to have been a saturnalia of enjoyment for the prisoner, who amid these savage orgies evidenced such exultation and mingled with them such nameless blasphemy and ribald jests, as at times to exhibit him rather as a demon than a man. It was his continual boast that by these barbarities he was destroying more Union soldiers than rebel generals were butchering on the battle-field. He claimed to be doing the work of the rebellion, and faithfully, in all his murderous cruelty and baseness, did he represent its spirit. It is by looking upon the cemeteries which have been filled from Libby, Belle Isle, Salisbury, Florence, and Andersonville, and other rebel prisons, and recalling the prolonged sufferings of the patriots who are sleeping there, that we can best understand the inner and real life of the rebellion, and the hellish criminality and brutality of the traitors who maintained it. For such crimes human power is absolutely impotent to enforce any adequate atonement.

It may be added, in conclusion, that the court before which the prisoner was tried was composed of officers high in rank, and eminent for their faithful services and probity of character, and that several of them were distinguished for their legal attainments. The investigation of the case was conducted throughout with patience and impartiality, and the conclusion reached is one from which the overwhelming volume of testimony left no escape. It is recommended that the sentence be executed.

J. HOLT,
Judge Advocate General.

ORDER OF THE PRESIDENT
[General Court-martial Orders No. 607.]

WAR DEPARTMENT, ADJUTANT GENERAL'S OFFICE,
Washington, November 6, 1865.

I. Before a military commission which convened at Washington, D. C., August 23, 1865, pursuant to paragraph 3, Special Orders No. 453, dated August 23, 1865, and paragraph 13, Special Orders No. 524, dated October 2, 1865, War Department, Adjutant General's Office, Washington, and of which Major General Lewis Wallace, United States volunteers, is president, was arraigned and tried Henry Wirz.

[Here follow the charges, specifications, findings, and sentence.]

*   *   *   *   *   *   *

II. The proceedings, findings, and sentence in the foregoing case having been submitted to the President of the United States, the following are his orders:

EXECUTIVE MANSION, *November 3, 1865.*

The proceedings, findings, and sentence of the court in the within case are approved, and it is ordered that the sentence be carried into execution, by the officer commanding the department of Washington, on Friday, the 10th day of November, 1865, between the hours of 6 o'clock a. m. and 12 o'clock noon.

ANDREW JOHNSON, *President.*

III. Major General C. C. Augur, commanding the department of Washington, is commanded to cause the foregoing sentence, in the case of Henry Wirz, to be duly executed, in accordance with the President's order.

IV. The military commission, of which Major General Lewis Wallace, United States volunteers, is president, is hereby dissolved.

By command of the President of the United States:

E. D. TOWNSEND,
Assistant Adjutant General.

Official:

E. D. TOWNSEND,
Assistant Adjutant General.

LETTER OF THE COMMANDING GENERAL DEPARTMENT OF WASHINGTON, REPORTING THE EXECUTION AND BURIAL OF HENRY WIRZ

HEADQUARTERS DEPARTMENT OF WASHINGTON,
Washington, D. C., November 11, 1865.

SIR: I have the honor to report that the sentence and orders of the President in the case of Henry Wirz, as promulgated in General Court-martial Orders No. 607, dated War Department, Adjutant General's Office, Washington, November 6, 1865, have been duly executed (between the hours of 10 and 11 a. m.) yesterday, November 10, and his body has been interred by the side of Atzerodt, in the arsenal grounds.

I am, general, very respectfully, your obedient servant,

C. C. AUGUR,
Major Gen. Vols., Commanding Department.

The ADJUTANT GENERAL *of the Army.*

NOTES

1. New Yorkers—hoodlums, thieves and wanted criminals from the slums of New York, who joined the Union Army for the $300 bounty paid by draft dodgers as legal substitutes.

2. Soldiers receiving the $300 bounty to substitute for drafted men, and who deserted at the first opportunity, only to reappear in the ranks under assumed names. Many men repeated this practice as many as four and five times. When they were caught, they were usually brought back in shackles.

3. The Crimean War, 1856–1858.

4. An herb grown in the south used for forage and manure. The seed of the plant is sometimes used for food.

5. During the 1860's and 1880's the Army Medical Museum in Washington had many exhibits showing this type of wound, especially from Indian arrowheads imbedded in the skull.

6. McElroy's figures on the British losses are in error; 2000 men were killed in the action including three generals, among them General Pakenham. General Andrew Jackson's losses were 13 killed and three wounded. The action lasted less than an hour.

7. McElroy's figure is correct. Most of the men died from the effects of scurvy and gangrene and malnutrition. There were also numerous mental cases.

8. McElroy's friend's full name was Bezaleel B. Andrews. He was nicknamed "Lale." He became a physician after the war.

9. Men whose terms of enlistment specified one hundred days (3-month volunteers).

10. A photograph on black japanned iron (tin) similar to a tintype.

11. McElroy is speaking in round figures. The exact total at one given time was 41,768 prisoners. This figure is probably correct.

12. Japanned tin.

13. McElroy claims that "few rebels had the requisite clerical skill" for such a job, that most could not read or write. It was therefore necessary that they detail prisoners who could.

14. General Benjamin Franklin Butler with his Army of the James was ordered to land at Bermuda Hundred, a small strip of land between the Appomattox and James rivers, and hold City Point as a base. On May 4th Butler, with 40,000 men, occupied City Point. Butler delayed too long and was attacked and disastrously defeated at Drewery's Bluff by Beauregard, who trapped Butler and his entire army and "bottled" them up until the end of the war.

15. These were made by simply filling 3-inch cannon balls with powder and fuses. These "homemade" grenades were used at Vicksburg and at Fort Wagner during the siege of Petersburg.

16. Sergeant Corbett, a reformed alcoholic and Bowery drifter, frequented Bowery missions. Corbett was with Colonel Baker's cavalry troop when it trapped John Wilkes Booth in Garrett's barn, and claimed to have fired the fatal shot that killed Booth. Though it was against orders, Corbett said that "Providence directed him to fire." Whether he did or whether Booth shot himself is still a mystery.

17. Hebraic—Benai Regesh or "Sons of Thunder" or an especially vociferous preacher.

18. Accumulated army pay.

19. McElroy means that the force of "Egypt's" fist was like a kick from a *healthy* mule.

20. McElroy refers to the painting "Death on a Pale Horse" by Asher B. Durand.

21. Grant's "Grand Strategy," a coordinated movement of all the Federal Armies, instead of the former uncoordinated movements practiced before he took command.

22. Federal forces engaged, 58,000; Confederate forces engaged, 40,000. Federal, killed and wounded, 12,000; Confederate, killed and wounded, 9,000. Total 21,000.

23. Sherman's campaign was a masterpiece of military maneuver. Johnston, employing the Roman Fabian's tactics of slow withdrawal, tried to hold Sherman by sudden slashing attacks. But Johnston's constant retreating originated a joke in Atlanta, to the effect that he "was preparing a fleet of transports to continue the retreat by water to the Bahamas."

24. New prisoners.

25. General John Bell Hood, an impetuous but loyal fighter bearing the wounds of former battles —the loss of an arm and a leg—borrowed a page from Stonewall Jackson's strategy at Chancellorsville, using the same maneuver against Sherman. But it was only a temporary triumph.

26. General John McPherson was one of the finest officers in the Army and one of the most capable. He was, perhaps, one of the best liked by officers and men alike. At the news of his death many soldiers cried. McPherson, it seems, was killed instantly by a bullet in the back when he mistakenly rode into a Confederate line while on a reconnaissance mission.

27. Spencer and Winchester repeating carbines which had first come into general use in 1864. The Springfield was the regulation single-shot musket.

28. Shortly after McElroy's book appeared, "Little Red Cap" whose real name was Ransom Powell, a Baltimorean, saw the book and contacted the author. For some time afterward, the two veterans of Andersonville corresponded with each other.

29. During the period of these five months—from May through September—the casualties at Andersonville, from all causes, amounted to 30,485, an average of 6,970 a month. The total figure is within 6,000 of the total casualty list of the Battle of Gettysburg; 37,000 in three days of fighting. Total number of men engaged, 163,000.

30. Ben Butler, known to the Southerners as "Beast Butler" for his questionable activities when he occupied New Orleans. Butler was the most feared and hated Federal officer in the entire South.

31. The battles of the Wilderness and Spotsylvania were the first battles Grant directed against Lee after taking supreme command of the Union Armies. The Wilderness was desperately fought in a vast expanse of tangled forest of briars, scrub oak and swamp, called "poison

fields," Spotsylvania was the result of Grant's famous "shift to the left"—an effort to place him-self between Lee and Richmond. The line of battle at the foremost salient took the form of a "mule shoe," the lines coming so close together that the men used their rifles as spears and clubs. For violent hand-to-hand action, Spotsylvania had no equal in the war.

32. An herb of the aster family used as a diaphoretic and tonic (ague weed).

33. The heavy, partly submerged trunk of a cypress tree.

34. The 6th Massachusetts Regiment was one of the first regiments to answer Lincoln's call for troops. The regiment was attacked by a group of hoodlums while passing through Baltimore. Several of the soldiers were wounded and one or two killed.

35. Captain Wirz was a native of Switzerland.

36. Major General George H. Thomas, or "Pap" as his men affectionately called him, engaged Hood's Army of Tennessee and, to all practical purposes, destroyed it as an army at Nashville, Tennessee, in one of the decisive battles of the war.

37. This is a strange role for Boston Corbett, who later capitalized on his fame as President Lincoln's avenger. Corbett became a Baptist Minister.

38. These derogatory terms originated during the march of General Irwin McDowell's Army to the first battle of Bull Run. They were applied to the undisciplined stragglers and skulkers who dropped out of ranks on the march to pick blackberries, boil coffee and "to wash their feet" in roadside streams and brooks.

39. By "able-bodied" McElroy means newly captured prisoners who had not yet undergone the full rigors of prison life.

40. The Etowah.

41. A term used by the prisoners meaning: to slip into the place of a man chosen for exchange. The prison authorities did not concern themselves too much with proof of identity.

42. A soldier fortunate enough to have his name on a list for exchange.

43. The annual Donnybrook Fair held in Ireland, noted for its riotous character, debauchery and fist fights.

44. General George B. McClellan, the Democratic nominee for President, stated in his letter of acceptance that he was for "a spirit of conciliation and compromise," but he never mentioned slavery. "But no peace can be permanent without Union," he said. McClellan had been ex-tremely popular with the Army of the Potomac. But he was not as well known to the men of the Western armies. It was this popularity that misled the Raiders into thinking the prisoners would vote for McClellan.

45. Edwin McMasters Stanton.

46. Major General Henry Wager Halleck, Chief of Staff.

47. Hood left Atlanta hoping that Sherman would follow him, and headed for Tennessee. He came upon the armies of Schofield at Franklin and Thomas at Nashville in November and De-cember. In two desperate battles, Hood's Army was almost annihilated. Federal losses—3,000 killed and wounded; Confederate losses—3,500 killed and wounded.

48. Savannah Exchange: the prisoners were taken to Annapolis before being treated, washed, fed and clothed, and were photographed as they were. Captain A. J. Russel was the photographer. The pictures were later published in the northern newspapers as propaganda.

49. One of the popular illustrated novels of the time.

50. In 1861, a popular phrase in the South was "that one gentleman could lick five Yankees." Throughout the war, the Southern armies gave ample proof of this statement.

51. After Atlanta, Hood thought he could lure Sherman out of Atlanta by striking out into Tennessee and that Sherman would follow him. But Sherman had other plans. Thomas and Schofield could take care of Hood in subordinate actions, while he, with the main force, "made Georgia howl." Sherman headed for Savannah and the sea in his famous march. The plan worked. Hood attacked Schofield and Thomas at Franklin and Nashville and wrecked his army.

52. Governor Joe Brown was an idiot, an unprincipled political demagogue. He refused to support the Confederacy and did more to wreck it than all the Union armies combined. He refused to let the Georgia Militia fight outside the State. Only when General Sherman was about to take Atlanta did he embrace the Confederate Cause as "ours."

53. Here McElroy is completely wrong. He omits General Wade Hampton, one of the finest officers in the entire Confederate Army, a gentleman and statesman of great ability. Wade Hampton and Robert E. Lee were of the same caliber.

54. Kershaw's and Perrin's South Carolina Brigades distinguished themselves at Gettysburg.

55. Slaves and the fertilizer discovered by Edmund Ruffin of Virginia, for the reclamation of worn-out soil was the "secret" McElroy mentions. Edmund Ruffin was reputed to be the man who fired the first shot at Fort Sumter.

56. These are the names of distinguished South Carolina families. Robert Barnwell Rhett was "the father of secession." Major Stephen Elliott had command of the garrison of Fort Sumter during the bombardment of 1863. General Gab. Manigault was State Ordnance Board officer during the action against Major Anderson at Fort Sumter in 1861.

57. The "Swamp Angel" was a rifled Parrott gun that fired a 200-pound shell. It was mounted on Morris Island, a marsh where the "mud was like liquid." General Q. A. Gilmore opened fire on Charleston with the "Swamp Angel," but the huge gun burst on the 36th shot; 17,000 pound Knox seacoast mortars, firing 300-pound shells, replaced it.

58. The Charleston Racecourse was used as a drill ground from the first days of the war.

59. Yellow fever epidemics broke out several times in Charleston since its founding in 1670. The worst epidemic appeared in 1856.

60. "Galvanizing" meant changing sides, enlisting in the Confederate Army. As a rule, these men were former bounty jumpers who found it comparatively safe in the southern ranks.

61. This is an example of how cavalry units, needed desperately for action with the army, were weakened by detaching squadrons for the purpose of guarding prisoners.

62. General Lewis Wallace was the distinguished author of the famous novel, *Ben Hur*.

63. Winder's orders.

64. The office of Provost Marshal in both the Union and Confederate Armies functioned in the same manner as our present day Military Police. The unit functioned as a policing organization within the army itself without authority to make arrests outside it. Winder assumed a dictatorship over it which embraced civilians as well as soldiers. In his hands it became a southern Gestapo until public opinion compelled Jefferson Davis to do something about his vicious, sadistic "pet."

ACKNOWLEDGMENTS

Grateful acknowledgment is forthcoming to the following people who lent me their valuable time and assistance. To them I extend my thanks and appreciation for their many kindnesses.

First to Anne Meredith, and to:

Milton Kaplan, *Assistant Curator, Print Division, Library of Congress, Washington, D.C.*

Miss Virginia Daiker, *Print Division, Library of Congress, Washington, D.C.*

Miss Shirley Spranger, *The New York Public Library*

Mr. Carl Schaller, *Superintendent, Andersonville, Military Cemetery and Park, Andersonville, Ga.*

Culver Service

Irene Glynn

Charles Criswell

973.7 McElroy, John
MCE
    This was
      Andersonville

DATE			